Education, Science and Knowledge Capitalism

A.C. (Tina) Besley, Michael A. Peters,
Cameron McCarthy, Fazal Rizvi
General Editors

Vol. 25

The Global Studies in Education series
is part of the Peter Lang Education list.
Every volume is peer reviewed and meets
the highest quality standards for content and production.

PETER LANG
New York • Washington, D.C./Baltimore • Bern
Frankfurt • Berlin • Brussels • Vienna • Oxford

Michael A. Peters

Education, Science and Knowledge Capitalism

Creativity and the
Promise of Openness

PETER LANG
New York • Washington, D.C./Baltimore • Bern
Frankfurt • Berlin • Brussels • Vienna • Oxford

Library of Congress Cataloging-in-Publication Data

Peters, Michael A., author.
Education, science and knowledge capitalism: creativity
and the promise of openness / Michael A. Peters.
pages cm. — (Global studies in education; vol. 25)
Includes bibliographical references and index.
1. Knowledge economy. 2. Education—Economic aspects. I. Title.
HD30.2.P476   303.48'33—dc23   2012039193
ISBN 978-1-4331-2058-9 (hardcover)
ISBN 978-1-4331-2057-2 (paperback)
ISBN 978-1-4539-0989-8 (e-book)
ISSN 2153-330X

Bibliographic information published by **Die Deutsche Nationalbibliothek**.
Die Deutsche Nationalbibliothek lists this publication in the "Deutsche
Nationalbibliografie"; detailed bibliographic data is available
on the Internet at http://dnb.d-nb.de/.

The paper in this book meets the guidelines for permanence and durability
of the Committee on Production Guidelines for Book Longevity
of the Council of Library Resources.

© 2013 Peter Lang Publishing, Inc., New York
29 Broadway, 18th floor, New York, NY 10006
www.peterlang.com

All rights reserved.
Reprint or reproduction, even partially, in all forms such as microfilm,
xerography, microfiche, microcard, and offset strictly prohibited.

Printed in the United States of America

Contents

Preface and Acknowledgments — vii
Introduction. Global Science and Knowledge Capitalism — 1

Part One | New Forms of Educational Capitalism

Chapter One. Cybernetic Capitalism, Informationalism and Cognitive Labor | *with Rodrigo Britez and Ergin Bulut* — 17
Chapter Two. Education, Creativity and the Economy of Passions: New Forms of Educational Capitalism — 43
Chapter Three. Greening the Knowledge Economy: Ecosophy, Ecology and Economy — 61
Chapter Four. Biocapitalism and the Politics of Life | *with Priya Venkatesan* — 93
Chapter Five. Bioeconomy and the Third Industrial Revolution in the Age of Synthetic Life | *with Priya Venkatesan* — 113
Chapter Six. Algorithmic Capitalism and Educational Futures — 119
Chapter Seven. Three Forms of Knowledge Economy: Learning, Creativity and Openness — 135

Part Two | The Emergence of the Global Science System and the Promise of Openness

Chapter Eight. The Rise of Global Science and the Emerging Political Economy of International Research Collaborations — 165
Chapter Nine. 'Knowledge Economy,' Economic Crisis and Cognitive Capitalism: Public Education and the Promise of Open Science — 191
Chapter Ten. 'Openness' and the Global Knowledge Commons: An Emerging Mode of Social Production for Education and Science — 217
Chapter Eleven. Open Education and the Open Science Economy — 231
Chapter Twelve. Digital Technologies in the Age of YouTube: Electronic Textualities, the Virtual Revolution and the Democratization of Knowledge | *with Peter Fitzsimons* — 255
Chapter Thirteen. Manifesto for Education in the Age of Cognitive Capitalism: Freedom, Creativity and Culture — 277

Index — 291

Preface and Acknowledgements

These essays were written over the last few years around the themes that I have tried to bring together in one book: New Forms of Educational Capitalism and The Emergence of the Global Science System and the Promise of Openness. I have brought these two themes together because the educational history of the late twentieth and early twenty-first centuries seems undeniably to signal the marketization, privatization and commercialization of knowledge and knowledge institutions and the best hope we have for reviving the public nature of institutions, of preserving the notion of public space and developing global civil society seems to me the promise inherent in forms of openness, especially as they are manifested in science, education and government. Openness is oriented toward change and experiment, collaboration and sharing, tolerance and the acceptance of criticism. It is one of the best hopes I believe for a non-hegemonic world. In the first part I outline some of the main forms of educational capitalism that point toward the future: biocapitalism, bioinformationalism, eco- or green capitalism, algorithmic capitalism. In the second half I try to develop a conception that demonstrates the promise of openness in realtion to the emerging global science and educational systems. I apologize in advance for overlaps among these articles.

My thanks to my coauthors of various chapters. Rodrigo Britez and Ergin Bulut were PhD students at the University of Illinois with whom I worked closely during the six years I was there. I enjoyed their company and relish the way in which ideas mattered to them. Priya Venkatesan coauthored chapters 4 and 5. We meet at Oxford University where I gave a paper on open science and immediately set to writing and collaborating on the two papers that comprise these chapters. It was exhilarating to work with Priya. Peter Fitzsimons, an old friend and colleague, coauthored Chapter 12. Peter is a person who gets things done and I can always rely on him to deliver. Of course, as they say, all the errors and imperfections are mine for which I bear sole responsibility.

The sources for the chapters are: "Cybernetic Capitalism, Informationalism and Cognitive Labor" (with Rodrigo Britez and Ergin Bulut) *Geopolitics, History, and International Relations* 1 (2), 2009; "Education, Creativity and the Economy of Passions: New Forms of Educational Capitalism", *Thesis* vol. 96 no. 1, 2009: 40-63; "Greening the Knowledge Economy: Ecosophy, Ecology and Economy", *International Handbook of Research on Environmental Education*, Chapter 46, pp. 493-501 (AERA, 2012); "Biocapitalism and the Politics of Life" (with Priva Venkatesan) *Geopolitics, History, and International Relations,* 2(2), 2011, pp. 100-122; "Bioeconomy and the Third Industrial Revolution in the Age of Synthetic Life" (with Priva Venkatesan) *Contemporary Readings in Law and Social Justice,* 2 (2), 2010: pp. 148-162; "Algorithmic Capitalism and Educational Futures" in M.A. Peters & Ergin Bulut (eds.) *Cognitive Capitalism, Education and Digital Labor,* New York, Peter Lang, 2011, pp. 245-258; "Three Forms of Knowledge Economy: Learning, Creativity and Openness" *British Journal of Educational Studies,* 58 (1), 2010, pp. 67-88; "The Rise of Global Science and the Emerging Political Economy of International Research Collaborations" *European Journal of Education,* 41 (2), 2006, pp. 255-244; "'Knowledge Economy,' Economic Crisis and Cognitive Capitalism: Public Education and the Promise of Open Science" in David Cole (ed.) *Surviving Economic Crises Through Education,* New York, Peters Lang, pp. 21-44; "'Openness' and the Global Knowledge Commons: An Emerging Mode of Social Production for Education and Science" in Huge Lauder, Michael Young, Harry Daniels, Maria Balarin & john Lowe (eds.) *Educating for the knowledge economy? : critical perspectives,* London, Routledge, 2012, 66-76; "Open Education and the Open Science Economy" *Yearbook of the National Society for the Study of Education,* Volume 108, Issue 2, pages 203–225, September 2009; "Digital Technologies in the Age of YouTube: Electronic Textualities, the Virtual Revolution and the Democratization of Knowledge" (with Peter Fitzsimons) *Geopolitcs, History, and International Relations,* 1, 2012, pp. 11-27; "Manifesto for Education in the Age of Cognitive Capitalism: Freedom, Creativity and Culture" *Economics, Management, and Financial Markets,* 6 (1), 2011, pp. 389-401.

Michael A. Peters
Hamilton, NZ
October, 2012

Introduction

Global Science and Knowledge Capitalism

Michael A. Peters

The emerging political economy of global science is a significant factor influencing development of national systems of innovation, and economic, social and cultural development, with the rise of multinational actors and a new mix of corporate, private/public and community involvement.[1] It is only since the 1960s with the development of research evaluation and increasing sophistication of bibliometrics and webometrics that it has been possible to map the emerging economy of global science, at least on a comparative national and continental basis.[2] The question of the political economy of world science and its geographic distribution cannot be easily separated from its measurement and evaluation or the pattern of journal ownership.

Increasingly, emphasis has fallen on the economics and productivity of science in both firms and higher education institutions, as policy-makers and politicians seek to foster innovation and to draw strong links between scientific performance and emerging economic structures (Crespi & Geuna, 2004, 2005). In these science policy discussions the accent often falls on measuring scientific productivity, on 'intellectual property' and the codification of knowledge, and on research collaboration, partnership and cooperation in regional, national and international contexts. Investment in science, engineering and technology has received strong attention from governments as the basis of the 'knowledge economy' and most governments now look to their international science policy strategy to emphasize national competitive advantage and to encourage research collaboration in global science projects.

Indeed, it is the age of *global science*, but not primarily in the sense of 'universal knowledge', which has characterized the liberal meta-narrative of 'free' science since its early development, where scientific findings or results are open to peer review, and public scrutiny and, in principle, are reproducible by others following the same procedures. The (older) liberal meta-narrative of science has now been submerged by official narratives based on an economic logic linking science to national purpose, economic policy, and national science policy priorities. In the era of 'post-normal' science (Funtowicz & Ravetz, 1992), where globalised corporate science dominates the horizon and scientific 'outputs' differ from the traditional peer-reviewed published scientific papers, quality assurance replaces 'truth' as the new regulative ideal. In contemporary science, policy regimes outputs often take the form of patents, unpublished consultancy, 'grey literature' or are covered by legal arrangement and 'lawyer-client confidentiality'. As a result, there are expressed concerns about the fate of scientific publishing. The rise of digitized publications has led to a counter-revolution in scholarly publishing where actual sales are recast into licences and commercial publishers are taking advantage of the growth of open archives (Guédon, 2001).

Global science as a term to describe the emerging *geography of scientific knowledge and collaboration* as an aspect of globalization and its new interconnectedness within a globalized world is a distinctly new phenomenon, although, judging by scholarly criteria, it still reflects a strong Western control and bias and is still heavily nationalistic and seen as a vital part of national culture and state economic policy. The emergence of 'global science' also reflects new global exigencies, new global problems and an enhanced global network of science communicative practice. Today, 'big science' projects require massive state and intergovernmental funding support in an era of intense international competition for knowledge assets, which has forced governments and institutions to collaborate with one another on certain issues. Global science in the form of international science agencies also recognizes the need for cooperation on a number of pressing common global issues that run across borders, such as global warming and other ecological problems, AIDS/HIV, other global diseases and virus outbreaks, natural species extinction, preservation of biomass features, and so on.

The term 'big science' actually dates back to the late 1950s when it was used to herald the transition from individual to team research and development. The term was employed to refer to large scale and instrument-expensive, mainly government-funded projects in basic science (high-energy physics), space research and military science, and also the shifts in science policy and funding after WWII. Derek J. de Solla Price (1963) in *Little Science, Big Science* applied publications analysis to the system of science communication providing the first systematic approach to the structure of modern science, helping to establish bibliometrics and scientometrics that later became essential in the evaluation of the productivity of scientific research.

On a world scale it is now possible to get some idea of *science distributions* in terms of academic papers for the first time. An issue of the UIS Bulletin on Science and Technology Statistics (UNESCO, 2005), published in collaboration with the Institut National de la Recherche Scientifique (INRS) (Montréal, Canada), presented a bibliometric analysis of 20 years of world scientific production from 1981 to 2000, as reflected by the publications indexed in the Science Citation Index (SCI). It indicated that

> In 2000 the SCI included a total of 584,982 papers, representing a 57.5% increase from 1981, when 371,346 papers were published worldwide. Authors with addresses in developed countries wrote 87.9% of the papers in 2000, a decrease from 93.6% in 1981. Developing countries, on the other hand, saw a steady increase in their share of scientific production: from 7.5% of world papers in 1981 to 17.1% in 2000.... Since 1981 the world map of publications changed significantly. North America lost the lead it had in 1996, and in 2000 produced 36.8% of the world total, a decrease from 41.4% in 1981. The opposite trend can be found in the European Union, which in 2000 published 40.2% of the world total, up from 32.8% in 1981. Japan went up from 6.9% to 10.7% in 2000. Collectively this 'triad' has therefore maintained its dominance, accounting for 81% of the world total of scientific publications in 2000, up from 72% in 1981.

The UIS Bulletin concluded that the developed world share of publications has declined while developing regions (Asia and Latin America) have expanded and Africa has stagnated. There is also clear evidence that there has been considerable growth in international collaboration.

In 2004 Britain's then Chief Scientist David A. King (2004) provided an analysis of the output and outcomes from research investment over the past decade, to measure the quality of research on national scales and to set it in an international context, reveals the unevenness of world distribution of science and ascendancy of a group of 31 countries[3] that accounted for 'more than 98% of the world's highly cited papers, defined by Thomson ISI as the most cited 1% by field and year of publication: the world's remaining 162 countries contributed less than 2% in total' (p. 311). His analysis revealed the overwhelming dominance of the United

States (whose share has declined), United Kingdom and Germany, and the fact that 'The nations with the most citations are pulling away from the rest of the world' (p. 311). He provided the following analysis:

> The countries occupying the top eight places in the science citation rank order...produced about 84.5% of the top 1% most cited publications between 1993 and 2001. The next nine countries produced 13%, and the final group share 2.5%. There is a stark disparity between the first and second divisions in the scientific impact of nations. Moreover, although my analysis includes only 31 of the world's 193 countries, these produce 97.5% of the world's most cited papers. (p. 314)

And King goes on to draw political conclusions about the distribution: 'South Africa, at 29th place in my rank ordering, is the only African country on the list. The Islamic countries are only represented by Iran at 30th (p. 314). Yet recent reports indicate national anxiety about the decline of US science.

The U.S. National Science Board's (2008) publication *Research and Development: Essential Foundation for U.S. Competiveness in a Global Economy* charts the decline since 2005 of Federal and industry support for basic research which accounted for 18% ($62B) of the $340B U.S. research budget in current dollars in 2006. The report comments:

> Federal obligations for academic research (both basic and applied) and especially in the current support for National Institutes of Health (NIH) (whose budget had previously doubled between the years 1998 to 2003) declined in real terms between 2004 and 2005 and are expected to decline further in 2006 and 2007. This is the first multiyear decline in Federal obligations for academic research since 1982.

The report also clearly shows the declining competiveness of U.S. science and technology: patents dropped from 55% in 1996 to 53% in 2005; and, 'Basic research articles published in peer-reviewed journals by authors from U.S. private industry peaked in 1995 and declined by 30% between 1995 and 2005.' The report goes on to say: 'The drop in physics publications was particularly dramatic: decreasing from nearly 1,000 publications in 1988 to 300 in 2005.' The loss in U.S. share and its decline of science and technology 'reflects the rapid rise in share by the East Asia-4 (comprising China, South Korea, Singapore, and Taiwan).' The architecture of world science is changing rapidly. The U.S. needs a comprehensive strategy based on an understanding of the globalization of science, the promotion of innovation through international collaboration and the global value chain if it is to remain competitive in the coming decades.[4]

There are clear signs that architecture of global science is shifting especially with the huge investment in research and the consequent growth of scientific publications in Asia. Adams and Wilsdon (2006) report that China's spending on research has increased by more than 20% per year, reaching 1.3% of GDP in 2005 and making it third in the global league table in research expenditure after U.S. and Japan. Science budgets in India have increased by the same annual percentage, adding some 2.5 million IT, engineering and life sciences graduates, 650,000, postgraduates and 6,000 PhDs every year.

The Royal Society has released its policy document entitled *Knowledge, Networks and Nations: Global Scientific Collaboration in the 21st Century* (2011) in March 2011 that reports on science as a global enterprise indicating that there are

> over 7 million researchers around the world, drawing on a combined international R&D spend of over US$1000 billion (a 45% increase since 2002), and reading and publishing in around 25,000 separate scientific journals per year. (p. 5)

The report reviews the changing patterns of science, and scientific collaboration aiming to identify the opportunities for international collaboration and to initiate a debate on how international scientific collaboration can be harnessed to tackle global problems more effectively. The first part of the report maps the changing architecture of global science and indicates that while the traditional 'scientific superpowers' still lead the field, China has overtaken Japan and Europe in terms of its publication output and is predicated to overtake the US by 2014. Emerging scientific hubs are supported by explicit government policy to support R&D with rapid developments in India, Brazil and new emergent scientific nations in the Middle East, Southeast Asia and North Africa, as well as a strengthening of the smaller European nations. The report concludes that it is 'an increasingly multipolar scientific world, in which the distribution of scientific activity is concentrated in a number of widely dispersed hubs' (p. 5).

The second part of the report focuses on the shifting patterns of international collaboration fueled by 'connections of people, through formal and informal channels, diaspora communities, virtual global networks and professional communities of shared interests' (p. 6) demonstrating an intensive new dynamics of networking that while still poorly understood brings significant benefits. *Knowledge, Networks and Nations* concludes with a set of recommendations to strengthen global science, calling for 'more creative, flexible and better resourced mechanisms to co-ordinate research across international networks and to ensure that scientists and science can fulfil their potential' (p. 6). The report concludes, perhaps predictably, that 'Understanding global science systems, their mechanisms and motivations, is essential if we are to harness the very best science to address global challenges and to secure the future of our species and our planet' (p. 6).

Historically, we have seen the small science era—Boyle's 'invisible college' 17th century Europe—and the professionalization in 18th century with Curie, Pasteur, and Volta. The disciplines evolved in 19th century and we saw a scientific nationalism develop in the 20th century with the rise of 'big science'. Today we are witnessing the rise of global science, a series of highly interconnected science hubs associated with strong publishing cities where scientists are highly mobile and science is organized from the bottom up in a series of international collaborations aided by governments and agencies. The new globalized science system indicated that seven major forces are increasingly responsible for structuring the emergent open global science system: *Openness, Networks, Collaboration, Emergence, Circulation, Stickiness (place), Distribution (virtual)* (Wagner, 2007).

The new open science economy demonstrates some advantages of smallness that utilizes and enhances the shift to international collaborative research with virtual organization of global science teams. Increasingly teams produce more papers and receive more citations (Wuchty et al., 2007). Big science has built-in irreversible constraints and can be bureaucratic and fragmented with communication difficulties and organization rigidities. It can be argued that excellence in science requires nimble, autonomous organizations—qualities more likely to be found in small research settings—and enhanced performance can occur through creation of several dozen small research organizations in interdisciplinary domains or in emerging fields. Dozens of scientists who made significant advances did so in organizations with fewer than 50 full-time researchers. In the past decade Nobel prizes have been awarded to scientists for work done in relatively small settings: Günter Blobel (physiology or medicine), Ahmed Zewail (chemistry), Paul Greengard (physiology or medicine), Andrew Fire (physiology or medicine), Roderick MacKinnon (chemistry) and Gerhard Ertl (chemistry) (Hollingsworth, 2008). Open source initiatives have facilitated the development of new models of scientific production and innovation where distributed peer-to-peer knowledge systems rival, the scope and quality of similar products produced by proprietary efforts. Open science demonstrates an "exemplar of a compound of 'private-collective' model of innovation" that contains elements of both proprietary and public models of knowledge production. Science 2.0 generally refers to new practices of scientists who post raw experimental results, nascent theories, claims of discovery and draft papers on the Web for others to see and comment on. Proponents say these "open access" practices make scientific progress more collaborative and therefore more productive. Rich text, highly interactive, user generated and socially active Internet (Web 2.0) has seen linear models of knowledge production giving way to more diffuse open ended and serendipitous knowledge processes.

Open science economy plays a *complementary* role with corporate & transnational science and implies strong role for governments. Increasingly, portal-based knowledge environments and global science gateways support collaborative science (see, e.g., Science.gov & Science.world). Cyber-mashups of very large data sets let users explore, analyze, and comprehend the science behind the information being streamed (Leigh & Brown, 2008). The World Wide Web has revolutionized how researchers from various disciplines collaborate over long distances especially in the Life Sciences, where interdisciplinary approaches are becoming increasingly powerful as a driver of both integration and discovery (with regard to data access, data quality, identity, and provenance) (Sagotsky et al., 2008). National science review and assessment to focus on formative role in developing distributed knowledge systems based on quality journal suites in disciplinary clusters with an ever finer mesh of in-built indicators which implies that the 'republic of science' is subject to new forms of governance.

Organization of This Book

This is a collection of essays most of which have been published previously. This work is an opportunity to bring them together into a coherent whole. I have been interested in the notion of knowledge economy and its role in development for many years well before I published the book *Building Knowledge Cultures: Education and development in the age of knowledge capitalism* coauthored with Tina Besley in 2006. That book discussed the notion of "knowledge cultures" in relation to claims for the new economy, social media and the communicative turn, as well as theorizing "knowledge cultures" within larger frameworks of discussion concerning the cultural economy and the politics of postmodernity. It focused on national policy constructions of the knowledge economy, "fast knowledge" and the role of the so-called new pedagogy and social learning under these conditions to argue for knowledge networks as development possibilities in relation to educational policy futures. It also used the term "knowledge capitalism" (as opposed to knowledge economy) as a way of focusing on the problematic nature of knowledge creation and knowledge production under conditions of capitalism. Knowledge capitalism (as well as knowledge economy) is a term that signals the production of knowledge from the viewpoint of capital (rather than labor or "knowledge workers"). It follows in the wake of mainstream neoclassical analysis of the economics of knowledge that were first raised by Friedrich von Hayek and Fritz Machlup at the Chicago School in the late 1950s and 1960s—a school that also resulted in Gary Becker's formulation of "human capital" that came to dominate education policy agendas.

Knowledge capitalism is a term like knowledge economy that is based on the assumption that capitalism has undergone a structural change. In *The Economics of Knowledge* Dominique Foray (2004: ix–x) entertains the hypothesis of knowledge-based economy as a structural transformation:

> the rapid creation of new knowledge and the improvement of access to the knowledge bases thus constituted, in every possible way (education, training, transfer of technological knowledge, diffusion of innovations), are factors increasing economic efficiency, innovation, the quality of goods and services, and equity between individuals, social categories, and generations....

And he goes on to remark on the nature of the term:

> The term *knowledge-based economy* also enables readers to fully understand a qualitative innovation in the organization and conduct of modern economic life—

namely, the factors determining the success of firms and national economies are more dependent than ever on the capacity to produce and use knowledge.

This is a situation that leads to the "polarization of labor markets" reflecting a bias in favor of qualified workers who hold jobs in "knowledge-intensive industries". The now-standard analysis demonstrates the increasing significance of scientific research, learning-by-doing, and industrial coordination as a step towards the historical emergence of the knowledge economy especially when combined with the emergence and diffusion of information and communication technologies.

One of the questions that emerges from this literature from a public policy viewpoint is how appropriate is the model of private knowledge production for state education and knowledge considered as a global public good. Foray explores this as a conflict between private motivation and the social use and distribution of knowledge and argues that there are good arguments for considering the direct production or subsidization of public goods ion the knowledge economy. In particular, externalities and network effects of open knowledge production seem to offer new avenues for knowledge creation and innovation, especially at a time when the latest crisis of Western economies becomes a structural lag on the innovation economy weakening it economic dynamism (Foray & Phelps, 2011).

Foray comments on knowledge capitalism and the strategy of innovation as a cure for a crisis-induced slow-down in economic dynamism from the point of view of capital and the needs of capitalism yet in a social economy, mediated and networked, that harnesses the power of collective labor, the symbolic economy speaks to the power of expressive labor as theorized by the concept of "cognitive capitalism" (Peters & Bulut, 2011). Cognitive capitalism—sometimes referred to as 'third capitalism,' after mercantilism and industrial capitalism—is an increasingly significant theory, given its focus on the socio-economic changes caused by Internet and Web 2.0 technologies that have transformed the mode of production and the nature of labor. The theory of cognitive capitalism has its origins in French and Italian thinkers, particularly Gilles Deleuze and Felix Guattari's *Capitalism and Schizophrenia*, Michel Foucault's work on the birth of biopower and Michael Hardt and Antonio Negri's *Empire and Multitude*, as well as the Italian Autonomist Marxist movement that had its origins in the Italian *operaismo* (workerism) of the 1960s. The concept and theory of cognitive capitalism has great significance for education at all levels.

With the decline of economic dynamism the emphasis falls on the radical innovation of network companies and the synergies produced through collaboration with research universities especially in the domain of open knowledge production and in areas of open education and open science. This is where intelligent public policy might focus its long-term financial investments. I have explored in a variety of books and papers (see Peters et al., 2010; Peters & Roberts, 2011). This question emerges how is it possible to marry two regimes of digital political economy: public knowledge production and the rise of new forms of openness in science and education on the one hand, and private knowledge production? Are these two inherently incompatible? To what extent do new forms of knowledge capitalism cannibalize the public digital domain and led increasingly to monopolization of infrastructure services and inevitably to the privatization and commodification of knowledge and education? Is there a way of developing innovation and entrepreneurial activity in the public domains of education and science that does not contract out core intellectual functions of the university?

The answers to these questions are complicated especially in view of the changing nature of science and the new partnerships between public and private, universities and multinationals companies. In particular, the new forms of capitalism that are all based on a new formalization—on computerization and "algorithmic capitalism"—and the development of economies of scale that result from personalization within large global digital systems such as Google and Facebook seem even more rapid forms of accumulation than anything compared with the industrial system.

The first section of this book is aimed at exploring the nature of new forms of capitalism—informationalism and biocapitalism—which I see as leading sectors that will constitute what I have called "bio-informational capitalism" (Peters, 2012). In the first group of chapters I detail new forms of capitalism and their effects on education. This is a rapidly changing game and I have only scratched the surface especially in relation to biocapitalism and bioeconomy. Basically, with the help of a couple of junior colleagues (Rodrigo Britez and Ergin Bulut) and Priva Venkatesan a post-doc specializing in genetics, I try to map the various new configurations of capitalism.

In the second section I begin to details the influence of these forms and also the promise of open knowledge production as it is manifested in open education and open science. These chapters represent only a beginning of a study of the political economy of openness and open knowledge production especially as it represents the basis for a renewal of the public sphere and especially public knowledge institutions that use and develop social media and social economic forms to harness intelligence and symbolic labor in the service of collective and public processes of knowledge creation. We are after all only at the very start of an interconnectedness and radical openness that increasingly will contest both knowledge capitalism and central state bureaucracy.

Notes

1. This editorial is based on an updated version of the seminar 'The Changing Atlas of World Science: Towards an Open Science Economy' delivered at the Bureau of Education Research Seminar Series, the University of Illinois, October 3, 2008.
2. The Science Citation Index provides bibliographic and citational information from 3,700 of the world's scientific and technical journals covering over one hundred disciplines. The expanded index available in an online version covers more than 5,800 journals. Comparable 'products' in the social sciences (SSCI) and humanities (A&HCI) cover, respectively, bibliographic information from 1,700 journals in fifty disciplines and 1,130 journals.
3. The countries are Australia, Austria, Belgium, Brazil, *Canada*, China, Denmark, Finland, *France*, *Germany*, Greece, India, Iran, Ireland, Israel, *Italy*, *Japan*, Luxembourg, the Netherlands, Poland, Portugal, *Russia*, Singapore, Spain, South Africa, South Korea, Sweden, Switzerland, Taiwan, the *United Kingdom* and the *United States* (with G8 countries in italics).
4. The author participated in a two-day follow-up workshop 'Developing Evaluations Approaches to International Collaborative Science and Engineering Activities' on July 28 and 29, 2008 at the National Science Foundation. The report can be accessed at the Sigma Xi website at the following URL: http://www.sigmaxi.org/programs/global/index.shtml.

References

Adams, J., & Wilsdon, J. (2006). *The new geography of science: UK research and international collaboration*. London, United Kingdom: Demos.

Crespi, G., & Geuna, A. (2004). *The productivity of science: An international analysis.* Report prepared for the Office of Science and Technology, Department of Trade and Industry. SPRU, University of Sussex. Retrieved from akgul.bilkent.edu.tr/inovasyon/crespiost2.pdf.

Crespi, G. & Geuna, A. (2005.) *Modelling and measuring scientific production: Results for a panel of OECD countries.* SPRU Electronic Working Paper Series, University of Sussex. Retrieved from www.sussex.ac.uk/spru/documents/sewp133.pdf.

Foray, D. (2004). *The economics of knowledge.* Cambridge, MA: MIT Press.

Foray, D., & Phelps, E. (2011). *The challenge of innovation in turbulent times.* Retrieved from http://infoscience.epfl.ch/record/170401/files/MTEI-WP-2011-002-Foray_Phelps_1.pdf?version=1.

Funtowicz, S. O., & Ravetz, J. R. (1992). Three types of risk assessment and the emergence of post-normal science. In S. Krimsky & Golding (Eds.), *Social theories of risk* (pp. 251–273). Westport, CT: Greenwood.

Guedon, J.-C. (2001). *In Oldenburg's long shadow: Librarians, research scientists, publishers, and the control of scientific publishing.* Retrieved from http://www.arl.org/arl/proceedings/138/guedon.html#v.

Hollingsworth, J. R., Müller, K. H., & Hollingsworth, E. J. (2008). China: The end of the science superpowers. *Nature, 454*, 412–413.

King, D. A. (2004). The scientific impact of nations: What different countries get for their research spending. *Nature, 430*, 311–316, Retrieved from www.nature.com/nature.

Leigh, J., & Brown, M. D. (2008). Cyber-commons: Merging real and virtual worlds. *Communications of the ACM, 51*(1), 82–85.

National Science Board (2008). *Research and development: Essential foundation for U.S. competiveness in a global economy.* Retrieved from http://www.nsf.gov/statistics/nsb0803/start.htm.

Peters, M. A. (2006). The rise of global science and the emerging political economy of international research collaborations. *European Journal of Education, 41*(2), 225–244.

Peters, M. A., & Besley, T. (A.C.) (2006). *Building knowledge cultures: Education and development in the age of knowledge capitalism.* Lanham, MD:, Rowman & Littlefield.

Peters, M. A., & Bulut, E. (Eds.). (2011). *Cognitive capitalism, education and the question of digital labor.* New York, NY: Peter Lang.

Peters, M. A., & Roberts, P. (2011). *The virtues of openness: Education, science and scholarship in a digital age.* Boulder, CO: Paradigm Publishers.

Ravetz, J. R. (1996). *Scientific knowledge and its social problems, with a new introduction by the author.* New Brunswick, NJ: Transaction Publishers. (Original work published 1971).

Royal Society, The. (2011). Knowledge, networks and nations: Global scientific collaboration in the 21st century. Retrieved from http://royalsociety.org/uploadedFiles/Royal_Society_Content/Influencing_Policy/Reports/2011-03-28-Knowledge-networks-nations.pdf.

Sagotsky J. A., et al. (2008). Life sciences and the web: A new era for collaboration. *Mol. Syst. Biol.* 4. Retrieved from http://www.ncbi.nlm.nih.gov/pmc/articles/ PMC2516361/.

UNESCO. (2005). What do bibliometric indicators tell us about world scientific output? *UIS Bulletin on Science and Technology Statistics, 2*(September). Retrieved from http://www.csiic.ca/PDF/UIS_bulletin_sept2005_EN.pdf

Wagner, C. (2008). *The new invisible college: Science for development.* New York, NY: Brookings Institution Press.

Wuchty, S., Jones, B. F., & Uzzi, B. (2007). The increasing dominance of teams in production of knowledge. *Science, 316*, 1036–1039.

Part One | New Forms of Educational Capitalism

Chapter 1

Cybernetic Capitalism, Informationalism and Cognitive Labor

Michael A. Peters, Rodrigo Britez, and Ergin Bulut

Cybernetics, Catastrophe, Chaos and Complexity

Modern cybernetics began with Norbert Weiner who defined the field with his 1948 book *Cybernetics: or Control and Communication in the Animal and the Machine* where he developed the science of information feedback systems linking control and communication in an understanding of the computer as 'ideal central nervous system to an apparatus for automatic control' (Wiener, 1948, p. 36) and, therefore, referring to the automatic control of animal and machine. The prehistory of the term can be traced back at least to Plato where *kybernētēs* meaning 'steersman' or 'governor' (from the Latin *gubernator*)—the same root as government—was used to refer governing of the city-state as an art based on the metaphor of the art of navigation or steering a ship. Thus, from the beginning the term was associated with politics and the art of government as well as with communication and organization. It is not surprising, then, that 'cybernetics' should be a significant theoretical term in global studies particularly with the growth of cognate terms derived from the root 'cyber' as a synonym for 'virtual' and emblematic of the global, such as 'cyberspace', 'cyberculture' and 'cyberpunk'.

In this context cybernetics has figured in global studies as a code word for global communications and media studies. As an epistemology related to systemics and systems philosophy the term as functioned as an approach for investigating a wide range of phenomena in information and communication theory, computer science and computer-based design environments, artificial intelligence, management, education, child-based psychology, human systems and consciousness studies, cognitive engineering and knowledge-based systems, 'sociocybernetics', human development, emergence and self-regulation, ecosystems, sustainable development, database and expert systems, health and medicine, musical and theatre performance, musicology, peace studies, multimedia, hypermedia and hypertext, collaborative decision-support systems, World Wide Web studies, cultural diversity, neural nets, software engineering, vision systems, global community, individual freedom and responsibility, urban revitalization, environmental design, and personal and spiritual development.

'Governing' as a major root meaning has been picked up in all major definitions including A.M. Ampere, the French scientist, who used it to refer to the science of government, W. Ross Ashby who talked of the 'art of steermanship' and Stafford Beer who talked of the science of effective organization. Other modern pioneers in the field tended to emphasize a more technical aspect of the study of systems: 'systems open to energy but closed to information' (Ashby); 'problems of control, recursiveness, and information' (Gregory Bateson); 'feedback as purposeful behaviour in man-machines and living organisms' (Ludwig von Bertalanffy); 'the deep nature of control' (Beer); 'relationship between endogenous goals and the external environment' (Peter Corning); 'circularity' (Heinz von Forster); 'the theory of interconnectedness of possible dynamic self-regulated systems' (G. Klaus); 'the art and science of human understanding' (Humberto Maturana); 'the study of justified intervention' (James Wilk).[1] Where one tradition emphasized circular causality in the design of computers and automata—and finds its intellectual expression in theories of computation, regulation and control' Another tradition, which emerged from human and social concerns, emphasizes epistemology—how we come to know—and explores theories of self-reference to understand such phenomena as autonomy, identity, and purpose' (ASC webpage).

Cybernetics is also broadly related to systems philosophy and theory and as Charles François (1999, p. 203) notes both function as 'a meta-language of concepts and models for transdisciplinarian use, still now evolving and far from being stabilized'. François (1999) provides a detailed history of systemics and cybernetics in terms of a series historical stages: First, Precursors (Before 1948)—the 'Prehistory of Systemic-Cybernetic Language'—going back to the Greeks and to Descartes in the modern world and ranging across the disciplines with important work in philosophy, mathematics, biology, psychology, linguistics, physiology, chemistry and so on (Hartmann, Leibnitz, Bernard, Ampère, Poincaré, Konig, Whitehead, Saussure, Christaller, Losch, Xenopol, Bertalanffy, Prigogine). Second, 'From Precursors to Pioneers (1948–1960)' beginning with Weiner who aimed to address the problem of prediction and control and the importance of feedback for corrective steering and mentioning Shannon and Weaver's (1949) *Mathematical Theory of Communication*, Von Bertalanffy's 1950 chapter 'An outline of general system theory', Kenneth Boulding's (1953) 'Spaceship Earth', von Neumann's theory of automata, Von Förster biological computer and his collaborators like Ashby (1956), Pask (1975) and Maturana who pursued questions in human learning, autopoiesis and cognition. François (1999) rightly devotes space to Prigogine (1955) on systemic and his escape from assumptions of thermodynamic models towards understanding dissipative structures in complex systems.[2] Third, 'Innovators (After 1960)' beginning with Simon's (1962) discussion of complexity, Miller's (1978) work on living systems, Maturana's work on autopoiesis, i.e., self-production, Mandelbrot's (1977) work on fractal forms, Zadeh (1965) work fuzzy sets and fuzzy logic, Thom's work on the theory of catastrophes, and the development of chaos theory. As François (1999, p. 214) writes:

> Chaos theory as the study of the irregular, unpredictable behaviour of deterministic non- linear systems is one of the most recent and important innovations in systemics. Complex systems are by nature non-linear, and accordingly they cannot be perfectly reduced to linear simplifications.

François also significantly details important work in ecology and economics mentioning Odum (1971), Daly (1973) on steady-state economy, Pimentel (1977) on the energy balance in agricultural production, among other working in the field. Fourth and finally, François (1999) examines 'Some Significant Recent Contributions (After 1985)' mentioning the Hungarian Csanyi's (1989) work on the 'replicative model of self-organization', Langton (1989) on AL, Sabeili's (1991) theory of processes, and McNeil (1993) on the possibility of a better synthesis between physical sciences and living systems. He ends by referencing Prat's (1964) work on the 'aura' (traces that remain after the demise of the system), Grassé on 'stigmergy'[3] (indirect communication taking place among individuals in social insect societies) and Gerard de Zeeuw (2000) on 'invisibility'.

In this full history we can see cybernetics passing through several phases: The Macy conferences that focused on the new science of cybernetics; catastrophe theory; chaos theory; and complexity theory. The Macy conferences were set up by Warren McCulloch under the auspices of the Macy Foundation from 1946–53 to develop a general science of the human mind and began in the first year studying self-regulating and neural networks moving through a variety of topics covering cybernetics, systems theory, integrative learning.[4] Heims (1993) provides an account of the Macy conferences as a set of dialogues that forged connections between wartime science and postwar social science transforming it through the centrality of the notion of circular causation and feedback and its naturalization through increased quantification. Heims demonstrates how Norbert Wiener, von Neumann, Margaret Mead, Gregory Bateson, Warren McCulloch, Kurt Lewin, Molly Harrower, and many others, shaped ideas in psychology, sociology, anthropology, and psychiatry during the war period.

If modern cybernetics was a child of the 1950s, catastrophe theory developed as a branch of bifurcation theory in the study of dynamical systems originating with the work of the French mathematician Rene Thom in the 1960s and developed by Christopher Zeeman in the 1970s. Catastrophes are bifurcations between different equilibria, or fixed point attractors and has been applied to capsizing boats at sea and bridge collapse. Chaos theory also describes certain aspects of dynamical systems, i.e., systems whose state evolve over time such as the 'butterfly effect' that exhibit characteristics highly sensitive to initial conditions even though they are deterministic systems (e.g., the weather).[5] Chaos theory goes back to Poincaré's work and was taken up mainly by mathematicians who tried to characterize reiterations in natural systems in terms of simply mathematic formulae. Both Edward Lorenz and Benoît Mandelbrot studied recurring patterns in nature—Lorenz on weather simulation and Mandelbrot (1975) on fractals in nature (objects whose irregularity is constant over different scales). Chaos theory which deals with non-linear deterministic systems has been applied in many disciplines but has been very successful in ecology for explaining chaotic dynamics. Victor MacGill[6] provides a nontechnical account of complexity theory: 'Complexity Theory and Chaos Theory studies systems that are too complex to accurately predict their future, but nevertheless exhibit underlying patterns that can help us cope in an increasingly complex world.' Complexity is concerned with theoretical foundations of computer science being concerned with the study of the *intrinsic complexity of computational tasks*[7] and rests on understanding the central role of randomness.

Systems theory in sociology as it was introduced through Parsonian functionalism (Parsons, 1951, 1977), developed in Luhmann's 'systemtheorie' (1995) and Immanuel Wallenstein's (1974) world system theory has been largely discredited and dismissed or superseded in an attempted new synthesis (Bailey, 1994; Bánáthy, 1996). Recently, scolars are rethinking systems theory (Pickel, 2006, 2007) empasizing 'mechanism' and focusing on related concepts such as 'emergentism' (Elder-Vass, 2007), 'self-organization' (Summers-Effler, 2007), 'complexity theory' (Walby, 2007), and 'evolutionary systems theory (Hofkirchner, 2007). John Urry (2005) introducing a special issue of *Theory Culture and Society* commented that the social and cultural sciences over the last few decades have experienced a number of incursions including Marxism of the 1970s, the linguistic and postmodern turns of the 1980s, and the body, performative and global culture turns of the 1990s.[8] Without commenting on the simple metaknowledge schema he introduces he then goes on to introduce the latest turn—'complexity'—which he describes as follows:

> This turn derives from developments over the past two decades or so within physics, biology, mathematics, ecology, chemistry and economics, from the revival of neo-vitalism in social thought (Fraser *et al.*, 2005), and from the emergence of a more general 'complex structure of feeling' that challenges some everyday notions of social order (Maasen and Weingart, 2000; Thrift, 1999).
>
> Within these scientific disciplines, an array of transformations took place, loosely known as chaos, complexity, non-linearity and dynamical systems analysis. There is a shift from reductionist analyses to those that involve the study of complex adaptive ('vital') matter that shows ordering but which remains on 'the edge of chaos'. Self-assembly at the nanoscale is a current example of new kinds of matter seen as involving emergent complex adaptive systems. At the nanoscale the laws of physics operate in different ways, especially in the way that molecules stick together and through self-assembly can form complex nanoscale structures that could be the basis of whole new products, industries and forms of 'life' (Jones, 2004). (Urry, 2005, p. 1)

It is, he says, in the 1990s that the social sciences 'go complex' which he dates from the 1996 Gulbenkian Commission on the Restructuring of the Social Sciences, chaired by Wallerstein and including non-linear scientist

Prigogine, who together wanted to break down some of the divisions between the social and natural sciences. Complexity thought he dates from the 1990s and also the global spread of 'complexity practices' and its popularizations, including applications to the social and cultural sciences.

The globalization of system analyses within and across the disciplines demands a complexity approach, but more importantly, it demonstrates that these complex systems operate at the level of infrastructure, code and content to enable certain freedoms while controlling others.

Complexity as an approach to knowledge and knowledge systems now recognizes both the develops of global systems architectures in (tele)communications and information with the development of *open knowledge production systems* that increasingly rest not only on the establishment of new and better platforms (sometimes called Web 2.0), the semantic web, new search algorithms and processes of digitization but also social processes and policies that foster *openness* as an overriding value as evidenced in the growth of open source, open access and open education and their convergences that characterize global knowledge communities that transcend borders of the nation-state. This seems to intimate new orders of global knowledge systems and cultures that portend a set of political and ethical values such as universal accessibility, rights to knowledge, and international knowledge rights to research results especially in the biosciences and other areas that have great potential to alleviate human suffering, disease and high infant mortality. Openness seems also to suggest political transparency and the norms of open inquiry, indeed, even *democracy* itself as both the basis of the logic of inquiry and the dissemination of its results (Peters & Roberts, 2009).

Contemporary Forms of Cybernetic Capitalism

Increasingly, cybernetics and its associated theories has become central in understanding the nature of networks and distributed systems in energy, politics and knowledge and also its significant in conceptualizing the knowledge-based economy. Economics itself as a discipline has become to recognize the importance of understanding systems rather than rational agents acting alone and pure rationality models of economic behaviour are being supplemented by economic theories that use complexity theory to predict and model transactions. More critical accounts of globalization emphasize a new form of global capitalism, as Teeple (1995, p. 7) remarks:

> Globalization can be defined as the arrival of 'self-generating capital' at the global level: that is, capital as capital, capital in the form of the transnational corporation, increasingly free of national loyalties, controls, and interests.

The 'financialization of capitalism' is a process that seems to have accompanied neoliberalism and globalization, representing a shift from production to financial services, proliferation of monopolistic multinational corporations and the financialization of the capital accumulation process (Foster, 2007). Nassim Taleb[9] and Benoit Mandelbrot (2004) joined forces to criticize the state of financial markets and the global economy, highlighting some of the key fallacies that have prevented the financial industry from correctly appreciating risk and anticipating the current crisis including, large and unexpected changes in dynamical systems that are difficult to predict, the difficulty of predicting risk based on historical experience of defaults and losses, the idea that consolidation and mergers of banks into larger entities makes them safer but in reality imperils whole financial system.[10]

Cybernetic capitalism is a system that has been shaped by the forces of formalization, mathematization and aestheticization beginning in the early twentieth century and associated with developments in mathematical theory, logic, physics, biology and information theory. Its new forms now exhibit themselves in the forms of finance capitalism, informationalism, knowledge capitalism and the learning economy with incipient nodal developments associated with the creative and open knowledge (and science) economies. The critical question in the wake of the collapse of the global finance system and the impending ecocrisis concerns whether capitalism can promote forms of social, ecological and economic sustainability.

'Cybernetic capitalism' is a term we use in order to distinguish a group of theories, or, better, positions, on the left that attempt to theorize the nature of the *new* capitalism. We can group these contributions as largely sociological and left-leaning and characterize them in terms of what they share with and differ from Marxist theory of industrial capitalism. Using kinship with Marxism we can generate the following rough groupings of recent work that we have systematically itemised as:

1. Informational capitalism
2. Cultural capitalism

3. Cognitive capitalism
4. Finance capitalism
5. Biocapitalism

There are strong overlaps and conceptual connections among these five broad categories categories and also some interesting differences within them. We will simply assert in this chapter that they are systematically related phenomena that grow out of the same forces of increasing formalization, mathematicization and aestheticization that have been in operation since the beginning of the twenieth century but that began to coalesce and impact after WWII with the development of cybernetics and a group of theories that developed to explain linear and nonlinear dynamical systems (catastrophe, chaos, complexity). These relationships and particularly the way in which they profile education are to be the subject of other chapters. This largely explains why we have adopted the general theoretical description of *'cybernetic capitalism'* as a means of grouping a set of recent theorizations together.

Group 1—Informational capitalism: The nature of information/knowledge 'Informational', 'Digital', 'Virtual', 'Cyber', 'Fast', 'High-tech' Castells, Shiller, Morris-Suzuki, Schmiede, Fuchs

1. *Informational capitalism*: Emerges from the work of Manuel Castells on the 'networked society'. Castells sees informationalism as a new technological paradigm (he speaks of a mode of development) characterized by "information generation, processing, and transmission" that have become "the fundamental sources of productivity and power" (Castells, 2000, p. 21). Morris-Suzuki (1997) and Schmiede (2006a, b) have used this term and Christian Fuchs (2007) also writes of an informational capitalism of *self-regulation*. Sometimes also referred to as the 'networked model' of capitalism.[11]

2. *Digital capitalism*: Emerges with Dan Schiller and Robert McChesney at the University of Illinois from a tradition Marxist political economy applied out of communication theory to questions of ownership of global communications. "networks are directly generalizing the social and cultural range of the capitalist economy as never before" (Schiller, 2000, p. xiv). See also Peter Glotz (1999).

3. *Cyber-Capitalism:* Dyer Witheford, N. *Cyber-Marx. Cycles and Circuits of Struggle in High Technology Capitalism* (1999).

4. *Knowledge Capitalism:* Michael A. Peters & Tina Besley, *Building Knowledge Cultures: Education and Development in the Age of Knowledge Capitalism* (2006); Sheila Slaughter & Gary Rhoades, *Academic Capitalism and the New Economy* (2004).

5. *Fast capitalism*: A term that was coined by Ben Agger (1989, 2004)—Also see the journal website of the same title.[12]
6. *Virtual capitalism*: the "combination of marketing and the new information technology will enable certain firms to obtain higher profit margins and larger market shares, and will thereby promote greater concentration and centralization of capital" (Dawson & Foster, 1998, p. 63).
7. *High-tech capitalism* (Haug 2003), or informatic capitalism (Fitzpatrick, 2002)—to focus on the computer as a guiding technology that has transformed the productive forces of capitalism and has enabled a globalized economy.

Group 2—Cultural capitalism: The change of culture 'new culture', 'knowing capitalism', 'new spirit', 'cultural economy'

8. *New culture of capitalism*: This strand emerges from work in the 'new geography' and sociology and is epitomized by Richard Sennett's (2007) *The Culture of New Capitalism*.
9. *Knowing Capitalism*—Epitomized by Nigel Thrift's (2006) *Knowing Capitalism*.
10. *The New Spirit of Capitalism*, Boltanski, L. and E. Chiapello (2005).
11. *Cultural economy* Michael Pryke and Paul du Gay.

Group 3—Cognitive capitalism: Immaterial labor 'cognitive capitalism', 'affective capitalism', 'immaterial labor'

12. *Cognitive Capitalism*—'Affective Labour is a key feature of the new mode of cognitive capitalism based on immaterial labour. It is a key aspect of a strategy based on autonomous peer production'.[13] Yann Moulier Boutang *Le capitalisme cognitif : La Nouvelle Grande Transformation*, (2007); Vercellone C. (ed.), *Capitalismo cognitivo*, (2006); De Angelis, M. and D. Harvie (2009) 'Cognitive Capitalism and the Rat Race: How capital measures ideas and affects in UK higher education'.
13. *Immaterial Labor*: Based on Deleuze and Guattari's *Anti-Oedipus: Schizophrenia and Capitalism* (1999); Negri & Hardt (2000, p. 290) argue that contemporary society is an Empire that is characterized by a singular global logic of capitalist domination that is based on immaterial labour. With the concept of immaterial labour Negri and Hardt introduce ideas of information society discourse into their Marxist account of contemporary capitalism. Immaterial labour would be labour "that creates immaterial products, such as knowledge, information, communication, a relationship, or an emotional response" (Hardt/Negri, 2005, p. 108; cf. also 2000, p. 280–303), or services, cultural products, knowledge (Hardt/Negri, 2000, p. 290).
14. *Affective Capitalism*—Massumi, B. (n.d.) 'The Future Birth of the Affective Fact';[14] *Immaterial and affective labor*, Emma Dowling, Rodrigo Nunes and Ben Trott (*Ephemera, 2007*); Juan Martín Prada, 'Economies of affectivity'[15] and Michael Hardt 'Affective Labor'.[16]

15. *Semio-capitalism—Precarious Rhapsody. Semio-capitalism and the Pathologies of the Post-Alpha Generation*, Franco Bernadi (2009).

Group 4—Finance capitalism: 'Financialization'

16. *Finance Capitalism*: John Bellamy Foster; Glyn, A. *Capitalism Unleashed: Finance Globalization and Welfare* (2006); Leyshon, A. and N. Thrift (2007) 'The Capitalization of Almost Everything: The Future of Finance and Capitalism'; Vestergaard, J. *Discipline in the Global Economy? International Finance and the End of Liberalism* (2008).

Group 5—Biocapitalism & Biopolitics

17. *Biocapitalism*: Based lossely on Foucault's work on governmentality and biopower, and Deleuze and Guattari's *Anti-Oedipus: Schizophrenia and Capitalism* (1999); Rajan, K. S. *Biocapital: The Constitution of Postgenomic Life* (2006); Biotechnology and the Spirit of Capitalism.[17]

In what follows we examine two of these groups, namely *informational capitalism* and *cognitive capitalism* and their differences and similarities in the final section.

Informational Capitalism

As Fuchs & Horak (2007) indicate the notion of informational capitalism was first introduced by Manuel Castells in his magnum opus *The Rise of the Network Society*. Castells describes contemporary processes in advance developed capitalist countries transforming the dominant systems of social production and organization of capitalist societies. In other words, those are processes of change that permit the reproduction of the 'fundamental logic' implicit in the capitalist system, but under a different rules, different social relations, different modalities of social organization (or morphology) and at a global scale, thus the emergence of a 'different kind of capitalism' (Stalder, 2006, p. 48). This is the focus of Castells analysis on the new economic globalization; the contemporary transformation of the capitalism system and its global expansion through new information technologies (Castells, 2000a). Hence, the assertion of the emergence of a 'new economy': an informational economy.

According to Castells, what is unique of this new economy is not merely its capitalist character, but the influence of technology, applied by economic actors to sustain social change. Technology, more precisely the integration of specific types of technologies in production processes helped to implement an alternative to the crisis of economic growth of 'profit making' in advance capitalist societies. Nevertheless, they also provide something more pervasive, a new 'technique', a new logic that goes beyond the realm of economics or economic analysis. More precisely, those changes are interrelated with the creation of new forms of social structural organization, and patterns of institutional transformation through networks.

One of the basic characteristics of contemporary globalization is the significant acceleration of interactions enabled by technology. Technologies of communication are shaping reality and reconfiguring world connectedness with a concentration of traffic in taking place between certain geographical nodes over others. Patterns of mobility and exchanges have always been mediated by technologies of communication.

Today, technologies of communication become globalizing forces through which projects of material integration of social spaces at a global scale became possible, allowing emergence of 'a new material basis for time-sharing on which dominant activities are manage through flows' (Stalder, 2006, p. 6). In other words, they have made possible projects of global material and social integration. For instances, transnational strategies of integration come to dominate the organization of economic activity through organizational networks (especially where corporations become transnational, finance activity becomes global, etc.).

Networks based on informational technologies are complex forms of organization that today dominate the way in which complex patterns interaction are organized in the world. The understanding of these processes of interconnectedness in terms of networks has the basic advantage of enabling an analysis 'based on flows, rather than isolated units, entities, and individuals' (Aneesh, 2006, p. 78) thereby allowing analysis of connectedness, of intrinsic interdependence (of economy, policy, society and culture) in terms of patterns of symbolic and material communication.

Precisely, Fuchs & Horak (2007) indicate that "the historical novelty is not that social relationships are networked, but that processes of production, power, hegemony, and struggles take on the form of transnational networks that are mediated by networked information- and communication technologies"(p. 12). As we observe, one of the main features of this "new economy" is the increasing importance of knowledge or information production what Castells denominated 'informationalism', this implies the emergence of an economy based on new forms of production and labor. In other words, knowledge, information and communication in the globalize world—as informationalism—is manifested in the increased importance of labor involved in the production of what Hardt and Negri (2000) denominated 'immaterial goods' (p. 290).

Concomitantly, the value labor changes from mechanical production to the primacy of 'symbolic analytical services', "data analysis, financial planning and most research and development jobs and occupations" (see Webb & Shirato, 2003). An example, is seem in the constant creation an recreation of products images through relentless marketing campaigns, the preeminence of financial markets, and the increasing dependence of manufacturing and agricultural activities from services occupations. This implies the emergence of two set of contradictory developments at the center of the social production systems emerging from informationalism: one based on a commodity economy and a gift economy (Fuchs, 2006). Fuchs indicates that the affordances facilitating new forms of collaborative knowledge production at the core of capitalism using new technologies are enabling the emergence of a parallel and antagonistic economic system: "an alternative economic model of a gift economy" (Fuchs, 2006).

Basically, due to the very nature of the requirements of open knowledge production and communication system, knowledge is extremely difficult to be transformed into a commodity as in the case of material goods. This is resulting in increasing conflicts between the forces of informational production and the still prevalent system of capitalist accumulation and relationship (Fuchs, 2006). Therefore, it is possible to observe the contentious contemporary struggles over the nature of information as a property. The strategies of capitalist accumulation that contemporary systems of information and communication favor are different from those observed during the industrial age. As Fuchs appears to indicate informationalism requires more democratic forms of participation and collaboration in the relationships of production of and accumulation of wealth in informational capitalist in ways that require that information should not be consider as a restricted property, but an unhindered component of social interactions.

As we indicate Castells "emphasizes this new capitalism is profoundly different from the one formed during the Industrial Revolution", in the sense that one of its main features it is of being largely "structured around networks of financial flows" (Capra, 2002, p. 136). In other words, financial capital becomes in the dominant sector of capital: "capital accumulation proceeds and its value making is generated, increasingly, in the global financial market enacted by information networks in the timeless space of financial flows" (Castells, 2000a, p. 503). Or, as Harvey (2005) could critically indicate, the solution of the problem of capital accumulation drew "heavily on surpluses extracted from the rest of the world through international flows and structural adjustment practices" (Harvey, 2005, pp. 29–31) sometimes following a process of extraction of capital not very different that those of the past (Harvey, 2005, p. 74).

However, Castells have argued with reiteration against this argument. For Castells the debate of technologic determinism or social determinism is a false one, or rather a mixed one. One of the focuses of Castells' argumentation through his work is not to emphasis in the relativity of technical design, but in the diversity of appropriations made by the actors and society. In other words, people appropriated technology; define its meaning and use in ways that the designers did not foresee. For example, the history of telephone, the internet, or the cell phone has shown that their main shared characteristic of technologies have being is malleability.

In particular those technologies like, internet, in which consumer are at the same time producers, are incredibly malleable in its applications. Moreover, it is crucial to understand that for Castells, the rise of the use of technological innovations, like internet in the '90s, is not merely defined by the technological innovation itself, but it is dependent in the ways that the consumer interests drive the implementation and use of those technologies.

On one hand is deterministic to certain extend in a limited sense, because without those technologies the current global economy it is not viable. On the other, on a broader sense is not deterministic because technologies do not determine society. In other words, is both, technology is society, meaning that technology is one dimension of society, a cultural dimension of society. It is important to note that of the main assumptions of Castells theory is based on the affirmation of the existence of a "dialectical interaction of social relations and technological innovation, or, in Castells's terminology modes of production and modes of development" (Stalder, 2006, p. 302). This point need some clarification to understand the nature of Castells's rupture with a traditional Marxian approach, for Castells there is not difference between modes of production and relations of production, in the sense that they are consider one dimension defined by the primacy of a particular type of organization of production and consumption. The emphasis is made in the organization of the relations of production and consumption not in the system of production and the relations of production.

Finally, this implies the emergence not merely a knowledge base economy but a knowledge base society and culture. In other words the transition from industrial towards informational capitalism is disestablishing the systems of capitalist relationships thus opening possibilities for transformation of a different world, maybe a better one. Transnational networked capitalism leading the current processes of economic globalization had generated process of accumulation not very different from those observe during the industrial age, with negative effects for many populations, at the same time that global emerging protest of civil societies groups attempts to steer more democratic forms of conceiving globalization. It is important to remember that the expansion of information networks in the form of global systems of transaction, and capitalism restructuring were and are still implement by centralize, authoritarian, mostly industrial working-oriented styles through many nations.

The consequences of the contradictory positions of the gift and proprietary economy are observed in sometimes overlapping forms in the ways in which labor and education is conceived today. The movement and organization of labor is profoundly affected and also the different levels the demands over the content and functions of higher education institutions, in which the learning value is now characterize by the "central role of knowledge, information, affect and communication" (Webb & Shirato, 2003, pp. 76–77), but whose main value characteristic is the potential access to venues of mobility. In other words, the potential entrée to nodes of activity and interaction, which, according to the type and changing hierarchy of higher education institution, allows individuals, states, and business, to be integrate, to participate or to exploit different flows generated by global networks. Higher education accreditation becomes a commodity to access to a set of strategic positions allowing employability and transnational networks of capitalism.

Accordingly, the economic activity and the wealth of countries become extremely dependent on people able to enter into those flows and its recruitment. In short, become increasingly linked to educated individuals able to participate in global process, to its recruitment, education and training. In those circumstances, higher educations institutions became linked to strategic sectors of the economy activity of countries through the international recruitment of skilled personal. Higher education institutions become with companies and research institutions in spaces of articulation of international networks of collaboration, and labor recruitment and the integral component of this global system of interactions. This is observed in the function of training of universities in the United States, and around the world, specifically in graduate institutions, which have become directly associated with the recruiting and searching of talent by advances companies.

All this indicate that "labor is internationalized" (Castells, 2001a, p. 196), at least in the most valuable positions. The ability to access those occupations "require not only the capacity to use information technology and process information, but also the ability to learn" (Castells & Himanen, 2002, pp. 1–2) to operate and generate a value in those global networks. Therefore, defining a new system of production in "which labor is redefine in its role as producer, and sharply differentiated according to workers' characteristics" (Castells, 2000, p. 372). In other words, higher education institutions generate accreditations as commodities, as in a proprietary economy, while the training that they provided is only useful if educate their graduates with skills to participate in the gift economy based on skills of participation very similar to those required in research collaborations at the academy. This contradiction and overlapping between these two trends is a relevant aspect of the complex capitalist system and society that is been created.

Cognitive Capitalism and Immaterial Labor

Richard Sennett's *The Corrosion of Character* describes the enormous difference between the lives of a Fordist worker Enrico and his flexible son Rico. Upon reading the book, one comes to recognize the extent to which work has been transformed. Even though the popular media remembers Karl Marx only during times of crisis, there are vibrant debates among Marxists themselves, regarding the transformation of work and labor processes. We should definitely take Michael Hardt and Antonio Negri into account among the prominent names of this debate. Yet, we believe a historical account about this concept would be useful before more contemporary ones.

Leopoldina Fortunati gives the names of Gabriel Tarde and Werner Sombart as far as reflections on immaterial labor after Marx are concerned. Fortunati states that Tarde's writings [*Les Lois de l'imitation* (1890) and *La Logique sociale* (1895)], "stressed the existence of other forces (or laws) acting on a socio-psychological level, such as imitation, the law of minimal effort, and innovation. In doing so he argued that the social teleology imposed by classical economists unaware of the true foothold of political economics was at fault for the omission of affections, and especially of desire, in analyses of valorization (spheres which were also neglected by subsequent Marxisms)" (Fortunati, 2007, p. 142). Sombart, on the other hand, in *Modern Capitalism* argued that immaterial labor was becoming more central to capitalism and laid down three reasons for the technological developments of the time:

> first of all, the objectification of technical knowledge, which ensured a continued control over new ideas or inventions, their transmission and with it the diffusion of knowledge; secondly, the systematization of technical knowledge which allowed for a systematic progression of knowledge and its enlargement; thirdly, the mathematization of technical knowledge. (Fortunati, 2007, p. 143)[18]

The revival of the contemporary versions of immaterial labor debates can be cohered around people including Antonio Negri, Michael Hardt and Maurizio Lazaratto, the journal *Futur Antérieur*. Nick Dyer-Witheford (2001) provides a smooth historical account of how these debates were chronologically shaped. Antonio Negri's writings (1988, 1989) on the "intellectual qualities of a post-Fordist proletariat enmeshed in the computers and communication networks of high-technology were intensified in the analysis of the general intellect (the socialized, collective, intelligence prophesied by the Marx of the *Grundrisse*) developed by the journal Futur Antérieur" (Dyer-Witheford, 2001, p. 70). As a precise definition of immaterial labor, we can refer to Lazzarato:

> Immaterial labor is defined as the labor that produces the informational and cultural content of the commodity. Informational content: related to big industry and tertiary sectors; skills involving cybernetics and computer control.... Cultural content: kind of activities involved in defining and fixing cultural and artistic standards, fashions, tastes, consumer norms and more strategically public opinion. (Lazzarato, 2006, p. 132)

The revival of these reflections reached its peak with the publication of Hardt and Negri's *Empire*. Underlining the shift from an industrial economy towards an informational economy, Hardt and Negri focus on how the nature of labor has changed within the framework of Toyotist model, as opposed to the Fordist one. In this new phase of global capitalism, "factories will maintain zero stock" (Hardt & Negri, 2000, p. 290) and immaterial labor will gain significance. Hardt and Negri define immaterial labor as one "that produces an immaterial good, such as a service, a cultural product, knowledge, or communication" (p. 290). According to Hardt and Negri, there are three types of immaterial labor:

> one is involved in an industrial production that has been informationalized and has incorporated communication technologies in a way that transforms the production process itself….Second is immaterial labor of analytical and symbolic tasks, which itself breaks down into creative and intelligent manipulation on the one hand and routine symbolic tasks on the other. Finally, a third type of immaterial labor involves the production and manipulation of affect and requires (virtual or actual) human contact, labor in the bodily mode. (Hardt & Negri, 2000, p. 293)[19]

As far as the rise of immaterial labor is concerned, Hardt and Negri stress a point of departure from a "Marxian political economy by which labor power is conceived as 'variable capital', that is, a force that is activated and made coherent only by capital" and argue that "today productivity, wealth, and the creation of social surpluses take the form of cooperative interactivity through linguistic, communicational, and affective networks" (p. 294). Thus, they argue, in this decentralized production, "the assembly line has been replaced by the network…workers can even stay at home…and these tendencies place labor in a weakened bargaining position" (Hardt & Negri, 2000, pp. 295–296). Hardt and Negri, when thinking about this assault on labor, argued that production and life have become quite inseparable. That is, in this flexible accumulation regime, "life is made to work for production and production is made to work for life" (Hardt & Negri, 2000, p. 32).[20]

Presumably, Hardt and Negri and others' analyses of immaterial labor was attacked for some obvious reasons in the sense that this new circuits of capital "look a lot less immaterial and intellectual to the female and Southern workers who do so much of the grueling physical toil demanded by a capitalist general intellect whose metropolitan headquarters" (Dyer-Witheford, 2001, p. 71; Dowling, 2007).

Despite these sound critiques, Dyer-Witheford acknowledges the increasing hegemony of immaterial labor along with other scholars, including Yann Moulier Boutang who has neatly classified certain characteristics of cognitive capitalism. Comparing cognitive capitalism with industrial capitalism, Boutang states that "in industrial capitalism, accumulation concerns mainly machines and the organization of work dealt with…whereas accumulation in cognitive capitalism rests on management of knowledge and production of innovation, hence on immaterial investments" (Boutang, 2007, p. 12).[21] Along with that, Boutang stresses the differences with regard to different entrepreneurs of industrial capitalism and cognitive capitalism. While the former is defined by his/her greed and pride of loneliness and "exception of founding father", the latter is marked by the desire for fame and "pride of cooperation and connectivity" (Boutang, 2007, p. 22). Here, the issue of cooperation and connectivity directly takes us to the classification we have tried to accomplish within the framework of this chapter. We have argued that the different capitalisms we have underlined have a lot in common. In this respect, immaterial labor, cooperation and informational capitalism all have overlapping features. As it is argued with respect to information, for instance, it is "hard to control in single places or by single owners, intangible and based on networks that negate individual ownership" (Fuchs, 2008a).[22] These features all have the potential for collaboration. However, it is exactly here that we might step back and be cautionary in terms of the 'cooperative or emancipatory' for two reasons: political economy and subjectivity. While the former is related to the fact that "the total assets of the top six knowledge corporations were 1132,41 billion US dollars in 2007 and are larger than the total African GDP" (Fuchs, 2008a, p. 284), the second has to do with how labor is subsumed within cyberspace thanks to the discourse around collaboration, fun and participation. In other words, what the participation of immaterial labor within cyberspace means has not been endorsed by critical theorists, who have underlined this potential but at the same time pointed to various mechanisms through which subsumption of labor is realized in cyberspace (Fuchs, 2008b, 2007, 2002). This cautionary stance is relevant to the realm of education, as well.

David Harvie, for instance, argues that the war over value has spread over not only factory but there are also attempts to quantify the value produced by immaterial labor, especially within the framework higher education, including techniques of "quantification, surveillance and standardization" (Harvie, 2008, 2000), (De Angelis & Harvie, 2009). Neoliberal restructuring of schooling in line with market demands has also resulted in the emergence of a global policy inflation around lifelong learning and educational credentials that would be commodified. As the assembly line with certain expected demands from the factory and workplace have disappeared, schooling built around industrial lines would have been rearranged, which would be asked to train students along the lines of the global knowledge economy and fluctuating market demands. However, the responsibility would be shared between the school and the individual. An awareness of these developments definitely takes us to the centrality of value creation to capitalism. That is, despite the changing nature of work and labor processes, value still represents "the life blood of capitalism", whether this or that (Rikowski, 2003). As it is also asserted, "the extraction of value from immaterial labor, much like that occurring at the zenith of Fordism in the automobile factories of Turin or Detroit, is not a friction-free matter" (Brophy & de Peuter, 2007, p. 179).

In this respect, one could argue that immaterial labor is quite material in terms of extraction of surplus value and exploitation and thus analyses based on the concept has to take an approach that is based on a layered and relational understanding of immaterial labor and the differential power relations among the people who exercise this kind of labor in their everyday lives, be it a creative design worker or the janitor who cleans his cutting-edge PC.

Conclusion

This chapter provides a synoptic view of what we have called 'cybernetic capitalism'—a term that attempts to capture the leading sector developments within modern capitalism and to profile the leading accounts of these developments. 'Third capitalism' (after mercantilism and industrialism) now relies on a systems architecture that draws on cybernetics and modern computing that connects five aspects of cybernetic capitalism: informational capitalism, cultural capitalism, cognitive capitalism, finance capitalism and biocapitalism. These five elements are interrelated. In this chapter we have identified the five elements but not described or analysed the interconnections among them. Clearly, there are obvious links among information, cognitive and cultural capitalism even though we are not claiming that the theorists who articulate these separate elements offer the same descriptions or that they agree in their characterizations. Finance and biocapitalism also employs similar methods and works off the same systems architectures: where the former is based on sophisticated mathematical modelling and search algorithms, the latter makes 'nature' and biogenetics central to the production process.

In this chapter, we have tried to underline the new features of where global capitalism is shifting towards. Among the different models, there are strong overlapping characteristics which coalesce around aesthetization, design and immateriality. Yet, there is one concept that is central to all of the types, including industrial capitalism. That is value. Value creation for the sake of it is still central to contemporary capitalism. That is, the universal contradiction, which might manifest itself differently in different localities, between capital and labor is still there and has diffused to every sphere of our lives. Thus, any attempt to define any novelty to these capitalisms should bear this in mind. Along with that, spatiality is another concept we have to bear in mind in the sense that not all the globe is going through these changes simultaneously. In other words, the shiny capitalism of any global city is only possible through different mechanisms of capital accumulation, either based on the modern slavery in the sweatshops of the third world or its own ghettoes.

Notes

1   See the American Society for Cybernetics (ASC) webpage for a full set of definitions at http://www.asc-cybernetics.org/foundations/definitions.htm.

2   Prigogine has an interest in time derived from the philosopher Bergson, and later from the physicists Boltzmann and Planck, where he developed a theorem on examples of systems which were highly organized and irreversible and applied it to the energetics of embryological evolution. His work in irreversible phenomena theory led him also to reconsider their insertion into classical and quantum dynamics and to the problem of the foundations of statistical mechanics. See his discussion of his work at http://nobelprize.org/nobel_prizes/chemistry/laureates/1977/prigogine-autobio.html.

3   For the literature on stigmergy and massive online collaboration see Susi & Ziemke (2001), Gregorio (2002) and Robles, Merelo & Gonzalez-Barahona (2005).

4   See the description at http://www.asc-cybernetics.org/foundations/history/ Macy-Summary.htm.
5   For a brief introduction see http://www.imho.com/grae/chaos/chaos.html.
6   See http://complexity.orconhosting.net.nz/.
7   See Oded Goldreich's webpage at http://www.wisdom.weizmann.ac.il/~oded/ cc.html.
8   The next section is based on Peters (2008).
9   See Taleb's homepage and publications at http://www.fooledbyrandomness.com/.
10 See the video interview at http://financemanila.net/2009/01/taleb-and-mandelbrot/.
11 See http://ideas.repec.org/a/nos/voprec/2003-8-10.html.
12 See http://www.fastcapitalism.com/.
13 See http://p2pfoundation.net/Affective_Capitalism.
14 See http://browse.reticular.info/text/collected/massumi.pdf.
15 See http://www.vinculo-a.net/english_site/text_prada.html.
16 See http://www.vinculo-a.net/english_site/text_hardt.html.
17 See http://www.thenewatlantis.com/publications/biotechnology-and-the-spirit-of-capitalism.
18 Fortunati also mentions the names of the human capital theorist Gary Becker, along with Michel Foucault (with his concepts biopower and biopolitics) and Deleuze and Guattari who considered human beings to be desiring machines (Fortunati, 2007, p. 144).
19 Hardt and Negri's comments about this third type of labor is worth questioning, in terms of its immateriality, though, since this affective labor can be regarded as quite material in terms of reproduction of labor power. Along with that, we have to acknowledge that the authors clarified this point in *Multitude: War and Democracy In the Age of Empire* by arguing that the labour itself is not immaterial. What is immaterial is the product or affects it creates (Hardt & Negri, 2004, p. 109).
20 For the same issue, Lazzarato would argue the following: "what modern management techniques are looking for is for the worker's soul to become part of the factory...workers are expected to become "active subjects" in the coordination of the various functions of production, instead of being subjected to it as simple command" (p. 133).
21 Boutang lists 22 main characteristics of cognitive capitalism, among which we can count: virtualization economy and increasing role of information, exploitation of the inventive force instead of the labor force, the fact that market precedes production, the blurring of the traditional division between capital and labor (Boutang, 2007, pp. 13-14).
22 Available at: http://fuchs.icts.sbg.ac.at/Fuchs_CriticalTheory.pdf.

References

Aneesh, A. (2006). *Virtual migration*. Durham, NC: Duke University Press.
Ashby, W. R. (1956). *An introduction to cybernetics*. London, United Kingdom: Chapman & Hall.

Bailey, K.D. (1994). *Sociology and the new systems theory: Toward a theoretical synthesis.* New York, NY: State of New York Press.

Bánáthy, B. (1996). *Designing social systems in a changing world.* New York, NY: Plenum.

Berardi, F. (2009). *Precarious rhapsody: Semio-capitalism and the pathologies of the post-alpha generation.* London, United Kingdom: Minor Compositions.

Bertalanffy, L. von (1950). An outline of general system theory. *British Journal for the Philosophy of Science 1*(2), 134–165.

Bohm-Bawerk, E. (2006). *Karl Marx and the close of his system.* London, United Kingdom: Porcupine Press.

Boltanski, L., & Chiapello, E. (2005). *The new spirit of capitalism.* (G. Elliott, Trans.). London, United Kingdom: Verso.

Boulding, K. (1953). Toward a general theory of growth. *Canadian Journal of Economics and Political Science, 19* (reprinted in General Systems Yearbook, vol. 1, 1956).

Boutang, Y. M. (2007, September). *Cognitive capitalism and entrepreneurship decline in industrial entrepreneurship and the rising of collective intelligence.* Paper presented at the Sage Hall Cornell University Capitalism and Entrepreneurship Conference, Ithaca, NY.

Brophy, E., & de Peuter, G. (2007). Immaterial labor, precarity, and recomposition. In C. McKercher & V. Mosco (Eds.), *Knowledge workers in the information society* (pp. 177–193). Idaho Falls, ID: Lexington Books.

Capra, F. (2002a). *The hidden connections: Integrating the biological, cognitive, and social dimensions of life into a science of sustainability.* New York, NY: Doubleday.

Capra, F. (2002b). *Where have all the flowers gone? Reflections on the spirit and legacy of the sixties.* Retrieved from http://www.fritjofcapra.net/articles120102.html

Castells, M. (1999). Flows, networks, and identities: A critical theory of the informational society. In M. Castells, R. Flecha, P. Freire, H. A. Giroux, D. Macedo, & P. Willis (Eds.), *Critical education in the new information age* (pp. 37–64). Lanham, MD: Rowman & Littlefield.

Castells, M. (2000a). *The rise of the network society* (2nd ed.). Malden, MA: Blackwell Publishers.

Castells, M. (2000b). Materials for an exploratory theory of the network society. *British Journal of Sociology, 51*(1), 5–24.

Castells, M. (2001a). Universities as dynamic systems of contradictory functions. In J. Muller, N. Cloete, & S. Badat (Eds.), *Challenges of globalisation* (pp. 206–223). Pinelands, South Africa: Maskew Miller Longman.

Castells, M. (2001b). Informationalism and the network society. In P. Himanen, *The hacker ethic and the spirit of informationalism* (pp. 155–178). New York, NY: Random House.

Castells, M. (2001c). *The internet galaxy: Reflections on the internet, business, and society.* New York, NY: Oxford University Press

Castells, M., & Himanen, P. (2002). *The information society and the welfare state: The Finnish model.* Oxford, United Kingdom: Oxford University Press.

Castells, M., & Ince, M. (2003). *Conversations with Manuel Castells.* Cambridge, United Kingdom: Polity Press.

Csanyi, V. (1989). The replicative model of self- organization. In G. J. Dalenoort (Ed.), *The paradigm of self-organization* (pp. 22–36). New York, NY: Gordon & Breach.

Daly, H. (1973). *Towards a steady-state economy.* San Francisco, CA: Freeman.

De Angelis, M. (2007). *The beginning of history: Value struggles and global capital.* London, United Kingdom: Pluto Press.

De Angelis, M., & Harvie, D. (2009). Cognitive capitalism and the rat race: How capital measures ideas and affects in UK higher education. *Historical Materialism, 17*, 3–30

Dowling, E. (2007). Producing the dining experience: Measure, subjectivity and the affective worker. *Ephemera, 7*(1), 117–132. Retrieved from http://www.ephemeraweb.org/

Dowling, E., Nunes, R., & Trott, B. (2007). Immaterial and affective labor. *Ephemera, 7*(1), 1–7. Retrieved from http://www.ephemeraweb.org/

Dyer-Witheford, N. (1999). *Cyber-Marx: Cycles and circuits of struggle in high technology capitalism.* Chicago, IL: University of Illinois Press.

Dyer-Witheford, N. (2001). Empire, immaterial labor, the new combinations, and the global worker. *Rethinking Marxism, 13*(3–4), 70–80. Retrieved from http://www.tandfonline.com/toc/rrmx20/13/3-4

Elder-Vass, D. (2007). Luhmann and Emergentism: Competing paradigms for social systems theory? *Philosophy of the Social Sciences, 37*(4), 408–432.

Fortunati, L. (2007) Immaterial labor and its machinization. *Ephemera, 7*(1), 139–157. Retrieved from http://www.cphemeraweb.org/

François, C. (1999). Systemics and cybernetics in a historical perspective. *Systems Research and Behavioral Science 16*, 203–219.

Fraser, M., Kember, S., & Lury, C. (Eds.) (2005) Inventive life: Approaches to the new vitalism. *Theory Culture & Society, 22*(1), 1–14.

Fuchs, C. (2002). Software engineering and the production of surplus value. *Cultural Logic.* Retrieved from http://clogic.eserver.org/2002/fuchs.html

Fuchs, C. (2006). *Strategies and forms of capital accumulation in transnational informational capitalism.* Retrieved from http://www.transform.or.at/images.Accumulation.pdf

Fuchs, C. (2007). Transnational space and the network society, *21st Century Society, 2*(1), 49–78.

Fuchs, C. (2008a, November). Towards a critical theory of information. In J. M. D. Nafria & F. S. Alemany (Eds.), *Qué es Información? (What Is Information?) Proceedings of the First International Meeting of Experts in Information Theories. An Interdisciplinary Approach (Primer Encuentro Internactional de Expertos Teorías de la Información. Un enfoque interdisciplinar)* (pp. 247–316.). León, Spain: Universidad de León.

Fuchs, C. (2008b). Book review of wikinomics: How mass collaboration changes everything. *International Journal of Communication, 2*, 1–11.

Fuchs, C., & Horak, E. (2007). Informational capitalism and the digital divide in Africa. *Masaryk University of Law and Technology, 1*(2), 11–32.

Glyn, A. (2006). *Capitalism unleashed: Finance globalization and welfare.* New York, NY: Oxford University Press.

Gregorio, J. (2002). Stigmergy and the worldwide web. *Bitworking* [web log], Retrieved from http://bitworking.org/news/Stigmergy

Hardt, M., & Negri, A.(2000). *Empire*. Cambridge, MA: Harvard University Press.

Hardt, M., & Negri, A. (2004). *Multitude: War and democracy in the age of empire*. New York, NY: Penguin Press.

Harvey, D. (2000). Time space compression and the postmodern condition. In D. Held & A. McGrew (Eds.), *The global transformation reader: An introduction to the globalization debate* (pp. 82–91). Cambridge, United Kingdom: Polity Press.

Harvey, D. (2005). *A brief history of neo liberalism*. New York, NY: Oxford University Press.

Harvie, D. (2000). Alienation, class and enclosure in UK universities. *Capital & Class, 71*(Summer), 103–132.

Harvie, D. (2008). Academic labor: Producing value and producing struggles. In T. Green, G. Rikowski, & H. Raduntz (Eds.), *Renewing dialogues in Marxism and education: Openings* (pp. 231–247). London, United Kingdom: Palgrave Macmillan.

Heims, S. J. (1993). *Constructing a social science for postwar America: The cybernetics group, 1946–1953*. London, United Kingdom: Cambridge University Press.

Hodfkirchner, W. (2007). A critical systems view of the internet. *Philosophy of the Social Sciences, 37*, 471–407.

Jones, R. (2004). *Soft machines: Nanotechnology and life*. New York, NY: Oxford University Press.

Langton, C. (Ed.). (1989). *Artificial life. Santa Fe Institute for Studies in the Sciences of Complexity*. Reading, MA: Addison-Wesley.

Law, J., & Urry, J. (2004). Enacting the social. *Economy and Society, 33*(3), 390–410.

Lazzarato, M. (2006). Immaterial Labor. In P. Virno, S. Buckley, & M. Hardt, (Eds.), *Radical tThought in Italy* (pp. 133–151). Minneapolis, MN: University of Minnesota Press.

Leyshon, A., & Thrift, N. (2007). The capitalization of almost everything: The future of finance and capitalism. *Theory, Culture & Society, 24*(7–8), 97–115.

Luhmann, N. (1995). *Social systems* (J. Bednarz, Jr. with D. Baecker, Trans.). Stanford, CA: Stanford University Press.

Maasen, S., & Weingart, P. (2000) *Metaphors and the dynamics of knowledge*. London, United Kingdom: Routledge.

Mance, E. A. (2008, July). *Solidarity economics*. Retrieved from http://turbulence.org.uk/turbulence-1/solidarity-economics/

Mandelbrot, B. (1975). *The fractal geometry of nature*. New York, NY: Freeman.

Mandelbrot, B. (1977). *Fractal forms, change and dimensions*. San Francisco, CA: Freeman.

Mandelbrot, B., & Hudson, R. L. (2004). *The (mis)behavior of markets: A fractal view of risk, ruin, and reward*. New York, NY: Basic Books.

Massumi, B. (n.d.). *The future birth of the affective fact*. Retrieved from http://browse.reticular.info/text/collected/massumi.pdf

Maturana, H., & Varela, F. (1980). *Autopoiesis and cognition*. Boston, MA: Reidel.

McNeil, D. H. (1993). Architectural criteria for a general theory of systems. In R. Packham (Ed.). *The ethical management of science as a system.* Hawkesbury, Australia: International Society for Systems Sciences.

Miller, J. G. (1978). *Living systems.* New York, NY: McGraw Hill.

Nowotny, H. (2005). The increase of complexity and its reduction emergent interfaces between the natural sciences, humanities and social sciences. *Theory, Culture & Society, 22*(5), 15–31.

Odum, H. (1971). *Environment, power and society.* New York, NY: Wiley.

Parsons, T. (1951). *The social system.* Glencoe, IL: Free Press.

Parsons, T. (1977). *Social systems and the evolution of action theory.* New York, NY: Free Press.

Pask, G. (1975). *The cybernetics of human learning and performance.* London, United Kingdom: Hutchinson.

Peters, M. A. (2008). Editorial: Complexity and knowledge systems. *Educational Philosophy and Theory, 40*(1), 1–3.

Peters, M. A., & Roberts, P. (2009). *The virtues of openness: Education and scholarship in a digital world.* Boulder, CO: Paradigm.

Pickel, A. (2006). *The problem of order in the global age: Systems and mechanisms.* New York, NY: Palgrave Macmillan.

Pickel, A. (2007). Rethinking systems theory: A programmatic introduction. *Philosophy of the Social Sciences, 37,* 391–407.

Pimentel, D. (1977). America's agricultural future. *The Economist, 21*(5), 15–19.

Power, D., & Scott, A. (Eds.). (2004). *Cultural industries and the production of culture.* London, United Kingdom: Routledge.

Prat, H. (1964). *Le champ unitaire en biologie.* Paris, France: Presses Universtaires de France.

Prigogine, I. (1955). *Thermodynamics of irreversible processes.* Springfield, IL: Thomas Press.

Rajan, K. S. (2006). *Biocapital: The constitution of postgenomic life.* Durham, NC: Duke University Press.

Rikowski, R. (2003). Value: The life blood of capitalism: Knowledge is the current key. *Policy Futures in Education, 1*(1), 160–178.

Robles, G., Merelo, J. J., & Gonzalez-Barahona, J. M. (2005). Self-organized development in libre software: a model based on the stigmergy concept. In *Proceedings of 6th International Workshop on Software Process Simulation and Modeling,* St. Louis, MO.

Sabeili, H. (1991). Process theory: a biological model of open systems. In *Proceedings of the 35th ISSS Meeting,* Ostersund, Sweden.

Sennett, R. (1999). *The corrosion of character: The personal consequences of work in the new capitalism.* New York, NY: W.W. Norton.

Shannon, C., & Weaver, W. (1949). *The mathematical theory of communication.* Urbana-Champaign, IL: University of Illinois Press,

Shirato, T., & Webb, J. (2003). *Understanding globalization.* London, United Kingdom: Sage.

Simon, H. A. (1962). The architecture of complexity (reprinted in *General Systems Yearbook,* Vol. X, 1965).

Slaughter, S. & Rhoades, G. (2004). *Academic capitalism and the new economy: Markets, states and higher education.* Baltimore, MD: The Johns Hopkins University Press.

Stalder, F. (2006). *Manuel Castells: The theory of the network society.* Malden, MA: Polity Press.

Summers-Effler, E. (2007). Vortexes of involvement: Social systems as turbulent flow. *Philosophy of the Social Sciences, 37,* 433–448.

Susi, T., & Ziemke, T. (2001). Social cognition, artefacts, and stigmergy: A comparative analysis of theoretical frameworks for the understanding of artefact-mediated collaborative activity. *Cognitive Systems Research, 2*(4), 273–290.

Teeple, G. (1995). *Globalization and the decline of social reform.* New York, NY, Humanities Press.

Terranova, T. (2004). *Network culture: Politics for the information age.* Ann Arbor, MI: Pluto Press.

Thom, R. (1975). *Structural stability and morphogenesis.* Reading, MA: Benjamin.

Urry, J. (2005). The complexity turn. *Theory, Culture & Society, 22*(5), 1–14.

Vercellone C. (Ed.). (2006). *Capitalismo cognitivo.* Rome: Manifestolibri.

Vestergaard, J. (2008). *Discipline in the global economy? International finance and the end of liberalism.* New York, NY: Routledge.

von Förster, H. (1981). *Observing systems.* Seaside, CA: Intersystems.

von Neumann, J. (1966). *Theory of self-producing automata.* Urbana-Champaign, IL: University of Illinois Press.

Walby, S. (2007). Complexity theory, systems theory, and multiple intersecting social inequalities. *Philosophy of the Social Sciences, 37*(4), 449–469.

Wallerstein, I. (1974). *The modern world system: Capitalist agriculture and the origins of the European world economy in the sixteenth century.* New York, NY: Academic Press.

Weiner, N. (1948). *Cybernetics or control and communication in the animal and the machine.* New York, NY: John Wiley & Sons.

Zadeh, L. (1965). Fuzzy sets. *Information and Control, 8,* 338–353.

Zeeuw, G. de (2000). Some problems in the observation of performance. In F. P. Luna (Ed.), *The performance of social systems: Perspectives and problems* (pp. 61–70). Dordrecht, the Netherlands: Kluwer Academic/Plenum Publishers.

Chapter 2

Education, Creativity and the Economy of Passions
New Forms of Educational Capitalism

Michael A. Peters

Introduction: The Creative Economy

The notion of the 'creative economy' is a concept and discourse that developed during the late 1990s and was strongly promoted by John Howkins (2002), a British media entrepreneur, who bases his analysis on the relationship between IP, creativity and money. Howkin's thesis is in part a rejuvenation and democratic reworking of the notion of entrepreneurship based on the understanding that it is ideas, people and things rather than land, labor or capital that have become the most important factors of production in the leading-edge liberal-capitalist economies. Howkins's thesis is echoed by Richard Florida (2002) in his *The Rise of the Creative Class* where he argues 'Human creativity is the ultimate economic resource' (p. xiii).

In one sense these new studies of the 'creative economy' grow out of a long gestation of blended discourses that go back at least to the early literatures in the economics of knowledge initiated by Friedrich von Hayek and Fritz Machlup in the 1940s and 1950s, to studies of the 'information economy' by Marc Porat in the late 1960s, and to the sociology of postindustrialism, a discourse developed differently by Daniel Bell and Alain Touraine in the early 1970s. The creative economy also highlights and builds upon important ideas given a distinctive formulation by Paul Romer under the aegis of endogenous growth theory in the 1990s, and aspects of the emerging literatures concerning national systems of innovations and entrepreneurship that figure in public policy formulation from the 1980s. Indeed, the notion of the 'creative economy' sits within a complicated and interconnected set of discourses that rapidly succeed, replace and overlap one another. This even set of literatures gave rise to the notion of the 'knowledge economy' that has dominated both national economic policy and development agendas since the early 1990s and has strong conceptual affinities with the creative economy.

The creative economy discourse combines elements from the earlier theories and formulations providing a recipe and policy mix that highlights creativity, innovation, distributive knowledge systems, social production and networking, the creative commons and the new communication technologies, along with an emphasis on the cultural and creative sector industries, cultural policy, and the emphasis on human and social capital formation especially through organizational learning, corporate training, and education at all levels. Buried in this discourse and its rapid uptake in public policy is an implicit account about the shifting nature of capitalism or at least of its leading sectors and also an attempt to promote and develop what I have called new forms of educational capitalism that cultivate a new spirit of enterprise and the enterprise curriculum, give a new emphasis to the entrepreneurial subject, encourage teaching for giftedness and creativity, prioritize accelerated and personal learning, and lend weight to 'consumer-citizens' and a new ethic of self-presentation and self-promotion (see Peters, 2004, 2005). This chapter provides an account of the creative economy in relation to education and the development of new forms of educational capitalism by reference to prevailing accounts of creativity. This chapter contrasts two accounts of creativity. The first I have called 'personal anarcho-aesthetics': it is the dominant model. This highly individualistic model emerged in the psychological literature at the turn of the century from sources in German idealism and Romanticism that emphasized the creative genius at one with Nature. It emphasizes the way in which creativity emerges from deep subconscious processes, involves the imagination, is anchored in the passions, cannot be directed and is beyond the rational control of the individual. This account has a close fit to business often as a form of 'brainstorming', 'mind-mapping' or 'strategic planning', and is closely associated with the figure of the risk-taking entrepreneur. This fit is not surprising given that Schumpeter's 'hero-entrepreneur' springs from the same Romantic sources as the creative genius (see Peters & Besley, 2007).

The second account I have called 'the design principle' and, by contrast to the first individualistic and irrational model, is both relational and social. This second account is more recent and tends to emerge in literatures that intersect between sociology, economics, technology and education. It surfaces in related ideas of 'social capital', 'situated learning', and 'P2P' (peer-to-peer) accounts of commons-based peer production. It is seen to be a product of social and networked environments—rich semiotic and intelligent environments in which everything speaks. It is also a product of knowledge systems design that allows a high degree of interaction and rests on principles of distributed knowledge and collective intelligence. This chapter traces the genealogies of these two contrasting accounts of creativity and their significance for educational practice before showing how both notions are strongly connected in accounts of new forms of capitalism that require a rethinking of the notion of creativity and its place in schools and institutions of higher education. The chapter begins by providing a context in terms of a history of the knowledge economy and the historical tendency toward aesthetic or designer capitalism.

Knowledge Economy and the Increasing Significance of Aesthetic Capitalism

For analytical purposes it is both possible and important to distinguish among the different and competing strands and readings of the knowledge economy. It is an important intellectual task not only to provide something of a chronological order for these readings but also to recognize their different assumptions and descriptions as well as their embedded political values. Clearly, not all are based on neoliberal orthodoxy and some predate neoliberalism while others provide a critique of the neoliberal project of globalization.

Table 1. History of the Knowledge Economy

1. Hayek's 1945 exploratory AER paper 'The Use of Knowledge in Society'[1] established the Austrian school perspective based on methodological individualism and the subjective theory of value;
2. Economic value of knowledge studies based on Fritz Machlup's[2] studies of the U.S. production and distribution of knowledge in the late 1950s and after;
3. Alain Touraine[3] and new social movements literature he helped develop forecasts a symbolic economy predicated on the industrialization of education and students as a new knowledge class;
4. Peter Drucker[4] focuses on the knowledge worker, the corporation as community and establishes the field of knowledge management;
5. 'Technological revolution' studies popularised by Daniel Bell[5] and Alvin Toffler[6] in the 1970s based on the sociology of postindustrialism;

Table 1. History of the Knowledge Economy *(continued)*

6. Jean-François Lyotard[7] brings together the postindustrial economy with postmodern culture to suggest the leading sciences and technologies are significantly all language-based;
7. Growth of knowledge management approaches (techno-centric, organizational & ecological) in the 1980s focus on the creation, distribution and transfer of knowledge and associated notions of intellectual capital;[8]
8. OECD's model of knowledge economy based on endogenous growth theory;[9]
9. The World Bank's 'Knowledge for Development' and 'Education for the Knowledge Economy';[10]
10. 'New economy' readings of the 1990s;[11]
11. The role of information in market;[12]
12. The learning economy based on Lundvall's work;[13]
13. The 'weightless' economy based on Danny Quah's work;[14]
14. Global information society derived from the World Summit (WSIS);[15]
15. Postmodern global systems theory based on network theory after Manuel Castells.[16]

One of the main threads running through these different conceptions is an increasing formalism of capitalism characterized by the mathematicization and aestheticization variously expressed by reference to the linguistic, communicative, information, cultural turns that have been observed in fields as disparate as economics, philosophy, sociology, communication and cultural studies (see Peters & Besley, 2006, especially Chapter 2). The descriptions abound—the symbolic economy; the sign economy, the information economy, the digital economy, the knowledge economy, the cultural economy, the creative economy, the aesthetic economy. They all point to the increasing significance of symbols and signs and their manipulation in encoding and decoding information flows that establish economic value-chains and encourage further technological innovation and diffusion. While the sources of the information or knowledge economy in its first theorizations can be traced to the 1960s it is not until the 1990s that the discourses of 'new economy', 'knowledge economy', and 'creative economy' are popularized and become policy metaphors, the latter two more in evidence after the dot.com bubble burst in 2001. This is my rough characterization of what I call 'Aesthetic or Designer Capitalism' in which the economy of information and ideas, and traditional and related notions of freedom, self-expression, and creativity become the central themes:

- 'The economization of culture and the culturalization of economics' (du Gay & Pryke, 2002) where 'Economic and symbolic processes are more than ever interlaced and interarticulated' (Lash & Urry, 1994, p. 64).
- The info-communicative turn based on digitalization, speed & compression—all new technologies significantly language-based (Lyotard, 1984).
- Underlying epistemologies of *design* for all knowledge systems including Web 2.0 and semantic web.
- Investment in human capital & emergence of immaterial labor—postmodern flexibilization facilitated by social networking' (Boltansky & Chiapello, 2005).
- Importance of intellectual assets & emergence of global intellectual property rights regimes—patents, copyright, trademarks, advertising, financial & consulting services, & education.
- Significance of electronic, databases & emergence of new media based on radical concordance of sound, text and image.
- Digital goods are nonrival, infinitely expansible, discrete, recombinant (Quah, 2001) & permit radical decentralization but also encourage geographically clusters and corridors based on face-to-face and tacit knowledge.
- Emergence of paradigm of social or cultural production (Benkler, 2006) where consumers are active co-creators.
- Organizational cultures structure cognition and affect and reconstitute situated knowledge practices and activities of fast 'knowing capitalism' (Thrift, 2005).
- Network systems that permit economies of scale and monopolistic tendencies even more dangerously than traditional industrial economies (witness the rapid rise of Microsoft and Google), tend towards either oligopolistic (e.g., broadcast media) or mass democratic (e.g., completely horizontal and deterritorialized) forms.

This is a sketch of a form of knowledge capitalism that with co-author Tina Besley I have discussed at length (Peters & Besley, 2006) together with its new educational forms and effects. Under the thematic of globalism, consumerism and empire, as Thomas M. Kemple (2007, p. 147) remarks 'a revived conceptual and critical vocabulary is emerging to account for—or discredit—the latest metamorphoses of "the new capitalism"' by which he means the works he seeks to review: one of Bourdieu's (2005) last works devoted to how '"the economy" cultivates particular modes of conduct...and "schemes of vision and division" (habitus in Bourdieu's terms) articulated within fields of struggle over forms of capital' (p. 148); Boltanski and Chiapello's (2005) *The New Spirit of Capitalism* represented by interactions among three dimensions justification / legitimation, social / artistic critique, and employability / profitability; and Nigel Thrift's (2005) *Knowing Capitalism* concerned with 'the actual business practice of "selling ideas"—that is, the pragmatic dissemination of knowledge and sites of performance of the new capitalism's many scripts' (p. 154). His Weberian interpretation insists on adding the Protestant values of autonomy and authenticity to Boltanski and Chiapello's schematization of the three latest mutations in the 'spirit of capitalism' (SC) since the late 19th century, thus:

SC1 (mid-18th century): pre-industrial ascetic work ethic infused with civic ideals

SC2 (late 19th century): industrial assembly-line production combined with social engineering

SC3 (mid-20th century): post-industrial restructuring in part provoked by counter-cultural values

SC4 (late 20th century): postmodern flexibilization facilitated by social networking (p. 152).

The story of these mutations, I would argue could easily be retold or narrativized in terms of the central value of creativity as it relates to evolving liberal notions of freedom and self-expression, the growing significance of printing, publishing and copyright in the sixteenth and seventeenth centuries, together with the institutionalization of science and the modern research university, and its increasing formalization (mathematicization, computerization and aestheticization) in the late twentieth century. Such a story would of course also draw connections and parallels between what I have called 'the opening of the book' (Peters, 2007)—the shift from closed to open textual environments—and the larger context of the development of the open society and so-called free trade, although not uncritically. Creativity as a value takes pride of place in this liberal metanarrative and through the Romantic Movement also begins to re-marry elements of culture with economy in 'cultural economy', often inflected with 'ideas', 'knowledge', 'innovation' and 'learning' (Archibugi & Lundvall, 2002; Lundvall, 1992; Lundvall & Johnson, 1994; Lundvall & Borra, 1999; David & Foray, 2003; Hartley, 2007).

Clearly, today there is a strong renewal of interest by politicians and policy-makers worldwide in the related notions of creativity and innovation, especially in relation to terms like 'the creative economy', 'knowledge economy', 'enterprise society', 'entrepreneurship' and 'national systems of innovation'. In its rawest form the notion of the Creative Economy emerges from a set of claims that suggests that the Industrial Economy is giving way to the Creative Economy based on the growing power of ideas and virtual value-chain—the turn from steel and hamburgers to software and intellectual property. In this context increasingly public policy latches onto the issues of copyright as an aspect of intellectual property, the control of piracy, new distribution systems, network literacy, public service content, the creative industries, new interoperability standards, the WIPO and the development agenda, WTO and trade, and the policy means to bring creativity and commerce together. At the same time this focus on creativity has exercised strong appeal to policy-makers who wish to link education more firmly to new forms of capitalism emphasizing how creativity must be taught, how educational theory and research can be used to improve student learning in mathematics, reading and science, and how different models of intelligence and creativity can inform educational practice.

Personal Anarcho-Aesthetics, Creativity and the Roots of Romanticism

> The highest demand that is made on an artist is this: that he be true to Nature, study her, imitate her, and produce something that resembles her phenomena. How great, how enormous, this demand is, is not always kept in mind; and the true artist himself learns it by experience only, in the course of his progressive development. Nature is separated from Art by an enormous chasm, which genius itself is unable to bridge without external assistance.
> —J. W. Goethe, 'Einleitung in die Propylaen', 1798, at http://web.archive.org/web/20000621124111/www.warwick.ac.uk/fac/arts/History/teaching/sem10/goethe.html

> The true source of art and of the beautiful is feeling. Feeling reveals the proper idea and aim of art, and points to the certain knowledge of the artist's intention, though the proof of this lies in practice rather than words.
> —Friedrich Schlegel, Extract from *Descriptions of Paintings*, 1802–1804

In *The Roots of Romanticism* Isaiah Berlin (1999), the Latvian-born political philosopher and historian of ideas who was to become one of the leading liberal thinkers of the twentieth century, shies away from the problem of definition and yet suggests that the romantic movement was a radical shift in values that occurred in the latter half of the eighteenth century. Berlin describes romanticism as 'the greatest single shift in the consciousness of the West that has occurred' (p. 1). The book consists of a series of lectures—The A.W. Mellon Lectures in the Fine Arts—that Berlin gave at the National Gallery of Art, Washington, D.C., in 1965 and broadcast by the BBC a year later. I turn first to Berlin on romanticism because I want to argue that 'creativity' as a concept that comes down to us in one dominant form is 'Romantic' to the core and that its kinship concept map has to be drawn against a background of related concepts—'genius', 'individualism', 'the artist', 'Nature', 'emotion' or 'feeling', 'infinity', 'aestheticism', 'the irrational', 'primitivism', 'mysticism', 'the visionary'—that makes up a general pattern of change that cannot be reduced to a textbook definition. 'Creativity' and the genealogy of the concept, at least in the West is part of a defining tradition, that is difficult to separate out the concept from the network that sustains and gives it life. It is also a grave error then to want to fish it up out of the pond and to dry it off before exhibiting it as the causal link to some other desirable political or economic state, say, 'innovation', or 'liberty', or 'imagination', that then can be analyzed, opened up, dissected, and reassembled for the brave new world of the postmodern creative state, school or economy.

This is how Defillippi et al. (2007, p. 511) describe the paradoxes of creativity and the organizational and management challenge of the cultural economy in a way that highlights the persistent significance of the Romantic account:

> The current shift towards knowledge-based societies has turned creativity into a source of strategic advantage in the contemporary managerial and political lexicon. Perhaps in the most pronounced fashion, Florida (2002, p. 4) even boldly claims that creativity '...is now the decisive source of competitive advantage' (for critiques of this position, see Kotkin, 2005; Peck, 2005). Since creativity is also popularly regarded as something genuinely spontaneous and irrational and hence, by its very definition, impossible to control, the current managerial infatuation with creativity as a strategic asset for gaining competitive advantage must be squared with empirical research and extant theory.

Usefully, the authors provide an extended account of the model that I am discussing and comment on the difficulties for the private sector knowledge management and by obvious implication also the difficulty facing curriculum planners, educational policy-makers and teachers who think there is an easy fit or translation from creativity in schools to innovation in the workplace:

> Creativity in the 'Western' tradition from Plato to Freud and Popper has mostly been regarded as something divergent, impulsive and 'messy' (De Bono, 1992: 2). This particular perception of creativity precipitated the assumption that creativity is embodied in a particular type of personality: the individual creative genius (Bilton & Leary, 2002: 54; Boden, 1994b). Emblematic accounts of irrational genius and spontaneous invention in science and art, such as Kekule's discovery of the benzene molecule while dozing in front of the fire, Coleridge's poem Kublai Khan or Picasso's painting of Guernica have served to illustrate this construal of creativity (Weisberg, 1993). In this romantic perception of the enigmatic eureka!-moment, a scientific approach to creativity is not just philosophically uninteresting, but impossible (Boden, 1994b: 3). (p. 512)

The Romantic period emphasized the self, creativity, imagination and the value of art in contrast to the Enlightenment emphasis on both rationalism and empiricism. As such philosophically Romanticism represents a shift from the objective to the subjective. Its roots can be found in the work of Jean-Jacques Rousseau and Immanuel Kant and later Johann Wolfgang von Goethe (1749-1832), Freidrich Wilhelm Joseph von Schelling (1775-1854), and George Wilhelm Friedrich Hegel (1770-1831) in Germany and Samuel Taylor Coleridge (1772-1834) and William Wordsworth (1770-1850) in Britain. Under these writers the imagination was elevated to a position as the supreme faculty of the mind. This contrasted distinctly with the traditional arguments for the supremacy of reason. The Romantics tended to define and to present the imagination as our ultimate "shaping" or creative power, the approximate human equivalent of the creative powers of nature or even deity. It is dynamic, an active, rather than passive power, with many functions. Imagination is the primary faculty for creating all art. On a broader scale, it is also the faculty that helps humans to constitute reality, for (as Wordsworth suggested), we not only perceive the world around us, but also in part create it. Uniting both reason and feeling (Coleridge described it with the paradoxical phrase, "intellectual intuition"), imagination is extolled as the ultimate synthesizing faculty, enabling humans to reconcile differences and opposites in the world of appearance. The reconciliation of opposites is a central ideal for the Romantics. Finally, imagination is inextricably bound up with the other two major concepts, for it is presumed to be the faculty which enables us to "read" nature as a system of symbols.

Today a number of literary theorists have called into question two major Romantic perceptions: that the literary text is a separate, individuated, living "organism"; and that the artist is a fiercely independent genius who creates original works of art. In current theory, the separate, "living" work has been dissolved into a sea of "intertextuality", derived from and part of a network or "archive" of other texts—the many different kinds of discourse that are part of any culture. In this view, too, the independently sovereign artist has been demoted from a heroic, consciously creative agent, to a collective "voice", more controlled than controlling, the intersection of other voices, other texts, ultimately dependent upon possibilities dictated by language systems, conventions, and institutionalized power structures. It is an irony of history, however, that the explosive appearance on the scene of these subversive ideas, delivered in what seemed to the establishment to be radical manifestoes, and written by linguistically powerful individuals, has recapitulated the revolutionary spirit and events of Romanticism itself.

Critiques of romanticism and subjectivism have been restated so many times that they may sound tired and repetitive to some. It might appear trite and even boring to keep remaking this case. But even so, discourses of subjectivism and romanticism continue to permeate interpretations of creativity. Nowhere is this clearer than in legal and economic definitions. In intellectual property law, for instance, we find that discourses of the author, romanticism, subjectivism, originality and genius are still rife. Given this, it is no surprise that sociologists will keep reminding us, pointing to the sociological "facts" of art and creativity.

Political economists take a different approach. They ask why these specious discourses of romanticism and subjectivism remain pervasive. And they argue that the reasons are clear-cut. Look no further than the commodification and privatization of artistic creativity. The story goes like this: in order to generate profit from art, creative products must be transformed into property that may be owned and exchanged by private profiteers. "Intellectual property rights", enforced by the state, are the mechanism for achieving this. Intellectual property requires a legal persona who "owns" the creative product in order to function: the "author". This legal fiction is the sovereign "individual", endowed with the power of creation, someone who "justifiably" has ownership rights over their creative goods and "deserves" to be handsomely rewarded. These creative goods, even though they were created in and out of the public, may then be owned by private entities (and not necessarily the "original creators") and removed from what we share in common. Then, as property, these creative products can be exchanged among private hands, and traded and consumed in the market place. Arts and Humanities departments in universities make room for "Marketing" and "Creative Industries" departments, where the value of creativity is reduced to its profitability.

In our view, the attempts of these networks to reinstate a "commons" in a world of capitalist privatization is a significant contemporary development. If nothing else, these networks create a vantage point from which we can view the profound increase in the commodification and privatization of our common creative life—where shared concepts and ideas are privatized and expropriated from the common by profit-makers. Thanks to them we are less likely to allow the marketing and PR of the creative industries fool us into thinking they are the true friends of creativity. Or convince us that sharing our creative work with one another is criminal. If anything, property is the corruption and the crime, an act of theft from the common substrate of creativity. Copyleft groups have created critique and resistance to the intellectual property regime. More positively, these networks have given us new possibilities. They are not only reactive, but productive: they make available new forms of subjectivity and life; they remind us that we only ever attain the possible by time and again reaching for the impossible; they are social laboratories. Let us hope, for a possible future of creativity to come.

Creativity and the Design Principle

Under the spell of the creative economy discourse there has been a flourishing of new accelerated learning methodologies together with a focus on giftedness and the design of learning programs for exceptional children. One strand of the emerging literature highlights the role of the creative, cultural and expressive arts, of performance and aesthetics in general, and the significant role of design as an underlying infrastructure or epistemology for the creative economy. Another strand focuses on the architecture and design associated with Web 2.0 and the semantic web and the way a host of new platforms enable Web-enabled knowledge services and knowledge trading as well as supporting innovation, creativity, collaboration, social production and information sharing (*MIT Sloan Management Review*, 2007; Mentzas et al., 2007). It is worth dwelling on this aspect further given that it prefigures one of the two accounts of creativity that I seek to contrast. As Greaves (2007, p. 94) has commented 'Web 2.0 isn't a precise term. It refers to a class of Web-based applications that were recognized ex post facto to share certain design patterns'. He refers to Tim O'Reilly's (2005) early characterization of Web 2.0 using a set of oppositions against classic Web techniques and design metaphors: between directories and tag systems, Web site stickiness and RSS syndication, content management systems and wikis, screen scraping and open Web APIs, personal Web pages and blogs, and client/server style publishing and massive user participation. He goes on to argue:

> Many exemplary Web 2.0-style applications and companies now exist, including Flickr, Wikipedia, YouTube, Six Apart, Technorati, Google, del.icio.us, Greasemonkey, MySpace, Facebook, Zimbra, and many others. Most Web 2.0 applications share common themes, including
>
> - weaving together different Web-accessible data and services (especially with UI technologies such as AJAX and powerful scripting languages such as Ruby on Rails);
> - depending on collective intelligence, social networks, and user-contributed content and tags;
> - addressing long-tail markets and scenarios (see Chris Anderson's article "The Long Tail" at www.wired.com/wired/archive/12.10/tail.html);
> - repurposing and remixing Web-based data; and
> - enhancing existing Web-based data with personalization capabilities, such as tailored feeds and contextual recommendation systems. (p. 95)

As Kwei-Jay Lin (2007, p. 101) indicates 'There is no one set of technologies that every Web 2.0 system uses':

> Many new technologies make the Web interface smooth and intuitive. Ajax, JavaScript, Cascading Style Sheets (CSS), Document Object Model (DOM), Extensible HTML (XHTML), XSL Transformations (XSLT)/XML, and Adobe Flash provide users with a rich and fun interactive experience without the drawbacks of most old Web applications. These technologies display and deliver Web services just like desktop software, making distributed processing difficulties invisible. Other new technologies make it easy for Web services to connect to multiple data and information sources. XML-RPC, Representational State Transfer (REST), RSS, Atom, mashups, and similar technologies facilitate the subscription, propagation, reuse, and intermixing of Web content. Perhaps the most important resource for Web 2.0 is the user. Providing friendly tools for user participation in content creation, consumption, and distribution has been the key to success (and failure) for many startups in the Web 2.0 era. Technologies such as blogs, wikis, podcasts, and vodcasts foster the growth of new

Web communities. Technologies are also in place to make Web sites more scalable. For example, Google and Yahoo! Process most requests in less than a second, and connections to popular user-based Web sites such as YouTube and Flickr are nearly effortless. (pp. 101–102)

It is these applications that have driven the likes of Lessig (2004) and Benkler (2006) to talk more broadly about the change in the mode of social production towards a new kind of freedom based on convergences between open course, open access, and the creative commons. Perhaps, more than any other this strand based around Web 2.0 developments with the democratic goal of encouraging all user-participants to create, share, distribute, and enjoy ideas and information, that brings commerce and creativity together in educational settings, not only in terms of education as a source and research center for creative applications for Web-based systems but also as spin-off university companies and, even more importantly, as a market subject to endless fashion gadgetry and redesign.

Notes

1. Hayek's 1945 paper (available at http://www.econlib.org/Library/Essays/hykKnw1.html) poses the problem of the rational economic order as 'the utilization of knowledge which is not given to anyone in its totality.' Hayek's paper was also conceived as part of the attack on the socialist calculation debate.
2. Machlup, a student of Von Mises and the Austrian school, came to the US in 1933 on a Rockefeller fellowship that took him to Columbia, Harvard, Stanford and Chicago. He held various visiting professorships at a number of US universities before accepted a post at Johns Hopkins in political economy in 1947, and later Princeton, where he completed work leading to the publication of *The Economic Review of the Patent System* (1958), *The Production and Distribution of Knowledge in the United States* (1962), and *Education and Economic Growth* (1970). He published the three volumes comprising *Information through the Printed Word: The Dissemination of Scholarly, Scientific, and Intellectual Knowledge* (1978) and the first three volumes of the projected ten volume series *Knowledge: Its Creation, Distribution, and Economic Significance* (1980, 1982, 1983).
3. See Alain Touraine's *The Post-Industrial Society*.
4. See Peter Drucker (1969, 1993).
5. In *The Coming of Post-Industrial Society* Daniel Bell (1973) argued that such a society would be based on information, the centrality of new science-based industries and managed by a new technical elite.
6. Alvin Toffler, the American futurist, predicted third-wave society based on knowledge production, diversity and demassification where 'prosumers' fulfill their own needs.

7 Jean-François Lyotard (1984) lists these as: 'phonology and theories of linguistics, problems of communication and cybernetics, modern theories of algebra and informatics, computers and their languages, problems of translation and the search for areas of compatibility among computer languages, problems of information storage and data banks, telematics and the perfection of intelligent terminals, to paradoxology'. These technical transformations have permanently altered the two principal functions of knowledge—research and the transmission of acquired learning.
8 See, e.g., Nonaka & Takeuchi (1995).
9 See OECD's (1996, 1997, 2001) early publications on the knowledge-based economy.
10 See the World Bank's 'Knowledge for Development' website at http://web.worldbank.org/WBSITE/EXTERNAL/WBI/WBIPROGRAMS/KFDLP/0,,menuPK:461238~pagePK:64156143~piPK:64154155~theSitePK:461198,00.html
11 See, e.g., Brenner (2002), Baily (2002), Temple (2002).
12 See Hayek's classic 1945 essay "The Use of Knowledge in Society" at http://www.econlib.org/library/Essays/hykKnw1.html.
13 See Lundvall (1992), Lundvall & Johnson (1994), Lundvall and Borra (1999).
14 See Danny Quah's personal webpage for a selection of recent papers at http://econ.lse.ac.uk/staff/dquah/index_own.html
15 See the WSIS website at http://www.itu.int/wsis/index.html
16 See, in particular, Castells (1996) and webpage at http://annenberg.usc.edu/Faculty/Communication/CastellsM.aspx#recentpubs

References

Archibugi, D., & Lundvall B.-A. (Eds.). (2002). *The globalizing learning economy*. New York, NY: Oxford University Press.

Baily, M. N. (2002). The new economy: Post mortem or second wind? *Journal of Economic Perspectives, 16*(2), 3-22.

Bell, D. (1974). *The coming of post-industrial society: A venture in social forecasting*. London, United Kingdom: Heinemann.

Benkler, Y. (2006). *The wealth of networks*. New Haven, CT: Yale University Press. Retrieved from http://www.benkler.org/Benkler_Wealth_Of_Networks.pdf

Berry, D., & Moss, G. 'Art, creativity, intellectual property and the commons: Can free/libre culture transform art?' Retrieved from http://www.freesoftwaremagazine.com/articles/focus-art_and_commons

Berry, D. M., & McCallion, M. (2005). Copyleft and copyright: New debates about the ownership of ideas. *Eye: The International Review of Graphic Design, 14*, 74-75.

Berry, D. M., & Moss, G. (2005). The libre culture manifesto. *Free Software Magazine*. Retrieved from http://www.freesoftwaremagazine.com/free_issues/issue_02/libre_manifesto/

Bilton, C., & Leary, R. (2002). What can managers do for creativity? Brokering creativity in the creative industries. *International Journal of Cultural Policy, 8*, 49-64.

Boden, M. A. (1994a). What is creativity? In M. A. Boden (Ed.), *Dimensions of creativity* (pp. 75–118). Cambridge, MA: MIT Press.

Boden, M. A. (1994b). Introduction. In M. A. Boden (Ed.), *Dimensions of creativity*. Cambridge, MA: MIT Press.

Boltanski, L., & Chiapello, È. (2005). *The new spirit of capitalism* (G. Elliott, Trans.). Brooklyn, NY: Verso.

Bourdieu, P. (1983). The field of cultural production: Or the economic world reversed, *Poetics, 12*, 311–356.

Bourdieu, P. (2005). *The social structures of the econ*omy (C. Turner, Trans.). Cambridge, United Kingdom: Polity Press.

Brenner, R. (2002). *The boom and the bubble: The US in the world economy.* London, United Kingdom: Verso.

Brown, J. S., & Duguid, P. (1991). Organizational learning and communities of practice: Towards a unified view of working, learning and innovation. *Organization Science, (2)1*, 40–57.

Castells, M. (1996). *The rise of the network society.* Oxford, United Kingdom: Blackwell.

Cooke, P. (2002). *Knowledge economies. clusters, learning and cooperative advantage.* London, United Kingdom: Routledge.

David, P., & Foray, D. (2003). Economic fundamentals of the knowledge society. *Policy Futures in Education, 1*, 20–49.

De Bono, E. (1992). *Serious creativity: Using the power of lateral thinking to create new ideas.* London, United Kingdom: Harper & Collins.

Defillippi, R., Grabher, G., & Jones, C. (2007). Introduction to paradoxes of creativity: managerial and organizational challenges in the cultural economy. *Journal of Organizational Behavior, 28*, 511–521.

Drucker, P. (1969). *The age of discontinuity; Guidelines to our changing society.* New York, NY: Harper & Row.

Drucker, P. (1993). *Post-capitalist society.* Oxford, United Kingdom: Butterworth Heinemann.

Du Gay, P. (1997). *Production of culture, cultures of production.* London, United Kingdom: Sage.

Florida, R. (2002). *The rise of the creative class.* New York, NY: Basic Books.

Freeman, C. (1995). The national system of innovation in historical perspective. *Cambridge Journal of Economics, 19*, 5–24.

Greaves, M. (2007). Semantic Web 2.0. *IEEE Intelligent Systems*, March/April, 94–96. Retrieved from www.computer.org/intelligent

Hartley, D. (2007). Organizational epistemology, education and social theory'. *British Journal of Sociology of Education, 28*(2), 195–208.

Hesmondhalgh, D. (2002). *The cultural industries.* London, United Kingdom: Sage.

Hesmondhalgh, D., & Pratt, A. C. (2005). Cultural industries and cultural policy. *International Journal of Cultural Policy, 11*, 1–13.

Howkins, J. (2002). *The creative economy: How people make money from ideas.* London, United Kingdom: Penguin

Kemple, T. M. (2007). Spirits of late capitalism. *Theory Culture Society, 24,* 147–159.

Kotkin, J. (2005). Uncool cities. *Prospect, 115.* Retrieved from http://www.prospectmagazine.co.uk/magazine/uncoolcities/

Kwei-Jay Lin. (2007). Building Web 2.0. *Computer, May,* 101–102.

Lessig, L. (2004). *Free culture: How big media uses technology and the law to lock down culture and control creativity.* New York, NY: Allen Lane.

Lundvall, B. A., & Borra, S. (1999). *The globalising learning economy: Implications for innovation policy.* Luxembourg, Luxembourg: Office for Official Publications of the European Communities.

Lundvall, B. A., & Johnson, B. (1994). The learning economy. *Journal of Industry Studies, 1,* 23–42.

Lundvall, B.-A. (Ed.). (1992). *National systems of innovation: Towards a theory of innovation and interactive learning.* London, United Kingdom: Pinter.

Lyotard, J.-F. (1984). *The postmodern condition* (G. Bennington & B. Massumi, Trans.). Minneapolis, MN: University of Minnesota Press.

Machlup, F. (1962) *The production and distribution of knowledge in the United States.* Princeton, NJ: Princeton University Press.

Mentzas, G., Kafentzis, K., & Georgolios, P. (2007). Knowledge services on the semantic web. *Communications of the ACM, 50*(10), 53–58.

MIT Sloan Management Review. (2007). The future of the web [Special Report, Spring]. *48*(3).

Nonaka, I., & Takeuchi, H. (1995). *The knowledge-creating company.* Oxford, United Kingdom: Oxford University Press.

O'Reilly, T. (2005). *What is web 2.0: Design patterns and business models for the next generation of software.* Retrieved from www.oreillynet.com/pub/a/oreilly/tim/news/2005/09/30/what-is-web-20.html

OECD. (1996). *The knowledge-based economy.* Paris, France: OECD Publications.

OECD. (1997). *National innovation systems.* Paris, France: OECD Publications

OECD. (2001). *OECD science, technology and industry scoreboard. Towards a knowledge-based economy.* Paris, France: OECD.

Peck, J. (2005). Struggling with the creative class. *International Journal of Urban and Regional Research, 29,* 740–770.

Peters, M., & Besley, T. (2006). *Building knowledge cultures: Education and development in the age of knowledge capitalism.* Lanham, MD: Rowman & Littlefield.

Peters, M., & Besley, T. (2007). Academic entrepreneurs and the creative economy. *Thesis Eleven 8*(1), 88–105.

Peters, M. A. (2007). Opening the book: From the closed to open text. *International Journal of the Book, 5*(1), 77–84

Peters, M. A. (2004). Citizen-consumers, social markets and the reform of the public service. *Policy Futures in Education, 2* (3 & 4), 621–632.

Peters, M. A. (2005). The new prudentialism in education: Actuarial rationality and the entrepreneurial self. *Educational Theory, 55*(2), 123–137.

Romer, P. M. (1986). Increasing returns and long-run growth. *Journal of Political Economy, 94*(5), 1002–1037.

Rooney, D., Hearn, G., Mandeville, T., & Joseph, R. (2003). *Public policy in knowledge-based economies: Foundations and frameworks.* Cheltenham, United Kingdom: Edward Elgar.

Scott, A. J., & Power, D. (2004). *Cultural industries and the production of culture.* London, United Kingdom: Routledge.

Temple, J. R. W. (2002). The assessment: The new economy. *Review of Economic Policy, 18*(3), 241–264.

Thrift, N. (2005). *Knowing capitalism.* London, United Kingdom: Sage.

Tödtling, F., Lehner, P., & Trippl, M. (2006). Innovation in knowledge intensive industries: The nature and geography of knowledge links. *European Planning Studies, 14*(8), 1035–1057.

Touraine, A. (1971). *The post-industrial society: Tomorrow's social history classes, conflicts and culture in the programmed society.* New York, NY: Random House.

Weisberg, R. W. (1993). *Creativity: Beyond the myth of genius.* New York, NY: Freeman.

Chapter 3

Greening the Knowledge Economy
Ecosophy, Ecology and Economy

Michael A. Peters

Introduction

This chapter argues that the most sustainable and 'productive' interface in advanced postindustrial societies in the twenty-first century will be that between the knowledge and the 'green economy'. It charts three forms of the knowledge economy—the 'creative', 'learning' 'open science' economy—each of which profiles education as a central activity and 'learning processes' as the source of intellectual energy driving the new educational environment and shaping emergent knowledge ecologies. It discusses the significance of network analysis as a broad methodology that provides the basis in terms of policy for yoking large systems together—ecosophy, ecology and economics and social, ecological, and economic sustainability. Finally, the chapter outlines the concept of 'greening the knowledge economy' as a basis for long-term sustainability.

I begin by discussing methodology in environmental educational research by employing an approach from green philosophy (ecosophy) and green political economy to examine some wider conceptual issues concerning learning processes within the 'knowledge economy.'[1] This constitutes 'wide-canvas research' with a visionary element that is designed to demonstrate the importance of philosophical research in relation to broad conceptual questions that attempt to look for the connections and integrations among ecosophy, ecology and economy in an approach that highlights education and learning as the central human activities that can enhance sustainability in its ecological, economic and educational forms. It is also an example of *linked-up policy* analysis (cf. linked-up government) based upon the understanding and integration of large systems. What this age demands more than ever is an understanding not simply of systems in natural, social and geo-political environments and their interrelations but also the logic of large-scale system events and their impacts for humanity. In the economic and political realm as social scientists we need to know more about the logic of large scale events governing system failures such as the collapse of the Soviet system in 1989 and the collapse of neoliberal global financial system in 2009. The social sciences have not been good at predicting or analyzing these kinds of events which demand a better interface between social and natural sciences and their mediation and understanding through new mathematical and computational theories of complex systems, of complexity and chaos, and of the difficulties with formal mathematical modeling and simulation.[2]

The approach in this chapter is an example of doing environmental education research with complex issues of conceptualization, contextualization, representation and legitimization. The approach is a combination of different methodologies and perspectives drawing on both philosophical scholarship and argument, and the tradition of radical political economy, applied to the contemporary policy problems of the knowledge economy and the role of education and learning within it. The chapter attempts to demonstrate the need for understanding the importance of philosophical argumentation to strategic research interests in environmental education and to building a case for understanding the concept of environment as a suitable perspective in order to trace the complex ecologies comprising knowledge societies and economies. The argument is made that the most sustainable and 'productive' interface in advanced postindustrial societies in the twenty-first century will be that between the knowledge and the 'green economy'— what I refer to as the 'greening of the knowledge economy'. This chapter also demonstrates the need for an eclectic, synthesizing, synoptic, vision-based and radically multidisciplinary approach that draws upon a range of methodologies such as network analysis and systems thinking especially in relation to distributed cognition, media, knowledge, pedagogy and energy systems.

President Barack Obama in his address on the U.S. economy at Georgetown University (Tuesday April 14, 2009) laid out five pillars of the new foundations for recovering the American dream: new rules for Wall Street and greater regulation of finance capitalism with less emphasis of manipulation of numbers and more emphasis on making; investment in education at all levels and the preparation of students for the twenty-first century; the promotion and investment in clean-green energy technologies designed to utilize renewable resources and promote energy efficiencies while reducing the dependency on Middle East oil; reforming the health care system (Medicare, Medicaid), reducing inflated costs and providing a system of universal provision; reducing the deficit and creating a sustainable economic future for America. For Obama's administration these five pillars are the basis of long-term economic sustainability signaling a deliberate move away from the speculative bubble of an unregulated neoliberal finance capitalism that led to the worst global recession since the end of WWII and historic number of foreclosures and job losses.

The so-called 'financialization of capitalism' led to the rise of speculative finance culture that benefited hedge fund and Wall Street financiers at the expense of the rest of the population causing credit and finance imbalances and system crises. The spectacular growth of finance capital based itself upon the selling of financial derivatives, credit-default swaps and securitized risk products. Managed hedge funds that were packaged and sold on resulted in overvalued assets and a labyrinthine maze where it was no longer possible to fathom who owned the risk any longer. This new speculative finance culture collapsed distinctions between commercial and investment banking (beginning with the rescinding of the 1933 Glass-Speigel Act in 1994) and gave way to excessive profits, massive fraud and a crisis of markets and financial institutions. It also imperiled the architecture and ecology of the whole global economy leading George Soros to call it the 'era of the destruction of capital'. Some thirty trillion was wiped off equity assets; a further thirty trillion was wiped off the books through lost production, the subprime mortgage market and bailout attempts to ring-fence other toxic assets. Together the financial crisis and global climate change and broader ecological challenges demand a new model of how America and the world pursues economic prosperity with a greater emphasis on long term sustainability, state-centric policies and greater regulation aimed at reinvestment in public infrastructure as well as education, health and renewal energy forms.

The neoliberal era had encouraged a form of socioeconomic evolution of wage-laboring 'man' of industrial capitalism into global postindustrial 'smart investor' with a balanced portfolio. The Obama ecological era promises to place the emphasis once again on an economic identity based of 'making' rather than 'speculating', on diligence, hard work and community rebuilding rather than becoming a landlord with a portfolio of investment properties, able to retire early and live off investment returns. For Middle America and for the UK middle class—so-called Anglo-American model of capitalism—the dream of easy returns from smart investment and continuous monitoring of stock markets has evaporated. By contrast the Obama era emphasizes an age of renewed collective responsibility based on ecological, market and social sustainability. The efficient market thesis has been replaced by an acknowledgement of market failure essential to both ecological economics and to the 'sign', symbolic or knowledge economy.

The chapter is structured into the three sections. First, it charts three forms of the knowledge economy—the 'creative', 'learning' 'open science' economy—each of which profiles education as a central activity and 'learning processes' as the source of intellectual energy driving the new educational environment and shaping emergent knowledge ecologies. Second, it briefly discusses the significance of network analysis as a broad methodology that provides the basis in terms of policy for yoking large systems together—ecosophy, ecology and economics and social, ecological, and economic sustainability. Third, the chapter outlines the concept of 'greening the knowledge economy' as a basis for long term sustainability.

Three Forms of the Knowledge Economy: Creativity, Learning and Open Science

It is important to distinguish a number of different strands and readings of the knowledge economy and important to do so because it provides a history of a policy idea and charts its ideological interpretations.[3] As will become obvious below the different strands of this discourse are radically diverse and include attempts to theorize not only 'knowledge economy' but also the parallel term 'knowledge society', and also attempts to relate these terms to wider and broader changes in the nature of capitalism, modernity and the global economy. Early attempts by Friedrich von Hayek (1937, 1945) to define the relations between economics and knowledge were followed by the economic value of knowledge studies of the production and distribution of knowledge in the U.S. by Fritz Machlup (1962). Both of these scholars were associated with the Austrian school of economics. Gary Becker (1964), a prominent member of the Chicago School, analyzed human capital with reference to education while Peter Drucker (1969), the management theorist, developed an emphasis on 'knowledge workers' coining the term in 1959 and founding the field of 'knowledge management'. Daniel Bell's (1973) sociology of postindustrialism emphasized the centrality of theoretical knowledge and the new science-based industries and Alain Touraine's (1971) *The Post-industrial Society* hypothesized students as a new social movement and predicted the 'programmed society'. Mark Granovetter (1973) theorized of the role of information in the market based on weak ties and social networks. Marc Porat (1977) defined 'the information society' in a series of publications for the US government and Alvin Toffler (1980), the futurist, talked of knowledge-based production in the 'Third Wave economy'. The French philosopher Jean-François Lyotard (1984) defined *The Postmodern Condition* as an age marked by the contingency, complexity, dispersal and distribution of knowledge and the Marxist geographer David Harvey (1989) analyzed large scale shifts from Fordist to flexible accumulation. James Coleman (1988) analyzed how social capital creates human capital and Pierre Bourdieu (1986) and Robert Putnam (2000) further developed the notion providing distinctive notions of cultural and social capital. The Stanford economist Paul Romer (1990) argued that growth is driven by technological change arising from intentional investment decisions where technology as an input is a nonrival, partially excludable good and the OECD's (1996), basing its work on Romer and endogenous growth theory, provided an influential model of the 'knowledge-based economy'. Meanwhile, Joseph Stiglitz (1999a) ex-chief economist developed the World Bank's *Knowledge for Development* and *Education for the Knowledge Economy* programs based on the notion that knowledge is a global public good. In the wake of these reports employers called for new workforce skillsets (*Partnership for 21st Century Skills*, 2008) and public policy applications and developments of the 'knowledge economy' concept began to appear in authoritative forms at the end of the decade (Hearn & Rooney, 2008).

What this brief history reveals is the different stages in the evolution of a discourse with parallel streams, often contradictory or opposing, with different ideological sources and different visions of economy and society. We can no longer simply hold that 'knowledge economy' or 'knowledge society' are simply neoliberal notions. They are complex and openly contested policy narratives based on metaphors that have emerged to described the trajectory of the rich liberal capitalist states and now function as generalized policy framework that permit local applications and forms of indigenization, depending on location, geopolitics, state actors, and a range of other variable factors.

The knowledge economy is also a concept undergoing rapid conceptual development. In the following three sections I have detailed three forms of the knowledge economy: the 'learning economy'; the 'creative economy'; and the 'open science economy'. Each of these has a special relationship to education and pedagogy and highlights the significance of learning processes within these larger conceptual policy frameworks. What this analysis demonstrates is the increasing dynamic differentiation of the concept and progressive new developments that distinguishes elements of the general concept.

The Learning Economy

The concept of the learning economy was coined and has been championed by Bengt-Åke Lundvall, a Swedish economist from Aalborg University, who uses the term to talk about a new context for European innovation policy.[4] Lundvall (1994, 2000, 2002) first used the concept in the mid 1990s in a series of working papers to discuss technological change, innovation and institutional learning directly applying it to the learning society and economy, to universities, and to education more generally in the 2000s, culminating in *How Europe's Economies Learn* (Lorenz & Lundvall, 2006) that focuses on diversity in European competence building systems, organization, labor markets and corporate governance and the links between education and science-industry. The concept and theory of the learning economy is a refinement of the knowledge economy based on the way a set of interlocking forces (ecologies) in information/knowledge intensities, distributed new social media, and greater computer networking and connectivity have contributed to the heightened significance of human capital formations, mode of social production and an emphasis on learning processes. Lundvall (1996) argues, for instance, that the growing frequency of so-called paradoxes in economic theory and of unsolved socioeconomic problems reflects that neither economic theory nor policy has been adapted to the fact that we have entered a new phase: the "Learning Economy."

In the learning economy it is the capacity to learn that increasingly determines the relative position of individuals, firms and national systems and Lundvall claims that the growing polarization in the OECD-labor markets is explained by the increasing importance of learning and the acceleration in the rate of change. *Sustainability* of these learning economies tendencies ultimately depends on the distribution of capabilities to learn. The OECD highlights the importance of skills and learning focusing on lifelong learning becoming the central element in a high-skills, high-wage jobs strategy. Lundvall distinguishes between information and knowledge; the former is logical, sequential and easily broken down into bits and transmitted by computer whereas the latter is associated with learning that is often a form of know-how and competencies based on tacit knowledge. An information or knowledge economy is quite different from a learning economy that is not tied to formal knowledge institutions and goes beyond formal propositional forms of knowing to the arena of routinised learning based on learning-by-doing or learning-by-using. Such a definition allows us to consider the types of learning associated with the process of working that emphasizes tacit, practical and embodied knowledge generated during the work process. One might also argue in a broader sense that the learning economy focuses on learning processes that are responsible for the production of knowledge.

Lundvall et al. (2008) argue that innovation is crucial to economic competitiveness and learning is crucial to innovation. They argue that knowledge is becoming obsolete more rapidly than before and that therefore firms and employees constantly have to learn and acquire new competencies, mostly learnt through experience. Lundvall and his colleagues argue that traditional schooling, isolated from society and organised according to traditional disciplines and educational cultures focusing on collaboration, interdisciplinarityand engagement with real-life problems are required to produce flexible workers who can successfully participate in the new economy.

A Note on Personal and Tacit Knowledge

The concept of the learning economy requires further examination especially in term of its predecessor theoretical element in the work of Polanyi on personal and tacit knowledge and as it contributes to a theory of educational practice. Michael Polyani's magnum opus is the book he published in 1962 entitled *Personal Knowledge: Towards a Post-Critical Philosophy* based on some thirteen papers he published during the period 1952–58 in journals like *The British Journal for the Philosophy of Science, Encounter, Science, The Lancet, Dialectica*, and *The Cambridge Journal*. The papers indicate something of the extraordinary range of thought, the diversity of thinking, and the target of his work: 'Skill and connoisseurship'; 'Passion and controversy in science'; 'Pure and applied science and their appropriate forms of organization'; 'The magic of Marxism'; 'On the introduction of science into moral subjects'; 'Stability of beliefs'; 'Scientific outlook: its sickness and cure'; 'Words, conception and science'; 'Beauty, elegance and reality in science'; 'Problem solving.'

Polyani's target was the delusion of complete objectivity as an ideal for the exact sciences and also the positivism, or more correctly, logical empiricism of the Vienna Circle, and Popper's falsificationism. This is in part the reason that Polyani subtitles his book 'a post-critical philosophy' because it was designed to take its readers beyond Popper's critical rationalism to the realm of personal knowledge which Polyani saw as a suitable substitute and ideal for science. Polyani tried to demonstrate the inherent personal dimension, both bias and judgment, in every action of the scientist through the structure of skill that is achieved by the observance of a set of rules not known by the person following them. He draws on Gestalt psychology to articulate a conception of subsidiary awareness and focal awareness and its connection with frameworks and tools. Personal knowledge thus has 'its roots in the subsidiary awareness of our body as merged in our focal awareness of external objects' which 'reveals not only the logical structure of personal knowledge but also its sources' (p. 60). Personal commitment is also implied by the fact that we make some things central to our focal awareness. The roots of personal knowledge that lie behind the exact sciences depend upon a commitment and responsibility which we cannot divest ourselves of even by setting up standards of objectivity or falsifiability. Polyani's analysis of skillful doing and knowing is the essence of a performance that relies of intellectual commitment that saves us from mere subjectivity.

Polyani admits 'the tacit component' as an indispensible element of learning that he constructs into three types—trick learning, sign-learning and latent learning—following Hilgard's (1956) *Theories of Learning*, Mowrer's (1950) *Learning Theory and Personality Dynamics*, and Tolman's (1932) *Purposive Behavior in Animals and Men* (see original work for references). Latent or tacit learning is the 'capacity for deriving from a latent knowledge of a situation a variety of appropriate routes or appropriate behavior amounts to a rudimentary logical operation' (p. 74). In short, it functions as a guide to problem solving. This is a position that Polyani tracks out by reference to Piaget's work on the principles of psychology and his studies of the cognitive developmental stages of children's thinking. The three types of learning correspond to an act of invention (trick learning), an act of observation (sign-learning) and an act of interpretation (latent learning) which are the active coefficients of articulation that Polyani spells out in the following form:

1. Nearly all knowledge by which man surpasses animals is acquired by the use of language.
2. The operations of language rely ultimately on our tacit intellectual powers which are continuous with those of the animals.[5]
3. These inarticulate acts of intelligence strife to satisfy self-set standards and reach conclusions by accrediting their own success. (p. 95)

The educated mind learns mostly through verbal media especially listening and speaking which is a latent kind of knowing. Polyani develops an approximation that traces the participation of the scientist to its personal coefficient in the origins of spoken utterance and the very active principles of animal life. Polyani outlines a theory of 'intellectual passions' which can only survive in a society where the values affirmed by those passions, such as the love of truth, are respected and become part of the cultural life shared by a community. Here Polyani's thesis comes very close to Thomas Kuhn's (1962) position in *The Structure of Scientific Revolutions* in articulating the conviviality required for the fellowship, trust and collaboration necessary for the cultivation of thought.

The Creative Economy

The conception of the creative economy emphasizes the creative industries and institutions as an interlocking sector producing cultural goods and services as a rapidly growing and key component of the new global knowledge economy. It refers to those broadly defined design industries and institutions that draw on the individual and increasingly collective resources of creativity, skill and talent that have strong potential for the generation of wealth and job creation through the development and exploitation of intellectual property. Both the idea and policies associated with it originate in the late 1990s and early 2000s in the work of Landry

(2000), Howkins (2001) and Florida (2002). Increasingly, the notion has been applied to education at all levels both in terms of the development of creative minds, the creative curriculum and universities as creative institutions. This section provides a broad conceptual understanding of the creative economy and its relation to education.

Today there is a strong renewal of interest by politicians and policymakers worldwide in the related notions of creativity and innovation, especially in relation to terms like 'the creative economy', 'knowledge economy', 'enterprise society', 'entrepreneurship' and 'national systems of innovation' (Baumol, 2002; Cowen, 2002; Scott & Urry, 1994). In its rawest form the notion of the creative economy emerges from a set of claims that suggests that the Industrial Economy is giving way to the Creative Economy based on the growing power of ideas and virtual value—the turn from steel and hamburgers to software and intellectual property. In this context increasingly policy latches onto the issues of copyright as an aspect of IP, piracy, distribution systems, network literacy, public service content, the creative industries, new interoperability standards, the WIPO and the development agenda, WTO and trade, and means to bring creativity and commerce together (Cowen, 2002; Shapiro & Varian, 1998; Davenport & Beck, 2001; Hughes, 1998; Netanel, 1996, 1998; Gordon, 1993; Lemley, 2005; Wagner, 2003).

At the same time this focus on creativity has exercised strong appeal to policymakers who wish to link education more firmly to new forms of capitalism emphasizing how creativity must be taught, how educational theory and research can be used to improve student learning in mathematics, reading and science, and how different models of intelligence and creativity can inform educational practice (Blythe, 2000). Under the spell of the creative economy discourse there has been a flourishing of new accelerated learning methodologies together with a focus on giftedness the design of learning programs for exceptional children.[6] One strand of the emerging literature highlights the role of the creative and expressive arts, of performance, of aesthetics in general, and the significant role of design as an underlying infrastructure for the creative economy (Caves, 2000; Frey & Pommerehne, 1989; Ginsburgh & Menger, 1996; Heilbrun & Gray, 2001; Hesmondhalgh, 2002).

There is now widespread agreement among economists, sociologists and policy analysts that creativity, design and innovation are at the heart of the global knowledge economy: together creativity, design and innovation define knowledge capitalism and its ability to continuously reinvent itself.[7] Together and in conjunction with new communications technologies they give expression to the essence of digital capitalism—the 'economy of ideas'—and to new architectures of mass collaboration that distinguish it as a new generic form of economy different in nature from industrial capitalism. The fact is that knowledge in its immaterial digitized informational form as sequences and value chains of 1s and 0s—ideas, concepts, functions, and abstractions—approaches the status of pure thought. Unlike other commodities it operates expansively to defy the law of scarcity that is fundamental to classical and neoclassical economics and to the traditional understanding of markets. A generation of economists have expressed this truth by emphasizing that knowledge is (almost) a global public good; it is non-rivalrous and barely excludable (Stiglitz, 1999b; Verschraegen & Schiltz, 2007). It is non-rivalrous in the sense that there is little or marginal cost to adding new users. In other words, knowledge and information, especially in digital form, cannot be consumed. The use of knowledge or information as digital goods can be distributed and shared at no extra cost and the distribution and sharing is likely to add to its value rather than to deplete it or use it up. This is the essence of the economics of file-sharing education; it is also the essence of new forms of distributed creativity, intelligence and innovation in an age of mass participation and collaboration (Brown and Duguid, 2000; Tapscott & Williams, 2006; Surowiecki, 2004).

The Open Science Economy

Yochai Benkler (2006), the Harvard law professor, theorizes fundamental changes in his book *The Wealth of Networks: How Social Production Transforms Markets and Freedom*. Benkler develops a vision of the good society based on access and distribution of information goods in a networked global information economy that places a high value on individual autonomy where within the public information space of the Internet and the information commons people have the individual means to pursue their own interests'.[8] He indicates that a set of related changes in the information technologies entailing new social practices of production has fundamentally changed how we make and exchange information, knowledge, and culture, and he envisages these newly emerging social practices as constituting a new information environment that gives individuals the freedom to take a more active role in the construction of public information and culture. The emergence of the global networked information economy made possible by increasingly cheaper processors linked as a pervasive network has created an information economy based on the production of information and culture that enables social and nonmarket or peer-to-peer production and exchange to play a, perhaps even, the central role.

Benkler's arguments chime with a number of others who have been working in the same area of the intellectual commons as a newly defined public space or laid the groundwork for doing so: Richard Stallman, John Perry Barlow, Larry Lessig, James Doyle and Pamela Stephenson. Stallman's (2002) collected essays in *Free Software, Free Society* originally written a couple of decades ago provides a discussion of the philosophy underlying the free software movement, including the GNU project and manifesto, the difference between 'free' and 'open' software, the concept of copyleft and the GNU General Public License. As Larry Lessig (2002, p. 10) writes: 'Every generation has its philosopher ... who captures the imagination of a time'. The philosopher who best captures our time, Lessig asserts, is Richard Stallman, who began as a computer programmer designing operating systems and came to define the freedom of code as the central pressing issue confronting a computer society. Free software is Stallman's answer to the question of control—'free' as in 'free speech', that is, free from control, transparent, and open to further development, change and innovation. Such freedom, then, is the basis of 'free laws', an economy of free code and the 'free society'. The principles demand openness and transparency that form the basis for control of code, for laws that guarantee this freedom and for government itself. Stallman argues that copyright is not defined as a natural right in the U.S. Constitution and he seeks to reduce it, arguing also for the distribution of scientific publishing in non-proprietary formats.

The fact is that the accumulated canon of patent and copyright law applies well to things but faces insuperable difficulties when applied to nonmaterial goods. Information increasingly separates itself from the material plane to exist merely in the ideational form as pure ideas. Digital technologies tend to eliminate the distinction between the idea and its expression in some physical form also erasing the legal jurisdictions of the physical world. Lessig (2004), building on earlier work (e.g., Lessig, 2001) argues that for an underlying conception of freedom and its protection as the basis for 'free culture', at the same time warning of the dangers of 'big media' in colonizing public media space. He emphasizes the way the Internet makes possible the efficient spread of content through peer-to-peer (p2p) file sharing in a way that does not respect traditional copyright and he warns us of the dangers to the kind of creativity that is the basis of cultural innovation. In *The Future of Ideas* (Lessig, 2002) describes how the Internet counterculture has encouraged an explosion of innovation and creativity and the legal architecture protecting it as a public space is now under threat.

In the same context we can also talk of James Boyle and Pamela Stephenson. Boyle is a law professor at Duke University and the co-founder of the Center for the Study of the Public Domain[9] established in 2002 with the mission to promote research and scholarship on the contributions of the public domain to speech, culture, science and innovation, to promote debate about the balance needed in our intellectual property system and to translate academic research into public policy solutions. Boyle (1997) argues that that we need a political economy of 'intellectual property'. Likening the Net to an environment and drawing on the politics of environmentalism he suggests 'our intellectual property discourse has structural tendencies towards over-protection, rather than under protection'. He claims that the 'public domain' is disappearing in an IP system built around the interests of the current stakeholders and the notion of the original author, around an over-deterministic practice of economic analysis and around a 'free speech' community that is under-sensitized to the dangers of private censorship.

He argues that a pay-as-you-read architecture will be inefficient and that such a system will '[l]ead to extraordinary monopoly and concentration in the software industry, as copyright and patent trump antitrust policy' and possibly legitimize the extension of 'intellectual property rights even further over living organisms, including the human genome, transgenic species and the like' as well as privatizing 'words, or aspects of images or texts that are currently in the public domain, to the detriment of public debate, education, equal access to information ...' (Boyle, 1997, n.p.).

Boyle is one of a number of scholars working in this area including Michael Carroll, Molly Shaffer Van Houweling, and Larry Lessig, along with the filmmakers, Eric Saltzman and Davis Guggenheim, the computer science expert Hal Abelson, and CEOs like Jimmy Wales (founder of Wikipedia), Laurie Racine (founder of dotSUB), Joi Ito (founder of Neotony) and John Buckman (founder of Magnatune.com) (and all members of Creative Commons).[10] Pamela Samuelson is another working on intellectual property and the public space. Stephenson (1996) in Wired's 'The Copyright Grab'[11] warned that President Clinton's white paper on intellectual property was a sellout of the public and a reward of supporters in the copyright industry.

'Henry' in the *Crooked Timber* seminar[12] on Benkler's *The Wealth of Networks* indicates how this recent literature maps onto 'to a broader tradition of thought; that of people like Jane Jacobs, James Scott, Richard Sennett and Iris Marion Young'. He acknowledges that the Internet enables us to engage with each other in new creative ways and 'to form networks of collaboration and of conversation, creating possibility conditions for the kinds of diversity and critical thinking that democratic theorists prize'. The essential point emphasized here, especially for the Left, is that these newly enabled forms of 'community' or 'conversation' are non-constraining and occur without central planning or the heavy-handed agency of the State. Henry suggests that three key norms—linking, attribution and authenticity—structure the blogosphere creating an economy built on 'gift exchange' and contemplates how even self-regulatory solutions tend to rigidify over time reducing spontaneity and introducing more formal rules and hierarchies.

To summarize: Information is the vital element in a 'new' politics and economy that links space, knowledge and capital in networked practices. Freedom is an essential ingredient in this equation if these network practices develop or transform themselves into knowledge cultures. The specific politics and eco-cybernetic rationalities that accompany an informational global capitalism comprised of new multinational edutainment agglomerations are clearly capable of colonizing the emergent ecology of info-social networks and preventing the development of knowledge cultures based on non-proprietary modes of knowledge production and exchange.

Complexity as an approach to knowledge and knowledge systems now recognizes both the development of global systems architectures in (tele)communications and information with the development of open knowledge production systems that increasingly rest not only on the establishment of new and better platforms (sometimes called Web 2.0), the semantic web, new search algorithms and processes of digitization.

Social processes and policies that foster *openness* as an overriding value as evidenced in the growth of open source, open access and open education and their convergences that characterize global knowledge communities that transcend borders of the nation-state. Openness seems also to suggest political transparency and the norms of open inquiry, indeed, even democracy itself as both the basis of the logic of inquiry and the dissemination of its results (Peters & Britez, 2009; Peters & Roberts, 2011). This is increasingly evident in forms of open science economy based on large-scale, international science portal systems that themselves are aimed at addressing large-scale natural systems attrition, rapid industrial depletion of natural ecosystems and environmental collapse and debasement.

A Note on Open Education

Open education develops around a successive series of utopian historical moments based on a set of similar ideas stemming from core Enlightenment concepts of freedom, equality, democracy and creativity.[13] The early history of open education consists political and psychological experiments conducted in special schools established in the early twentieth century (Neil, 1960; Rogers, 1969; Illich, 1972). The movement from the very beginning thus was shaped by contemporary political and psychological theory that attempted to provide alternatives to the mainstream, connected to and exemplified a form of society and set of institutions that was seen as politically desirable. These early ideas also significantly involved an analysis of the space and architecture of schools and the associated idea of freedom of movement underwent considerable refinement and development over the course of the twentieth century.

An important aspect concerned not only the analysis of architecture but the overcoming of distance in a form of distance education that began in the late nineteenth century through correspondence and progressed through various media eras including that of radio and television. Open education consisted of several strands and movements that often coalesced and overlapped to create a complex skein that despite the complexity was able to rapidly avail itself of new communication and information technologies in the last decade of the twentieth century and to identify itself more broadly with the new convergences among open source, open access, and open courseware movements. It was as though the open education movement in its infancy required the technological infrastructure to emerge as a major new paradigm rather than a set of small-scale and experimental alternatives or a form of distance education.

The model of technology-based distance education really received its impetus in the 1960s when the Open University in the UK was established founded on the idea that communications technology could extend advanced degree learning to those people who for a variety of reasons could not easily attend campus universities. It has been immensely influential as a model for other countries and distance education flourished in the 1970s and picked up new open education dimensions with the introduction of local area network environments.[14]

Open courseware (OCW) is very much a feature of the twenty first century. MIT, one of the first universities to introduce OCW, announced its intention in the *New York Times* in 2001, formed the OpenCourseWare Consortium in 2005, and by 2007 published virtually all its courses online.[15] MIT is only one example of the OpenCourseWare movement, an important player, but nevertheless, only one institution amongst many.[16] Most recently the Cape Town Open Education Declaration mentions the variety of openly licensed course materials, including lessons, games, software and other teaching and learning materials that contribute to making education more accessible and help shape and give effect to a 'participatory culture of learning, creating, sharing and cooperation' necessary for knowledge societies. It goes on to provide a statement based on a three-pronged strategy designed to support 'open educational technology, open sharing of teaching practices and other approaches that promote the broader cause of open education'.[17]

The open education movement and paradigm has arrived: it emerges from a complex historical background and its futures are intimately tied not only to open source, open access and open publishing movements but also to the concept of the open society itself (Peters & Britez, 2008; Iiyoshi and Kumar, 2008).

The Logic of Networks

Network logic is increasingly the basis of economic transactions and social life.[18] The fact is that neoclassical economics does not understand this new logic. Network logic embodies a set of rules for the ordering, distribution and dissemination of knowledge and information and help to structure new forms of organization, decision making, coordination and collective action. In communication networks the dynamic of information is one of openness and with the right kinds of transparency it would be possible to rebuild trust in public institutions. New communication networks also permit increased capacity for increased coordination such as that evidenced in the 'open access' and 'creative commons' movements, which also links with innovation considered as a networked endeavor. There are important implications here for regulation, accountability and ownership, and dwell on 'network citizens' who will be able 'to participate in the creation of new decision-making capabilities as well as understanding their informal power and responsibilities' (McCarthy et al., 2002). Power structures the contours of networks determining the entry points and conditions that define structural advantage (Castells, 2002).

The network perspective entails viewing natural and social systems as networks—molecules as networks of atoms, brains as neural networks, organisms as networks of cells, organizations as networks of jobs, economics as networks of organizations, and ecologies as networks of organisms. Thus, it is not just the composition of elements of the system but rather how they are configured and what kind of relations exist. Network analysis is, therefore, non-reductionistic and holistic with an emergent-properties orientation. In this perspective the structure of the system largely determines the outcomes or performance of the system and the individual position in the system determines both the opportunities and constraints encountered. Against the mainstream then the network perspective is non-atomistic and non-independent, where individual are studied as they are embedded in the web of social relations and have direct influence on one another.[19]

In this context it is important to note that the concept of information considered in terms of today's scholarship in biology still is open to interpretation and checking even though its role is central. This is also a technical issue that requires careful scrutiny. João Queiroz, Claus Emmeche and Charbel Niño El-Hani (2005) adopting a semiotic approach reassesses and reconsiders the role of information in living systems, stating:

'Information' is a concept which is very important but problematic in biology (see Oyama, 2000; Stuart, 1985; Sarka, 1996; Griffiths, 2001; Jablonka, 2002).

The concept of information in biology has been recently a topic of substantial discussion (see, e.g., Maynard Smith, 2000; Godfrey-Smith, 2000; Sarkar, 2000; Sterelny, 2000; Wynnie, 2000; Jablonka, 2002; Adami, 2004). Furthermore, the evolution of new kinds of information and information interpretation systems in living beings has received a great deal of attention recently (see, e.g., Jablonka, 1994; Jablonka & Szathmáry, 1995; Maynard Smith & Szathmáry, 1995, 1999; Jablonka, Lamb & Avital, 1998). It is even the case that the evolution of different ways of storing, transmitting, and interpreting 'information' can be treated as a major theme in the history of life (Maynard Smith & Szathmáry, 1995, 1999; Jablonka, 2002).[20]

The network approach lends itself to interesting applications in political economy. For example, Mark Granovetter (1985) argues that the concept of *homo economicus* in economics is extremely under socialized because it ignores the importance of personal contacts and social networks, that is, the embeddedness of economic transactions in social relations. By doing so, economics ignores the incentives to mutual cooperation and its individualism based on rational choice theory is unable to provide an analysis of flows of information between actors which are used to make decisions of mutual gain and are endogenous to the social network. He argues that 'the behavior and institutions to be analyzed are so constrained by ongoing relationships that to construe them as independent is a grievous misunderstanding' (p. 481). He goes on to argue 'Despite the apparent contrast between under- and oversocialized views, we should note an irony of great theoretical importance: both have in common a conception of action and decision carried out by atomized actors. In the under socialized account, atomization results from narrow pursuit of self-interest; in the over socialized one, from the fact that behavioral patterns have an internalized and ongoing social relations thus have only peripheral effects on behavior' (p. 485).

The assumption of fully rational agents pursuing their own self-interest must be embedded in the social networks in which they are involved and make decisions. Granovetter's views reinforce what has now become widely known that many beneficial economic transactions are constituted by informal means involving trust, reputation, cooperation, and obligation (see also Granovetter, 1973, 1983). Social scientists like Coleman (1988) and Putnam (1993, 2000) have argued that social interactions and network closure—dense connections between network participants—are key determinants in fostering trust and cooperative relationships.

The concept of the network was developed in the 1920s to describe communities of organisms linked through food webs and its use became extended to all systems levels: cells as networks of molecules; organisms as networks of cells; ecosystems as networks of individual organisms (Capra, 1996; Barabasi, 2002). The network pattern is one of the very basic patterns of organization of all living systems whose key characteristics is self-generation—the continual production, reproduction, repair and regeneration of the network. This is where an ecological economics must be properly based. The notion of networks also has recently been used to describe society and to analyze a new social structure based on networking as a new form of organization (Castells, 1996, 2002). On the strong view social networks are self-generating networks of communication that unlike biological networks operate in the non-material realm of meaning rather than matter yet like biological networks they form multiple feedback loops, which become self-generating, producing a shared or common context of meaning that we call culture. It is through this networked culture that individuals acquire their identities as members of the social network (Capra, 2002, 2004; Bateson, 1973). Castells argues that the proper identification of our society is in terms of its specific networked social structure, which provides the structural basis for globalization, the form of new organization (including political institutions), and the reconstruction of civil society.

The new science of networks offers strong methodological and epistemological promise across the social sciences with an apparently easy applications to economics and education with a focus on learning and knowledge networks, especially where these connect with issues of 'innovation' and come into play within a 'knowledge economy'. Network science also has gathered a new fillip with the application of statistical modeling and developments in discrete mathematics to 'small-world' analysis of complex systems—a form of analysis that is described as 'new' and taken to depart in terms of its scope and power from traditional social network analysis. In short, network theory is pictured as attaining the status of a mega-paradigm in the social sciences as a form of social theory and analyses that in part gains its epistemological status from the influence of Gestalt psychology and European structuralism promising a kind of empiricism which is both holistic and relational, and, thus, poses a challenge to all forms of epistemological atomism based on the individual as the basic unit of analysis, including rational choice theory.

Both Gestalt psychology and structuralism that spawned relational, systems and genetic epistemologies offered not only a relational account of structures (of the whole and its parts) but also seemed to offer the possibility of accounting for the genesis and transformation of structures. Yet the tangled genealogies of the emergence of the field are difficult to describe and there is doubt over to what extent we might talk of the different strands of network theory as comprising a coherent program or even sharing similar epistemological assumptions. Network theory has also been referred as a 'new science' (Watts, 2004) characterized in terms of the mathematicization of method especially in relation to 'small world' analysis of complex networks, yet it is not clear where formalization of methods, led by mathematicians and physicists, actually constitute a 'new science' in the same way that any formalization of a discipline, say, for example economics, constitutes a 'new science'.

There are interesting similarities and a core set of shared concepts between policy discourses of the knowledge economy and the green economy that provide useful, new, and constructive economic imaginaries. These new imaginaries at the social scientific utilize an interdisciplinary set of concepts, theories and approaches that has the potential to map a new reality and evolutionary stage in cultural and economic development of networked post-industrial societies.

Greening the Knowledge Economy

The Postmodern Critique of Neoliberalism

The postmodern critique is not merely a negative account of neoclassical assumptions or simply an updating of economics according to the debates of the 1980s and after. It also constitutes a positive moment that provides important directions for the future. I have called these directions the 'greening the knowledge economy' by which I mean a constellation after the 'second industrial divide' of a synergistic relation between two mega-trends, imperatives and forces that acting upon one another become a significant trajectory for postindustrial economies. The tradition of economics of information and knowledge now is a well-documented field that coalesces with other disciplines to define the discourse of the knowledge economy (Peters & Besley, 2006; Peters, 2008). This discourse both predates and postdates neoliberalism although it has also been given a neoliberal reading by world policy agencies like the World Bank based on a version of human capital theory with investment in key competencies and neoliberal restructuring of education based on principles of deregulation, privatization and the introduction of student loans.

The neoliberal reading is also sometimes associated with the growth of sign economies and financialization of the global economy (Forster, 2007). Yet the neoliberal reading is only one reading and it does not analyze or identify the notion of knowledge as a global public good that demands government intervention designed to protect the public domain. The neoliberal reading does not take into account or try to explain the fundamental differences between the traditional industrial economy and the knowledge economy except by reference to pure rationality assumptions that do not sit well or apply within networked environments or merging distributive knowledge ecologies. In these 'ecological' environments none of the elements of *homo economicus* focusing on individuality, rationality and self-interest apply. The neoliberal reading does not understand how knowledge as a commodity behaves differently from other commodities. Neither does it recognize the parallel discourse of the 'knowledge society' that begins in the sociological literature on post-industrialism in the early 1960s which is often directed at concerns about new forms of stratification, universal access to knowledge and the role and significance of knowledge workers and institutions (Peters & Besley, 2006). Finally, the neoliberal reading is stuck temporally in the 1990s and does not take account of the movement towards various forms of the open economy signified in the creative economy, the learning economy, the open science economy (see Peters, 2009a,b).

Conceptions of the Green Economy

Perhaps most importantly the neoliberal reading does not recognize the way in which conceptions of the green economy now offer both new strategic and policy directions in ways that reinforce and interact dynamically with the knowledge economy.[21] Brian Milani (2000), for instance, in his *Designing the Green Economy: The Postindustrial Alternative to Corporate Globalization* argues that the ecological economy is an authentic postindustrialism based on principles of regeneration and sustainability aimed at quality of life, community rebuilding and environmental renewal. The green economy is based on the recognition of ecological principles of self-organization, protection of diversity, and the enhancement of network flows.[22] Neoclassical economics based on rationalistic and reductionist assumptions does not have the conceptual or philosophical resources to recognize the significance of natural assets, their relational contexts and their renewable and dynamic environments that pre-supposed elements of the ecosystem: throughput, distributive development, feedback and scale (see Daly, 2003). Founded on the work of Kenneth E. Boulding (1978), Nicholas Georgescu-Roegen's bio-economics (1971; see also Mayumi, 2001), and Hermann Daly (1999) ecological economics addresses the interdependence of human economies and natural ecosystems and has strong connections with both green economics and ecology with the focus on networks.[23]

Environmental Ethics: From Anthropocentrism to Systems[24]

As the renowned theoretical physicist, Stephen Hawking indicates in a lecture 'On the Beginning of Time': 'All the evidence seems to indicate, that the universe has not existed forever, but that it had a beginning, about 15 billion years ago. This is probably the most remarkable discovery of modern cosmology. Yet it is now taken for granted.'[25] He outlines how the discussion whether or not the universe had a beginning persisted through the nineteenth and twentieth centuries and was conducted on the basis of theology and philosophy on the basis of anthropocentric assumptions with little consideration of observational evidence partly because of the poor unreliability of cosmological evidence up until very recently. 'Big Bang,' the name for a cosmological model of the universe coined by Fred Hoyle for a theory he did not believe, began with observations by Edwin Hubble and his discovery of evidence for the continuous expansion of the universe. In essence, the theory is based notably on observations of the Cosmic Microwave Background Radiation, large-scale structures, and the *redshifts* of distant supernovae (Ross, 2008). The technical details need not detain us here as there are many good accounts of the standard model. What is important for our purposes is to note the shift from a set of anthropocentric assumptions to a theory based on observation and its importance for providing an observational and empirical basis for an environmental ethics based on the existence, life, scale and longevity of the sun at the centre of our solar system. This feature requires some comment because it is an unusual claim to consider the way in which empirical matters to some extent determine the philosophical nature of environmental ethics even where the notion of ethics in relation to the environment is also unclear. Yet it seems clear that environmental ethics as the theory of environmental right conduct or the environmental good *life* (where the notion of life itself is, definitionally, at stake) rests fundamentally upon the notion of 'environment' and how we understand it.

Environmental ethics has been slow to develop and has suffered from anthropocentrism or 'human-centeredness' embedded in traditional Western ethical thinking that has assigned intrinsic value only to human beings considered as separate moral entities from their supporting environment. The difficulty is whether such anthropocentric accounts can reconceive the relations between human beings and their environment and if so, whether the concept of environment might be taken in an extraterrestrial sense as applying to our solar system with the sun at the center. This seems more like the environmental package that has a kind of systemic wholeness and integrity as a system with the energy source at its center without which life would not be possible.

If we are to accept this more inclusive notion of environment that decenters Earth within the solar system, then the notion of environment has to be renegotiated as one that dynamically also includes the lifespan of the solar system. One of the advantages of this definitional move is to resituate human beings in relation to the 'environment' out of which they emerged in a number of evolutionary steps towards complex intelligent life forms and systems, and into which they will finally remerged. When environmental ethics emerged in the 1970s it began to call for a change of values based on ecological understandings that emphasized the interconnectivity of all life and thereby issues a challenge to theological, philosophical and scientific accounts that posited individual moral agents as separate from and logically prior to their environment. This challenge drew on early environmental studies, and prompted the emergence of ecology as a formal discipline and deep ecology, as well as feminist, new animism, and later social ecology and bioregional accounts, sought to dislodge anthropocentric accounts that gave intrinsic value to human beings at the expense of the moral value of living systems (Brenan & Lo, 2008). While this insight does not establish what kind of environmental ethical theory one should adopt it does establish the *prima facie* case that traditional theories of ethics have been unable to talk about the environment in ethical terms. This is largely because they have been bolstered by deep anthropocentric assumptions that are embedded in earlier modern, scientific accounts of 'nature', and also in the nature of industrial capitalism (White, 1967; Merchant, 1990).

Ecopolitics and Green Capitalism as Foci of Environmental Education

Ecopolitics must come to terms with the scramble for resources that increasingly dominate the competitive motivations and long range resource planning of the major industrial world powers. There are a myriad of new threats to the environment that have been successfully spelled out by ecophilosophers that have already begun to impact upon the world in all their facets. First, there is the depletion of non-renewable resources and, in particular, oil, gas, timber and minerals. Second, and in related-fashion, is the energy crisis itself upon which the rapidly industrializing countries and the developed world depend. Third, is the rise of China and India with their prodigious appetites that will match the U.S. within a few decades in a rapacious demand for more of everything that triggers resource scrambles and the heavy investment in resource-rich regions such as Africa. Fourth, global climate change will have the greatest impact upon the world's poorest countries, multiplying the risk of conflict and resource wars. With these trends and possible scenarios only a better understanding of the environment can save us and the planet. A better understanding of the earth's environmental system is essential if scientists in concert with politicians, policy-makers and business leaders are to promote green exchange and to ascertain whether green capitalism strategies that aim at long-term sustainability are possible.

The energy crisis may be a blessing in disguise for the U.S. Jeremy Rifkin (2003) envisions a new economy powered by hydrogen that will fundamentally change the nature of our market, political and social institutions as we approach the end of the fossil-fuel era, with inescapable consequences for industrial society. New hydrogen fuel-cells are now being pioneered which together with the design principles of smart information technologies can provide new distributed forms of energy use. Thomas Friedman (2008) also argues the crisis can lead to reinvestment in infrastructure and alternative energy sources in the cause of nation building. Education has an important role to play in the new energy economy both in terms of changing worldview and the promotion of a green economy but also in terms of R&D's contribution to energy efficiency, battery storage and new forms of renewable energy.

At this stage of the world's development with space travel, planetary exploration, satellite communications systems in space, and scientific probing of the beginnings of the universe, the concept of 'environment' itself needs radical extension to the solar system and universe. Increasingly, although it is still early days, the earth needs to be thought not just as 'Gaia,' as an organic living system but also as part of a larger, more broadly embracing environmental system. The notion that the environment is a dynamic concept, of which we are a part, is the central understanding of a greening of capitalism. Sustainable prosperity becomes possible with a shift to knowledge and creative economies based on services and clean, efficient technologies, although the ecological society depends on a broad consensus over the nature of the market and the economic system: What are the conflicts between the market and ecological economics (Daly & Farley, 2004)? Does sustainability imply 'limits' and to what extent (Greenwood, 2007)? Can Green Capitalism 2.0 solve the looming bio crisis within the constraints of a green mixed economy? 'Natural capital', the self-renewing ecosystem on which all wealth depends, is the basis of green capitalism and we need to develop democratic and participatory means by which to encourage and pursue it. This is one of the great tasks facing education at all levels in the twenty-first century.

Notes

1. The derivation of the English meaning of the prefix 'eco' is based on the French *eco-*, Latin *-oeco* from the Greek *[oikos]* meaning *'house', 'household'* or *'dwelling place'*. Ernst Haeckel used the term 'ecology' (*oikos-logos*) in the 1870s to describe the relationship of living organisms to their environment. Economy is also derived from the Greek *oikos* together with *nomos* (law; regulate) and *nomia* (stewardship, managing). *A Dictionary of Prefixes, Suffixes, and Combining Forms* based on *Webster's Third New International Dictionary Unabridged*, 2002 (p. 16), gives the following entry: 'ec- or eco- also oec- or oeco- or oiko- combining form earlier also *yco-*, fr. MF ? LL@ MF *yco-*, fr. LL *oeco-, oiko-*, fr. Gk *oik-, oiko-*, fr. *oikos* house, habitation1 a : household *eco*nomy: 1b : economic and *eco*-cultural: 2 : habitat or environment esp. as a factor significantly influencing the mode of life or the course of development *eco*species: *eco*system: *ec*ad: 3 *ec-* or *eco-* : ecological or environmental *eco*catastrophe', at http://www.spellingbee.com/pre_suf_comb.pdf. There are good reasons both ety-

mological and conceptual for examining the root prefix constructions of 'ecosophy', 'ecological' and 'economy'. This chapter draws on Peters (2009), Peters and Araya (2009), and Peters and Hung (2009). See also Peters and Besley (2006), Peters (2007), Kapitzke and Peters (2007), and Peters, Marginson and Murphy (2009).

2. Complexity theory is a broad term used for a research approach to problems in diverse disciplines (physics, chemistry, molecular biology, meteorology, economics, sociology, psychology and neuroscience) based on non-linear, nondeterministic systems evolution. Cybernetic, catastrophe, chaos and complexity are forms of thinking that historically have attempted to theorize these phenomena (see, e.g., Prigogine, 1997; Cilliers, 1998; Amaral & Ottino, 2004). In particular, see the special issue and monograph *Complexity and the Philosophy of Education* in Mason (2008); and my essay 'Complexity and Knowledge Systems' (Peters, 2008).

3. This list is based on Michael A. Peters, Simon Marginson, and Peter Murphy (2008) as it was compiled for *New Learning: A Charter for Change in Education* at http://education.illinois.edu/newlearning/.

4. For Lundvall's publications see his webpage at http://www.business.aau.dk/ike/members/bal.html.

5. This section is based on my entry in *New Learning: A Charter for Change in Education* at http://education.illinois.edu/newlearning/ but see Peters, Marginson, and Murphy (2009).

6. See The Center for Accelerated learning at http://www.alcenter.com/; see, e.g., *The Framework for Gifted Education* at http://education.qld.gov.au/publication/production/reports/pdfs/giftedandtalfwrk.pdf.

7. For innovation theory see the Swedish economist Bengt-Åke Lundvall's webpage at http://www.business.aau.dk/ike/members/bal.html and especially his concept of 'the learning economy' (above).

8. See Benkler's homepage at http://www.benkler.org/ where he outlines his research in terms of a set of general theoretical problems, including: Cooperation and Human Systems Design (how we understand the dynamics of human cooperation through work in many disciplines, from experimental economics, evolutionary biology, and computer science, to organizational sociology and anthropology, and how we can synthesize this body of work into an approach to designing human systems: be they technical platforms, business processes, or law); Commons-based information production and exchange (sustainability and comparative efficiency); and, Freedom, justice, and the organization of information production on nonproprietary principles (normative analysis of the implications of commons-based production and exchange of information and culture). Many of his papers are available online.

9. See http://www.law.duke.edu/cspd/.

10. See http://creativecommons.org/.

11. See http://www.wired.com/wired/archive/4.01/white.paper_pr.html.

12. See http://crookedtimber.org/category/benkler-seminar/.

13. This section is based on my entry in *New Learning: A Charter for Change in Education* at http://education.illinois.edu/newlearning/.
14. See, for example, the Indian Open Schooling Network (IOSN) at http://www.nos.org/iosn.htm, the National Institute of Open Schooling at http://www.nos.org/, and Open School BC (British Columbia) at http://www.pss.gov.bc.ca/osbc/.
15. See http://www.ocwconsortium.org/index.php?option=com_content&task=view&id=15&Itemid=29.
16. See the OpenCourseWare Consortium for the full list of participating countries and list of courses at http://www.ocwconsortium.org/.
17. The full declaration can be found at http://www.capetowndeclaration.org /read-the-declaration.
18. See the huge and growing field of network economics at http://www2.sims.berkeley.edu/resources/infoecon/Networks.html.
19. This basic description is taken from http://www.analytictech.com/networks/topics.htm.
20. Please refer to the original articles for references.
21. Obama's green capitalism based on green energy policies is in part a response to the problem of global climate change but also, I would argue, also an ecological understanding of the global financial crisis and the undesirable network effects of financialization of the global economy. Obama's policies offer the possibility for a new wave of growth based on clean-green technologies for a low-carbon economy and forms of economic sustainability based on renewal resources.
22. See the website on green economics at http://www.greeneconomics.net/ and the site on ecological economics at http://www.greeneconomics.net/.
23. See http://en.wikipedia.org/wiki/Ecological_economics.
24. This section and the draws on Peters and Hung (2009) and my entries in *New Learning: A Charter for Change in Education* at http://education.illinois.edu/newlearning/.
25. See http://www.hawking.org.uk/lectures/bot.html.

References

Adami, C. (2004). Information theory in molecular biology. *Physics of Life Reviews 1*: 3–22.

Amaral, L. A. N., & Ottino, J. M. (2004). Complex networks: Augmenting the framework for the study of complex networks. *European Physical Journal, B*(38), 147–162.

Barabasi, A.-L. (2002). *Linked: The new science of networks*. New York: Perseus Publishing.

Bateson, G. (1972). *Steps to an ecology of mind: Collected essays in anthropology, psychiatry, evolution and epistemology.* New York, NY: Chandler.

Baumol, W. J. (2002). *The free-market innovation machine: Analyzing the growth miracle of capitalism.* Princeton, NJ: Princeton University Press.

Becker, G. S. (1993). *Human capital: A theoretical and empirical analysis, with special reference to education* (3rd ed.). Chicago, IL: University of Chicago Press.

Benkler, Y. (2006). *The wealth of networks: How social production transforms markets and freedom.* New Haven, CT: Yale University Press.

Blythe, M. (2000). *Creative learning futures: Literature review of training and development needs in the creative industries.* Retrieved from http://www.cadise.ac.uk/projects/creativelearning/New_Lit.doc.

Boulding, K. (1978). *Ecodynamics: A new theory of societal evolution.* Beverly Hills, CA: Sage.

Bourdieu, P. (1986). The forms of capital (R. Nice, Trans.). In J. F. Richardson (Ed.), *Handbook of theory of research for sociology of education* (pp. 241–258). Westport, CT: Greenwood Press.

Boyle, J. (1997). *A politics of intellectual property: Environmentalism for the net?* Retrieved from: http://www.james-boyle.com/.

Brennan, A., & Lo, Y. S. (2008). Environmental ethics. In *Stanford encyclopaedia of philosophy.* Retrieved from http://plato.stanford.edu/entries/ethics-environmental/

Brown, J. S., & Duguid, P. (2000). *The social life of information.* Boston, MA: Harvard Business School Press.

Capra, F. (1996). *The web of life. A new synthesis of mind and matter.* London: Harper Collins.

Capra, F. (2002). Living networks. In H. McCarthy, P. Miller, & P, Skidmore (Eds.), *Network logic: Who governs in an interconnected world?* At http://www.demos.co.uk/catalogue/networks/.

Capra, F. (2004). *Hidden connections.* London: Harper Collins.

Castells, M. (1996). *The rise of the network society.* Oxford: Blackwell.

Castells, M. (1997). *The power of identity: Economy, society and culture.* Oxford: Blackwell.

Castells, M. (2002). Afterword: Why networks matter. In H. McCarthy, P. Miller, & P, Skidmore (Eds.), *Network logic: Who governs in an interconnected world?* At http://www.demos.co.uk/catalogue/networks/.

Caves, R. E. (2000). *Creative industries: Contracts between art and commerce.* Cambridge, MA: Harvard University Press.

Cilliers, P. (1998). *Complexity and postmodernism: Understanding complex systems.* London, United Kingdom: Routledge.

Coleman, J. S. (1988). Social capital in the creation of human capital. *American Journal of Sociology, 94*(Supplement), 95–120.

Cowen, T. (2002). *Creative destruction: How globalization is changing the world's cultures.* Princeton, NJ: Princeton University Press.

Daly, H. (1999). *Ecological economics and the ecology of economics.* London: Edward Elgar.

Daly, H. E., & Farley, J. (2003). *Ecological economics: principles and applications.* Washington, DC: Island Press.

Greenwood, D. (2007). The halfway house: Democracy, complexity, and the limits to markets in green political economy. *Environmental Politics, 16*(1), 73–91.

Davenport, T., & Beck, J. (2001). *The attention economy: Understanding the new economy of business.* Cambridge, MA: Harvard Business School Press.

Drucker, P. (1969). *The age of discontinuity: Guidelines to our changing society.* New York, NY: Harper & Row.

Florida, R. (2002). *The rise of the creative class.* New York, NY: Basic Books.

Forster, J. B. (2007). The financialization of capitalism. In *Monthly Review 58*(11), April, 1–12.

Friedman, T. (2008). *Hot, flat and crowded: Why we need a green revolution—and how it can renew America.* London, United Kingdom: Farrar, Straus & Giroux.

Frey, B. S., & Pommerehne, W. W. (1989). *Muses and markets: Explorations in the economics of the arts.* Cambridge, MA: Blackwell.

Frey, B. (2000). *Arts and economics: Analysis and cultural policy.* New York, NY: Springer.

Friedman, T. (2008). *Hot, flat and crowded: Why we need a green revolution—and how it can renew America.* London: Farrar, Straus, and Giroux.

Georgescu-Roegen, N. (1971). *The entropy law and the economic process.* Cambridge, MA: Harvard University Press.

Ginsburgh, V. A., & Menger, P. M. (Eds.). (1996). *Economics of the arts.* Amsterdam, the Netherlands: North Holland.

Gitlin, T. (2001). Having a riot. *Newsweek,* July 23, 48–49.

Godfrey-Smith, P. (2000). Information, arbitrariness, and selection: Comments on Maynard Smith. *Philosophy of Science 67*(2), 202–207.

Gordon, W. J. (1993). A property right in self-expression: Equality and individualism in the natural law of intellectual property. *Yale Law Journal, 102*(7), 1568–1572.

Granovetter, M. S. (1973). The strength of weak ties. *American Journal of Sociology, 78*(6), 1360–1380.

Granovetter, M. (1985). Economic action and social structure: The problem of embeddedness. *American Journal of Sociology, 91*(3), 481–510.

Griffiths, P. (2001). Genetic information: A metaphor in search of a theory. *Philosophy of Science 68*(3), 394–403.

Hardt, M., & Negri, A. (2001). What the protesters in Genoa want. *The New York Times,* available at http://www.nytimes.com/2001/07/20/opinion/what-the-protesters-in-genoa-want.html.

Hayek, F. A. (1937). Economics and knowledge. (Presidential address delivered before the London Economic Club, November 10, 1936); Reprinted in *Economica IV* (new ser., 1937) (pp. 33–54.) Retrieved from http://mises.org/page/1411

Hayek, F. A. (1945). The use of knowledge in society. *The American Economic Review, 35*(4), 519–30.

Heilbrun, J., & Gray, C. M. (2001). *The economics of art and culture* (2nd ed.). New York, NY: Cambridge University Press.

Hermann, E. D., & Farley, J. (2004). *Ecological economics: Principles and applications.* New York, NY: Island Press.

Hesmondhalgh, D. (2002). *The cultural industries.* Thousand Oaks, CA: Sage.

Howkins, J. (2001). *The creative economy: How people make money from ideas.* London, United Kingdom: Allen Lane.

Hughes, J. (1988). The philosophy of intellectual property. *Georgetown Law Journal, 77*, 337–344.

Iiyoshi, T., & Vijay Kumar, M. S. (2008). *Opening up education: The collective advancement of education through open technology, open content, and open knowledge.* Cambridge, MA: MIT Press.

Illich, I. (1972). *Deschooling society.* New York, NY: Marion Boyars Publishers.

Jablonka, E. (1994). Inheritance systems and the evolution of new levels of individuality. *Journal of Theoretical Biology 170*: 301–309.

Jablonka, E. (2002). Information: Its interpretation, its inheritance, and its sharing. *Philosophy of Science 69*, 578–605.

Jablonka, E., Lamb, M. J., & Avital, E. (1998). Lamarckian' mechanisms in Darwinian evolution. *Trends in Ecology and Evolution 13*, 206–210.

Jablonka, E., & Szathmáry, E. (1995). The evolution of information storage and heredity. *Trends in Ecology and Evolution 10*, 206–211.

Kapitzke, C., & Peters, M. A. (Eds.) (2006). *Global knowledge cultures.* Rotterdam, the Netherlands: Sense Publishers.

Kuhn, T. S. (1962). *The structure of scientific revolutions.* Chicago, IL: University of Chicago Press.

Landry, C. (2000). *The creative city: A toolkit for urban innovators.* London, United Kingdom: Earthscan Florida.

Lash, S., & Urry, J. (1994). *Economies of signs and space.* Thousand Oaks, CA: Sage.

Lemley, M. A. (2005). Property, intellectual property, and free riding. *Texas Law Review, 83*, 1031–1075.

Lorenz, E., & Lundvall, B.-Å. (Eds.) (2006). *How Europe's economies learn.* Oxford, United Kingdom: Oxford University Press.

Lundvall, B.-Å. (1996), *The social dimension of the learning economy.* [DRUID Working Papers, 96-1], Copenhagen Business School, Department of Industrial Economics and Strategy/Aalborg University, Department of Business Studies.

Lundvall, B.-Å. (2000, May). *The learning economy: Implications for the knowledge base of health and education systems.* Paper presented at the High-level Seminar on Production, Mediation and Use of Knowledge in the Education and Health Sectors, Paris, France. Retrieved from http://www.business.aau.dk/~esa/evolution/ducmaster/druldstuff/druidthemeC/papers/health.pdf

Lundvall, B.-Å. (2002). *The university in the learning economy.* (DRUID Working Paper No. 02-06.). Retrieved from http://www3.druid.dk/wp/20020006.pdf.

Lundvall, B.-Å. & Johnson, B. (1994). The learning economy. *Journal of Industry Studies, 1*(2), 23-42.

Lundvall, B.-Å., Rasmussen, P., & Lorenz, E. (2008). Education in the learning economy: A European perspective. *Policy Futures in Education, 6*(6), 681-700.

Machlup, F. (1962). *The production and distribution of knowledge in the United States.* Princeton, NJ: Princeton University Press.

Mason, M. (Ed.), (2008). Complexity theory and the philosophy of education. *Educational Philosophy and Theory, Special Issues, 40*(1). Oxford, United Kingdom: Blackwell.

Maynard Smith, J. (2000).The concept of information in biology. *Philosophy of Science 67*(2), 177-194.

Maynard Smith, J., & Szathmáry, E. (1995). *The major transitions in evolution.* Oxford: W. H. Freeman.

Mayumi, K. (2001). *The origins of ecological economics: The bioeconomics of Georgescu-Roegen.* Routledge, Taylor & Francis.

McCarthy, H., Miller, P., & Skidmore, P. (Eds.) (2002). *Network logic: Who governs in an interconnected world?* At http://www.demos.co.uk/catalogue/networks/.

Merchant, C. (1990). *The death of nature: Women, ecology, and the scientific revolution.* New York, NY: HarperOne.

Milani, B. (2000). *Designing the green economy: The postindustrial alternative to corporate globalization.* Lanham, MD: Rowman & Littlefield.

Neill, A. S. (1960). *Summerhill: A radical approach to child rearing.* London, United Kingdom: Hart Pub Co.

Netanel, N. W. (1996). Copyright and a democratic civil society. *Yale Law Journal, 106,* 347-362.

Netanel, N. W. (1998). Asserting copyright's democratic principles in the global arena. *Vanderbilt Law Review, 51,* 272-276.

Organisation for Economic Co-operation and Development. (1996). *The knowledge-based economy.* Paris, France: OECD Publishing.

Oyama, S. (2000). *The ontogeny of information: Developmental systems and evolution. 2nd Ed.* Cambridge, UK: Cambridge University Press.

Peters, M. A. (2007). *Knowledge economy, development and the future of higher education.* Rotterdam, the Netherlands: Sense Publishers.

Peters, M. A. (2008). Complexity and knowledge systems. In M. Mason (Ed.), *Complexity theory and the philosophy of education (Educational philosophy and theory special issue)* (pp. 1-3). Oxford, United Kingdom: Blackwell.

Peters, M. A. (2009). Knowledge economy and scientific communication: Emerging paradigms of 'open knowledge production' and 'open education.' In M. Simons, M. Olssen, & M. A. Peters (Eds.), *Re-reading education policies: A handbook studying the policy agenda of the 21st century* (pp. 311-336). Rotterdam, the Netherlands: Sense Publishers.

Peters, M. A. (2010). Three forms of knowledge economy: Learning, creativity, openness. *British Journal of Educational Studies, 58*(1), 67–88.

Peters, M. A., & Araya, D. (2009). Network logic: An ecological approach to knowledge and learning. In M. McKenzie, H. Bai, B. Jickling, & P. Hart (Eds.), *Fields of green: Reimagining education.* New Jersey, NJ: Hampton Press.

Peters, M. A., & Besley, T. (A. C.) (2006). *Building knowledge cultures: Education and development in the age of knowledge capitalism.* Boulder, CO: Rowman & Littlefield.

Peters, M. A., & Britez, R. (2008). *Open education and education for openness.* Rotterdam, the Netherlands: Sense Publishers.

Peters, M. A., & Hung, R. (2009). Solar ethics: A new paradigm for environmental ethics? In E. J. Gonzalez-Gaudiano, & M.A. Peters (Eds.) *Environmental education today: Identity, politics and citizenship.* Rotterdam, the Netherlands: Sense Publishers.

Peters, M. A., Marginson, S., & Murphy, P. (2009). *Creativity and the global knowledge economy.* New York, NY: Peter Lang.

Peters, M.A., & Roberts, P. (2009). *The virtues of openness.* Boulder, CO: Paradigm Publishers.

Polk-Wagner, R. (2003). Information wants to be free: Intellectual property and the mythologies of control. *Columbia Law Review, 103,* 1001–1003.

Polyani, M. (1967). *The tacit dimension.* Chicago, IL: University of Chicago Press.

Polyani, M. (1997). *Science, economics and philosophy: Selected papers of Michael Polanyi.* Edited with an introduction by R. T. Allen. New Brunswick, NJ: Transaction Publishers.

Porat, M. (1977). *The information economy.* Washington, DC: US Department of Commerce.

Prigogine, I. (1997). *The end of certainty.* New York, NY: The Free Press.

Putnam, R. (2000). *Bowling alone: The collapse and revival of American community.* New York, NY: Simon & Schuster.

Putnam, R. with Leonardi, R. & Nanetti, R. (1993). *Making democracy work: Civic traditions in modern Italy.* Princeton, NJ: Princeton University Press.

Queiroz, J., Emmeche, C., & El-Hani, C. N. (2005). Information and semiosis in living systems: A semiotic Approach. *SEED 5*(1) [Semiotics, Energy, Evolution. September 2005], 60–90.

Rifkin, J. (2002). *Hydrogen economy. The creation of the world-wide energy web and the redistribution of power on Earth.* New York, NY: Putnam.

Rifkin, J. (2003). *The hydrogen economy.* New York, NY: Tarcher.

Rogers, C. (1994). *Freedom to learn* (3rd ed.). New York, NY: Prentice Hall.

Romer, P. M. (1990). Endogenous technological change. *Journal of Political Economy, 98,* 71–102.

Ross, M. (2008). Expansion of the universe: Standard big bang model. Retrieved from http://arxiv.org/ PS_cache/arxiv/pdf/0802/0802.2005v1.pdf

Sachs, W. (1991). Environment and development: The story of a dangerous liaison. *The Ecologist 21*(6), 252–257.

Sarkar, S. (1996). Biological information: A skeptical look at some central dogmas of molecular biology. In S. Sarkar (Ed.), *The philosophy and history of molecular biology: New perspectives.* Dordrecht: Kluwer.

Sarkar, S. (2000). Information in genetics and developmental biology: Comments on Maynard Smith. *Philosophy of Science 67*(2), 208–213.

Shapiro, C., & Varian, H. (1998). *Information rules: A strategic guide to the network economy.* Cambridge, MA: Harvard Business School Press.

Sterelny, K. (2000). The 'genetic program' program: A commentary on Maynard Smith on information in biology. *Philosophy of Science 67*(2), 195–201.

Stiglitz, J. E. (1999a). Knowledge for development: Economic science, economic policy, and economic advice [Keynote Address]. *Proceedings from the Annual Bank Conference on Development Economics 1998* (pp. 9–58). Washington, DC: World Bank.

Stiglitz, J. E. (1999b). Knowledge as a global public good. *Global Public Goods, July,* 308–326.

Stuart, C. I. J. M. (1985). Bio-informational equivalence. *Journal of Theoretical Biology 113,* 611–636.

Surowiecki, J. (2004). *The wisdom of crowds: Why the many are smarter than the few and how collective wisdom shapes business, economies, societies and nations.* New York, NY: Doubleday.

Tapscott, D., & Williams, A. (2006). *Wikinomics: How mass collaboration changes everything.* New York, NY: Portfolio (Penguin).

Toffler, A. (1980). *The third wave.* New York, NY: Bantam Books.

Touraine, A. (1971). *The post-industrial society: Tomorrow's social history: Classes conflicts and culture in the programmed society* (L. Mayhew, Trans.). New York, NY: Random House.

UNEP (United Nations Environment Programme). (2009). *A global green New Deal,* prepared by Edward B. Barbier. At www.unep.ch/.../Green%20Economy/UNEP%20Policy%20Brief%20Eng.pdf.

Verschraegen, G., & Schiltz, M. (2007). Knowledge as a global public good: The role and importance of open access. *Societies Without Borders, 2*(2), 157–174.

Watts, D. (2003). *Six degrees: The science of a connected age.* New York, NY: W.W. Norton & Company.

White, L. (1967). The historical roots of our ecological crisis. *Science, 55,* 1203–1207.

Wynnie, J. A. (2000). Information and structure in molecular biology: Comments on Maynard Smith. *Philosophy of Science 67*(3), 517–526.

Chapter 4

Biocapitalism and the Politics of Life

Michael A. Peters and Priya Venkatesan

> For millennia, man remained what he was for Aristotle: a living animal with the additional capacity for a political existence; modern man is an animal whose politics places his existence as a living being in question.
> —Michel Foucault (1978),
> *History of sexuality: The will to knowledge* (p. 143)

> The concept of "life" must constitute the subject of the coming philosophy.
> —Giorgio Agamben (1999),
> *Potentialities: Collected essays in philosophy* (p. 238)

> A new economic space has been delineated—the bioeconomy—and a new form of capital—biocapital.
> —Nicholas Rose (2009), *The politics of life itself:*
> *Biomedicine, power, and subjectivity in the twenty-first century* (p. 6)

Introduction

The term 'biocapitalism' recently has emerged to map the growing significance of the life sciences and biotechnology as an innovation within late capitalism that controls, changes and experiments with the material basis of life. Biocapitalism or 'genomic capitalism' has it has sometimes been called (Rajan, 2003) increasingly is seen as the new funding priority for public good science and the basis of the new genetic revolution symbolized by the significance and 'success' of the Human Genome Project. We argue that genomics research represents a phase of global biocapitalism (Baber, 2008) and while some scientists have expressed reservations, including Richard Lewontin (2000), Stephen Jay Gould (1996) and others have adopted a rejectionist stance (e.g., Vandana Shiva, 1989), the scientific community, multinationals and government funding agencies have expressed a kind of utopian perfectionism about the prospect of biotech, on the one hand, together with nascent theories about the possibilities of a new age of genetic self-renewing capitalism, on the other. As Baber (2008) notes James Watson, Mr. DNA, and Richard Gibbs, Director of the Human Genome Project sequencing center at Baylor College of Medicine both herald the promise of the genomics revolution, epitomizing a form of human perfectionism. Genetics has moved from the margins of science to the center of medicine and the basis of a new kind of biocapitalism in less than fifty years.

This chapter first examines the rise of the new biology before providing some data on the rise of biocapital in the US. In the next section of the chapter we spell out the connection between biocapital and biocapitalism, and then provide an analysis of the relationship between biocapitalism and neoliberalism by reference to the work of Michel Foucault and especially his comments on the Freiburg School of neoliberalism. The final sections of the chapter examine Foucault's call for struggle and the promissory ethics of biocapital.

The Rise of the New Biology

The word 'gene' was not used until the early 1900s when Mendel's work was rediscovered. Watson and Crick postulated the double helix structure of DNA in 1953 and DNA became the universal language of life. Only in the 1970s did scientists discover gene splicing techniques and recombinant DNA technology which rapidly became the basis for human gene therapy. During the 1970s human reproductive technology moved from in vitro fertilization to the storage of frozen human embryos and scientists also began cloning experiments with carrots, mice, cows, and sheep developing a set of industries based on GMO. In 1993 Robert Stillman and Jerry Hall cloned human embryos. The Human Genome Project was launched in 1990 and completed in 2003. Craig Venter using the controversial shot gun sequencing completed mapping the human genome in the year 2000 and in 2007 published the first complete (six-billion-letter) genome of an individual human being (himself). In 2008 the draft corn genome sequence was completed, only the third plant genome to be completed, after Arabidopsis and rice and the President signed the Genetic Information Nondiscrimination Act into law.

In the annual Richard Dimbleby Lecture given on the BBC in December 2007 Craig Venter spoke of 'A DNA-driven World' suggested that the future of our society depended upon an understanding of biology and going so far as to argue:

> the future of life depends not only in our ability to understand and use DNA, but also, perhaps in creating new synthetic life forms, that is, life which is forged not by Darwinian evolution but created by human intelligence.

BIOCAPITALISM AND THE POLITICS OF LIFE

Craig Venter is one of the new breed of bio-informational entrepreneurs in a form of capitalism that brings together two strains of research in genomic biology and bioinformatics in a way that has only become possible since James Watson and Francis Crick described the double helical structure of DNA in 1953 and the genetic code was cracked in 1966, two significant discoveries that signal the modern era of genetics. Venter founded The Institute for Genomic Research (TIGR) in 1992 which is now part of the Craig Venter Institute (http://www.jcvi.org/) established in 2006 as a not-for-profit research organization. Venter is the renowned scientist first to sequence the human genome in 2001 and he published the first complete (six-billion-letter) genome of an individual in 2007 (his own). His Institute describes its research as focusing on human genomic medicine, infectious disease, plant, microbial and environmental genomics, synthetic biology and biological energy, bioinformatics, and software engineering. It is in particular his research on synthetic biology and the assembly of the complete synthetic 582,970 bp *Mycoplasma genitalium* JCVI 1.0 genome that has created a great deal of media interest.

> We're actually starting at a new point: we've been digitizing biology, and now we're trying to go from that digital code into a new phase of biology, with designing and synthesizing life. So, we've always been trying to ask big questions. "What is life?" is something that I think many biologists have been trying to understand at various levels. We've tried various approaches, paring it down to minimal components. We've been digitizing it now for almost 20 years. When we sequenced the human genome, it was going from the analog world of biology into the digital world of the computer. Now we're trying to ask, can we regenerate life, or can we create new life, out of this digital universe?

Carl R. Woese (2004) argues that the old molecular biology has run its course and that the new biology with an appropriate vision of the living world, in a reciprocal relationship with physics, can become a fundamental science that defines the nature of reality and teaches how to live in harmony with the rest of the living world. Woese (2004) argues for the displacement of a reductionistic molecular biology which conceptually cannot recognize or account for biocomplexity and he searches for a new synthetic vision that is holistic and no longer looks at the organism as a 'molecular machine'. He goes on to tell a story about a biology released from reductionism and determinism that is able to look at cellular evolution without the old constraints. He puts the alternative both succinctly and forcefully:

> In the last several decades we have seen the molecular reductionist reformulation of biology grind to a halt, its vision of the future spent, leaving us with only a gigantic whirring biotechnology machine. Biology today is little more than an engineering discipline. Thus, biology is at the point where it must choose between two paths: either continue on its current track, in which case it will become mired in the present, in application, or break free of reductionist hegemony, reintegrate itself, and press forward once more as a fundamental science. The latter course means an emphasis on holistic, "nonlinear," emergent biology—with understanding evolution and the nature of biological form as the primary, defining goals of a new biology.

Writing with Nigel Goldenfield in the journal *Nature* (Goldenfield & Woese, 2007), Woese argues that just as 'satellite-based astronomy has...overthrown our most cherished ideas of cosmology, especially those relating to the size, dynamics and composition of the Universe' so too the convergence of fresh theoretical ideas in evolution and the coming avalanche of genomic data will profoundly alter our understanding of the biosphere—and is likely to lead to revision of concepts such as species, organism and evolution.' Their argument is that horizontal gene transfer (HGT) indicates that 'microbial behavior must be understood as predominantly cooperative' rather than microbes seen as organisms characterized by individual or discrete genomic properties.

Other scientists like Freeman Dyson, the theoretical physicist, mathematician and professor emeritus at Princeton University, have remarked that the twenty-first century will be the century of biology. Already 'Biology is now bigger than physics, as measured by the size of budgets, by the size of the workforce, or by the output of major discoveries' and 'Biology is also more important than physics, as measured by its economic consequences, by its ethical implications, or by its effects on human welfare.' In 'Our Biotech Future' (2007) written for the *New York Review of Books*, Dyson claims that the Darwinian paradigm is over because we have moved into an era of cultural evolution characterized by a new interdependence and the open source exchange model of innovation that speeds up evolution and puts is directly under the control of human being:

> Now, after three billion years, the Darwinian interlude is over. It was an interlude between two periods of horizontal gene transfer. The epoch of Darwinian

evolution based on competition between species ended about ten thousand years ago, when a single species, Homo sapiens, began to dominate and reorganize the biosphere. Since that time, cultural evolution has replaced biological evolution as the main driving force of change. Cultural evolution is not Darwinian. Cultures spread by horizontal transfer of ideas more than by genetic inheritance. Cultural evolution is running a thousand times faster than Darwinian evolution, taking us into a new era of cultural interdependence which we call globalization. And now, as Homo sapiens domesticates the new biotechnology, we are reviving the ancient pre-Darwinian practice of horizontal gene transfer, moving genes easily from microbes to plants and animals, blurring the boundaries between species. We are moving rapidly into the post-Darwinian era, when species other than our own will no longer exist, and the rules of Open Source sharing will be extended from the exchange of software to the exchange of genes. Then the evolution of life will once again be communal, as it was in the good old days before separate species and intellectual property were invented. (Dyson, 2007, para. 14)

Many of the claims made in the name of the new biology such as the creation of synthetic life have occasioned a number of influential reports on the ethics of genetic engineering and bioethics more broadly, including the full range of issues concerning: cloning, sex predetermination and the legal and moral implications of reproductive technologies, designer babies, stem cell research, personalized medicine, gene therapy, and the creation of synthetic life (Singer & Viens, 2008).

Dyson goes on to predict that the 'domestication' of biotechnology will dominate our lives in the next fifty years by which he means domesticated, small, and user-friendly as opposed to being owned and controlled by large pharmaceutical and agribusiness corporations such as Monsanto who have breached our trust by putting 'genes for poisonous pesticides into food crops'. Domestication through small-scale domestic experiments will 'give us an explosion of diversity of new living creatures, rather than the monoculture crops that the big corporations prefer'. But in this optimistic scenario he holds back from contemplating the advance and control of biocapitalism.

Mapping Biocapital

Biocapital has become a strong force in society. The biotech sector is rapidly expanding in ways that encompass the notion of biocapital as the French historian-philosopher Michel Foucault conceived of it. The very emergence of the term "the bioeconomy" brings into existence a new space for thought and action: a complex made up of biotech companies working on everything from therapeutic stem cells to DNA paternity testing, pharmaceutical companies, manufacturers of machinery, equipment, reagents, and much more. "Biocapital" has become constitutive terms within "the bioeconomy."

According to Nikolas Rose (2009), contemporary molecular biomedicine requires commitment of funds on a large scale over many years before achieving a return: the purchase of expensive equipment, the maintenance of well-staffed laboratories, a multiplication of clinical trials, financial commitments to measures required to meet regulatory hurdles. Increasingly such investment comes from venture capital provided to private corporations who also seek to raise funds on the stock market. Hence it is subject to all the exigencies of capitalizations, such as the obligations of profit, and the demands of shareholder value. The laboratory and factory are intrinsically interlinked (Rose, 2009, pp. 17–18).

The burgeoning genomics industry serves as one example. Genomics—the pursuit of unraveling the mysteries of the DNA double-helix, the fundamental blueprint of life—may very well transform twenty-first century medical care, much as the automobile industry changed transportation. With Silicon Valley startups Complete Genomics and Pacific Biosciences at the forefront, the genomics industry suddenly seems racing toward a new era of delivering truly personalized medicine. PacBio recently received $68 million in new funding, including a strategic investment from the agricultural giant Monsanto, underscoring genomics' potential impact on food production, biofuels and biodiversity (Harris, 2009).

Biotechnologies refers to the use of cellular and biomolecular processes to make products for the market and really constitutes a collection of technologies that exploits DNA as the basic cellular unit that unites the living world at all levels and provides a foundation for biology. The biotech industry emerged in the 1970s based largely on a new recombinant DNA techniques creating more than 200 new therapies and vaccines, with many more in drug trials. The industry includes fields of agricultural, environmental, industrial biotech as well as DNA fingerprinting.

The biotech industry is regulated by the U.S. Food and Drug Administration (FDA), the Environmental Protection Agency (EPA) and the Department of Agriculture (USDA). As of December 31, 2006, there were

1,452 biotechnology companies in the United States, of which 336 were publicly held. Market capitalization, the total value of publicly traded biotech companies (U.S.) at market prices, was $360 billion as of late April 2008 (based on stocks tracked by BioWorld). The biotechnology industry has mushroomed since 1992, with U.S. health care biotech revenues from publicly traded companies rising from $8 billion in 1992 to $58.8 billion in 2006. Biotechnology is one of the most research-intensive industries in the world. U.S. publicly traded biotech companies spent $27.1 billion on research and development in 2006. There were 180,000 employed in U.S. biotech companies in 2006. In 1982, recombinant human insulin became the first biotech therapy to earn FDA approval. The product was developed by Genentech and Eli Lilly and Co. Corporate partnering has been critical to biotech success. According to BioWorld, in 2007 biotechnology companies struck 417 new partnerships with pharmaceutical companies and 473 deals with fellow biotech companies. The industry also saw 126 mergers and acquisitions. Most biotechnology companies are young companies developing their first products and depend on investor capital for survival. According to BioWorld, biotechnology attracted more than $24.8 billion in financing in 2007 and raised more than $100 billion in the five-year span of 2003–2007. The biosciences—including all life-sciences activities—employed 1.3 million people in the United States in 2006 and generated an additional 7.5 million related jobs. The average annual wage of U.S. bioscience workers was $71,000 in 2006, more than $29,000 greater than the average private-sector annual wage. U.S. publicly traded biotech companies alone spent $27.1 billion on research and development in 2006 (*Growing the Nation's Biotech Sector: State Bioscience Initiatives*, 2006).[1] The estimated figure for biotech industry globally in the double-digit trillions.

However, this description does not adequately portray a vision of the life science industry borne out an analysis of the bioeconomy. In fact, it is the promissory quality of biotech that is reflexively extending it rather than real gains in profit or productivity. The work of Kaushik Sunder Rajan and Melinda Cooper highlights how this quality of promise gave life to the industry initially by allowing the capitalization on financial promise, which then became the backbone of its growth. The flight into financialization is the speculative response to crisis—a faith-driven attempt to relaunch the accumulation of surplus value at a higher level of returns, in the hope that production will at some point follow. This is the prophetic, promissory moment of capitalist restructuring, the kind of utopia that is celebrated in neoliberal theories of growth. The creation of surplus population, of a life not worth the costs of its own reproduction, is strictly contemporaneous with the capitalist promise of more abundant life (Cooper, 2008, pp. 60–61). Consequently, biopolitics is the strategic coordination of these power relations in order to extract a surplus of power from living beings (Lazzarato). According to Cooper, the debtor nation status of United States is unequivocally related to this illusion of growth and output in the biotech sector. "In this way capital's dream of promissory self-regeneration finds in counterpart in a form of directly embodied debt peonage" (Cooper, 2008, p. 150).

Biotech industries have developed around the major tolls of bioprocessing that uses living cells to create cultures; recombinant DNA technology to effect genetic modification in selection and breeding; monoclonal antibodies uses immune-system cells to make proteins called *antibodies*, which help the body to destroy foreign invaders such as viruses or bacteria; cloning used to generate identical molecules, cells, plants or animals; protein engineering; biosensors couple with microelectronics to measure nutritional value, pollutants, etc.; nanotechnology involves miniaturization similar to microelectronics, microchips and microcircuits that may engineer DNA as the information storage molecule for the next generation of computers; microarrays allows for the analysis of thousands of DNA or protein molecules, or tissue samples, on a single 'chip'. Now synthetic biologists are working to develop a set of 'standard parts' that can be used (and reused) to build biological systems and to reverse engineer and redesign biological parts and a simple natural bacterium with the prospect of personalized medicine, new forms of healthcare diagnostics and therapeutics, and also the prospect of regenerative medicine.[2] Biotechnology also promises much in the areas of crop and food production, alternative energy, and many other applications.

In 1999 *Time* magazine ran a cover called 'the biotech century' with the following storyline:

> Ring farewell to the century of physics, the one in which we split the atom and turned silicon into computing power. It's time to ring in the century of biotechnology. Just as the discovery of the electron in 1897 was a seminal event for the 20th century, the seeds for the 21st century were spawned in 1953, when James Watson blurted out to Francis Crick how four nucleic acids could pair to form the self-copying code of a DNA molecule. Now we're just a few years away from one

of the most important breakthroughs of all time: deciphering the human genome, the 100,000 genes encoded by 3 billion chemical pairs in our DNA.

The story also predicted that 'The 20th century's revolution in infotechnology will thereby merge with the 21st century's revolution in biotechnology'. Jeremy Rifkin (1998) wrote of convergent forces that heralded an emergent technological revolution that would enable us to remake ourselves and reorganize life at the genetic level. He saw that the new biology could alter the conditions for global agriculture and help to remediate the world's ecosystems, and through the marriage of genes and computers change the basis for civilization, signaling the end of the industrial era.

Rifkin suggest that there are seven strands that make up the 'operational matrix' of the Biotech Century and the paradigm shift from nurture to nature and the shift from the communication age to the bioindustrial age including the to identify, isolate and recombine DNA to be used as a raw material; the race to fund, patent and commercialize bio-science; a 'laboratory-conceived second Genesis' with the release of engineered life forms back into the natural environment; the eugenics and the human genome project at the National Institute of Health; the computerization of the genetic code the use of DNA instead of silicon in microchips. For Rifkin this constitutes a new cosmology that is challenging the Darwinian view of nature: 'The ability to reduce all biological organisms and ecosystems to information and then to use that information to overcome the limitations of time and space is the ultimate dream of biotechnology' (p. 217).

Yet as Falkner (2007) 'reports rising public concern about GM food, coupled with efforts to create precautionary international regulation of GMO trade, have put a brake on the worldwide spread of food biotechnology'. Falkner suggests that 'Despite its early successes, the birth of the biotechnology century has been more troubled than could have been foreseen ten or twenty years ago. In Europe and elsewhere, global corporate power has been met with new forms of transnational social power and state efforts to create a global regulatory framework'.

Biocapital/Biocapitalism

Alongside the biologists and other scientists it is important to consult and work of social scientists and social theoreticians who can directly address questions of power and political economy. Kaushik Sunder Rajan (2003, p. 88) identifies the main features of biocapitalism as:

1. a breathless rhetoric of speed, implying seamless flows of information, tempered by speed bumps in the form of ownerships through patent protection;
2. mobile and unpredictable strategic terrains of conflict and co-operation between different companies and types of companies as well as between companies and public-funded scientists and institutions;
3. the establishment of new forms of contractual alliance such as consortia that destabilize the commodity status of information while instantiating the gift regime as a logical, strategic and ethical mode of corporate functioning;
4. the emergence of forms of symbolic capital through confluences of advertising excess and ethical embodification; and
5. the emergence of new biosocialities and subjectivities that are always-already embedded in the logic of the market—a logic which is itself very much at stake in the strategic articulations of biocapitalism.

Stefan Helmreich (2008, p. 463), in a comprehensive overview of the social science contribution, charts the uses of the many related concepts that social science scholars have used to describe the political economy of the new biology and its societal consequences. He writes:

> Scholars in anthropology, sociology, history, and literary theory have generated a variety of concepts: biovalue, genetic capital, the biotech mode of (re)production, the organic phase of capitalism, genomic capital, life as surplus, the bioeconomy, and, perhaps most prominently, biocapital, which term is becoming the prevailing coin in academic exchanges about contemporary unions of biological science with profit-oriented enterprise. Articulations of biocapital and its kin are various enough that a taxonomy of species of biocapital may be in order.

And he goes on to suggest 'Scholarship in the social and cultural study of biology has suggested that in the age of biotechnology, when the substances and promises of biological materials, particularly stem cells and genomes, are increasingly inserted into projects of product-making and profit-seeking, we are witnessing the rise of a novel kind of capital: 'biocapital'. Biocapital and biocapitalism, Helmreich (2008) argues extends Foucault's notion of 'biopower' to include the governance 'no longer only individuals and populations—the twin poles of Foucault's biopower—but also cells, molecules, genomes, and genes'.

In the course of a review of Kaushik Sunder Rajan's (2006) *Biocapital: The Constitution of Postgenomic Life* and Nikolas Rose's (2007) *The Politics of Life Itself: Biomedicine, Power, and Subjectivity in the Twenty-First Century* he maps the origins of biocapital beginning with Marx and Webber,

BIOCAPITALISM AND THE POLITICS OF LIFE   103

traversing through Foucault, feminist scholars Olivia Harris and Kate Young, Edward Yoxen's (1981) 'Life as a productive force', Hortense Spillers, Jack Kloppenburg, Paul Rabinow, Marilyn Strathern, ecologist Walter V. Reid on 'bioprospecting', Harriet Ritvo, Donna Haraway (1997), Vandana Shiva (1997) on Biopiracy, Hannah Landecker, Catherine Waldby's biovalue, Chaia Heller's organic phase of capitalism, Mike Fortun's (2008) appreciate of genomics as a speculative science, Margaret Lock's attention to the body, Nikolas Rose's (2001) 'bioeconomics', Sarah Franklin and Margaret Lock's definition of biocapital, Charis Thompson's biotech mode of (re)production, Kaushik Sunder Rajan's 'genomic capital', Cori Hayden, Eugene Thacker's The Global Genome, Rajan's (2006) Biocapital, Adriana Petryna, Andrew Lakoff, and Arthur Kleinman's (2006) Global Pharmaceuticals, Sarah Franklin's (2007) Dolly Mixtures, Joseph Dumit's (2007) 'surplus health', and Melinda Cooper in 'Life, autopoiesis, debt: inventing the bioeconomy'.

In this 'tentative genealogy' he identifies two important clusters:

> One cluster—loosely around Sarah Franklin, Margaret Lock, and Charis Thompson, and drawing significantly on Marilyn Strathern, Donna Haraway, and Paul Rabinow— might be called Marxist feminist. Here the binary of production versus reproduction is key, as are questions to do with sex/gender and race (particularly in work about reproductive technology). The remaking of boundaries between nature and culture is a central concern—one reason that attention to the changing substances and generativities of biology, emblematized by Hannah Landecker's work on the history of tissue culture, is also a signature feature of this scholarship. A second cluster—around Kaushik Sunder Rajan, Eugene Thacker, and Michael Fortun, and drawing in diverse measure on Haraway and Rabinow— pays close attention to questions of meaning, though less to biomatter as such. Focusing on questions of information management and speculation, this scholarship has a Weberian flavour. Call it Weberian Marxist; relations of production are described alongside accountings of ethical Subjectivity. (p. 471)

Helmreich maintains that the two schools of thinking on biocapital have distinct orientations in that they represent two views: one view (formalist) sees a common rational logic underlying all exchange, while the other (substantivist) sees logics of exchange in relation to the cultural values that motivates them. He proceeds to embrace the formalist formulation based on Marx's description of the circulation of money as capital as a model for understanding the biotech imagination:

B–C–B0, where B stands for biomaterial, C for its fashioning into a commodity through laboratory and legal instruments, and B0 for the biocapital produced at the end of this process, with 0 the value added through the instrumentalization of the initial biomaterial.

Biocapitalism and Neoliberalism

The promise of biocapital is related to neoliberalism in terms of governmentality of the state and governance of the self. This is can be transposed onto Foucault's extrapolations on power and ethics, respectively. Among Foucault's great insight in his work on governmentality was the critical link he observed in liberalism between the governance of the self and government of the state. The question of government concerns Foucault in that for his governmentality studies, politics were inseparable in its modern forms both from biology—biopower and the government of the living—and truth and subjectivity (Peters, 2009).

The advent of patent laws to encourage biotech intellectual property, the risky financial investment into biotech companies in hopes of profit and productivity and private funding into biotech research, creating the new scientist-entrepreneur, have culminated in the enormity of biocapital. Nikolas Rose argues that the spirit of biocapital is directly related to a somatic ethics, in which our very corporeality is affected by the bioeconomy, creating biochemical ("neurochemical") selves (Rose, 2007). Our argument is not so much that biocapital constitutes a new conception of the natural body, but that the growing biotech sector exists at a crucial nexus between government, power and ethics whereby biopolitical strategies, which led to the formation of the biotech industry, are leading to "states of domination." These states of domination are fluid and reversible and serve as a potential focal point whereby ethical action can transform these states into spaces of creativity, resistance and culture. In this section we track the Frieberg School of German ordoliberalism that Foucault developed in *La Naissance de la Biopolitique* in terms of neoliberalism's contribution to biocapital and then develop how this notion of biocapitalism fits in with biopolitical strategies of power. We then formulate how Foucault's call to ethical action would allow for resistance against these strategies and conclude with biocapital's potential to effect creativity rather than contribute to states of domination through the Foucauldian notion of "care of the self."

The Freiburg School of Neoliberalism and Biocapital

Maurizio Lazzarato in 'Biopolitics/Bioeconomics: a politics of multiplicity' comments on the texts of the late Foucault—*Security, Territory, Population* and *The Birth of Biopolitics*—that enables a new understanding of the history of liberalism and its genealogy and 'effectively present a way of reading capitalism which differs from Marxism, from political philosophy and from political economy at once'. Maurizo Lazzarato in "From Biopower to Biopolitics" catalogs Foucauldian thought on the subjectivation of the subject in the context of power relations. In effect, Foucault interprets the introduction of "life into history" constructively because it presents the opportunity to propose a new ontology, one that begins with the body and its potential that regards the "political subject as an ethical one" against the prevailing tradition of Western thought which understands it as a "subject of law." Historically, the socialization of the forces that political economy attempts to govern calls sovereign power into crises; these forces compel the biopolitical technologies of government into an "immanence" one that grows increasingly extensive with society. This socialization always forces power to unfold in *dispositifs* that are both complementary and incompatible and that express an immanent transcendence in our actuality (Lazzarato).

For the Frieburg School the market order, as a non-discriminating, a privilege-free order of competition, is in and by itself an ethical order. As far as the need for "social insurance" is concerned, the Frieburg ordoliberals recognizes that the competitive market can be, and should be, combined with a system of minimal income of guarantees. They insisted though that such social insurance provisions must be of a nondiscriminating, privilege-free nature and must not be provided in ways that corrupt the fundamental ethical principle of the market order namely its privilege free nature. The problem of neoliberalism is knowledge of how to exercise global political power based on the principles of a market economy and he suggests that a major transformation occurred with the association between the principle of the market economy and the political principle of laissez-faire that presented itself through a theory of pure competition (Peters, 2009).

Foucault also examines the emergence in post-war Germany of what calls "politique de société" and the ordoliberal critique of the welfare state where society is modeled on the enterprise society, and enterprise society and the good society to be seen as one and the same. The concept of order is the central concept in the Freiburg School as it is the basis of an understanding of economic constitution or the rules of the game, upon which economies or economic systems are based. Eucken insisted that all economic activity necessarily takes place within a historically evolved framework of rules and institutions and that one improves the economy by improving the economic constitution or the institutional framework within which economic activity takes place. This was, in effect, the attempt to create conditions under which the invisible hand that Adam Smith had described can be expected to do its work (Peters, 2009).

Thus, the logic of the free market is subsumed by governmental technologies in the spirit of neoliberalism. Neoliberal economic growth and neoliberal governmentality have served as the lynchpin for biotech expansion. The penetrability of the biotech sector into society is one that serves in turn to promote the interests of free enterprise. The free market presumably ensures individual freedoms according to German ordoliberalism, however, Foucault qualifies this notion of freedom in the context of neoliberalism. In the way of understanding power and social relations there really is a "freedom" (an autonomy and independence) of the forces in play, but it is rather a freedom that is constituted as "the power to deprive others." Power is a mode of action upon "acting subjects" upon "free subjects, insofar as they are free" (Lazzarato, n. d.).

"States of domination" are characterized by the institutional stabilization of strategic relations, by the fact that the mobility, the potential reversibility and instability of power relations, of actions upon actions is limited. The asymmetric relations within every social relation crystallize and lose the freedom, the fluidity and the reversibility of strategic relations. Foucault places governmental technologies that is to say the set of practices that constitute, define, organize and instrumentalize the strategies that individuals in their freedom can use in dealing with each other between strategic relations and states of domination (Lazzarato, n. d.).

Foucault's Call for Struggle

For Foucault, governmental technologies play a central role in power relations, because it is through these technologies that the opening and closing of strategic games is possible; through their exercise strategic relations become either crystallized and fixed in asymmetric institutionalized relations (states of domination), or they open up to the creation of subjectivities that escape biopolitical power in fluid and reversible relations. The ethico-political struggle takes on its full meaning at the frontier between strategic relations and states of domination on the terrain of governmental technologies. Ethical action, then, is concentrated upon the crux of the relation between strategic relations and governmental technologies, and it has two principal goals:

1. To permit, by providing rules and techniques to manage the relationships established with the self and with others, the interplay of strategic relations with the minimum possible domination,
2. To augment their freedom, their mobility and reversibility in the exercise of power because these are the prerequisites of resistance and creation. (Lazzarato, n. d.)

Neoliberalism and the Promissory Ethics of Biocapital

While biocapital has the promissory capability to create profit, we add that it also has the potential to produce resistance to "states of domination" and the power to effect creativity against biopolitical strategies. The leaders of the Silicon Valley genomics industry engage in the traditional discourse of biotech creating economic productivity and becoming a medical panacea in order to promote genomics technologies and financial investiture in those technologies. Many industry CEOs and CTOs state that medicine will no longer be the same with the advent of genomics technologies and the industry will produce jobs, productivity and profit. Yet the potential of the genomics and biotech industry is more expansive, and is inescapably linked to an ethics of the technologies of the self that go beyond Foucauldian disciplinary technologies.

This is nowhere more clearly seen than in the biotech sector. Stuart Murray explores a novel philosophy of ethical care in the face of burgeoning biomedical technologies. Murray develops and applies Foucault's late work on the "care of the self." In this understanding of "care," he suggests that we might work towards an ethical self that is more commensurable both with recent theoretical views on subjectivity and—more pressingly—with the challenges of emergent biotechnologies. [He shows] how this Foucaultian "care of the self" is incommensurate with the care that we find in the "self-care" paradigm. In other words, the model of selfhood that emerges in Foucault's "care of the self" must be sharply distinguished from the more traditional self of "self-care" conceived under the aegis of liberal humanism. Only the [care of the self] can sustain an ethical politics; only [this] can help us once again to question the good life. The "care of the self,"...might be one way to begin to move...toward a different discourse on subjectivity—one that does not anxiously attempt to reinstate a sovereign, autonomous, and rational agent."

Murray continues that "[t]o be clear, 'care of the self' should be seen as a social and political project that does not condemn new genomic technologies out of hand; instead, it would be a critical project that returns us to the question of the self and the question of care in the pursuit of the good life. In other words, it would vitalize the questioning relation that the self has with itself, and it will look beyond, to question the kinds of subjects that emergent biotechnologies will inaugurate. It would refuse the absolute identity and oneness of the questioning self. It would keep this self-self relation open and dynamic—chiasmatic—rather than closing it epistemically or morally through reductionist genetic terminologies or other biotechnical fundamentalisms. In effect, I am arguing that being human necessitates an ethical openness that biotechnologies—in many of their current discursive formulations at least—threaten to close rhetorically."

However, Murray adds that "this is not to deny that biotechnologies could, in fact, foster a rhetorical and ethical openness. To take the example of NRTs [new reproductive technologies], we might look to the ways that traditional kinship norms have been challenged and new conceptions of the family have emerged as a result. While these effects are promising, I believe they are rare; more frequently, we find a kind of operational bad faith in which biotechnologies are used instrumentally, and end up underwriting the fiction of a sovereign, rational, and autonomous subject. This is disastrous because such a fiction—surely hubristic—will blind us to the wider effects of our actions. Better, then, to proceed with an avowed unknowingness, rather than with the certainty of epistemic and moral closure that so often accompanies Science" (S. Murray, 2007).

This conception of the "care of the self," which S. Murray articulates, allows one to move beyond the strategical categories of biocapital's state of domination toward one of creativity and fluidity. Novel forms of expression have already begun to emerge in the form of genomic art. In their relation to the bioeconomy, genomic art transforms the capital of biotechnology into Deleuzian artistic capital. However, even further, biocapital is not merely a manifestation of political and economic power but a consolidation of novel forms of subjectivity in its incorporation of technological posthuman strategies. In this incorporation, humanity finds sites of Foucauldian resistance and creativity that mobilize biocapital strategies of growth. The ethic of the "care of the self" founds itself on biocapital's energies, energies that traverse the spectrum of the novel technologies it is producing. Much like Foucault may have, we see the potential of genomics technologies in the form of biocapital creating sites of resistance among individuals in forming new notions of extra-corporeal subjectivity that displace notions of the transcendental Being and Cogito, leading to reversibility in the exercise of power.

Notes

1   See the full report at http://www.bio.org/local/battelle2006/.
2   Much of the data and information was gleaned from *Guide to Biotechnology 2008* at http://bio.org/speeches/pubs/er/BiotechGuide2008.pdf.

References

Agamben, G. (1998). *Homo sacer: Sovereign power and bare life* (D. Heller-Roazen, Trans.). Stanford, CA: Stanford University Press.

Agamben, G. (1999). *Potentialities: Collected essays in philosophy* (D. Heller-Roazen, Trans.) Stanford, CA: Stanford University Press.

Baber, Z. (2008) Global DNA: Genomics, the nation-state and globalisation. *Asian Journal of Social Science, 36*, 104–119.

Benson, P. (2008). Good clean tobacco: Philip Morris, biocapitalism, and the social course of stigma in North Carolina. *American Ethnologist, 35*(3), 357–379.

Boyd, W. (2003). Wonderful potencies? Deep structure and the problem of monopoly in agricultural biotechnology. In R. A. Schurman & D. D. T. Kelso (Eds.), *Engineering trouble: Biotechnology and its discontents* (pp. 24–62). Berkeley, CA: University of California Press.

Cambrosio, A., Limoges, C., Courtial, J. P., & Laville, F. (1993). Historical scientometrics? Mapping over 70 years of biological safety research with coword analysis. *Scientometrics, 27*(2), 119–143.

Cohen, L. (2005). Operability, bioavailability, and exception. In A. Ong & S. Collier (Eds.), *Global assemblages: Technology, politics, and ethics as anthropological problems* (pp. 124–143). Malden, MA: Blackwell.

Comaroff, J., & Comaroff, J. L. (2000). Millennial capitalism: First thoughts on a second coming. *Public Culture, 12*(2), 291–343.

Cooper, M. (2007). Life, autopoiesis, debt: Inventing the bioeconomy. *Distinktion, 14*, 25–43.

Cooper, M. (2008). *Life as surplus: Biotechnology and capitalism in the neoliberal era*. Seattle, WA: University of Washington Press.

Dumit, J. (2012). Prescription maximization and the accumulation of surplus health in the pharmaceutical industry: the_biomarx_experiment. In K. Sunder Rajan (Ed.), *Lively capital: biotechnologies, ethics, and governance in global markets* (pp. 45-92). Durham, NC: Duke University Press.

Dyson, F. (2007). *Our biotech futures*. Retrieved from http://www.nybooks.com.

Ewald, F. (1986). *L'Etat providence*. Paris, France: Grasset et Fasquelle.

Falkner, R. (2007, June). *The troubled birth of the biotechnology century: Global corporate power and its limits*. Paper presented at the annual meeting of the International Studies Association 48th annual convention, Chicago, IL. Retrieved from http://convention3. allacademic.com/meta/p_mla_apa_research_citation/1/7/9/7/7/p179778_index.html.

Foucault, M. (1978). *The history of sexuality Vol. 1*. New York, NY: Vintage.

Foucault, M. (1979). *The history of sexuality, Vol. 2*. London, United Kingdom: Allen Lane.

Foucault, M. (2003). *"Society must be defended": Lectures at the collège de France, 1975-76*. (D. Macey, Trans.). London, United Kingdom: Allen Lane.

Franklin, S. (1997). Dolly: A new form of transgenic breedwealth. *Environmental Values*, 6(4), 427-437.

Franklin, S. (2003). Ethical biocapital. In S. Franklin, & M. Lock (Eds.), *Remaking life and death: Toward an anthropology of the biosciences* (pp. 97-127). Santa Fe, NM: SAR Press.

Franklin, S. (2006). Bio-economies: Biowealth from the inside out. *Development*, 49(4), 97-101.

Franklin, S., & Lock, M. (Eds.). (2003). Animation and cessation. In *Remaking life and death: Toward an anthropology of the biosciences* (pp. 3-22). Santa Fe, NM: SAR Press.

Franklin, S., & Ragone, H. (Eds.). (1998). *Introduction, reproducing reproduction: Kinship, power, and technological innovation*. Philadelphia, PA: University of Pennsylvania Press.

Fullwiley, D. (2007). The molecularization of race: institutionalizing human difference in pharmacogenetics research. *Science as Culture*, 16(1), 1-30.

Gibson-Graham, J. K. (1996). *The end of capitalism (as we knew it): A feminist critique of political economy*. Oxford, United Kingdom: Blackwell.

Goldenfeld, N., & Woese, C. (2007). Biology's next revolution. *Nature*, 445(7126), 1-3.

Gould, S. (1996). *The Mismeasure of man*. New York, NY: Norton.

Haraway, D. (1997). *Modest_Witness@Second_Millennium.FemaleMan_Meets_Onco Mouse™: Feminism and technoscience*. New York, NY: Routledge.

Haraway, D. (2007). *When species meet*. Minneapolis, MN: University of Minnesota Press.

Harris, O., & Young, K. (1981). Engendered structures: some problems in the analysis of reproduction. In J. S. Kahn & J. R. Llobera (Eds.), *The anthropology of pre-capitalist societies* (pp. 109-147). London, United Kingdom: Macmillan.

Hayden, C. (2003). *When nature goes public: The making and unmaking of bioprospecting in Mexico*. Princeton, NJ: Princeton University Press.

Heller, C. (2001). McDonalds, MTV, and Monsanto: Resisting biotechnology in the age of informational capital. In B. Tokar (Ed.), *Redesigning life? The worldwide challenge to genetic engineering* (pp. 405–419). London, United Kingdom: Zed Books.

Helmreich, S. (2007). Blue-green capital, biotechnological circulation and an oceanic imaginary: A critique of biopolitical economy. *BioSocieties, 2*(3), 287–302.

Helmreich, S. (2008). Species of Biocapital. *Science as Culture, 17*(4), 463–478.

Jasanoff, S. (2005). *Designs on nature: science and democracy in Europe and the United States*. Princeton, NJ: Princeton University Press.

Kloppenburg, J. (1988). *First the seed: The political economy of plant biotechnology, 1492–2000*. Cambridge, United Kingdom: Cambridge University Press.

Koenig, B., Lee, S. S., & Richardson, S. S. (Eds.). (2008). *Revisiting race in a genomic age (studies in medical anthropology)*. New Brunswick, NJ: Rutgers University Press.

Larsen, L. (2005). Speaking truth to biopower: on the genealogy of bioeconomy. *Distinktion, 14*, 9–24.

Lawrence, C. (2001). The other kidney: Biopolitics beyond recognition. *Body Society, 7*(2–3), 9–29.

Lazzarato, M. (2004). *Les révolutions du capitalisme*. Paris, France: Empêcheurs de Penser en Rond.

Lazzarato, M. (n.d.). *From biopower to biopolitics*. Retrieved from http://www.generation-online.org/c/fcbiopolitics.htm

Lewontin, R. (2000). *The triple helix: Gene, organism, environment.* Cambridge, MA: Harvard University Press.

Marx, K. (1867). *Capital* (vol. 1). London, United Kingdom: Penguin.

Murray, S (2007) Care and the self: biotechnology, reproduction, and the good life. *Philosophy, Ethics, and Humanities in Medicine 2*:6. Retrieved from http://www.pehmed.com/content/2/1/6

Negri, A., & Hardt, M. (2001). *Empire*. Cambridge, MA: Harvard University Press.

Negri, A., & Hardt, M. (2004). *Multitude: War and democracy in the age of empire*. New York, NY: Penguin Press.

Peters, M. (2009). Neoliberal governmentality: Foucault on the birth of biopolitics. In M. A. Peters, T. Besley, M. Olssen, S. Maurer, & S. Weber (Eds.), *Governmentality studies in education*. Rotterdam, the Netherlands: Sense Publishers.

Rabinow, P. (1992). Artificiality and enlightenment: From sociobiology to biosociality. In J. Crary & S. Kwinter (Eds.), *Incorporations* (pp. 234–252). New York, NY: Zone.

Rajan, K. (2003). Genomic capital: Public cultures and market logics of corporate biotechnology. *Science as Culture, 12*(1), 87–121.

Ranklin, S. (2007). *Dolly mixtures: The remaking of genealogy*. Durham, NC: Duke University Press.

Reid, W. (1993). Bioprospecting: A force for sustainable development. *Environmental Science Technology, 27*(9), 1730–1732.

Rose, N. (2001). The politics of life itself. *Theory, Culture & Society, 18*(6), 1–30.

Rose, N. (2007). *The politics of life itself: Biomedicine, power, and subjectivity in the twenty-first Century.* Princeton, NJ: Princeton University Press.

Scheper-Hughes, N. (2001). Commodity fetishism in organs trafficking. *Body and Society, 7*(2–3), 31–62.

Shiva, V. (1997). *Biopiracy: The plunder of nature and knowledge.* New York, NY: Zed Books.

Shiva, V. (1989). *Staying alive: Women, ecology and development.* London, United Kingdom: Zed.

Singer, P., & Viens, A. (2008). *Cambridge textbook of bioethics.* Cambridge, United Kingdom: Cambridge University Press.

Spillers, H. (1987). Mama's baby, papa's maybe: An American grammar book. *Diacritics, 17*(2), 65–81.

Stengers, I. (2003). *Cosmopolitiques II, 2ème tome.* Paris, France: La Découverte.

Stoyle, J. (2005). Stem cells: Where the newest technology meets the oldest profession. *Theology & sexuality, 11*(2), 77–96.

Strathern, M. (1992a). *After nature: English kinship in the late twentieth century.* Cambridge, United Kingdom: Cambridge University Press.

Strathern, M. (1992b). *Reproducing the future: Anthropology, kinship, and the new reproductive technologies.* New York, NY: Routledge.

Sunder Rajan, K. (2003). Genomic capital: Public cultures and market logics of corporate biotechnology. *Science as Culture, 12*(1), 87–121.

Sunder Rajan, K. (2006). *Biocapital: The constitution of postgenomic life.* Durham, NC: Duke University Press.

Sunder Rajan, K. (Ed.). (2012). *Lively Capital: Biotechnologies, ethics, and governance in global markets.* Durham, NC: Duke University Press.

Thacker, E. (2005). *The global genome: Biotechnology, politics, and culture.* Cambridge, MA: MIT Press.

Virno, P. (2004). *A grammar of the multitude* (I. Bertoletti, J. Cascaito, & A. Casson, Trans.). New York, NY: Semiotext(e).

Waldby, C. (2000). *The visible human project: Informatic bodies and posthuman medicine.* London, United Kingdom: Routledge.

Waldby, C., & Mitchell, R. (2006). *Tissue economies: Blood, organs, and cell lines in late capitalism.* Durham, NC: Duke University Press.

Woese, C. R. (2004). A new biology for a new century. *Microbiology and Molecular Biology Reviews, 68*(2), 173–186.

Wright, S. (1994). *Molecular politics: Developing American and British regulatory policy for genetic engineering, 1972–1982.* Chicago, IL: University of Chicago Press.

Yoxen, E. (1981). Life as a productive force: Capitalizing upon research in molecular biology. In L. Levidow & R. Young (Eds.), *Science, technology, and the labour process* (pp. 66–122). London, United Kingdom: Blackrose Press.

Chapter 5

Bioeconomy and Third Industrial Revolution in the Age of Synthetic Life

Michael A. Peters and Priya Venkatesan

> A new economic space has been delineated—the bioeconomy—and a new form of capital—biocapital.
> —Nicholas Rose (2009), *The Politics of Life Itself: Biomedicine, Power, and Subjectivity in the Twenty-First Century* (p. 6)

Introduction: the creation of synthetic life

Daniel G. Gibson and his twenty-four colleagues[1] at the Craig Venter Institute published their pathbreaking paper 'Creation of a Bacterial Cell Controlled by a Chemically Synthesized Genome' in *Science* on May 20, 2010.[2] In the abstract they report:

> the design, synthesis and assembly of the 1.08- Mbp *Mycoplasma mycoides* JCVI-syn1.0 genome starting from digitized genome sequence information and its transplantation into a *Mycoplasma capricolum* recipient cell to create new *Mycoplasma mycoides* cells that are controlled only by the synthetic chromosome. The only DNA in the cells is the designed synthetic DNA sequence, including "watermark" sequences and other designed gene deletions and polymorphisms, and mutations acquired during the building process. The new cells have expected phenotypic properties and are capable of continuous self-replication.

Their research demonstrates new advances in reading the genetic code enhanced through the digitization of genomic information leading to new computational and experimental paradigms and, in particular, the reproduction of a complete genetic system by chemical synthesis starting with only the digitized DNA sequence contained in a computer. Synthetic genomic design is a young science really only developed since the mid 1990s and the creation of a new synthetic cell—new life called 'Synthia'—now heralds a brave new world based on the 'new biology' that has the potential to transform all aspects of life, economic and society as we know it. For the first time in biological history humankind has design and created synthetic life. Some see this as a major system-event in evolutionary development and others building on this understanding describe both the benefits in preventive medicine, ecological management, and promotion of green economy. For many it comes with deep ethical problems centered on questions of who creates and manufactures new synthetic life and for what purposes.

One begins to get a picture of the significance of this new creation by how it was described in the popular press. The *Guardian* reported:

> Scientists have created the world's first synthetic life form in a landmark experiment that paves the way for designer organisms that are built rather than evolved. The controversial feat, which has occupied 20 scientists for more than 10 years at an estimated cost of $40m, was described by one researcher as 'a defining moment in biology' Craig Venter, the pioneering US geneticist behind the experiment, said the achievement heralds the dawn of a new era in which new life is made to benefit humanity, starting with bacteria that churn out biofuels, soak up carbon dioxide from the atmosphere and even manufacture vaccines. (http://www.guardian.co.uk/science/2010/may/20/craig-venter-synthetic-life-form)

The BBC reported the event in a range of video and radio interviews, blogs, and articles, some critical of the entrepreneurial private science promoted by the Craig Venter Institute, while others, like the Science in Action series, focused on explaining the processes involved or examined the response from ethicists and religious organizations (http://www.bbc.co.uk/search/craig_venter).

Arthur L. Caplan in a guest blog for *Scientific American* begins his column with:

> Is life special, so special that we cannot understand it, much less create it? Are living things endowed with some sort of special power, force or property that distinguishes the inorganic from the organic, the living from the dead? Can life be nothing more than the precise interaction of physical stuff? (http://www.scientificamerican.com/blog/post.cfm?id=now-aint-that-special-the-implicati-2010-05-20)

Caplan then goes on to explain the fact that Venter's team has created a new living cell bacterium 'from a set of genes they decoded, artificially combined and then stuck into the cored out remains of the bacterium of another species. In other words, they created a living thing from man-

made parts. Or, in more important words, they created a novel life form from man-made parts'.
He ends by emphasizing the benefits for mankind thus:

> Synthetic biology should permit scientists to make microbes that solve many of our most pressing problems. Building bacteria that digest oil and chemical pollution from leaks and spills or eat cholesterol and other dangerous substances that accumulate in our bodies is all to the good.

Perhaps Susan Watts video story for the BBC—Assessing the impact of Venter's 'synthetic life'—was most factually accurate. Her story begins with the following:

> "Synthetic life" is new science and a new technology rolled into one. The aim is to create a whole new biological toolkit—organisms with artificially added DNA instructing them to exude cleaner oils, or novel drugs or vaccines. (http://www.bbc.co.uk/blogs/newsnight/susanwatts/2010/05/assessing_the_impact_of_venter.html)

In this chapter we begin to assess the importance of the genetic advance represented by the creation of new synthetic cell-life for bioeconomy and education considered in a broad sense, briefly focusing on the biotech industry as third industrial revolution, green capitalism and synthetic biology as new aspect of knowledge economy, the development of synthetic distributed intelligence based on organic computers, biotech modernity and education, and the effects of non-human digital labor. This chapter tries to scope some of the most important issues of the genomic revolution and its impacts on knowledge economy and education.

The biotech industry as third industrial revolution

The representation of genomic science in the popular media is in need of analysis especially in the way it sensationalizes the easy-to-spot ethical problems playing up public fears and avoiding the tough conceptual work that requires some further understanding of change in the nature of science ('technoscience') and its use of computers for synthesizing DNA, the emerging political economy of private science and the economic consequences of the genomic revolution.

These issues might be captures and elaborated in the concept of 'bioeconomy' or 'biocapitalism':

> The term 'biocapitalism' recently has emerged to map the growing significance of the life sciences and biotechnology as an innovation within late capitalism that controls, changes and experiments with the material basis of life. Biocapitalism or 'genomic capitalism' has it has sometimes been called (Rajan, 2003) increasingly is seen as the new funding priority for public good science and the basis of the new genetic revolution symbolized by the significance and 'success' of the Human Genome Project. Clearly, genomics research represents a phase of global biocapitalism (Baber, 2008) and while some scientists have expressed reservations, including Richard Lewontin (2000), Stephen Jay Gould (1996) and others have adopted a rejectionist stance (e.g., Vandana Shiva, 1989), the scientific community, multinationals and government funding agencies have expressed a kind of utopian perfectionism about the prospect of biotech, on the one hand, together with nascent theories about the possibilities of a new age of genetic self-renewing capitalism, on the other. As Baber (2008) notes James Watson, Mr. DNA, and Richard Gibbs, Director of the Human Genome Project sequencing centre at Baylor College of Medicine both herald the promise of the genomics revolution, epitomizing a form of human perfectionism. Genetics has moved from the margins of science to the center of medicine and will become the basis of a new kind of biocapitalism in less than fifty years. (Peters & Venkatesan, 2010, p. 100)

Nicolas Wade writing in *The New York Times*, one of the few journalist to draw attention to the company structure producing the research, quotes Venter who described the converted cell as 'the first self-replicating species we've had on the planet whose parent is a computer'. He reports that Venter states 'This is a philosophical advance as much as a technical advance,' suggesting that the 'synthetic cell' raised new questions about the nature of life. Wade continues 'Other scientists agree that he has achieved a technical feat in synthesizing the largest piece of DNA so far —a million units in length—and in making it accurate enough to substitute for the cell's own DNA' (http://www.nytimes.com/2010/05/21/science/21cell.html).

What is interesting about Wade's account is that besides describing the processes involved he notes the business interests involved. The company Blue Heron supplied the DNA and Synthetic Genomics, a company that Venter established, funded the project to the tune of some $40 million and has a contract with Exxon to generate biofuels from algae where Exxon is prepared to spend up to $600 million if all its milestones are met.

Synthetic Genomics Inc. (SGI) is a private company founded by Venter in 2005 to commercialize genomic-driven technologies. The company sponsors fundamental research at the J. Craig Venter Institute, a not-for-profit organization with more than 400 scientists working on a variety of genomic research. Venter teamed up with Nobel Laureate Hamilton O. Smith, M.D., to sponsor biotech research in synthetic biology and to commercialize its results. Their company site provides the following background:

> In the last two decades the field of genomics has undergone a rapid transformation, with scientific discoveries coming at an ever-dazzling pace. These breakthroughs were made possible by advances in underlying enabling technologies such as high-throughput DNA sequencing, high-performance computing and bioinformatics. These advances, many of which are directly attributable to the innovation of Dr. Venter and his teams, have enabled researchers to readily sequence and analyze the genetic code. So far the genomes of more than a thousand organisms and millions of genes have been discovered, with many available in public databases. (http://www.syntheticgenomics.com/about/genesis.html)

The website provides a company history detailing Venter's global ocean sampling and development of a synthetic genome, as well as its company genesis: the appointment of Aristides A.N. Patrinos, Ph.D., former director of the Office of Biological and Environmental Research at the U.S. Department of Energy's Office of Science; the opening its La Jolla, CA, facilities; the collaboration with BP to develop and commercialize microbial-enhanced solutions to increase the conversion and recovery of subsurface hydrocarbons; and the collaboration with ACGT Sdn Bhd to develop more high-yielding and disease-resistant plant feedstocks.

The company describes its activities in terms of three ongoing projects:

- Designing metabolic pathways for the production of biochemicals and next generation biofuels from a variety of feedstocks
- Developing biological solutions to increase the conversion and recovery rates of subsurface hydrocarbons
- Developing advanced plant feedstocks and microbial agents for agriculture
- And they describe their scientific capabilities as including: synthetic biology/genomics, environmental genomics, plant genomics, microbiology, bioinformatics, genome engineering, analytical chemistry, fuel chemistry, and biochemistry and assay development. (http://www.syntheticgenomics.com/what/ourscience.html)

The J. Craig Venter Institute describes in more research-oriented detail the advances and capabilities of genomic science including all forms of genomic medicine, treatment of infectious diseases, microbial and environmental genomics, plant genomics, and synthetic biology and bioenergy. This broad research agenda in essence describes the ways in which the new biology will drive the green economy in the near future.

Notes

1. Daniel G. Gibson, John I. Glass, Carole Lartigue, Vladimir N. Noskov, Ray-Yuan Chuang, Mikkel A. Algire, Gwynedd A. Benders, Michael G. Montague, Li Ma, Monzia M. Moodie, Chuck Merryman, Sanjay Vashee, Radha Krishnakumar, Nacyra Assad-Garcia, Cynthia Andrews-Pfannkoch, Evgeniya A. Denisova, Lei Young, Zhi-Qing Qi, Thomas H. Segall-Shapiro, Christopher H. Calvey, Prashanth P. Parmar, Clyde A. Hutchison, III, Hamilton O. Smith, J. Craig Venter.
2. See the full-text paper at http://www.sciencemag.org/cgi/rapidpdf/science.1190719v1.pdf.

Reference

Peters, M. A. & Venkatesan, P. (2010). Biocapitalism and the politics of life. *Geopolitics, History, and International Relations, 2*(2), 100–122.

Chapter 6

Algorithmic Capitalism and Educational Futures

Michael A. Peters

> The word *algorithm* comes from the name of the 9th century Persian Muslim mathematician Abu Abdullah Muhammad ibn Musa Al-Khwarizmi. The word *algorism* originally referred only to the rules of performing arithmetic using Hindu-Arabic numerals but evolved via European Latin translation of Al-Khwarizmi's name into *algorithm* by the 18th century. The use of the word evolved to include all definite procedures for solving problems or performing tasks.
>
> —*History of Algorithms and Algorithmics*
> http://www.scriptol.com/programming/algorithm-history.php

> Khwarizmi, Abu Jafar Muhammad ibn Musa al- (d. ca. 850): Mathematician, astronomer, and geographer. Synthesized extant Hellenic, Sanskritic, and cuneiform traditions to develop algebra, a term derived from the title of one of his books (containing the term al-jabr, meaning "forcing" [numbers]). Introduced Arabic numerals into the Latin West, based on a place-value decimal system developed from Indian sources. The word algorithm is derived from a Latin corruption of his name.
>
> —*Oxford Islamic Studies Online*
> http://www.oxfordislamicstudies.com/article/opr/t125/e1305

Introduction: Algorithmic trading and cloud capitalism

The Report of the Staffs of the CFTC and SEC to the Joint Advisory Committee on Emerging Regulatory Issues "Findings Regarding the Market Events of May 6, 2010"[1] begins:

> On May 6, 2010, the prices of many U.S.-based equity products experienced an extraordinarily rapid decline and recovery. That afternoon, major equity indices in both the futures and securities markets, each already down over 4% from their prior-day close, suddenly plummeted a further 5-6% in a matter of minutes before rebounding almost as quickly. (p. 1)

The Report provides a compelling account of that turbulent day: 'At 2:32 p.m., against this backdrop of unusually high volatility and thinning liquidity, a large fundamental5 trader (a mutual fund complex) initiated a sell program to sell a total of 75,000 E-Mini contracts (valued at approximately $4.1 billion) as a hedge to an existing equity position' (p. 2). The report indicates that liquidity crises ensued because a large trader used an automated execution algorithm ("Sell Algorithm") that was programmed to trade large volume (E-Mini contracts) with regard only to volume rather than price or time and the Sell Algorithm was executed rapidly in the period of twenty minutes resulting in one the three largest single-day price movements in the history of the stock market. Under the heading 'Lesson Learned' the Report suggests that 'under stressed market conditions, the automated execution of a large sell order can trigger extreme price movements, especially if the automated execution algorithm does not take prices into account. Moreover, the interaction between automated execution programs and algorithmic trading strategies can quickly erode liquidity and result in disorderly markets.' The report also goes on to comment on the way May 6 market volatility is a 'reminder of the interconnectedness of our derivatives and securities markets' and the 'nature of the cross-market trading activity'. The report concludes 'Of final note, the events of May 6 clearly demonstrate the importance of data in today's world of fully automated trading strategies and systems. This is further complicated by the many sources of data that must be aggregated in order to form a complete picture of the markets upon which decisions to trade can be based.'

Algorithmic capitalism and its dominance of the market increasingly across all asset classes has truly arrived. Rob Iati (July 10, 2009) writing for Advanced Trading asserts:

> Algorithms account for more than 25% of all shares traded by the buy side today—a number steadily rising for several years now. However, the incredible capabilities offered by technology have given meteoric rise to a relative few high-frequency proprietary trading firms that now wield far greater influence on the markets today than most people recognize. The familiar names of Lehman, Bear and Merrill are being replaced by less familiar ones like Wolverine, IMC and Getco... high-frequency trading firms, which represent approximately 2% of the 20,000 or so trading firms operating in the U.S. markets today, account for 73% of all U.S. equity trading volume.[2]

Iati indicates that value of high-frequency algorithmic trading relies on 'a real-time, collocated, high-frequency trading platform...where data is collected and orders are created and routed to execution venues in sub-millisecond times.'

Algorithmic capitalism is an aspect of informationalism or informational capitalism or 'cybernetic capitalism', a terms that I prefer because it speaks to the genealogy of postmodern capitalism and recognizes more precisely the cybernetic systems similarities among various sectors of the postindustrial capitalist economy in its third phases of development—from mercantilism, industrialism to cybernetics—linking the growth of the multinational info-utilities (e.g., Google, Microsoft, Amazon) and their spectacular growth in the last twenty years, with developments in biocapitalism and the informatization of biology, and fundamental changes taking place with algorithmic trading and the development of so-called financialization.

It is in this context that we can talk of 'cloud capitalism' that is recentralizing the Net and creating large scale monopolies in the knowledge economy, on a vastly larger scale than anything imagined possible in the industrial era. Take for example Google's project of digitizing millions of books that will make its digital library bigger than the Library of Congress. By doing so as Charles Leadbeater (2010) argues "Google will acquire huge power over the future of publishing. It will be able to head off potential competition from other databases of digital books." As he goes on to explain: "Google is the first and most successful exponent of a new kind of economic power: cloud capitalism." He suggests that the internet that the cloud capitalists want to give us is quite different from that of the "information superhighway" or "cyberspace":

> In cloud computing, our data—emails, documents, pictures, songs and software—will be stored remotely in a digital cloud hanging above us, always there to access from any device: computer, television, games console, hand-held and mobile. We should be able to draw down as much or as little of the shared cloud as we need. (http://www.guardian.co.uk/technology/2010/feb/07/cloud-computing-google-apple)

Leadbeater raises questions about the way cloud capitalism aims at complete control that ultimately excludes other databases while maximizing revenues and the capacity of clouds to hold vast amounts of data on us that occludes the interests of citizens and eludes the control of governments. We might see 'cloud capitalism' as an aspect of a wider phenomena of cognitive or cybernetic capitalism.

Cybernetic and cognitive capitalism

Cybernetic capitalism is a system that has been shaped by the forces of formalization, mathematization and aestheticization beginning in the early twentieth century and associated with developments in mathematical theory, logic, physics, biology and information theory. Its new forms now exhibit themselves in finance capitalism, informationalism, knowledge capitalism and the learning economy with incipient nodal developments associated with the creative and open knowledge (and science) economies. The critical question in the wake of the collapse of the global finance system and the impending eco-crisis concerns whether capitalism can promote forms of social, ecological and economic sustainability.

'Cybernetic capitalism' is a term we use in order to distinguish a group of theories, or, better, positions, on the Left that attempt to theorize the nature of the *new* capitalism (Peters, Britez, & Bulut, 2010). We group these contributions as largely sociological and Left-leaning characterizing them in terms of what they share with and how they differ from the Marxist theory of industrial capitalism. Using a kinship with Marxism we can generate the following rough groupings of recent work that we have systematically categorized as:

1. Informational capitalism
2. Cultural capitalism
3. Cognitive capitalism
4. Finance capitalism
5. Biocapitalism

There are strong overlaps and conceptual connections among these five broad categories and also some interesting differences within them. They are systematically related phenomena that grow out of the same forces of increasing *formalization, mathematicization* and *aestheticization* that have been in operation since the beginning of the twentieth century but that began to coalesce and impact after WWII with the development of cybernetics and a group of theories that developed to explain linear and nonlinear dynamical systems (catastrophe, chaos, complexity). These relationships and particularly the way in which they profile education is the concern for this chapter. We have categorized, referenced and discussed aspects of cybernetic capitalism in a series of

ALGORITHMIC CAPITALISM AND EDUCATIONAL FUTURES 123

other papers (Peters, 2010; Peters, Britez, & Bulut, 2010; Peters & Britez, 2010; Peters & Venkatesan, 2011a & b).

Cognitive capitalism is another label for a range of contemporary capitalism that represents a change in the regime of accumulation and new modes of knowledge production that highlight immaterial or digital production. The production of intangible goods and services that conflates the traditional categories of political economy blurring the boundaries between consumption, information, cognition, and communication issued from the pervasive use of new information and communication technologies. As Franco Berardi Bifo (2010) in 'Cognitarian Subjectivation' argues:

> Recent years have witnessed a new techno-social framework of contemporary subjectivation. And I would like to ask whether a process of autonomous, collective self-definition is possible in the present age. The concept of 'general intellect' associated with Italian post-operaist thought in the 1990s (Paolo Virno, Maurizio Lazzarato, Christian Marazzi) emphasizes the interaction between labor and language: social labor is the endless recombination of myriad fragments producing, elaborating, distributing, and decoding signs and informational units of all kinds. Every semiotic segment produced by the information worker must meet and match innumerable other semiotic segments in order to form the combinatory frame of the info-commodity, semiocapital. (http://worker01.e-flux.com/pdf/article_183.pdf)

This new semiocapital, Bifo argues, puts neuro-psychic energies to work. It is a theme that has been thematized also by Warren Neidich (2009) who credits Lazzarato and reads it back onto Deleuze's 'societies of control'.

> In the words of Maurizio Lazzarato, "In the societies of control, power relations come to be expressed through the action at a distance of one mind on another, through the brain's power to affect and become affected, which is mediated and enriched by technology....The institutions of the societies of control are thus characterised by the use of technologies acting at a distance, rather than of mechanical technologies (societies of sovereignty) or thermodynamic technologies (disciplinary societies).... First, in the transition from the Disciplinary Society to the Society of Control and onward to what Lazzarato refers to as noo-politics, the focus of power and the technology at its disposal is not directed toward the materiality of the body but, instead, its psychic life, particularly its memories and attention, recognising that the mind and the body are inextricably linked through voluntary and involuntary, somatic and autonomic, striated and smooth conditions...

He extends this idea to develop a new focus of sovereignty—neural plasticity as a generator of fields of difference that produced by post-Fordist deregulation—he goes on to argue that 'these new forms of the social as a multiplicity, formulated in the conditions of post-Fordist labour, produce the conditions of the dynamic, manifold, and metastable brain and mind', Biopower and algorithmic synoptic power produce new forms of informational transnationalism within capitalism while producing also new forms of reistance. Who would have thought the political uses of Facebook, a technology that began as a rating platform of female students within US privileged universities could also serve as a contagion of rebellion against dictators in the Muslim worlds in places like Tunisia, Egypt and Yemen?

Clearly, if something like what Lazzarato and Bifo indicates is an accurate description of conditions for labor under post-Fordism then education—school, community colleges and universities—are the sites for the proliferation of cognitive capitalism and also resistance to it. As Neidich (2006) succinctly summarizes in an earlier paper 'The Neurobiopolitics of Global Consciousness':

> [Where] the disciplinary society is constructed through a dissemination of social command by diffuse networks of machinic assemblages... that regulate each subject's customs, habits and productive practice the society of control operates within the domain of intensive cultural apparati characterised by the Riemannian spaces, rhizomatic logics and folded temporality induced by the multiplicity of flows that characterise our global world post-internet.

Deleuze makes a classification of three specific kinds of power: sovereign power, disciplinary power and 'control' of communication and views the third kind of power as becoming hegemonic, a form of domination that, paradoxically, is both more total than any previous form, extending even to speech and imagination. According to Deleuze (1989a,b) we now live in a universe that could be described as metacinematic and his classification of images implies a new kind of camera consciousness that determines our subjectivities and perceptions selves. We live in a visual culture that is always moving and changing and each image is always connected to an assemblage of affects and forces.

The New Logic and Culture of Social Media[3]

In the Oscar-winning 'The Social Network' Mark Zuckerberg, the founder of Facebook, is portrayed as someone who rips off an idea from two Harvard student colleagues (the Winklevoss twins) who want to create a virtual community and exploit the brand of Harvard. The film is directed by David Fincher featuring Jesse Eisenberg, Andrew Garfield and Justin Timberlake among others, based on a screenplay by Aaron Sorkin who adapts Ben Mezich's (2009) *The Accidental Billionaires*. Mezich subtitles the book *The Founding of Facebook, A Tale of Sex, Money, Genius, and Betrayal* and insists that while written as in the narrative style it is not a work of fiction. As he says in the 'Author's Note': *'The Accidental Billionaires* is a dramatic, narrative account based on dozens of interviews, hundreds of sources, and thousands of pages of documents, including records from several court proceedings' (p. 1). The film has won critical acclaim yet while called 'The Social Network' really focuses on the personality of Zuckerberg (perhaps unfairly) and the resulting lawsuits rather than on the social phenomenon of Facebook beyond the fact that it starts as a mechanism for rating the attractiveness of female students at Harvard. Perhaps this is philosophical enough? The movie begins in 2003 when Zuckerberg hacks into halls of residence to download details and photos and while he is punished for this act the idea of a social networking site is born and he soon devotes himself to exploiting the idea and building the network. We witness the building of a vast network as the idea is financed and the network grows, finally shifting to a site in the Silicon Valley. The oft-quoted observation that with one billion users Facebook is the fourth largest country in the world really misses the point about globalization and networks which are now no longer geographically-based. As some technology writers pointed out the film was 'anti-social', 'anti-geek' and misogynistic—Zuckerberg himself ironically is portrayed as someone almost autistic in his anti-social behavior—yet highlighted the intellectual property issues that established as Larry Lessig has pointed out the idea of the social network is not patentable and that the code written for Facebook (where the real innovation is) was Zuckerberg's.

Facebook was launched in 2004 as a social network service. It is estimated that over 40% of the US population has a Facebook account and that in one month in October 2010 Facebook had over 135 million unique visitors. Facebook's value has been estimated to be $41 billion and has become the third largest US web company after Google and Amazon. Along with Microsoft and eBay these web companies increasingly define the new landscape cybernetic capitalism. Facebook employs some 1,700 people in twelve countries and heads the list of over 200 social networking sites (excluding dating online websites).[4] The focus of these social networks run across the spectrum of social activities: websites for sports, gaming, nationalities, ethnic groups, mothers, Afro-Americans, green and social activists, investment groups, communities, sex groups, photo-sharing, movies, colleges and schools, religious-based groups, alumni associations, charity, travel and so on. Indeed, a list of social networking sites reveals well over 200 social networking sites[5] with some established as early as 1995 predating the establishment of Facebook by almost a decade. Many like Academia.edu, Classmates.com, TeachStreet, Tuenti, and LinkedIn are specifically professional and educational sites; others focus on business.

In *An Anthropological Introduction to YouTube,* Michael Wesch (2008) indicates that YouTube produced more hours of broadcasting in six months than ABC has since it began broadcasting in 1948, that is, YouTube adds 9,232 hours every day, the equivalent of 200,000 three-minute videos, without producers and most of the material is new.[6] YouTube was launched in 2005. Wesch (2007) in his video "Web 2.0...The Machine Is Using Us"[7] argues the Web 'is no longer just about information; it's about connecting people' and user-generated organization, distribution and commentary (blogging) of material so that we are living in a whole different mediascape based on the understanding media means *mediating* human relationships, not content, especially among the 18-24 age group, which is emblematic of a 'participatory culture' of drag and drop editing, and remixing, sometimes as many times as 2000.

The language of the new social media is easily programmable given its algorithmic character and its numerical coding allows for the automation of many of its functions including media creation. New media are variable and interactive and no longer tied to technologies of exact reproduction such as copying (Manovitch, 2000). They are part of a wider paradigm and system that Castells (2000) calls 'informational capitalism' which is a new technological paradigm and mode of development characterized by information generation, processing, and transmission that have become the fundamental sources of productivity and power.

More and more of this information that is the raw material of knowledge capitalism is increasingly either image-based or comes to us in the form of images. We now live in a socially networked universe in which the material conditions for the formation, circulation, and utilization of knowledge and learning are rapidly changing from an industrial to information and media-based economy. Increasingly the emphasis has fallen on knowledge, learning and media systems and networks that depend upon the acquisition of new skills of image manipulation and understanding as a central aspect of development considered in personal, community, regional, national and global contexts.

These mega-trends signal both changes in the production and consumption of symbolic visual goods and also associated changes in their contexts of use. The radical concordance of image, text and sound, and development of new information and knowledge infrastructures have encouraged the emergence of a global media networks linked with telecommunications that signal the emergence of a Euro-American consumer culture based on the rise of edutainment media a set of information utility conglomerates.

Jonathan Beller (2006) argues that cinema and other media formations including the internet as media platform, are de-territorialized factories in which spectators works or perform value-productive labor. The cinematic mode of production (CMP) is an exploitation of the sociality that characterizes a spectator economy. The question is whether we have already moved beyond spectatorship and the spectator economy to one now centered on new social media and a social mode of production that requires collaboration and co-creation as a matter of participation and entry.

The logic of free software as it underwrites social media has breathed new life into new facets of culture from music to politics, engendering what Christopher Kelty (2008) calls a recursive public—one that is *'vitally concerned with the material and practical maintenance and modification of the technical, legal, practical, and conceptual means of its own existence as a public'* (p. 3). In this new social media culture the individual imagination is harnessed in forms of hyper textual forms of multicreation that ties the expressive to politics and to democratic action, transforming and reshaping the de-territorialized community as one a global polis with shifting and temporary alliances mobilized for particular causes and social movements and political events.

Commons-based peer production is also an economic system of text and image production facilitated by the infrastructure of the Internet that encourages collaboration among individuals who share information, knowledge or cultural goods often without relying on the market pricing or corporate bureaucracies to coordinate their common enterprise. This might be true of open social media that has come to characterize open science and open education but not all social media is open in this sense. Indeed. Only a tiny proportion of social media is open and the difference between commercialization and non-commercialization is a critical question that goes to the heart of education. Some argue that open science demonstrates an 'exemplar of a compound of "private-collective" model of innovation' that contains elements of both proprietary and public models of knowledge production (von Hippel & von Krogh, 2003; von Krogh & von Hippel, 2003). Yet others maintain that the expansion of a patenting culture undermines the norms of open science (Rhoten & Powell, 2007; Peters & Roberts, 2011).

As code for greater political and economic freedoms the concept of openness symbolizes the development of a myriad of open public global spaces that serves as host for new forms of international collaboration in research, scholarship, innovation, creativity and expression. The movement toward greater openness represents a change of philosophy, ethos, and government and a set of interrelated and complex changes that transform markets altering the modes of production and consumption, ushering in a new era based on the values of openness: an ethic of sharing and peer-to-peer collaboration enabled through new architectures of participation. These changes indicate a broader shift from the underlying industrial mode of production—a 'productionist' metaphysics—to a postindustrial mode of consumption as use, reuse, and modification where new logics of social media structure different patterns of cultural consumption and symbolic analysis becomes a habitual and daily creative activity. The economics of openness constructs a new language of "presuming" and "produsage" in order to capture the open participation, collective co-creativity, communal evaluation, and commons-based production of social and public goods. Information is the vital element in the "new" politics and economy that links space, knowledge, and capital in networked practices and freedom is the essential ingredient in this equation if these network practices are to develop or transform themselves into 'knowledge cultures' (Peters & Besley, 2006).

In terms of economic and political systems much also has been written recently about openness as a new hybridized mode of production. Thus, openness has emerged as an alternative mode of *social* production based on the growing and overlapping complexities of open source, open access and open archiving and open publishing. It has become a leading source of innovation in the world global digital economy increasingly adopted by world governments, international agencies and multinationals as well as leading educational institutions. It is clear that the Free Software and 'open source' movements constitute a radical non-propertarian alternative to traditional methods of text production and distribution. This alternative non-proprietary method of cultural exchange threatens traditional models and the legal and institutional means used to restrict creativity, innovation and the free exchange of ideas. In terms of a model of communication there has been a gradual shift from content to code in the openness, access, use, reuse and modification reflecting a radical personalization that has made these open characteristics and principles increasingly the basis of the cultural sphere.

The fundamental distinction between social media and industrial media is that the former is a platform for social interaction and the new web-based technologies that are highly accessible, scalable, and user-friendly turning communication into dialogue and promoting the exchange of user-generated sharable content. This new media ecology contrasts strongly with the old one-way broadcast industrial media that is tied into a transmission model and is rarely dialogical or interactive although industrial media do now try to make concession to the new demand for interactivity via blogs, emails, and associated websites.

Web 2.0 technologies enhance creativity, communications, secure information sharing, collaboration and functionality of the web based on openness (open standards, open platforms), innovation, and evolution of web-culture communities. The applications of technologies of openness to education are still in their infancy (Peters & Britez, 2008) and the logic of new open systems outstrips that of our educational institutions built for the industrial age. These web 2.0 technologies (web as platform) are based on new architectures of participation and collaboration, promote social media and social networking, increasingly encourage wiki-collaborations based on the 'wisdom of the crowd' (Surowiecki, 2004) and mass innovation (Leadbeater, 2009).

These new communications technologies are based on the economics of file-sharing that promote mass customization and the personalization of services (Peters, 2009) based of the co-production of knowledge goods and services where the user is increasingly seen as as co-designer or co-creator integrated into value creation process. The growing interconnectedness of the Web has also passed into a new phase that Tim Berners-Lee calls 'linked data', an aspect of the 'semantic web' used to describe a method of exposing, sharing, and connecting data.[8]

There is a set of emerging open knowledge ecologies that can be briefly noted and sketched by observing that MIT adopts OpenCourseWare in 2001;[9] the Budapest OA statement;[10] National Institute of Health (NIH) adopts an open access policy requiring every scientist who receives an NIH research grant, and who publishes the results in a peer-reviewed journal, to deposit a digital copy of the article in PubMed Central (PMC),[11] the online digital library maintained by the NIH; The Ithaka Report *University Publishing in a Digital Age* (2007)[12] talks of both of 'creation of new formats made possible by digital technologies...will enable real-time dissemination, collaboration, dynamically-updated content, and usage of new media' and 'alternative distribution models (institutional repositories, pre-print servers, open access journals) have also arisen with the aim to broaden access, reduce costs, and enable open sharing of content' (p. 4); and Harvard mandates open self-archiving (February 14, 2008).[13]

The fact is that there are some major moves towards openness policies in regard to adoption of open source, open access, open archiving and open publishing.[14] Yet the openness of the Internet runs deeper and can be described in terms of an overlapping set of characteristics: *open standards*—TCP/IP, HTML, HTTP, interoperability, open processes, end to end principle, no centralized control; *open source software*—extended development community, alterable source code, flexible, personalizable; open access to networks; *open spectrum*—new source of wireless Internet broadband; *open availability of information*—free distribution of digital goods threatens intellectual property regime; DMCA, DRM; *open governance*—extraterritoriality, multilateral, self-regulation. All of these characteristics are in the process of development and emergence and educational and pedagogical possibilities are also still open to development, manipulation and control.

The Googlization of Education

One post in response to Siva Vaidhyanathan's *The Googlization of Higher Education* succinctly summarizes the argument and recognizes the high stakes involved:

> The official mission of Google is "to organize the world's information and make it universally accessible." That is also the goals of colleges throughout the world. As institutions increasingly surrender information organization and technology functions to Google, is the academy surrendering its function and goals to a private corporation?[15]

Interestingly the official mission does not say "to make inordinate profits off the backs of others" yet in a companion paper *The Googlization of Universities* Siva Vaidhyanathan (2009) begins:

> The relationship between Google and the world's universities is more than close. It is uncomfortably familial. Google has moved to establish, embellish, or replace many core university services such as library databases, search interfaces, and e-mail servers. Its server space and computing power opened up new avenues for academic research. Google Scholar has allowed non-scholars to discover academic research. Google Book Search radically transformed the vision and daily practices of university libraries. Through its voracious efforts to include more of everything under its brand, Google fostered a more seamless, democratized, global, cosmopolitan information ecosystem. But it also contributed to the commercialization of higher education and the erosion of standards of information quality.

He documents the googlization of students, of scholarship, of book learning and of research to argue that universities must reverse the terms of the relationship to impose their values. It's a theme that Vaidhyanathan (2011) follows up with *The Googlization of Everything* that addresses three questions: What does the world look like through the lens of Google? How is Google's ubiquity affecting the production and dissemination of knowledge? and how has the corporation altered the rules and practices that govern other companies, institutions, and states? He writes:

> Google dominates the World Wide Web. There was never an election to determine the Web's rulers. No state appointed Google its proxy, its proconsul, or viceroy. Google just stepped into the void when no other authority was willing or able to make the Web stable, usable, and trustworthy. This was a quite nec-

essary step at the time. The question is whether Google's dominance is the best situation for the future of our information ecosystem.

Vaidhyanathan (2011) argues that Google is a Web search-engine service "But as the most successful supplier of Web-based advertising, Google is now an advertising company first and foremost." He suggests that currently major search engines do not 'read' for meaning, they are purely navigational and while the industry pursues semantic search which takes into account contextual meanings of search items semantic analysis is still not advanced enough to take away Google's market position. One of the most significant arguments against Google is what economist call the free rider problem and Vaidhyanathan (2011) claims that Google rides for free on the creative work and investment of others; he reports that even Rupert Murdoch has complained of Google's ability to monetize the Web. And he also mentions the political interference of YouTube since its acquisition in 2006.

Perhaps most tellingly Vaidhyanathan (2011) challenges the neoliberal presumption that market forces can best solve problems and suggests that:

> It had its roots in two prominent ideologies: techno-fundamentalism, an optimistic belief in the power of technology to solve problems...and market fundamentalism, the notion that most problems are better (at least more efficiently) solved by the actions of private parties rather than by state oversight or investment.

And he goes on to argue:

> Our dependence on Google is the result of an elaborate political fraud, but it is far from the most pernicious result of that fraud. Google has deftly capitalized on a thirty-year tradition of "public failure," chiefly in the United States but in much of the rest of the world as well. Public failure is the mirror image of market failure. Markets fail when they can't organize to supply an essential public good, such as education, or have no incentive to prevent a clear harm to the public, such as pollution. Market failure is the chief justification for public intervention.

Vaidhyanathan's argument here is one ultimately against neoliberal in relation to global public knowledge goods but the theory of cognitive capitalism provides us with a 'stage' theory of the changing nature of

ALGORITHMIC CAPITALISM AND EDUCATIONAL FUTURES

capitalism that helps us better to understand the logic of knowledge capitalism that operates on the basis of arrhythmic logics to expand a universe of information accessibility while changing the nature of the regime of accumulation and creating giant global info-utilities that make its profits of the back of the creative endeavors of others at the same time posing as corporation dedicated to the commonweal. Educational futures require a global transnational public investment in infrastructures that stand against both the monopolization and privatization of knowledge and education.

Notes

1   See http://www.sec.gov/news/studies/2010/marketevents-report.pdf. Release September 30, 2010. Acronyms are CFTC: Commodity Futures Trading Commission; SEC: Securities & Exchange Commission.
2   See http://advancedtrading.com/algorithms/showArticle.jhtml?articleID=218401501.
3   This section draws on Peters & Roberts (2011) and Peters (2010).
4   See the full list at http://en.wikipedia.org/wiki/List_of_social_networking_websites.
5   See the list provided at http://en.wikipedia.org/wiki/List_of_social_networking_websites. See also the top 500 sites at http://www.alexa.com/topsites.
6   See http://www.youtube.com/watch?v=TPAO IZ4_hU.
7   See http://www.youtube.com/watch?v=6gmP4nk0EOE.
8   See the Web Design Issues Note by Berners-Lee at http://www.w3.org/Design Issues/LinkedData.html; see the whitepaper at http://virtuoso.openlinksw.com/Whitepapers/html/VirtLinkedDataDeployment.html; and Berners-Lee on the next Web at TED (video) at http://www.ted.com/index.php/talks/tim_berners_lee_on_the_next_web.html.
9   See http://ocw.mit.edu/OcwWeb/web/about/history/.
10 See http://www.soros.org/openaccess.
11 See http://www.pubmedcentral.nih.gov/.
12 See http://www.ithaka.org/ithaka-s-r/strategy/Ithaka%20University%20Publishing%20Report.pdf.
13 See Peter Suber's note on this event at http://www.earlham.edu/~peters/fos/newsletter/03-02-08.htm.
14 See *Foundations of Openness: Evaluating aspects of openness in software projects*, A collaboration between Waugh Partners & OSS Watch (2008), Oxford, at http://pipka.org/blog/2008/07/23/the-foundations-of-openness/; see also Open Technology at http://tomw.net.au/moodle/ and Foundations of Open (Australia) at http://brianna.modernthings.org/article/103/foundations-of-open-australia-2020-local-summit.

15 See http://blog10.facultyacademy.org/2010/04/19/the-googlization-of-higher-education/.

References

Beller, J. (2006). *The cinematic mode of production*. Dartmouth, MA: University Press of New England.

Deleuze, G. (1989a). *Cinema: The movement image* (H. Tomlinson & B. Habberjam, Trans.). Minneapolis, MN: University of Minnesota Press.

Deleuze, G. (1989b). *The time image* (H. Tomlinson & R. Galeta, Trans.). Minneapolis, MN: University of Minnesota Press.

Peters, M. A. (2010). Three forms of knowledge economy: Learning, creativity, openness, *British Journal of Educational Studies, 58*(1), 67–88.

Peters, M. A., & Venkatesan, P. (2011a). Biocapitalism and the politics of life. *Geopolitics, History and International Relations, 2*(2), 100–122.

Peters, M. A., & Venkatesan, P. (2011b). Bioeconomy and the third industrial revolution in the age of synthetic life. *Contemporary Readings in Law and Social Justice, 2*(2), 148–162.

Peters, M. A., & Britez, R. (2010). Ecopolitics of the 'green economy': Environmentalism and education. *The Journal of Academic Research in Economics, 2*(1), 21–36. Retrieved from http://econpapers.repec.org/article/shcjaresh/

Peters, M. A., Britez, R., & Bulut, E. (2010). Cybernetic capitalism, informationalism, and cognitive labor. *Geopolitics, History and International relations, 1*(2), 11–40.

Vaidhyanathan, S. (2009). *The Googlization of universities.* Retrieved from http://www.nea.org/assets/img/PubAlmanac/ALM_09_06.pdf

Vaidhyanathan, S. (2011). *The googlization of everything (and why we should worry).* Berkeley, CA: University of California Press.

Chapter 7

Three Forms of the Knowledge Economy
Learning, Creativity and Openness

Michael A. Peters

Introduction

It is important to distinguish a number of different strands and readings of the knowledge economy and important to do so because it provides a history of a policy idea and charts its ideological interpretations.[1] The different strands of this discourse are radically diverse and include attempts to theorise not only knowledge economy but also the parallel term 'knowledge society', and also the attempts to relate these terms to wider and broader changes in the nature of capitalism, modernity and the global economy. Early attempts by Friedrich von Hayek (1937, 1945) to define the relations between economics and knowledge were followed by the economic value of knowledge studies of the production and distribution of knowledge in the USA by Fritz Machlup (1962). Both of these scholars were associated with the Austrian school of economics. Gary Becker (1964) a prominent member of the Chicago School analysed human capital with reference to education while Peter Drucker (1969), the management theorist, developed an emphasis on 'knowledge workers' coining the term in 1959 and founding the field of 'knowledge management'. In a different vein, Daniel Bell's (1973) sociology of postindustrialism emphasised the centrality of theoretical knowledge and the new science-based industries and Alain Touraine's (1971) *The Post-industrial Society* hypothesised students as a new social movement and predicted the 'programmed society'.

In the 1970s, '80s and '90s there were various attempts by theorists from different disciplines to theorise aspects of the emerging economy. There is no space to discuss their work here but only to mention examples of the diverse literature. Mark Granovetter (1973) theorised of the role of information in the market based on weak ties and social networks. Marc Porat (1977) defined 'the information society' in a series of publications for the US government and Alvin Toffler (1980), the futurist, talked of knowledge-based production in the 'Third Wave economy'. The French philosopher Jean-François Lyotard (1984) defined *The Postmodern Condition* as an age marked by the contingency, complexity, dispersal and distribution of knowledge and the Marxist geographer David Harvey (1989) analysed large-scale shifts from Fordist to flexible accumulation in contemporary capitalism.

James Coleman (1988) analysed how social capital creates human capital and Pierre Bourdieu (1986) and Robert Putnam (2000) further developed the notion providing distinctive notions of cultural and social capital. The Stanford economist Paul Romer (1990) argued that growth is driven by technological change arising from intentional investment decisions where technology as an input is a nonrival, partially excludable good and the OECD (1996), basing its work on Romer and endogenous growth theory, provided an influential policy model of the 'knowledge-based economy'. Meanwhile Joseph Stiglitz (1999), ex-chief economist, developed the World Bank's *Knowledge for Development* and *Education for the Knowledge Economy* programmes based on the notion that knowledge is a global public good.[2] In the wake of these reports employers called for new workforce skill sets (Partnership for 21st Century Skills, 2008) and public policy applications and developments of the 'knowledge economy' concept began to appear in authoritative policy anthologies at the end of the decade (Hearn & Rooney, 2008).

This demonstrates that since the Second World War theorists from different perspectives and disciplines have simultaneously tried to analyse and describe certain deep-seated and structurally transformative tendencies in Western capitalism, society and modernity to move to a form of post-industrial economy that focuses on the production and consumption of knowledge and symbolic goods as a higher-order economic activity that encompasses and affects the entire economy and society (Foray, 2000). While they differ on its societal effects and impacts these theorists agree on the epochal nature of this deep economic transformation and the way in which it represents an ongoing automation and technologisation of processes of scientific communication, including access, distribution and dissemination that lie at the heart of knowledge creation.

What this brief potted history reveals is the different stages in the evolution of a discourse with parallel streams in economics and sociology, often contradictory or opposing, with different ideological sources, separate conceptual histories and different visions of economy and society. We can no longer simply hold that 'knowledge economy' or 'knowledge society' are *neoliberal notions* and ignore their descriptive and analytical force. They are complex and openly contested policy descriptions that have emerged to described the trajectory of the rich liberal capitalist states and now function as a generalised world policy framework that permit local applications and forms of indigenisation of associated concepts and policies, depending on location, the geopolitical climate, state actors and a range of other factors, including labour politics. Rather than discuss the origin and ideological basis of the knowledge economy which I have done elsewhere (see Peters & Besley, 2006) I want to focus on recent developments and applications of the concept that depend upon processes of education and learning directly.

The term 'knowledge economy' is a concept undergoing further conceptual development. In the following sections I have detailed three forms of the knowledge economy: the 'learning economy'; the 'creative economy'; and the 'open knowledge economy'. Each of these has a special relationship to education and pedagogy and highlights the significance of learning processes within these larger policy frameworks. What this analysis demonstrates is the increasing and dynamic differentiation of the concept and progressive new developments that distinguish and refine elements of the general concept. What also is clear is that the main strands of the analysis of the knowledge economy draw on overlapping literatures in economics, sociology and philosophy, and together share some underlying general concepts concerning economic, social or epistemic shifts that characterise modes of economy and social organization and large-scale global, geopolitical historical periodisations—agricultural-industrial-postindustrial-knowledge 'economy' and 'society'—that map onto more general debates concerning European 'modernity', 'postmodernity' that more recently mention global or historical 'multiple (post)modernities', and a set of broader philosophical debates that employ the terms 'modernism', 'postmodernism', and 'antimodernism'.

The Learning Economy

The concept of the learning economy was first coined and has been championed by Bengt-ÅkeLundvall, a Swedish economist from Aalborg University, who uses the term to talk about a new context for European innovation policy.³ Lundvall (1994, 2003) first used the concept in the mid 1990s in a series of working papers to discuss technological change, innovation and institutional learning directly applying it to the learning society and economy, to universities, and to education more generally in the 2000s, culminating in *How Europe's Economies Learn* (Lorenz & Lundvall, 2006) that focuses on diversity in European competence building systems, organisation, labour markets and corporate governance and the links between education and science-industry. The concept and theory of the learning economy is a refinement of the 'knowledge economy' concept based on the way a set of interlocking forces (ecologies) in information/knowledge intensities, distributed new social media, and greater computer networking and connectivity have contributed to the heightened significance of human capital formations, mode of social production and an emphasis on learning processes. Lundvall (1996) argues, for instance, that

> the growing frequency of so-called paradoxes in economic theory and of unsolved socioeconomic problems reflects that neither economic theory nor policy has been adapted to the fact that we have entered a new phase: the 'Learning Economy'.

In the learning economy it is the capacity to learn that increasingly determines the relative position of individuals, firms and national systems and Lundvall claims that the growing polarisation in the OECD-labour markets is explained by the increasing importance of learning and the acceleration in the rate of change. *Sustainability* of these learning economy tendencies ultimately depends on the distribution of capabilities to learn. The OECD highlights the importance of skills and learning, focusing on lifelong learning becoming the central element in a high-skills, high-wage jobs strategy. Lundvall distinguishes between information and knowledge; the former is logical, sequential and easily broken down into bits and transmitted by computer whereas the latter is associated with learning that is often a form of know-how and competencies based on tacit knowledge. An information or knowledge economy is quite different from a learning economy that is not tied to formal knowledge institutions and goes beyond formal propositional forms of knowing to the arena of routine learning based on learning-by-doing or learning-by-using. Such a definition allows us to consider the types of learning associated with the process of working that emphasises tacit, practical and embodied knowledge generated during the work process. One might also argue in a broader sense that the learning economy focuses on learning processes that are responsible for the production of knowledge.

Lundvall et al. argue that innovation is crucial to economic competitiveness and learning is crucial to innovation. They argue that knowledge is becoming obsolete more rapidly than before and that therefore firms and employees constantly have to learn and acquire new competencies, mostly learnt through experience. Lundvall and his colleagues argue that traditional schooling isolated from society and organised according to traditional disciplines and educational cultures focusing on collaboration, interdisciplinarity and engagement with real-life problems are required to produce flexible workers who can successfully participate in the new economy. Learning in this conception is not an end in itself but only in the service of innovation policy and focused on processes of institutional learning within firms which it is assumed can easily be applied and transferred to schools. Lundvall is influenced by Pasinetti's (1981) work and his distinction between *producer learning* linked to productivity growth and *consumer learning* connected to consumers' adoption of new consumption goods is an attempt to understand value creation. Lundvall also emphasises 'learning by doing' and 'learning by using' after Kenneth Arrow (1962) to talk about the need of firms and the workforce to engage in building new competencies in order to survive global competition. To this he adds 'learning by interacting' (Lundvall, 1988) which purportedly has the effect of transforming local learning into general knowledge. In the context of the EU's emphasis on creativity and innovation Lundvall has focused on innovation as an interactive learning process and the relation of the national innovation system to science and technology policies with a focus on knowledge management design and strategies. This provides an interesting and useful macroeconomic context for understanding the centrality and significance of various forms of *organisational learning* for the national economy as a whole but limited application to formal systems of education or to understanding the nature of academic knowledge and its transformation from propositional learning to learning by doing. Lundvall's formulations have proved influential and helpful and has also given greater profile to the significance of 'learning processes' but fails to link with the considerable literature in education on learning theory or to view learning processes as central to broader visions of society and politics.

The Creative Economy[4]

The conception of the creative economy emphasises the creative industries and institutions as an interlocking sector producing cultural goods and services as a rapidly growing and key component of the new global knowledge economy. It refers to those broadly defined design industries and institutions that draw on the individual and increasingly collective resources of creativity, skill and talent that have strong potential for the generation of wealth and job creation through the development and exploitation of intellectual property. Both the idea and policies associated with it originate in the late 1990s and early 2000s in the work of Charles Landry, John Howkins and Richard Florida. Increasingly, the notion has been applied to education at all levels both in terms of the development of creative minds, the creative curriculum and universities as creative institutions. This section provides a broad conceptual understanding of the creative economy and its relation to education.

Today there is a strong renewal of interest by politicians and policy-makers worldwide in the related notions of creativity and innovation, especially in relation to terms like 'the creative economy', 'knowledge economy', 'enterprise society', 'entrepreneurship' and 'national systems of innovation' (Baumol, 2002; Cowen, 2002; Scott & Urry, 1994). In its rawest form the notion of the creative economy emerges from a set of claims that suggests that the Industrial Economy is giving way to the Creative Economy based on the growing power of ideas and virtual value—the turn from steel and hamburgers to software and intellectual property (Florida, 2002; Howkins, 2001; Landry, 2000).

In this context increasingly policy latches onto the issues of copyright as an aspect of IP, piracy, distribution systems, network literacy, public service content, the creative industries, new interoperability standards, the WIPO and the development agenda, WTO and trade, and means to bring creativity and commerce together (Cowen, 2002; Davenport and Beck, 2001; Gordon, 1993; Hughes, 1988; Lemley, 2005; Netanel, 1996, 1998; Shapiro & Varian, 1998). At the same time this focus on creativity has exercised strong appeal to policy-makers who wish to link education more firmly to new forms of capitalism emphasising how creativity must be taught, how educational theory and research can be used to improve student learning in mathematics, reading and science, and how different models of intelligence and creativity can inform educational practice (Blythe, 2000). Under the spell of the creative economy discourse there has been a flourishing of new accelerated learning methodologies together with a focus on giftedness and the design of learning programmes for exceptional children.[5] One strand of the emerging literature highlights the role of the creative and expressive arts, of performance, of aesthetics in general, and the significant role of design as an underlying infrastructure for the creative economy (Caves, 2000; Frey & Pommerehne, 1989; Ginsburgh & Menger, 1996; Heilbrun & Gray, 2001; Hesmondhalgh, 2002).

There is now widespread agreement among economists, sociologists and policy analysts that creativity, design and innovation are at the heart of the global knowledge economy: together creativity, design and innovation define knowledge capitalism and its ability to continuously reinvent itself.[6] Together and in conjunction with new communications technologies they give expression to the essence of digital capitalism— the 'economy of ideas'—and to new architectures of mass collaboration that distinguish it as a new generic form of economy different in nature from industrial capitalism. The fact is that knowledge in its immaterial digitised informational form as sequences and value chains of 1s and 0s—ideas, concepts, functions, and abstractions—approaches the status of pure thought. Unlike other commodities it operates expansively to defy the law of scarcity that is fundamental to classical and neoclassical economics and to the traditional understanding of markets. A generation of economists have expressed this truth by emphasising that knowledge is (almost) a global public good; it is non-rivalrous and barely excludable (Stiglitz, 1999; Verschraegen & Schiltz, 2007). It is non-rivalrous in the sense that there is little or marginal cost to adding new users. In other words, knowledge and information, especially in digital form, cannot be consumed. The use of knowledge or information as digital goods can be distributed and shared at no extra cost and the distribution and sharing is likely to add to its value rather than to deplete it or use it up. This is the essence of the economics of file-sharing education; it is also the essence of new forms of distributed creativity, intelligence and innovation in an age of mass participation and collaboration (Brown & Duguid, 2000; Surowiecki, 2004; Tapscott & Williams, 2006).

The United Nations (2008, p. 3) *Creative Economy Report* views the creative economy as a new development paradigm that is able to link all aspects of the economy together in a way that provides new growth opportunities for developing countries.

> A new development paradigm is emerging that links the economy and culture, embracing economic, cultural, technological and social aspects of development at both the macro and micro levels. Central to the new paradigm is the fact that creativity, knowledge and access to information are increasingly recognized as powerful engines driving economic growth and promoting development in a globalizing world. The emerging creative economy has become a leading component of economic growth, employment, trade and innovation, and social cohesion in most advanced economies. Unfortunately, however, the large majority of developing countries are not yet able to harness their creative capacity for development. This is a reflection of weaknesses both in domestic policy and in the business environment, and global systemic biases. Nevertheless, the creative economy offers to developing countries a feasible option and new opportunities to leapfrog into emerging high-growth areas of the world economy.

This is a comprehensive report by a group that was set up by the Secretary-General of the United Nations Conference on Trade and Development (UNCTAD) in 2004 in the context of preparations for the High-level Panel on Creative Industries and Development, held during the UNCTADXI Ministerial Conference, and it provides a useful introduction to the concept and context of the creative economy including its development dimension, as well as focusing on its analysis and measurement, its role in international trade and the importance of intellectual property. Curiously, this report has little to say directly about education per se or its link with development, which is a major weakness.

Much of the literature concerning education and the creative economy emphasises the role of the arts in economic development and the need for building forms of cultural, social and public entrepreneurship. The problem is that beyond the formulation of concepts such as 'creative industries', 'creative cities' and 'creative class' little analysis has been made of creativity in schools apart from fostering instrumental versions of creativity or simply regarding 'education, training and skills' as one aspect of the creative economy. There is still a long way to go in theorising and developing policies that encourage creativity in schools predicated on new forms of social media and better understanding of new media and knowledge ecologies that democratise access to knowledge, decentralize organisational and authority structures, encourage a greater personalisation and autonomy of learning while promoting new forms of 'collective intelligence' and peer learning based on a new ethic of participation and collaboration (Caron & Caronia, 2007; Ito, 2006, 2008; Lave & Wenger, 1991; Peters, 2009a).[7]

The Open Knowledge Economy

Bill Gates (2006, p. 3) uses the term *information democracy* to signal the public world of information available globally that ordinary citizens can access through a PC. Gates says: 'While information wants to be free, knowledge is much "stickier"—harder to communicate, more subjective, less easy to define'. And he indicates that as software gets smarter it will help people synthesise and manage knowledge. He mentions a range of technologies like OneNote that promote consilience and just-in-time information—'technologies that infuse online data with meaning and context'. Gates's argument is another demonstration of a kind of technological determinism, yet the general point he raises—the changing relationship between democracy and information—has a venerable past in democratic theory and plays a strong role in educational theory and practice. In some quarters the term has come to mean no more than *information sharing* with attention directed towards different models— dictatorship, anarchy, democracy, and embassy—that might be employed in businesses to enhance productivity and in education to foster participation and collaboration.

At the 2007 World Economic Forum in Davos, Switzerland, the participants—among them, Gordon Brown and Rupert Murdoch— acknowledged that the ground rules for democratic societies have been permanently altered by an 'explosion of self-expression' (Murdoch) and a changed economy of information (Brown) that favors the individual active consumer-citizen or 'prosumer' who through the Internet accesses or creates blogs and bypasses much of the media mainstream. This new media thrives on a constant streaming torrent of opinion with millions of 'information transactions' that breaks stories, circulates endless commentaries and opinions but also 'gets the facts out there' (Murdoch) via a kind of public scrutiny that acts as a source of constant feedback. No government, no state, now is immune to information; what is more, no state or government can police or control information borders although state and corporate surveillance remains a real threat not only to privacy but also basic democratic rights. The 'information state' is thus the first politically porous state that with all its contradictions, mutations and imperfections looks the most likely model for a world public space.

Information and knowledge have always been central to accounts of democracy from its early modern formulations, where the emphasis was placed on the necessity of an informed or educated citizenry, through to more recent movements like that of open government which began in the 1960s. Open government opposed reason of state, state secrecy and national security, often popularized as 'big brother' and 'faceless bureaucracy', with a system of public accountability based on principles of freedom of information. The presumption of openness, political transparency and the demand for public scrutiny at all levels found favor with a range of different groups pressing for democratic freedoms in the 1960s, first in the USA, with countries in Europe and Australasia following in the 1970s and 1980s, respectively. Much of this demand and struggle found its way into legislation designed to enact 'freedom of information' that regulates and controls public access to government records. Freedom of information is sometimes tied to the historic right, enshrined in Article 19 of the Declaration of Human Rights, to the universal right to freedom of opinion and expression without interference. Generally, such legislation became part of the establishment of an ombudsman office that represents the interest of the public against government departments (Peters, 2009b).

Even before the movement for open government, democratic theory held a special place for the free press and assumed a benign relationship between the media, democracy, citizenship and education. On some accounts processes of media globalization have diminished the public sphere as the centralization of media control and the intensification of ownership and commercialization has led to the growth of the media transnational conglomerates. Media outputs become trivial through 'edutainment' and commercialism, thus serving market rather than citizenship needs. With the democratization of media a new paradigm of communication has emerged that seems to facilitate individual interactivity and enhance democracy, autonomy and justice. Yochai Benkler (2003, 2006) has been at the forefront of a movement that argues the political economy of the sphere of liberal communication has now changed with the radical decentralization of information production. The new paradigm of social production in the networked global information economy has diminished the significance of the corporate and transnational media conglomerates to create meaning, to influence the public agenda, and to control the format (soundbites) of news discussions. This is part of Benkler's argument for an enhancement of democracy and education. It is an argument that also places strong emphasis on the logic of decentralization, such that no individual actor (person or corporation) can exercise control over the totality, and allows individuals to 'build their own window on the world' and to invent the pathways, the sequences, the topics and the logic of performance that determines the next link. In Benkler's terms the individual access and user (inter)activity alleviates the 'autonomy deficit by an exclusively proprietary communications system'.

Finally, Benkler (2003) identifies the third leg of his argument concerning 'justice' where he states succinctly:

> Commons in information and communications facilities are no panacea for inequality in initial endowments, but they do provide a relatively simple and sustainable way of giving everyone equal access to one important set of resources. Second, commons in communications infrastructure provide a transactional setting that ameliorates some of the inequalities in transactional capabilities that Ackerman identifies as a focus for liberal redistribution.

Benkler and Nissenbaum (2006) go a step further to develop an argument concerning the relationship between commons-based peer production and virtue, combining two lines of inquiry—commons-based peer production and philosophy of technology where moral and political values can be seen to be inherent in technical design (Flanagan et al., 2005).

Commons-based peer production not only challenges the traditional basis of hierarchical economic management but also neoliberal theories based on the revival on *homo economicus* with its controlling assumptions of rationality, individuality and self-interest. It is the self-interest assumption that they problematise. Benkler and Nissenbaum (2006, pp. 394–395) suggest that:

> the emergence of peer production offers an opportunity for more people to engage in practices that permit them to exhibit and experience virtuous behavior. We posit: (a) that a society that provides opportunities for virtuous behavior is one that is more conducive to virtuous individuals; and (b) that the practice of effective virtuous behavior may lead to more people adopting virtues as their own, or as attributes of what they see as their self-definition. The central thesis

of this chapter is that socio-technical systems of commons-based peer production offer not only a remarkable medium of production for various kinds of information goods but serve as a context for positive character formation.

A range of initiatives and movements, including Free and Open Source Software, Open Access and Wikipedia, now tend to throw into question neoliberal assumptions within the global network information economy. The empirical fact is that self-interest is an inadequate explanation for the active engagement of millions of users worldwide who contribute without monetary reward in these projects and many thousands of smaller ones. The implications of this changed political economy for education has barely been registered.

Benkler (2006) theorizes fundamental changes to liberal society and economy in *The Wealth of Networks: How Social Production Transforms Markets and Freedom*. Benkler develops a vision of the good society based on access and distribution of information goods in a networked global information economy that places a high value on individual autonomy where within the public information space of the Internet and the information commons people have the individual means to pursue their own interests.[8] He indicates that a set of related changes in the information technologies entailing new social practices of production has fundamentally changed how we make and exchange information, knowledge and culture, and he envisages these newly emerging social practices as constituting a new information environment that gives individuals the freedom to take a more active role in the construction of public information and culture. The emergence of the global networked information economy made possible by increasingly cheaper processors linked as a pervasive network has created an information economy based on the production of information and culture that enables social and nonmarket or peer-to-peer production and exchange to play a, perhaps even, the central role.

Benkler's arguments chime with a number of others who have been working in the same area of the intellectual commons as a newly defined public space or laid the groundwork for doing so: Richard Stallman, John Perry Barlow, Larry Lessig, James Doyle and Pamela Samuelson. Stallman's (2002) collected essays in *Free Software, Free Society* originally written a couple of decades ago provides a discussion of the philosophy underlying the free software movement, including the GNU project and manifesto, the difference between 'free' and 'open' software, the concept of copyleft and the GNU General Public License. As Larry Lessig (2002, p. 10) writes, 'Every generation has its philosopher...who captures the imagination of a time'. The philosopher who best captures our time, Lessig asserts, is Richard Stallman, who began as a computer programmer designing operating systems and came to define the freedom of code as the central pressing issue confronting a computer society. Free software is Stallman's answer to the question of control—'free' as in 'free speech', that is, free from control, transparent, and open to further development, change and innovation. Such freedom, then, is the basis of 'free laws', an economy of free code and the 'free society'. The principles demand openness and transparency that form the basis for control of code, for laws that guarantee this freedom and for government itself. Stallman argues that copyright is not defined as a natural right in the US. Constitution and he seeks to reduce it, arguing also for the distribution of scientific publishing in non-proprietary formats.

The fact is the accumulated canon of patent and copyright law applies well to things but faces insuperable difficulties when applied to nonmaterial goods. Information increasingly separates itself from the material plane to exist merely in the ideational form as pure ideas. Digital technologies tend to eliminate the distinction between the idea and its expression in some physical form also 'erasing the legal jurisdictions of the physical world'. Lessig (2004), building on earlier work (e.g., Lessig, 2001), argues that for an underlying conception of freedom and its protection as the basis for 'free culture', at the same time warning of the dangers of 'big media' in colonizing public media space. He emphasizes the way the Internet makes possible the efficient spread of content through peer-to- peer (p2p) file-sharing in a way that does not respect traditional copyright and he warns us of the dangers to the kind of creativity that is the basis of cultural innovation. In *The Future of Ideas* Lessig (2002) describes how the Internet counter-culture has encouraged an explosion of innovation and creativity and the legal architecture protecting it as a public space is now under threat.

In the same context we can also talk of James Boyle and Pamela Samuelson. Boyle is a law professor at Duke University and the co-founder of the Center for the Study of the Public Domain[9] established in 2002 with the mission to promote research and scholarship on the contributions of the public domain to speech, culture, science and innovation, to promote debate about the balance needed in our intellectual property system and to translate academic research into public policy solutions. Boyle (1997) argues that we need a political economy of 'intellectual property'. Likening the Net to an environment and drawing on the politics of environmentalism he suggests 'our intellectual property discourse has structural tendencies towards over-protection, rather than under-protection'. He claims that the 'public domain' is disappearing in an IP system built around the interests of the current stakeholders and the notion of the original author, an over-deterministic practice of economic analysis and a 'free speech' community that is under-sensitized to the dangers of private censorship.

He argues that a pay-as-you-read architecture will be inefficient and that such a system will 'Lead to extraordinary monopoly and concentration in the software industry, as copyright and patent trump antitrust policy' and possibly legitimize the extension of 'intellectual property rights even further over living organisms, including the human genome, transgenic species and the like' as well as privatizing 'words, or aspects of images or texts that are currently in the public domain, to the detriment of public debate, education, equal access to information ...' (Boyle, 1997, n.p.). Boyle is one of a number of scholars working in this area including Michael Carroll, Molly Shaffer Van Houweling and Larry Lessig, along with the filmmakers Eric Saltzman and Davis Guggenheim, the computer science expert Hal Abelson, and CEOs like Jimmy Wales (founder of Wikipedia), Laurie Racine (founder of dotSUB), Joi Ito (founder of Neotony) and John Buckman (founder of Magnatune.com) (and all members of Creative Commons[10]). Pamela Samuelson is another working on intellectual property and the public space. Samuelson's piece in *Wired's* 'The Copyright Grab'[11] warned that President Clinton's white paper on intellectual property was a sellout of the public and a reward of supporters in the copyright industry.

'Henry' in the *Crooked Timber* seminar[12] on Benkler's *The Wealth of Networks* indicates how this recent literature maps onto 'a broader tradition of thought; that of people like Jane Jacobs, James Scott, Richard Sennett and Iris Marion Young'. He acknowledges that the Internet enables us to engage with each other in new creative ways and 'to form networks of collaboration and of conversation, creating possibility conditions for the kinds of diversity and critical thinking that democratic theorists prize'. The essential point emphasized here, especially for the Left, is that these newly enabled forms of 'community' or 'conversation' are non-constraining and occur without central planning or the heavy-handed agency of the State. Henry suggests that three key norms—linking, attribution and authenticity—structure the blogosphere creating an economy built on 'gift exchange' and contemplates how even self-regulatory solutions tend to rigidify over time, reducing spontaneity and introducing more formal rules and hierarchies.

To summarize: Information is the vital element in a 'new' politics and economy that links space, knowledge and capital in networked practices. Freedom is an essential ingredient in this equation if these network practices develop or transform themselves into knowledge cultures. The specific politics and eco-cybernetic rationalities that accompany an informational global capitalism comprised of new multinational edutainment agglomerations are clearly capable of colonizing the emergent ecology of info-social networks and preventing the development of knowledge cultures based on non-proprietary modes of knowledge production and exchange.

Complexity as an approach to knowledge and knowledge systems now recognizes both the development of global systems architectures in (tele)communications and information with the development of open knowledge production systems that increasingly rest not only on the establishment of new and better platforms (sometimes called Web 2.0), the semantic web, new search algorithms and processes of digitization. Social processes and policies that foster *openness* as an overriding value as evidenced in the growth of open source, open access and open education and their convergences that characterize global knowledge communities that transcend borders of the nation-state. Openness seems also to suggest political transparency and the norms of open inquiry, indeed, even democracy itself as both the basis of the logic of inquiry and the dissemination of its results (Peters & Britez, 2009; Peters & Roberts, 2010). This is increasingly evident in forms of open science economy based on large-scale, international science portal systems that themselves are aimed at addressing large-scale natural systems attrition, rapid industrial depletion of natural ecosystems and environmental collapse and debasement.

The Promise of Open Education

Open education develops around a successive series of utopian historical moments based on a set of similar ideas stemming from core Enlightenment concepts of freedom, equality, democracy and creativity.[13] The early history of open education consists of political and psychological experiments conducted in special schools established in the early twentieth century (Illich, 1972; Neil, 1960; Rogers, 1969). The movement from the very beginning thus was shaped by contemporary political and psychological theory that attempted to provide alternatives to the mainstream, connected to and exemplified a form of society and set of institutions that was seen as politically desirable. These early ideas also significantly involved an analysis of the space and architecture of schools, and the associated idea of freedom of movement underwent considerable refinement and development over the course of the twentieth century.

An important aspect concerned not only the analysis of architecture but the overcoming of distance in a form of distance education that began in the late nineteenth century through correspondence and progressed through various media eras including that of radio and television. Open education consisted of several strands and movements that often coalesced and overlapped to create a complex skein that despite the complexity was able to rapidly avail itself of new communication and information technologies in the last decade of the twentieth century and to identify itself more broadly with the new convergences among open source, open access, and open courseware movements. It was as though the open education movement in its infancy required the technological infrastructure to emerge as a major new paradigm rather than a set of small-scale and experimental alternatives or a form of distance education.

The model of technology-based distance education really received its impetus in the 1960s when the Open University in the UK was established founded on the idea that communications technology could extend advanced degree learning to those people who for a variety of reasons could not easily attend campus universities. It has been immensely influential as a model for other countries, and distance education flourished in the 1970s and picked up new open education dimensions with the introduction of local area network environments.[14] Open courseware (OCW) is very much a feature of the twenty-first century. The Massachusetts Institute of Technology (MIT), one of the first universities to introduce OCW, announced its intention in the *New York Times* in 2001, formed the OpenCourseWare Consortium in 2005, and by

2007 published virtually all its courses online.[15] MIT is only one example of the OpenCourseWare movement, an important player, but nevertheless, only one institution amongst many.[16] Most recently the Cape Town Open Education Declaration mentions the variety of openly licensed course materials, including lessons, games, software and other teaching and learning materials that contribute to making education more accessible and help shape and give effect to a 'participatory culture of learning, creating, sharing and cooperation' necessary for knowledge societies. It goes on to provide a statement based on a three-pronged strategy designed to support 'open educational technology, open sharing of teaching practices and other approaches that promote the broader cause of open education'.[17] The open education movement and paradigm has arrived: it emerges from a complex historical background and its futures are intimately tied not only to open source, open access and open publishing movements but also to the concept of the open society itself (Iiyoshi & Kumar, 2008 ; Peters & Britez, 2009).

The Open Science Economy

Openness has become a complex code word for a variety of digital trends and movements and has emerged as an alternative mode of 'social production' based on the growing and overlapping complexities of open source, open access, open archiving, open publishing and open science. Openness in this sense refers to open source models of scientific communication, knowledge distribution and educational development although it has a number of deeper registers that refer more widely to government ('open government'), society ('open society'), economy ('open economy') and even psychology (openness as one of the five traits of personality theory). The concept and evolving set of practices has profound consequences for education at all levels. 'Openness' has become a leading source of innovation in the world global digital economy increasingly adopted by world governments, international agencies and multinationals as well as leading educational institutions as a means of promoting scientific inquiry and international collaboration. It is clear that the Free Software and 'open source' movements constitute a radical non-propertarian (i.e., social) alternative to traditional methods of text and symbolic production, distribution, archiving, access and dissemination. This alternative non-proprietary model of cultural production and exchange threatens traditional models of intellectual property and it challenges the major legal and institutional means such as copyright currently used to restrict creativity, innovation and the free exchange of ideas.

As previously mentioned MIT was one of the first universities to introduce OCW, forming the OpenCourseWare Consortium in 2005 and by 2007 published virtually all its courses online.[18] The OCW Consortium advertises itself in the following terms emphasizing one aspect of alternative educational globalization—the distribution and free exchange of course content and also potentially a major source for the internationalization of curriculum:

> An OpenCourseWare is a free and open digital publication of high quality educational materials, organized as courses. The OpenCourseWare Consortium is a collaboration of more than 200 higher education institutions and associated organizations from around the world creating a broad and deep body of open educational content using a shared model. The mission of the OpenCourseWare Consortium is to advance education and empower people worldwide through opencourseware.

On February 14, 2008, Harvard University adopted a policy that requires faculty members to allow the university to make their scholarly articles available free online. The new policy makes Harvard the first university in the United States to *mandate* open access to its faculty members' research publications and marks the beginning of a new era that will encourage other US universities to do the same. The Harvard policy is a move to disseminate faculty research and scholarship and to give the University a worldwide license to make each faculty member's scholarly articles available globally. In effect the new policy establishes a global scholarly publishing system that allows scholars to use and distribute their own work giving them greater control over these aspects of scholarly production. Harvard's open-access repository makes scholarly research available worldwide for free while the faculty member retains the copyright of the article.

Harvard University is not alone; both the National Institutes of Health (NIH) and the European Research Council have recently adopted similar open access mandates putting pressure on other government agencies in the US and governments abroad to do the same. In a clear sense this is the beginning of a mega-trend that will make intellectual research and teaching resources freely available worldwide and encourage forms of education based on open source, open access, open archiving and open publishing models as well as supporting burgeoning initiatives like the Creative Commons project,[19] the P2P Foundation[20], the Public Knowledge Project[21] that supports Open Journal Systems, and the Open Knowledge Foundation,[22] to mention only a few.

To summarize, openness is a new mode of social production that has become a leading source of innovation in the world global digital economy and constitutes a radical non-propertarian alternative to traditional methods of text production, dissemination and distribution. In terms of a model of communication there has been a gradual shift from content to code in the openness, access, use, reuse and modification reflecting a radical personalization that has made these open characteristics and principles increasingly the basis of the cultural sphere. So open source and open access has been developed and applied in open publishing, open archiving and open music, constituting the hallmarks of 'open culture'.

Open cultures are built on radically decentralized digital systems that promote public participation. As I argued above, openness more broadly suggests political transparency and the norms of open inquiry. In other words, certain institutional forms are required to promote the organization of knowledge which enhance its free flow, the mode of open criticism, testing and validation characteristic of science-based institutions, and the non-ideological replication, trial and error ethos that typifies the scientific method consonant with an open community of inquiry.

New models of open science are rapidly developing based on mode 2.0 with greater interdisciplinarity and 'flattening' of geocentric science centers and knowledge flows toward global teams. Correspondingly there is a reversal from close conduit peer review to open source public scrutiny and increased use of open source data analysis, management of large databases, and sharing (bioinformatics). Science publishing has undergone a sea change with changes in creation, production and consumption of scholarly resources—'creation of new formats made possible by digital technologies, ultimately allowing scholars to work in deeply integrated electronic research and publishing environments that will enable real-time dissemination, collaboration, dynamically-updated content, and usage of new media' and 'alternative distribution models (institutional repositories, pre-print servers, open access journals) have also arisen with the aim to broaden access, reduce costs, and enable open sharing of content' (Ithaka Report, 2007, p. 4).[23] The new models of open science are to some extent in opposition or conflict with expanded protection of IP. Open source initiatives have facilitated the development of new models of production and innovation. The public and nonprofit sectors have called for alternative approaches dedicated to public knowledge redistribution and dissemination. Now distributed peer-to-peer knowledge systems rival the scope and quality of similar products produced by proprietary efforts, where speed of diffusion of open source projects is an obvious advantage. The successful projects occur in both software and open source biology. Open access science has focused on making peer-reviewed, online research and scholarship freely accessible to a broader population (including digitized back issues). Open science demonstrates an 'exemplar of a compound of "private-collective" model of innovation' that contains elements of both proprietary and public models of knowledge production (Von Hippel & von Krogh, 2003). Rhoten and Powell (2007) ask 'does the expansion of a patenting culture undermine the norms of open science? Does the intensification of patenting accelerate or retard the development of basic and commercial research?'

As *Scientific American* (2008) acknowledges, the emergence of Science 2.0:

> generally refers to new practices of scientists who post raw experimental results, nascent theories, claims of discovery and draft papers on the Web for others to see and comment on. Proponents say these "open access" practices make scientific progress more collaborative and therefore more productive. Critics say scientists who put preliminary findings online risk having others copy or exploit the work to gain credit or even patents. Despite pros and cons, Science 2.0 sites are beginning to proliferate; one notable example is the OpenWetWare project started by biological engineers at the Massachusetts Institute of Technology.

Waldrop (2008) demonstrates that rich-text, highly interactive, user-generated and socially active Internet (Web 2.0) has seen linear models of knowledge production giving way to more diffuse open ended and serendipitous knowledge processes.

Open science economy plays a complementary role with corporate and transnational science and implies a strong role for governments. Increasingly, portal-based knowledge environments and global science gateways support collaborative science (Schuchardt et al., 2007; see, for instance, Science.gov and Science.world). Cyber-mashups of very large data sets let users explore, analyze, and comprehend the science behind the information being streamed. The World Wide Web has revolutionized how researchers from various disciplines collaborate over long distances especially in the Life Sciences, where interdisciplinary approaches are becoming increasingly powerful as a driver of both integration and discovery (with regard to data access, data quality, identity, and provenance) (Sagotsky et al., 2008). National science review and assessment focuses on formative role in developing distributed knowledge systems based on quality journal suites in disciplinary clusters with an ever finer mesh of in-built indicators. Meanwhile economists argue that open source software can be an engine of economic growth (see David, 2003; Etzkowitz, 1997, 2003, 2008; Garzarelli et al., 2008) and clearly the notion of open science economy has the strong potential to become one of the leading sectors of the knowledge economy.

Conclusion

Education debates need to be centered on the changing concepts of the knowledge economy and to systematically address questions of:

- the 'learning economy' in a way that links education and schooling to national innovation without embracing a crude economic instrumentalism;
- the 'creative economy' without reducing creativity to innovation and schooling simply to a question of enhanced productivity, and in a way that recognizes and utilizes the prospects of new social media and learning ecologies that promote greater personalization, participation and peer collaboration;
- the 'open knowledge economy' that understands the public benefits of open knowledge production for education, science and democracy.

These questions have become pressing at a time when the prevailing neoliberal policy credo has been discredited and policy makers look for a new development paradigm that is sustainable in the long term.

Notes

1. This list is based on Michael A. Peters, Simon Marginson and Peter Murphy (2008) as it was compiled for *New Learning: A Charter for Change in Education* at http://education.illinois.edu/newlearning/.
2. These two World Bank programmes have been very influential. For both associated websites, see http://web.worldbank.org/WBSITE/EXTERNAL/WBI/WBIPROGRAMS/KFDLP/0,,menuPK:461238~pagePK:64156143~piPK:64154155~theSitePK: 461198,00. html and

http://web.worldbank.org/WBSITE/EXTERNAL/TOPICS/EXTEDUCATION/0,,content MDK: 20161496~menuPK:540092~page PK:148956~ piPK:216618~theSite PK: 282386, 00.html

3. For Lundvall's publications, see his webpage at http://www.business.aau.dk/ike/members/bal.html.

4. This section is based on my entry in *New Learning: A Charter for Change in Education* at http://education.illinois.edu/newlearning/ but see Peters, Marginson and Murphy (2009).

5 See The Center for Accelerated Learning at http://www.alcenter.com/; see e.g., *The Framework for Gifted Education* at http://education.qld.gov.au/publication/production/reports/pdfs/giftedandtalfwrk.pdf.

6 For innovation theory, see the Swedish economist Bengt-ÅkeLundvall's webpage at http://www.business.aau.dk/ike/members/bal.html and especially his concept of 'the learning economy' (above).

7 See also the education section of the P2P Foundation at http://p2pfoundation.net/Category:Education.

8 See Benkler's homepage at http://www.benkler.org/ where he outlines his research in terms of a set of general theoretical problems, including Cooperation and Human Systems Design (how we understand the dynamics of human cooperation through work in many disciplines, from experimental economics, evolutionary biology, and computer science, to organizational sociology and anthropology, and how we can synthesize this body of work into an approach to designing human systems: be they technical platforms, business processes, or law); Commons-based information production and exchange (sustainability and comparative efficiency); and, Freedom, justice, and the organization of information production on nonproprietary principles (Normative analysis of the implications of commons-based production and exchange of information and culture). Many of his papers are available online.

9 See http://www.law.duke.edu/cspd/.

10 See http://creativecommons.org/.

11 See http://www.wired.com/wired/archive/4.01/white.paper_pr.html.

12 See http://crookedtimber.org/category/benkler-seminar/.

13 This section is based on my entry in *New Learning: A Charter for Change in Education* at http://education.illinois.edu/newlearning/.

14 See, for example, the Indian Open Schooling Network (IOSN) at http://www.nos.org/iosn.htm, the National Institute of Open Schooling at http://www.nos.org/, and Open School BC (British Columbia) at http://www.pss.gov.bc.ca/osbc/.

15 See http://www.ocwconsortium.org/index.php?option=com_content&task=view&id=15&Itemid=29.

16 See the OpenCourseWare Consortium for the full list of participating countries and list of courses at http://www.ocwconsortium.org/.

17 The full declaration can be found at http://www.capetowndeclaration.org/read-the-declaration.
18 See the OCW website at http://www.ocwconsortium.org/.
19 See http://creativecommons.org/.
20 See http://p2pfoundation.net/The_Foundation_for_P2P_Alternatives.
21 See http://pkp.sfu.ca/.
22 See http://www.okfn.org/.
23 See, for instance, the *Journal of Visualized Experiments* at http://www.jove.com/.

References

Arrow, K. J. (1962). The economic implications of learning by doing. *Review of Economic Studies, 29*(3), 155–173.

Baumol, W. J. (2002). *The free-market innovation machine: Analyzing the growth miracle of capitalism*. Princeton, NJ: Princeton University Press.

Becker, G. (1993). *Human capital: A theoretical and empirical analysis, with special reference to education* (3rd ed.). Chicago, IL: University of Chicago Press. (Original work published 1964)

Bell, D. (1973). *The coming of post-industrial society: A venture in social forecasting*. New York, NY: Basic Books.

Benkler, Y. (2003). *Freedom in the commons: Towards a political economy of information*. Retrieved from http://www.law.duke.edu/shell/cite.pl?52+Duke+L.+J.+1245.

Benkler, Y. (2006). *The wealth of networks: How social production transforms markets and freedom*. New Haven, CT: Yale University Press.

Benkler, Y., & Nissenbaum, H. (2006). Commons-based peer production and virtue. *The Journal of Political Philosophy, 14*(4), 394–419.

Blythe, M. (2000). *Creative learning futures: Literature review of training and development needs in the creative industries*. Retrieved from http://www.cadise.ac.uk/projects/creativelearning/New_Lit.doc.

Bourdieu, P. (1986). The forms of capital (R. Nice, Trans.). In J. F. Richardson (Ed.), *Handbook of theory of research for sociology of education* (pp. 241–258). Westport, CT: Greenwood Press.

Boyle, J. (1997). *A politics of intellectual property: Environmentalism for the net?* Retrieved from http://www.james-boyle.com/.

Brown, J. S., & Duguid, P. (2000). *The social life of information*. Boston, MA: Harvard Business School Press.

Caron, A. H., & Caronia, L. (2007). *Moving cultures: Mobile communications in everyday life*. Montreal, Canada: McGill-Queens University Press.

Caves, R.E. (2000). *Creative industries: Contracts between art and commerce*. Cambridge, MA: Harvard University Press.

Coleman, J. (1988). Social capital in the creation of human capital. *American Journal of Sociology, 94*(Supplement), 95–120.

Cowen, T. (2002). *Creative destruction: How globalization is changing the world's culture.* Princeton, NJ: Princeton University Press.

Davenport, T., & Beck, J. (2001). *The attention economy: Understanding the new economy of business.* Cambridge, MA: Harvard Business School Press.

David, P. A. (2003). *The economic logic of 'open science' and the balance between private property rights and the public domain in scientific data and information: A primer.* Retrieved from http://129.3.20.41/eps/dev/papers/0502/0502006.pdf.

Drucker, P. (1969). *The age of discontinuity: Guidelines to our changing society.* New York, NY: Harper Row.

Etzkowitz, H. (1997). The entrepreneurial university and the emergence of democratic corporatism. In H. Etzkowitz and L. Leydesdorff (Eds.), *Universities and the global knowledge economy: A triple helix of university-industry-government relations* (pp. 141–154). London, United Kingdom: Continuum.

Etzkowitz, H. (2003). Innovation in innovation: The triple helix of university-industry-government relations. *Social Science Information, 42*(3), 293–337.

Etzkowitz, H. (2008). *The triple helix: University-industry-government innovation in action.* London, United Kingdom: Routledge.

Flanagan, H., & Nissenbaum, H. (2005). *Embodying values in technology: Theory and practice.* Retrieved from http://www.nyu.edu/projects/nissenbaum/papers/Nissenbaum-VID.4-25.pdf.

Florida, R. (2002). *The rise of the creative class.* New York, NY: Basic Books.

Foray, D. (2000). *The economics of knowledge.* Cambridge, MA: MIT Press.

Frey, B. S., & Pommerehne, W. W. (1989). *Muses and markets: Explorations in the economics of the arts.* Cambridge, MA: Blackwell.

Garzarelli, G., Limam, Y. R., & Thomassen, B. (2008). Open source software and economic growth: A classical division of labor perspective. *Information Technology for Development, 14*(2), 116–135.

Gates, B. (2006). The road ahead. *Newsweek,* January 25. Retrieved from http://www.msnbc.msn.com/id/11020787/.

Ginsburgh, V. A., & Menger, P.-M. (Eds.). (1996). *Economics of the arts.* Amsterdam, the Netherlands: North Holland.

Gordon, W. J. (1993). A property right in self-expression: Equality and individualism in the natural law of intellectual property. *Yale Law Journal, 102*(1533), 1568–1572.

Granovetter, M. (1973). The strength of weak ties. *American Journal of Sociology 78*(6), 1360–1380.

Harvey, D. (1989). *The condition of postmodernity.* Oxford, United Kingdom: Blackwell.

Hayek, F. (1937). *Economics and knowledge* (Presidential address delivered before the London Economic Club, November 10, 1936). Reprinted in *Economica, 4,* 33–54.

Hayek, F. (1945). The use of knowledge in society. *The American Economic Review, 35*(4), 519–530.

Hearn, G., & Rooney, D. (Eds.). (2008). *Knowledge policy: Challenges for the twenty first century.* Cheltenham, United Kingdom: Edward Elgar.

Heilbrun, J., & Gray, C. M. (2001). *The economics of art and culture* (2nd ed.). Cambridge, United Kingdom: Cambridge University Press.

Hesmondhalgh, D. (2002). *The cultural industries.* Thousand Oaks, CA: Sage.

Howkins, J. (2001). *The creative economy: How people make money from ideas.* London, United Kingdom: Allen Lane.

Iiyoshi, T., & Kumar, V. (2008). *Opening up education: The collective advancement of education through open technology, open content, and open knowledge.* Cambridge, MA: MIT Press.

Illich, I. (1972). *Deschooling society.* Harmondsworth, United Kingdom: Penguin.

Ithaka Harbors, Inc. (2007) *University publishing in a digital age.* Retrieved from http://www.ithaka.org/strategic-services/university-publishing.

Ito, M. (2006). Japanese media mixes and amateur cultural exchange. In D. Buckingham & R. Willett (Eds.), *Digital generations* (pp 49–66). Mahwah, NJ: Lawrence Erlbaum.

Ito, M. (2008). Mobilizing the imagination in everyday play: The case of Japanese media mixes. In K. Drotner & S. Livingstone (Eds.), *International handbook of children, media, and culture.* Draft manuscript retrieved from http://www.itofisher.com/mito/.

Landry, C. (2000). *The creative city: A toolkit for urban innovators.* London, United Kingdom: Earthscan.

Lave, J., & Wenger, E. (1991) *Situated learning: Legitimate peripheral participation.* New York, NY: Cambridge University Press.

Lemley, M. A. (2005). Property, intellectual property, and free riding. *Texas Law Review 83*, 1031–1104.

Lessig, L. (2001). *Code: And other laws of cyberspace.* New York, NY: Basic Books.

Lessig, L. (2002). *The future of ideas: The fate of the commons in a connected world.* New York, NY: Random House.

Lessig, L. (2004). *Free culture: How big media uses technology and the law to lock down culture and control creativity.* New York, NY: Allen Lane.

Lessig, L. (2006). *Code: Version 2.0.* New York, NY: Basic Books.

Lorenz, E., & Lundvall, B.-Å. (Eds.). (2006). *How Europe's economies learn.* Oxford, United Kingdom: Oxford University Press.

Lundvall, B.-Å. (1988). Innovation as an interactive process—from user-producer interaction to national systems of innovation. In G. Dosi (Ed.), *Technology and economic theory.* London, United Kingdom: Pinter.

Lundvall, B.-Å. (2003). Why the new economy is a learning economy. *Economia e Politica Industriale: Journal of Industrial and Business Economics, 117,* 173–185.

Lundvall, B.-A., & Borra, S. (1999). *The globalising learning economy: Implications for innovation policy*. Luxemburg: Office for Official Publications of the European Communities.

Lundvall, B.-A., & Johnson, B. (1994). The learning economy. *Journal of Industry Studies, 1*, 23–42.

Lyotard, J.-F. (1984). *The postmodern condition: A report on knowledge* (G. Bennington & B. Massumi, Trans.). Manchester, United Kingdom: Manchester University Press.

Machlup, F. (1962). *The production and distribution of knowledge in the United States*. Princeton, NJ: Princeton University Press.

Marginson, S., Murphy, P., & Peters, M. A. (2009). *Global creation: Space, connection and universities in the age of the knowledge economy*. New York, NY: Peter Lang.

Neil, A. S. (1960). *Summerhill: A radical approach to child rearing*. New York, NY: Hart Publishing.

Netanel, N. W. (1996). Copyright and a democratic civil society. *Yale Law Journal, 106*(283), 347–362.

Netanel, N. W. (1998). Asserting copyright's democratic principles in the global arena. *Vanderbilt Law Review, 51*(217), 272–276.

OECD. (1996). *The knowledge-based economy*. Paris, France: OECD.

Partnership for 21st Century Skills. (2008). Retrieved from http://www.p21.org.

Pasinetti, L. (1981). *Structural change and economic growth*. Cambridge, United Kingdom: Cambridge University Press.

Peters, M. A. (2007). *Knowledge economy, development and the future of higher education*. Rotterdam, the Netherlands: Sense.

Peters, M. A., & Besley, T. A. C. (2006). *Building knowledge cultures: Education and development in the age of knowledge capitalism*. Boulder, CO: Rowman and Littlefield.

Peters, M. A., & Britez, R. (Eds.). (2009). *Open education and education for openness*. Rotterdam, the Netherlands: Sense.

Peters, M. A., Marginson, S., & Murphy, P. (2009). *Creativity and the global knowledge economy*. New York, NY: Peter Lang.

Peters, M. A., & Roberts, P. (2011). *The virtues of openness: Education and scholarship in a digital age*. Boulder, CO: Paradigm.

Porat, M. (1977). *The information economy*. Washington, DC: US Department of Commerce.

Putnam, R. (2000). *Bowling alone: The collapse and revival of American community*. New York, NY: Simon and Schuster.

Rhoten, D., & Powell, W.W. (2007). The frontiers of intellectual property: Expanded protection versus new models of open science. *Annual Review of Law and Social Science, 3*, 345–373.

Rogers, C. (1969). *Freedom to learn*. New York, NY: Merrill.

Romer, P.M. (1990). Endogenous technological change. *Journal of Political Economy, 98*, 71–102.

Schuchardt, K., Pancerella, C., Rahn, L. A., Didier, B., Kodeboyina, D., Leahy, D., et al. (2007). Portal-based knowledge environment for collaborative science. *Concurrency Computation Practice and Experience, 19*(12), 1703–1716.

Scott, L., & Urry, J. (1994). *Economies of signs and space.* London, United Kingdom: Sage.

Shapiro, C., & Varian, H. (1998). *Information rules: A strategic guide to the network economy.* Cambridge, MA: Harvard Business School Press.

Stallman, R. (2002). *Free software, free society: Selected essays of Richard M. Stallman.* Boston, MA: GNU Press. Retrieved from http://www.gnu.org/philosophy/fsfs/rms-essays.pdf.

Stiglitz, J. (1999). *Knowledge as a global public good.* Retrieved from http://www.worldbank.org/knowledge/chiefecon/articles/undpk2/.

Stiglitz, J. (1999). *Knowledge for development: Economic science, economic policy, and economic advice.* Proceedings from the Annual Bank Conference on Development Economics 1998, World Bank, Washington, D.C. Keynote Address: 9–58.

Surowiecki, J. (2004). *The wisdom of crowds: Why the many are smarter than the few and how collective wisdom shapes business, economies, societies and nations.* Harpswell, ME: Anchor.

Tapscott, D., & Williams, A.D. (2007). *Wikinomics: How mass collaboration changes everything.* New York, NY: Penguin.

Toffler, A. (1980). *The third wave.* New York, NY: Bantam Books.

Touraine, A. (1971). *The post-industrial society: Tomorrow's social history; Classes conflicts and culture in the programmed society* (L. Mayhew, Trans.). New York, NY: Random House.

United Nations. (2008). *The creative economy report.* Retrieved from http://www.unctad.org/en/docs/ditc20082cer_en.pdf.

Verschraegen, G., & Schiltz, M. (2007). Knowledge as a global public good: The role and importance of open access. *Societies Without Borders, 2*(2), 157–174.

Von Hippel, E., & von Krogh, G. (2003). Open source software and the 'private-collective' innovation model: Issues for organization science. *Organization Science, 14*(2), 209–223.

Waldrop, M. M. (2008). Science 2.0. *Scientific American, 298*(5). Retrieved from http://www.sciam.com/article.cfm?id=science-2-point-0-great-new-tool-or-great-risk.

Part Two | The Emergence of the Global Science System and the Promise of Openness

Chapter 8

The Rise of Global Science and the Emerging Political Economy of International Research Collaborations[1]

Michael A. Peters

> Truth...and utility are the very same things.
> —Francis Bacon, *New Organon*, I, Aphorism 124

Introduction

Increasingly, emphasis has fallen on the economics and productivity of science in both firms and higher education institutions, as policy-makers and politicians seek to foster innovation and to draw strong links between scientific performance and emerging economic structures (Crespi & Geuna, 2004, 2005). In these science policy discussions the accent often falls on measuring scientific productivity, on 'intellectual property' and the codification of knowledge, and on research collaboration, partnership and cooperation in regional, national and international contexts. Investment in science, engineering and technology has received strong attention from governments as the basis of the 'knowledge economy' and most governments now look to their international science policy strategy to emphasise national competitive advantage and to encourage research collaboration in global science projects.

Indeed, it is the age of global science, but not primarily in the sense of 'universal knowledge', which has characterised the liberal meta-narrative of 'free' science since its early development, where scientific findings or results are open to peer review, and public scrutiny and, in principle, are reproducible by others following the same procedures.[2] It is the age of global science but not necessarily in the sense of 'international' collaboration (part of the same liberal meta-narrative) as, say, the incipient norms of free exchange of ideas, free inquiry and collaboration developed during the so-called 'scientific revolution' and period of classical science when 'scientists',[3] particularly within Europe, travelled to meet one another and to share their ideas. This was the period when learned societies were established and the first journals flourished with the growth of publishing during the seventeenth and eighteenth centuries, helping both to generate the international exchange of theories, concepts, methods and discoveries, and to aid the processes of research collaboration. This (older) liberal meta-narrative of science has now been submerged by official narratives based on an economic logic linking science to national purpose, economic policy, and national science policy priorities. In the era of 'post-normal' science (Funtowicz & Ravetz, 1992), where globalised corporate science dominates the horizon and scientific 'outputs' differ from the traditional peer-reviewed published scientific papers, quality assurance replaces 'truth' as the new regulative ideal. In contemporary science, policy regimes outputs often take the form of patents, unpublished consultancy, 'grey literature' or are covered by legal arrangement and 'lawyer-client confidentiality'. As a result, there are expressed concerns about the fate of scientific publishing. The rise of digitised publications has led to a counter-revolution in scholarly publishing where actual sales are recast into licences and commercial publishers are taking advantage of the growth of open archives (Guédon, 2001). The Select Committee on Science and Technology in the United Kingdom Parliament (2003), for example, has urged the adoption of a new government strategy to address the problem of increasing journal prices imposed by commercial publishers, recommending 'that all UK higher education institutions establish institutional repositories on which their published output can be stored and from which it can be read, free of charge, online'.[4]

Global science as a term to describe the emerging geography of scientific knowledge and collaboration as an aspect of globalisation and its new interconnectedness within a globalised world is a distinctly new phenomenon, although, judging by scholarly criteria, it still reflects a strong Western control and bias and is still heavily nationalistic and seen as a vital part of national culture and state economic policy. In modern Baconian statecraft, science belongs to a knowledge economy and is the source of innovation and growth in productivity. To a large extent, the developing infrastructure of global science is an outgrowth of earlier historical conditions, particularly, the industrial-military research complex established during the two world wars and extended through nuclear escalation and the space race of the Cold War, and the incipient infrastructure provided by 'colonial science' of the European expansionist era (arguably the first globalisation of science). On one reading, the term global science reflects an extension of the 'old' liberal (as opposed to the market-driven neo-liberal) ideology of 'universal free knowledge' based on exchange and peer review that developed with the emergence of the modern research university in the nineteenth century.Yet it is also clear that it also smacks of 'imperial science—science in the service of the empire—which strongly motivated Francis Bacon's new philosophy and the views of the founders of the Royal Society in the seventeenth century during the early institutionalisation of British science. At the same time, the emergence of 'global science' also reflects new global exigencies, new global problems and an enhanced global network of science communicative practice.

Today, big science projects require massive state and intergovernmental funding support in an era of intense international competition for knowledge assets, which has forced governments and institutions to collaborate with one another on certain issues. Global science in the form of international science agencies also recognises the need for cooperation on a number of pressing common global issues that run across borders, such as global warming and other ecological problems, AIDS/HIV, other global diseases and virus outbreaks, natural species extinction, preservation of biomass features, etc. This chapter provides a first attempt to theorise international research collaboration in the emerging age of global science. It adopts an historical perspective and an implicit sociological history of modern science (Rehbock, 2001; Teich, 1996). It begins by examining three 'moments' in the history of science—classical science, colonial science, and 'big' science. These are three illustrative moments in an extended chronology of science that might register other episodes such as 'industrial science', 'Cold War science', and the rise of multinational corporate science, without implying anything too profound about the temporal logic of the development of science or narratives of the emergence of world science that might be crafted from these dates, events and discoveries.

In this chapter, I adopt an explicit history of science that rests on a chronology to a large extent driven by scientific-technical innovation based on emerging scientific methodologies and technologies. It is a history that is, therefore, materialist and centered on the emergence of scientific practices but is not technologically deterministic. For example, in this regard we might talk of methodologies in the sixteenth and seventeenth centuries, including the emergence of systematic observation, classification, systematization, systematic experimentation and quantification, and the formulation of laws of nature. By contrast, we can mention the systematic collection and detailed description of new fauna, flora, and the exploitation of new world 'resources', including the development of principled scientific sampling (and the first systematic ethnographies) during the expansionist era of colonial science (e.g., Chambers & Gillespie, 2000). Given the space, we could also elaborate the technical break-throughs of steam, electric power and microelectronics and their relationship to new scientific developments in the period of industrial science. We could also detail the developments of modern physics and, in particular, the advent of nuclear and particle physics and the emergence of the industrial-science-military complex that developed during the two world wars (Greenhill, 2000). It would be important also to chronicle the technical developments of Cold War science that briefly saw the emergence of a science-public relationship in the atomic scientists' movement before anticommunist ideology, loyalty tests and surveillance destroyed it (Wang, 2002). In turn, we could document the developments in the computerization and mathematicization of communication that helped to enable international research collaboration in the era of 'big' science. Any attempt to work programmatically with these 'moments' needs also to consider the rise of multinational science contemporaneous with the rise of global science and with the advent of globalization (Dickson, 1999; Tudge, 2004).[5]

This historiographical reconstruction is Heideggerian in inspiration in that it frames the question of the history of science in terms of successive eras that metaphysically determine 'what is' (e.g., Glazebrook, 2000; see also Busch, 2000). These periods serve as ontological templates but against Heidegger I argue that science and technology are constituted through and by social, economic and political forces. I do entertain with Heidegger a reversal of the standard historiography of science. In terms of the received view technology is something that stands in a subsidiary, instrumental, and temporal relation with modern science. Modern physical science begins in the seventeenth century, historically it is seen as achieving a kind of takeoff by 1750, and its institutionalization through learned societies, royal societies and universities also dates from that period. 'Machinic technology', by contrast, chronologically speaking, begins in the eighteenth century and is pictured essentially as the 'handmaiden' to science: it is regarded as an application of 'pure' science or applied science.

Heidegger, however, reverses the chronological order of the received view. He distinguishes technology in its various manifestations from its essence, which is not technological, and describes this essence by returning to the Greek concept of techne, which relates to the activities and skills of the artisan. The essence of technology, Heidegger maintains, is a poiesis or 'bringing forth' which is grounded in revealing (aletheia). As he says: 'The essence of modern technology shows itself in what we call Enframing....It is the way in which the real reveals itself as standing-reserve' (Heidegger, 1977, p. 23). This has been referred to as a 'productionist metaphysics' because the concept of 'standing reserve' refers to resources which are stored in anticipation of consumption. For Heidegger, the essence of technology is part of the broader project of understanding the relation of this mode of objectifying experience to the tradition of Western metaphysics, which means that the question concerning technology cannot be thought apart from the critique of Western metaphysics.[6]

This is to tell a story (admittedly highly truncated and abridged)—to craft a narrative—about the emergence of global science that de-emphasizes the traditional historical picture that highlights Western origins for I would want to elaborate the sources of pre-classical or ancient science by discussing cultural exchange and hybridization among Phoenician, Egyptian, Arabian, Chinese, and Indian scientists rather than solely in terms of the Ancient Greeks, and to adopt an historical framework that emphasizes the connection of scientific development to other political, economic and social forces (such as colonialism and the Cold War). Of course, it is not possible to elaborate all of these concerns in one chapter. My concern here is to suggest an alternative reading and merely to suggest another sketch, another history, in programmatic terms, that allows us to investigate the rise of global science as a relatively new phenomenon and the emerging politics of international research collaborations.

This chapter, thus, does not deal directly with universities but rather focuses on the history of science and research networks from a sociological viewpoint that takes questions in political economy as significant in understanding both past and present science formations and especially the current emerging geography of science. One reviewer described this chapter as a 'chronotopology', a term I like very much because it emphasizes both the temporal and the spatial dimensions. The chapter, then, serves in this special issue of EJE to provide a context and historical reach, and raises some questions about universities in the rise of global science and the leading role European scientists are playing in this new global configuration. The chapter focuses primarily on the natural sciences, although it is not meant to imply that the same kinds of arguments cannot be advanced with regard to the social sciences.[7]

The social sciences also played a crucial role in the service of empire and one can also document the changes in their typology in relation to the 'industrial' and 'Cold War' periodisations. The positive social sciences entertained a strong inter-dependence and symbiosis with developing forms of industrial and welfare capitalism, as clearly evidenced by the growth of Tayloristic management science, industrial psychology, and welfare-oriented sociology and social work. The rise of political economy (later, politics and economics), geography, cartography, anthropology, psychology and sociology (among others) as disciplines oriented towards the state, as well as the rise of statistics (stateistics), provided the political and economic framework within which the contribution of the natural sciences and its role in the service of empire were theorised. This was certainly true of the early accounts provided by Thomas Hobbes of the problem of social and political order and the need for science. While the institutionalization of the social sciences was slower and often followed developments in the natural sciences (including, the formalization and mathematicization of method), it is impossible and undesirable to separate off the social sciences from the natural sciences in the processes of historical and disciplinary formation. The rise of global social science, however, is another story and takes different forms to natural science, yet it is also open to similar historiographical treatment.[8] A contemporary feature of this interdependence can be seen in the transformed relations between social science and natural science after Kuhn's (1970) *The Structure of Scientific Revolutions* that led to historical and cultural studies of science (e.g., Bloor, 1991 [1976]; Fuller, 1993), the displacement of the 'enchantment of science', and the ensuing 'science wars' that were sparked by the Sokal affair (Sokal, 1996; Sokal & Bricmont, 1998).

Three 'Moments' in the Rise of Global Science

Most theories of globalization—including Marxism, modernization, dependency, world systems, and commodity-chain theories—do not speak to the issue of the globalization of science, even although officially the 'free exchange' of knowledge among scientists has been the overwhelming orientation of universities well before the term 'globalization' was first coined. Global science has its modern origins in 'colonial science' when academic infrastructures for knowledge traffic were first laid down, although there was also a strong but highly circumscribed tradition of scientific cooperation among European countries during the Enlightenment. In this section, I chart three historical 'moments' of the rise of global science, beginning with the scientific revolution and age of classical science, moving to colonial science and to the emergence of 'big' science in the late twentieth century.[9] In each case, I will provide only the briefest of profiles, as each of these moments in the history of science has a massive and growing literature devoted to it. Each moment is treated externally rather than internally; it is a sociological and political history of science rather than a philosophy of science that I am attempting for this provides the important political economy of international research collaborations. The emphasis falls on the geography of science—an aspect largely ignored in the literature. These historical interpretations, then, are merely illustrative and evocative.

First Sketch: Classical Science

The life of science in its recognisable modern form dates from the Royal Society, which was preceded by the Philosophical College. A group of scientists in London, including Robert Moray, Robert Boyle, John Wilkins, John Wallis, John Evelyn, Christopher Wren and William Petty, began holding regular meetings in 1645. They were inspired by induction and experimental science, the ethos of which had been explored by Francis Bacon (1561–1626) a generation earlier in utopian works like *The Advancement of Learning* (1605), *Novum Organum* (1620), *The New Atlantis* (1626). The two salient aspects of Bacon's new philosophy of nature, both its experimentalism based on induction and its pragmatism committed to the extension of human power through the exploitation of natural phenomena, were derived from the traditions of alchemy, natural magic and religion (Henry, 2002). As Lord Chancellor, Bacon was first to discuss the organization and bureaucracy of modern science based on a new 'administration of learning' he set out in the *Advancement of Learning* and *New Organon*. His ideas were highly influential, championed by Newton, popularized by the Royal Society—and figured centrally in Thomas Sprat's *The History of the Royal Society* (1667)—and celebrated by the philosophes of the French Enlightenment.

While Bacon, the Renaissance man, travelled little outside England, members of the Royal Society, established in 1660, had strong contacts in Europe and travelled to meet other scientists. The 'European tour' was then fashionable for the upper classes and Boyle, for instance, spent part of his education in Lyons and Florence, and was in the city in 1642 when Galileo died. Learning Greek, Latin, French and Italian enabled English scientists to read the works of Copernicus, Kepler, Mersenne Galileo, Gilbert, Descartes, Pascal, Cavalieri, Roberval, Torricelli, and many others.

To take one notable example, Voltaire (1694–1778) took refuge in London in 1726 for two years after being exiled from Paris and in his letters later wrote of English tolerance and freedom of speech. He wrote of the changed scene in London in comparison with Paris and compared Descartes and Newton (Letter XIV: On Descartes and Newton). He also commented directly on Bacon's 'new philosophy' in *Novum Scientiarum Organum*, regarding him as the 'father of experimental philosophy', and wrote of Locke, Newton's 'attraction', optics and geometry, as well as the Royal Society, of which he observes:

> The English had an Academy of Sciences many years before us, but then it is not under such prudent regulations as ours, the only reason of which very possibly is, because it was founded before the Academy of Paris; for had it been founded after, it would very probably have adopted some of the sage laws of the former and improved upon others.

And he goes on to compare the Royal Society with the Academy in the following terms:

> A seat in the Academy at Paris is a small but secure fortune to a geometrician or a chemist; but this is so far from being the case at London, that the several members of the Royal Society are at a continual, though indeed small expense. Any man in England who declares himself a lover of the mathematics and natural philosophy, and expresses an inclination to be a member of the Royal Society, is immediately elected into it. But in France it is not enough that a man who aspires to the honour of being a member of the Academy, and of receiving the royal stipend, has a love for the sciences; he must at the same time be deeply skilled in them, and is obliged to dispute the seat with competitors who are so

much the more formidable as they are fired by a principle of glory, by interest, by the difficulty itself, and by that inflexibility of mind which is generally found in those who devote themselves to that pertinacious study, the mathematics.[10]

The development of learned societies in Europe[11]—from the establishment of the Compagnie du Gai Sçavoir in 1323—was contemporaneous with the establishment of the early medieval universities in Bologna, Paris, Padua, St Andrews, Oxford, Cambridge, and Glasgow in the eleventh, twelfth and thirteenth centuries. Both learned societies and universities slowly developed the norms of cooperation and textual conventions in scholarly activities that were inherited by the modern research university in the early nineteenth century, beginning with the establishment of the University of Berlin in 1810.

The Academy of Science, modeled on the Royal Society, was founded in Paris in 1666 and similar societies were established in Dublin (1683), St. Petersburg (1725), Stockholm (1739), and Edinburgh (1783). Learned societies, in particular, were responsible for the publication of scientific findings and issued the first academic journals that institutionalized the norms of scholarships, including ownership of an idea and priority of discovery, as well as societal recognition and membership of a scientific community. A model of scientific communication gradually became established as printing and publishing industries developed and helped to shape the scientific analytical method by rationalizing research methods, sharing theories and methods among scientists from different countries, and gradually establishing an international 'scientific community'. By 1700 there were already 30 journals and by 1800 hundreds of scientific journals existed.

Henry Oldenburg, the Secretary of the Royal Society, issued the first edition of *Philosophical Transactions* in 1665. The Royal Society was based in London, first in Gresham College and later in Crane Court, and remained very much a local and English phenomenon, although seventeenth century British science, epitomized by Newton, was based on the works of his European predecessors and, therefore, presupposed the transport and geographical spread of scientific ideas in the form of books and other published means such as journals. The learned societies represented a new form of cooperation that bypassed politics and religion and established norms for independent inquiry, collaborative research and discussion, and methods for replication and verification.

The *Philosophical Transactions of the Royal Society* was the first serial publication of a learned society. As Fjällbrant (1997) notes:

> It was a medium for publication of new observations and original experiments in science, mostly carried out by the Fellows of the Society. This was a monthly publication of scientific material, together with book reviews and with space for discussions between people holding differing scientific opinions. The *Philosophical Transactions of the Royal Society* provided a model for subsequent publications of scientific academies throughout Europe. It was translated into French—*Transactions philosophique de la Societé royale de Londres*—*de 1731 à 1744*. The *Histoire de l'Académie royale des sciences, Paris (1666–1699)* is one example of a publication modelled on the *Philosophical Transactions*.

Journals of the learned societies contained reviews of scientific work and reprints, especially in translation. Fjällbrant (1997) argues 'The learned societies were concerned with spread and diffusion of scientific knowledge' and indicates significantly that scientific journals were also published by private 'commercial' interests:

> the *Giornale de' Letterati* which was modelled on *Journal des Sçavans*, was published in Rome from 1668 to 1681. In contrast the *Acta Erutditorum* first published in Leipzig in 1682, editor Otto Mencke, followed the pattern of the *Philosophical Transactions of the Royal Society*. The *Acta Eruditorum* contained many papers by Leibnitz on his work on the calculus. There was a slow growth in the publication of scientific journals in the eighteenth century with some five new titles published between 1700 and 1750, followed by a more rapid growth in the second half of the century, with some seventy new titles including such well known titles as *Annales de Chimie (et de Physique)*,1790; *Annalen der Physik*, 1799. The oldest Swedish technical journal is *Daedalus Hyperboreus* by Swedenborg, 1716–1718. The journal *Jernkontorets annaler* was first published in 1817 and *Tidskrift för teknologie och tillämpad naturlära* was published in Gothenburg 1859–1866. Journals were supplemented by letters (important in pre-journal days), newspapers, books and scientific anagrams.

These developments in the institutionalization of science simultaneously were part and parcel of the first wave of colonial expansion and conquest by the European powers. For example, the botanist Joseph Banks (1743–1820), in the second generation of the Royal Society, and as its longest serving president (1778– 1820), travelled to Newfoundland and Labrador in 1776 to collect samples and was made a member of the Royal Society the same year. Two years later he accompanied Captain

Cook on his expedition to Tahiti organized by the Royal Society to observe the transit of Venus and later visited and made observations in South America, New Zealand, Australia, and Iceland. He founded the Royal Horticultural Society, became Superintendant of the Royal Botanical Gardens at Kew and a member of the Board of Longitude, and was a member of both the Trade and Coin Committees of the Privy Council.[12]

On the first *HMS Endeavour* journey in 1768 (to 1770) Banks identified and documented around 1,400 plants and more than 1,000 animals previously unknown to European science. Banks's specimen collection accounted for some 110 new genera and 1,300 new species. In his capacity as scientist-botanist and director of Kew Gardens, he made use of the plant specimens that he had brought back from various parts of the empire. Banks helped to organize the *Bounty* voyage of William Bligh, in part to obtain Tahitian breadfruit and establish it as a food source in the West Indies. (In 1779 and 1785 he recommended establishing colonies on the east coast of Australia.) He maintained a strong correspondence with Benjamin Franklin and was one of the first vice-presidents of the Linnean Society founded in 1800 after Carl Linneaus, the great Swedish naturalist who developed a system of classification based on a binomial system that Banks used to classify his specimens.

Both Linneaus and Banks brought back specimens for the benefit of their national economies, placing science at the very center of trade and politics and forging an interdependent relationship between scientific inquiry and the State that still endures (see Gascoigne, 1994, 1998). Unquestionably, this is the basis of national science institutions, the establishment and integration of national science systems, and later the development of science policy—public good science—as an indispensable aspect of the modern State.

Second Sketch: Colonial Science

Questions of hegemony in science cannot be separated from the history of 'colonial science', 'science and empire' or 'imperial science'. Indeed, as many scholars have pointed out in the burgeoning literature on colonial science that has developed rapidly since the mid-1980s, the rise of modern science is inextricably intertwined with the story of European colonial expansion since the later fifteenth century and took specific cultural forms in the first and second waves depending on territories, the colonizer-colonized relationship, and a myriad of other relevant factors. Indeed, global science, it might be argued, had its origins in imperial science, where science contributed to colonial development and administration, not only to facilitate the exploitation of native natural resources but also to administer local populations. The early infrastructures for the emergence of global science, for its incipient knowledge systems in taxonomic classifications, its field-testing in local sites, its data-gathering activities, and for its educational base, importation of ideas and spurious ideologies (based on 'race' and gender), and for its means and methods of exchange and eventual recruitment of scientific personnel.

There is now a massive and growing literature on 'colonial science', which is not easy to summarize given its many different threads since it was established as a field in the 1980s.[13] Cultural studies of science question its value-neutral stance. Harding (2003), for instance, provides the feminist critique along these lines, in an argument that in many respects parallels the cultural critique:

> The method of western modern sciences was supposed to generate value-neutral, objective, disinterested facts about nature's order. Yet feminist analyses have shown how these methods and facts have been permeated by gendered values and interests. To be sure, this is so to different degrees and in different ways for different sciences. Nevertheless, standard ways of conceptualizing and practicing scientific method appear to leave research incapable of achieving cultural neutrality in principle, not just in practice. Moreover, gender analyses have shown how in at least some research contexts cultural neutrality is undesirable; culture is also productive of knowledge, not just an obstacle to it. Which people get to do science can influence what we will know about the world.

Goonatilake (1995) talks of global science in terms of three registers that start from this critique: Viewing science without eurocentric blinkers explains how science was active in the ancient world outside Europe; examples of mining for contemporary science identify medicine, mathematics and psychology as areas where ancient science might contribute; more imaginative explorations suggests how ancient science could contribute to future technology.

Recent studies have focused on 'scientific' readings of the colonial experience and emphasised environment, ecology, diseases and medical topography as major categories of inquiry into the 'objective' nature of science and its power relations in colonial expansion.[14] These studies are not of a piece and should not be interpreted straightforwardly as an attack on the objectivity of science or its efficacy, although they do indicate that the origins and development of global science certainly have their roots in colonial science, and that cultural and institutional contexts help to shape the constitution of knowledge.

Building on these studies, Warwick Anderson, in a provocative paper, talks of 'Postcolonial Technoscience',[15] suggesting that:

> A postcolonial perspective suggests fresh ways to study the changing political economies of capitalism and science, the mutual reorganization of the global and the local, the increasing transnational traffic of people, practices, technologies, and contemporary contests over intellectual property. The term 'postcolonial' thus refers both to new configurations of technoscience and to the critical modes of analysis that identify them. We hope that a closer engagement of science studies with postcolonial studies will allow us to question technoscience differently, find more heterogeneous sources, and reveal more fully the patterns of local transactions that give rise to global, or universalist, claims.

His essay is an exploration of 'the turbulence and uncertainty of contemporary global flows of knowledge and practice'. It is clear that 'colonial science' studies and cultural studies of science have provided strong historical evidence of the role of science in the service of empire—not only its contribution to the exploration, navigation and the mapping of the 'new world', but also to the economic exploitation of the biota and governance of its peoples.

Third Sketch: Emergence of 'Big Science' and European Collaboration

The term 'big science' actually dates back to the late 1950s when it was used to herald the transition from individual to team research and development. The term was employed to refer to large-scale and instrument-expensive, mainly government-funded projects in basic science (high-energy physics), space research and military science, and also the shifts in science policy and funding after WWII.[16] Derek J. de Solla Price (1963) in Little Science, Big Science applied publications analysis to the system of science communication providing the first systematic approach to the structure of modern science, helping to establish bibliometrics and scientometrics that later became essential in the evaluation of the productivity of scientific research.[17]

In conceptualizing 'big science', the OECD Global Science Forum[18] puts it this way:

> Big Science is global. Research and development in medicine, technology, engineering, chemistry, biology and physics have long since overrun national borders, in part because no single government has the time, money or indeed skills that such work demands. Projects, from the International Space Station to building particle colliders and light sources, or semi-conductor research: all thrive on global co-operation. It was not always so. Governments, scientists and investors have often been wary of each other, with co-operation tending to take place on an ad hoc basis.

The OECD puts an emphasis on 'Big Science' and adduces a resources-based reason as the imperative driving global cooperation. Yet global science per se does not reduce simply to 'big science', even though it may account for genuine attempts to build international cooperation and adopt a strategic approach to collaborative partnerships at the extra-national level.

Bilateral and regional science and technology relations, of course, go back a long way, relatively speaking. In the early 1950s, the European Laboratory for Particle Physics (CERN) in Geneva was the result of cooperation among European governments which now has member scientists from both European and non-European countries. The European Science Foundation[19] was created in 1974 and established a scientific network in the early 1980s for the coordination of European science based in various subject group areas such as Physical and Engineering Sciences and Life, Environmental and Earth Sciences. In the early 1990s, the ESF also set up research linkages with Asia and APEC established protocols for scientific cooperation amongst its members.[20] Scientists, sponsored by world organizations like UNESCO and FAO, have set up global research programs, based on obvious cross-border exigencies. Earth scientists, in particular, have been instrumental in establishing international research programs dealing with the dynamics of the earth system such as the Global Climatic Observation System,[21] the Global Ocean Observation System[22] and the Global Terrestrial Observation System.[23]

Yet these recent examples of extra-national scientific collaboration do not take account of the many smaller institutional exchanges and partnerships, the development of university consortia for across-the-board cooperation, or firm and firm/university partnerships. Nor does it take account of the increasingly multinational-driven corporate nature of international research by world conglomerates like Monsanto and other biotech companies or the large pharmaceutical or drug companies. Some of these partnership arrangements and examples of multinational science probably fit better into theories of globalization than traditional university-based collaborations.

The emergence of global science, thus, can be seen to conform to both the global business model based on the market and the science model based on free exchange of give and take. The development economist, Amartya Sen (2002, p. 51), for instance, makes the following contrast that is essential to understanding the different kinds of associations needed for development:

> Contrast the sharing that underpins science with the transactional nature of market relations. The market mechanism is not only an important social institution, it is also an organizational ideology. Its success—perceived as well as real—can help stifle independent thinking about interactive relations of other kinds, including that of give and take. The gaps it leaves are worth filling since sharing is not only crucial to science, it is also central to development.

Not only does he contrast science with the market but he argues for a position that views science as a global tradition, avoiding the 'anti-Western' globalization sentiments as well as Western chauvinism and a proprietary approach to 'Western science', explaining that Western science drew on a world heritage (e.g., the mathematics of Al-Khwarizmi). Yet Sen does not contemplate the rise of global science or the complex ways in which it proceeds on mixed models integrating both traditional 'science sharing' (as he calls it) and market relations, especially evident in the emerging international regime of 'intellectual property' rights through the WTO. In a sense he avoids the difficult question of scientific hegemony based on private and cultural ownership of scientific discoveries, inventions, and insights (see, e.g., Tudge, 2004).

Global Science and Research Collaboration

It is clear that the age of global science has arrived. This is manifested not only in the growth of multinational corporate science but also mandated in administrative and organisational structures that are both regional and rhetorically also 'global'. For instance, Euroscience was founded in 1997 to 'provide an open forum for debate on science and technology; strengthen the links between science and society; contribute to the creation of an integrated space for science and technology in Europe; influence science and technology policies'.[24] Framework 6 for funding of science in Europe is approximately 16.27 billion euros, an increase of 17% over the previous Framework 5. This funding programme constitutes an estimated 5% of the research budget of EU countries overall and yet is seen to play a crucial role in structuring European research by defining the aims of European science and funding collaborative activity among scientists in Europe. Of the seven programme areas biotechnology and information technology account for well over 40% of total funding, with the rest shared by nuclear energy, nanotechnology, aeronautics, food safety, and sustainable development and global change (see also Simons & Featherstone, 2000).

At the same time, US science policy and science advocacy now cluster around the buzz words 'bioinformatics', 'Bose condensates', 'genomics', 'nano-technology', 'supersymmetries', and 'wavelets' with increases in the science budget, the reorganisation of science councils under Clinton and an increasing politicisation of domestic science issues under Bush (Bromley & Lubell, 2003).

Meanwhile, administrators like Bruce M. Alberts, as president of the National Academy of Sciences, called for a 'global science'. Alberts (1998, p. 26) writes:

> A major aim of the National Academy of Sciences (NAS) is to strengthen the ties between scientists and their institutions around the world. Our goal is to create a scientific network that becomes a central element in the interactions between nations, increasing the level of rationality in international discourse while enhancing the influence of scientists everywhere in the decision making processes of their own governments.

It is clear that the communications technologies are crucial to the strategy for enhanced collaboration. Alberts indicates that 'Electronic communication networks make possible a new kind of worm science' and he emphasizes 'that we are only at the very beginning of the communications revolution' promising greater commercialization with attendant benefits for the developing world (p. 27). He also mentions that the National Research Council (the operating arm of NAS and the National

Academy of Engineering) will attempt to prepare an international science road map to help the State Department.

An NSB report 'Toward a More Effective Role for the US Government in International Science and Engineering', as Paula Park reports (2002, p. 8), 'encourages agencies to evaluate whether new immigration and intellectual property policies and regulations will affect international science cooperation' and emphasizes, quoting Eamon Kelly, chairman of the NSB that 'the future of the developing countries rests on their ability to adapt to a culture of science and technology in the 21st century'. Further, Hal Cohen (2003) also indicates that scientists themselves are organizing global structures. The International Council of Scientific Unions created in 1931 has been recently renamed the International Council for Science. It has established several programs, including one in biology (1964–1974). Current programs include the International Geosphere-Biosphere Programme and the World Climate Research Programme (following the Kyoto Protocol).

Going back to the late 1980s the OECD tried to establish a set of guidelines covering all aspects of international relations in science (Dickson, 1987, p. 743) which included a focus on 'the extent to which each country should contribute to the world's basic research effort and the conditions under which foreign research workers are permitted to attend scientific meetings'. Much of the initiative under the Reagan administration emphasized the policing and protection of intellectual property rights within GATS and, later, WTO protocols. Within these emerging structures of global science, collaboration takes many different forms. Increasingly, under neo-liberalism it presupposes a competitive relationship that is the main form of collaboration, for instance, between Europe and the US. This normally revolves around the shared investment of personnel and resources and is directed at cutting-edge science and technology. Increasingly also, public–private partnerships take on an international dimension especially in relation to aeronautics and space research. Over and above these international forms there are collaborative relationships that are not premised on competitive criteria but rather take on forms of 'cooperation' or 'assistance' that fall within traditional development aid categories.

There is a third category, perhaps, other than non-competitive and market collaboration which is implied in Alberts (1998) and has been a feature of US science policy since the 1960s. It is the relation between expertise and governance. This form draws networks back to their funding bases and organizational homes in universities and laboratories and raises interestingly questions concerning the reorganization of the university in a shift from knowledge to expertise.[25]

In discussing developments of the emerging world knowledge system and, in particular, the structures of international research collaboration it is necessary to locate the merging systems within the historical context, a context that reveals the politics and competitive nature of collaboration and the leading position of the US-Europe constellation. In the age of knowledge capitalism where knowledge increasingly is seen to be the basis of national competitive advantage, the emphasis has fallen on the policing and reinforcement of intellectual property rights regimes and on forms of knowledge hoarding, especially with the growth of multinational science and the privatization of science funding regimes. While there are encouraging signs that India and China (especially, relating to foodstuffs, information science and the production of microchips, and recently space research) are developing more of a competitive science base, their science sectors pale into insignificance when compared to the West. Some concern has been expressed recently by Western governments, especially in the US, of the increasing outsourcing of R&D functions, especially the training of technicians and scientists who work for much less money and also on contract without the normal employment benefits of Western scientists. There are some forms of global science and associated forms of international collaboration that have been established or are being established that take on the more traditional liberal justifications of science and emphasize its status as a global public good (Stiglitz, 1999).

Be that as it may, it is clear that there is a diversity of forms, that they have emerged out of existing infrastructures and histories that strongly reflect politics, not merely the arms industry and its relation to the industrial-military research complex, but also past colonial origins and the continuing nature of many of the colonial relationships in forms that develop new 'neo-imperial' forms based around trading agreements or work against this hegemony to establish science as part of the basis of global social democracy harnessed in the service of global civil society and based on the needs of the world's population.

Universities encourage both competitive and non-competitive forms of international collaboration but increasingly with the historic downturn in state funding of higher education in the US and the development of nearly 200 science research parks[26] nationwide, with an emphasis on venture capital funding of spin-off companies, patents of university discoveries, and the attraction of leading multinationals on campus, the latter is giving way to the former as institutions struggle to diversify their funding bases. A major question is whether the funds accrued from competitive forms of collaboration will be used to help support and subsidise non-competitive forms of collaboration, and, therefore, whether the university can subscribe to twin legitimating discourses that embrace social justice goals as well as accommodating for-profit motives. Yet it may well be that technology-dependent 'sharable goods' as one form of social production and exchange (Benkler, 2004), alongside the state and the market, will emerge as a third mode of organizing economic production, bringing in its wake changes in the material conditions of production of the networked information economy that encourage non-propriety forms of academic production and facilitate international research collaboration.

Notes

1. I would like to thank Nicholas Burbules, Martin Lawn and anonymous reviewers of EJE for useful comments on the structure and contents of an earlier version of this chapter. This chapter first appeared in *European Journal of Education*, Vol. 41, No. 2, 2006.
2. 'Truths' established through these scientific norms have, thus, always been considered universal or so some positivist philosophers of science maintain—and there is some sense to this claim, although its content is notoriously difficult to unpack. The problem of truth of scientific knowledge in this respect is especially difficult to fathom, given the competing accounts of truth and their (different) role within the sciences (natural and social). The easy philosophical examples tend to abstract individual statements from their theory contexts; yet the 'truth' of theories in science is more complex as scholars like Popper, Lakatos and Feyerabend have demonstrated, suggesting that it serves as a regulative ideal. I do not want to deny 'truth' of scientific knowledge or its 'universality' yet I want to emphasize that questions of truth and validity should not obscure that the institutionalization of science has strongly reflected patterns of national, corporate and multinational interests.
3. I have put the word *scientist* in inverted commas because the term was not used until relatively recently, after the institutionalization of natural philosophy and the professionalization of science. Most 'scientists' in the period of the institutionalization of science were often wealthy gentleman amateurs, like Joseph Banks, for instance, who became president of the Royal Society nearly 120 years after its establishment. On biographies of Fellows of the RS, see 1679 and for a broader ac-

count of 'antebellum American science' see, e.g., Clark Elliot's review and bibliography at http://home.earthlink.net/~claelliott/index.html.
4. Lyotard (1984) raised similar questions a generation ago. See my *Education and the Postmodern Condition* (Peters, 1996) and, more recently, *Building Knowledge Cultures* (Peters & Besley, 2006).
5. This is a hugely under-researched field (history of multinational science), which is seemingly ignored in the globalization literature. A good starting point is 3 and the list of resources 'The Impacts of Multinational Corporations' at http://www.lib.berkeley.edu/BUSI/pdfs/multiCorp.pdf 'IMPACTS%20 OF%20MULTINATIONAL%20CORPORATIONS%3A'#search.
6. Much more could be said here about the history and historiography of science, a discourse which would need to include reference to Kuhn's (1962) distinction between 'normal' and 'revolutionary' science but also the assumptions underlying the historical context of Kuhn's own writings at Harvard during the Cold War (see Fuller, 2000).
7. The Editor remarked: [The social] "sciences" have been very important for building the nation state, leading to the consequences you describe. See, for example, Wagner, P., & Wittrock, B. (1991) States, institutions, and discourses: A comparative perspective on the structuration of the social sciences. In P. Wagner, B. Wittrock, & R. Whitley (Eds.), *Discourses on society. The shaping of the social science disciplines* (pp. 331–357). Dordrecht, the Netherlands: Kluwer. Or Peter Wagner's (2001) *A history and theory of the social sciences*. I am not sure whether this area of research would alter your argument but it is necessary to it.
8. In *Les mots et les choses—une archéologie des sciences humaines* (1966) (The Order of Things: An Archaeology of the Human Sciences), Foucault develops the claim that all periods of history possessed certain underlying conditions of truth constituting what was acceptable as 'scientific' discourse in the human sciences. He argued that these conditions of discourse changed over time, in major and relatively sudden shifts, or epistemes. While Foucault never applied this model to the natural sciences, scholars like Rouse (1987) have attempted to do so.
9. There is a story to be told of the 'globalisation' of science in the Ancient World, not only of the Ancient Babylon and Egypt, and Greco-Roman culture, but also Byzantium, the Islamic World, China and India; and, the exchanges and 'transport' of ideas between these worlds that often mirrored trade patterns. For some resources see *The Internet History of Science Sourcebook* at http://www.fordham.edu/halsall/science/sciencesbook.html.
10. For the full set of Voltaire's letters on the English, including those mentioned in the text, see http://www.fordham.edu/halsall/mod/1778voltaire-lettres. html.
11. See http://www.scholarly-societies.org/1599andearlier.html.
12. Some of his papers are available in digitised form on the website of the National Library of Australia at http://nla.gov.au/nla.ms-ms9. See also *The Papers of Sir Joseph Banks* by the State Library of New South Wales at http://www.sl.nsw.gov.au/ banks/

THE RISE OF GLOBAL SCIENCE 185

13. See, for instance, Goonatilake (1984, 1995), Nandy (1988), Petitjean, et al. (1992), Watson-Verran & Turnbull (1995), Harding (1993, 1998, 2003). The Sciences and Empires mail list as an 'unmoderated' list was established and is operated by the Sciences et Empires Groupe, a Commission of the International Congress of the History of Science. The group was founded at an international meeting held at UNESCO in Paris in April, 1990 under the theme 'Sciences and Empires: European Expansion and Scientific Development of Asia, Africa, America and Oceania', and includes Patrick Petitjean, Catherine Jami, Anne Marie Moulin, Kapil Raj, Deepak Kumar, Venni Krishna, Roland Waast, Mic Worboys, and Silvia Figueiroa as members. See also the bibliography by Pratik Chakrabarti 'Knowledge, Science and Empire' at http://www.history.ox.ac.uk/hsmt/courses_reading/advanced_papers/biblios/knowledge_science_empire.pdf.

14. This literature is also huge and I can only indicate some of the relevant studies: Arnold & Guha (1996), Crosby (1986, 2004), Gadgil & Guha (1995), Grove (1995, 1997), Arnold (1988, 1993), Harrison (1994, 1999), Bewell (1999).

15. See his paper at http://sts.nthu.edu.tw/~tsts/W-paper/Poco_Techno_Final_ms%5B1%5DWarwick.htm, *Social Studies of Science*, 32, (5-6), 643-658.

16. For an introduction to the literature on changes to sciences after WWII, see, for instance, Alexei Kojevnikov course at http://www.aip.org/history/syllabi/ postwar.htm.

17. Price's studies were continued in two directions: Eugene Garfield (1970, 1972) developed more sophisticated measures of quality using citations and Jerome R. Ravetz (1996) observed that the processes of peer review are 'informal', not themselves normally submitted to open scrutiny and review, and open to a variety of abuses, including bias and plagiarism. Bibliometric indicators based on the SCI while having limitations, nevertheless, are probably the best indicators of world science output. A recent UNESCO Institute for Statistics (UIS) report states: 'In 2000, the SCI included a total of 584,982 papers, representing a 57.5% increase from 1981, when 371,346 papers were published worldwide. Authors with addresses in developed countries 5 wrote 87.9% of the papers in 2000, a decrease from 93.6% in 1981. Developing countries, on the other hand, saw a steady increase in their share of scientific production: from 7.5% of world papers in 1981 to 17.1% in 2000'. North America has lost its 1996 lead producing 36.8% of papers in 2000, with most gains in the EU and Asia (particularly Japan). Significantly, the report also mentions that international collaborations in the 20 years from 1981 has also increased: 'The proportion of publications from authors in developed countries co-signed with authors in other countries has risen more than three times from 6.0% to 20.4% between 1981 and 2000, and in developing countries the share of collaborative papers doubled from 15.1% to 30.8%'.

18. The OECD Global Science Forum started as the 'Megascience Forum' in 1992, focusing on Big Science projects (ultra high-energy neutrinos electron accelerator facilities, nuclear physics and global biodiversity) and was expanded as the Global Science Forum in 1999 with the aim of addressing more basic issues (e.g., short-

pulse lasers, neuro-informatics, outer space airwaves). See OECD Observer at http://www.oecdobserver.org/news/fullstory.php/aid/1019/Global_science.html. On OECD best practices for establishing scientific cooperation and managing large-scale projects, see http:// www.oecd.org/department/0,2688,en_2649_34319_1_1_1_1_1,00.html.

19. See the ESF website at http://www.esf.org.
20. See the ASEM Science and Technology Ministers' Meeting, on which some of this chapter is based, at http://europa.eu.int/comm/external_relations/asem/min_other_meeting/sc_tech_comque.htm and also Connecting Asia Pacific and Europe (CAPE) 1998 at http://www.dante.net/cape/-cape.html.
21. See http://www.epa.gov/geoss/.
22. See http://ioc.unesco.org/goos/.
23. See http://www.fao.org/gtos/.
24. See http://www.euroscience.org/about.htm. See also the European Science Foundation at http://www.esf.org/.
25. I am indebted to Martin Lawn for making this observation to me almost in these words.
26. See the Association of University Research Parks' website at http://www.aurp.net/.

References

Alberts, B. M. (1998). Toward a global science. *Issues in Science and Technology, 14*, 25–28.

Arnold, D., & Guha, R. (Eds.). (1996). *Nature, culture, imperialism: Essays on the environmental history of South Asia.* Oxford, United Kingdom: Oxford University Press.

Arnold, D. (Ed.). (1988). *Imperial medicine and indigenous societies.* Manchester, United Kingdom: Manchester University Press.

Arnold, D. (1993). *Colonizing the body: State medicine and epidemic disease in nineteenth-century India.* Berkeley, CA: University of California Press.

Benkler, Y. (2004). Sharing nicely: On shareable goods and the emergence of sharing as a modality of economic production. *The Yale Law Journal, 114*, 273–358. Retrieved from http://www.yalelawjournal.org/pdf/1142/ Benkler_FINAL_YLJ114-2.pdf

Bewell, A. (1999). *Romanticism and colonial disease.* Baltimore, MD: The Johns Hopkins University Press.

Bloor, D. (1991). *Knowledge and social imagery.* Chicago, IL: University of Chicago Press. (Original work published 1976).

Bricmont, J., & Sokal, A. D. (1998). *Fashionable nonsense: Post-modern intellectuals' abuse of science.* New York, NY: Picador.

Bromley, A. D., & Lubell, M. S. (2003). Science's growing political strength. *Issues in Science and Technology, 19*, 13–16.

Busch, P. (2000). Nietzsche's political critique of modern science. *Perspectives on Political Science, 29*, 197–210.

Chambers, D. W., & Gillespie, R. (2000). Locality in the history of science: Colonial science, technoscience, and indigenous knowledge. *Osiris*, Annual, 221–242.

Cohen, H. (2003). ICSU: International council for Science. *The Scientist, 8,* 14–15.

Crespi, G., & Geuna, A. (2004). *The productivity of science: An international analysis.* A report commissioned by the OST-DTI. Brighton, United Kingdom: SPRU; University of Sussex. Retrieved from http://www.sussex.ac.uk/spru/publications/reports/CrespiOST.pdf

Crespi, G., & Geuna, A. (2005). *Modelling and measuring scientific production: Results for a panel of OECD countries.* Brighton, United Kingdom: SPRU, University of Sussex.

Crosby, A. (1986). *The Columbian exchange: Biological and cultural consequences of 1492.* Cambridge, United Kingdom: Cambridge University Press.

Crosby, A. (2004). *Ecological imperialism: The biological expansion of Europe, 900– 1900.* Cambridge, United Kingdom: Cambridge University Press.

Dickson, D. (1987). OECD to set rules for international science. *Science, 238*(4828), 743–744.

Dickson, D. (1999). Open house or closed shop? *UNESCO Courier,* May, 25–27. Retrieved from http://findarticles.com/p/articles/mi_m1310/is_1999_May/ai_54738744/

Fjallbrant, N. (1997). *Scholarly communication: Historical development and new possibilities.* Retrieved from http://www.iqtul.org/conference/proceedings/vol07/papers/full/nfpaper.html

Fuller, S. (1993). *Philosophy, rhetoric and the end of knowledge: The coming of science and technology studies.* Madison, WI: University of Wisconsin Press.

Fuller, S. (2000). *Thomas Kuhn: A philosophical history for our times.* Chicago, IL: University of Chicago Press.

Funtowicz, S. O., & Ravetz, J. R. (1992). Three types of risk assessment and the emergence of post-normal science. In S. Krimsky & Golding (Eds.), *Social theories of risk* (pp. 251–273). Westport, CT: Greenwood.

Gadgil, M., & Guha, R. (1995). *Ecology and equity: The use and abuse of nature in contemporary India.* New Delhi, India: Penguin Books India.

Garfield, E. (1970). Citation indexing for studying science. *Nature, 227,* 669–671.

Garfield, E. (1972). Citation analysis as a tool in journal evaluation. *Science, 178*(4060), 471–479.

Gascoigne, J. (1994). *Banks and the English Enlightenment: Useful knowledge and polite culture.* Cambridge, United Kingdom: Cambridge University Press.

Gascoigne, J. (1998). *Science in the service of empire: Joseph Banks, the British state and the uses of science in the age of revolution.* Cambridge, United Kingdom: Cambridge University Press.

Glazebrook, T. (2000). *Heidegger's philosophy of science.* New York, NY: Fordham University Press.

Goonatilake, S. (1984). *Aborted discovery: Science and creativity in the third world.* London, United Kingdom: Zed.

Goonatilake, S. (1995). *Toward a global science: Mining civilizational knowledge.* New Delhi, India: Vistaar Publications.

Greenhill, K. M. (2000). American science policy since World War II. *Polity, 32,* 633–645.

Grove, R. (1997). *Ecology, climate, and empire: Colonialism and global environmental history.* Cambridge, United Kingdom: White Horse Press.

Grove, R. H. (1995). *Green imperialism: Colonial expansion, Tropical island Edens and the origins of environmentalism, 1600–1860.* Cambridge, United Kingdom: Cambridge University Press.

Guedon, J.-C. (2001). *In Oldenburg's long shadow: Librarians, research scientists, publishers, and the control of scientific publishing.* Retrieved from http://www.arl.org/resources/pubs/mmproceedings/138guedon.shtml

Harding, S. (Ed.) (1993). *The 'racial' economy of science.* Bloomington, IN: Indiana University Press.

Harding, S. (1998). *Is science multicultural?* Bloomington, IN: Indiana University Press.

Harding, S. (2003). *Science and technology in a multicultural and postcolonial world: Gender issues.* Retrieved from http://www.zemargraphics.com/biopolitics_web/HardingGOLDBERG.pdf

Harrison, M. (1994). *Public health in British India: Anglo-Indian preventive medicine, 1857–1914.* Cambridge, United Kingdom: Cambridge University Press.

Harrison, M. (1999). *Climates and constitutions: Health, race, environment and British imperialism in India 1600–1850.* Oxford, United Kingdom: Oxford University Press.

Heidegger, M. (1977). *The question concerning technology* (W. Lovitt, Trans.). New York, NY: Harper and Row.

Henry, J. (2002). *Knowledge is power: How magic, the government and an apocalyptic vision inspired Francis Bacon to create modern science.* Cambridge, United Kingdom: Icon Books.

Kuhn, T. (1962). *The structure of scientific revolutions.* Chicago, IL: University of Chicago Press.

Kuhn, T. S. (1970). *The structure of scientific revolutions* (2nd ed.). Chicago, IL: University of Chicago Press.

Lyotard, J.-F. (1984). *The postmodern condition: A report on knowledge.* Manchester, United Kingdom: Manchester University Press.

Nandy, A. (Ed.). (1988). *Science, hegemony, and violence: A requiem for modernity.* Retrieved from http://www.arvindguptatoys.com/arvindgupta/hegemony-nandy.pdf

Park, P. (2002). Toward a United Nations of science: US science board calls for more than international collaboration funding. *The Scientist, 16*(10), 8–10.

Peters, M. A., & Besley, T. (2006). *Building knowledge cultures.* Boulder, CO: Rowman & Littlefield.

Peters, M. A. (Ed.). (1996). *Education and the postmodern condition.* Westport, CT: Bergin & Garvey.

Petitjean, P., Jami, K., & Moulin, A. M. (1992). *Science and empires: Historical studies about scientific development and European expansion*. Dordrecht, the Netherlands: Kluwer.

Price, D. J. de Solla (1963). *Little science, big science*. New York, NY: Columbia University Press.

Ravetz, J. R. (1996). *Scientific knowledge and its social problems*. New Brunswick, NJ: Transaction Publishers. (Original work published 1971)

Rehbock, P. I. (2001). Globalizing the history of science. *Journal of World History, 12*, 183-193.

Rouse, J. (1987). *Knowledge and power: Toward a political philosophy of science*. Ithaca, NY: Cornell University Press.

Science and Technology Select Committee. (2004, July). *Scientific publications: Free for all?* (Report No. 10, Vol. 1; House of Commons Science and Technology Select Committee Session 2003-2004). Retrieved from UK Parliament, publications and records website:
http://www.publications.parliament.uk/pa/cm200304/cmselect/cmsctech/399/399.pdf

Sen, A. (2002). The science of give and take. *New Scientist, 174*, 51-54.

Simons, K., & Featherstone, C. (2000). Science in Europe. *Science, 290*(5494), 1099-1101.

Sokal, A. D. (1996). Transgressing the boundaries. *Social Text, 14*, 217-252.

Stiglitz, J. (1999). *Knowledge as a global public good*. Washington, DC: World Bank. Retrieved from http://www.worldbank.org/knowledge/chiefecon/articles/undpk2/index.htm

Teich, M. (1996). The 20th-century scientific-technical revolution. *History Today, 46*(11), 27-34.

Tudge, C. (2004). The honesty of science is being compromised at every turn: Can we still rely on what scientists tell us? Alas, no. Their conferences and papers are sponsored by industry, their bad results are concealed, their jobs are threatened if they step out of line. *New Statesman, 133*, 29- 32.

Wagner, P. (2004). *A history and theory of the social sciences: Not all that is solid melts into air*. Thousand Oaks, CA: Sage.

Wagner, P., & Wittrock, B. (1991). States, institutions and discourses: A comparative perspective on the structruration of the social sciences. In P. Wagner, B. Wittrock, & R. Whitley (Eds.), *Discourses on society: The shaping of the social science disciplines* (pp. 331-357). Dardrecht, the Netherlands: Kluwer.

Wang, J. (2002). Scientists and the problem of the public in Cold War America, 1945-1960. *Osiris, 17*, 323-349.

Watson-Verran, H., & Turnbull, D. (1995) Science and other indigenous knowledge systems. In S. Jasanoff, G. E. Markle, J. C. Peterson, & T. Pinch (Eds.), *Handbook of science and technology studies* (pp. 115-139). Thousand Oaks, CA: Sage.

Chapter 9

'Knowledge Economy,' Economic Crisis and Cognitive Capitalism
Public Education and the Promise of Open Science

Michael A. Peters

Introduction

In a recent paper, 'Forms of Knowledge Economy: Learning, Creativity, Openness', I identified three discernibly separate but interrelated developmental strands of the 'knowledge economy' based around the notions of (1) The Learning Economy, based on the work of Bengt-Åke Lundvall; (2) The Creative Economy, based on the work of Charles Landry, John Howkins and Richard Florida; (3) The Open Science Economy, based on recent technological developments in promoting the openness of scientific communication (Peters, 2010a).[1] This conception has been part of an ongoing engagement with the discourse of the knowledge economy that views it as a structural transformation of western capitalism, a third stage of development after *mercantile capitalism*, a doctrine that characterizing the period 1500–1800 based on the the premise that national wealth and power were best served by increasing exports and collecting precious metals in return (Coleman, 1969; Miller, 1988), and *industrial capitalism*, that replaced the replaced the merchant as a dominant actor in the capitalist system with the industrialist and established a factory system of manufacturing based on a complex division of labor. David Hume and Adam Smith were among a new group of economic theorists that questioned the fundamental mercantile belief that the amount of the world's wealth remained constant and that a state could only increase its wealth at the expense of another state. Knowledge capitalism, by contrast, is another transformation of capitalism. The term 'knowledge capitalism' emerged only recently to describe the transition to the so-called 'knowledge economy'. Knowledge capitalism and knowledge economy are twin terms that can be traced at the level of public policy to a series of reports that emerged in the late 1990s by the Organisation for Economic Co-operation and Development (1996) and the World Bank (1998), before they were taken up as a policy template by world governments in the late 1990s. In terms of these reports, education is reconfigured as a massively undervalued form of knowledge capital that will determine the future of work, the destiny of knowledge institutions and the shape of society in the years to come (Peters, 2003, 2007; Peters & Besley, 2006).

These three forms of knowledge economy and their associated discourses represent three recent related but different conceptions of the knowledge economy, each with clear significance and implications for education and education policy. They indicate that there have been different national policy constructions of the knowledge economy. I argue that the last conception based on openness provides a model of radically non-propertarian form that incorporates both 'open education' and 'open science' economies and provides a radical alternative to neoliberal conceptions in providing a way to respond positively to the Great Recession by establishing and encouraging open science and education as part of the global knowledge commons. These developments of openness can be understood as an extension of arguments for the public good in a global context, of knowledge and education as global public goods, and as a necessary platform for the promotion of global civil society.

'Knowledge Economy' and Emergent Forms of Knowledge Capitalism

In the genealogy of 'knowledge economy it is important to distinguish a number of different strands and readings of the knowledge economy and important to do so because it provides a history of a policy idea and charts its ideological interpretations. The different strands of this discourse are radically diverse and include attempts to theorize not only knowledge economy but also the parallel term 'knowledge society', and also the attempts to relate these terms to wider and broader changes in the nature of capitalism, modernity and the global economy.

Theorists from different political perspectives and disciplines have simultaneously tried to analyze and describe certain deep-seated and structurally transformative tendencies in Western capitalism, society and modernity to move to a form of post-industrial economy that focuses on the production and consumption of knowledge and symbolic goods as a higher-order economic activity that encompasses and affects the entire economy and society. In these studies we should recognize certain long-term structural tendencies of increased *formalization* that transform both the production and consumption of symbolic goods. These are all tendencies towards increasing (in)formalization and abstraction centered on the sign, symbol and the image including a set of overlapping processes that transform knowledge production—informatization, mathematization, digitalization—together with process that transform consumption—culturalization and aestheticization. Most recently, capitalism has begun to exploit the reproduction of new synthetic life in terms of a set of biological processes. These are the leading processes transforming contemporary postmodern capitalism that rely on new forms of systems (cybernetic) capitalism based on design principles with the capacity to make new connections among old structures; to form areas of exquisitely precise specialization for recognizing patterns in information; and the ability to learn to recruit and connect information from these areas automatically.

Theoretical studies of U.S. 'knowledge economy' have proceeded from different assumptions, focusing on technological development, the economic value of knowledge, the role of information in the market and the emergence of postmodern global systems theory:

- 'Technological revolution' studies, e.g., Daniel Bell's (1973) *Postindustrial Society* and Alvin Toffler's (1980) *The Third Wave* predicted a radical break.
- Economic value of knowledge, e.g., Fritz Machlup (1962) *The Production and Distribution of Knowledge in the U.S.*; Marc Porat (1977) *The Information Economy*.
- Role of information in market, e.g., Mark Granovetter (1985) (economic transaction are embedded in web of complex social relations; economic actions undertaken for economic and non-economic reasons; institutions constraining economic interactions are socially constructed).
- Postmodern global systems theory, e.g., Manuel Castells (2000) emergence of networks as basic unit.

Jean-François Lyotard (1984, [1979]) was one of the first to recognize 'postmodern capitalism' in his initital formulation: 'Our working hypothesis is that the status of knowledge is altered as societies enter what is known as the postindustrial age and cultures enter what is known as the postmodern age'. He writes of the significance of language related developments as being essential and the leading technologies of the new capitalist system:

> For the last forty years the "leading" sciences and technologies have had to do with language: phonology and theories of linguistics, problems of communication and cybernetics, modern theories of algebra and informatics, computers and their languages, problems of translation and the search for areas of compatibility among computer languages, problems of information storage and data banks, telematics and the perfection of intelligent terminals, to paradoxology.

He also warned us that economic powers have reached the point of imperiling the stability of the state through new forms of the circulation of capital that go by the generic name of *multi-national corporations.*

Fredric Jameson's (1991, p. 55) *Postmodernism, or The Cultural Logic of Late Capitalism* (Jameson wrote the foreword to Lyotard's work on the postmodern condition) remarked on the shift in ideological premises of these discourses:

> Theories of the postmodern—whether celebratory or couched in the language of moral revulsion and denunciation—bear a strong family resemblance to all those more ambitious sociological generalizations which, at much the same time, bring us the news of the arrival and inauguration of a whole new type of society, most famously baptized "postindustrial society" (Daniel Bell). Often also designated consumer society, media society, information society, electronic society or high tech, and the like. Such theories have the obvious ideological mission of demonstrating, to their own relief, that the new social formation in question no longer obeys the laws of classical capitalism, namely, the primacy of industrial production and the omnipresence of class struggle.

There have been different formulations that try to capture these tendencies including perhaps the most recognized as informationalism or *informational capitalism* that emerges from the work of Manuel Castells on the 'networked society'. Castells (2000) sees informationalism as a new technological paradigm (he speaks of a mode of development) characterized by "information generation, processing, and transmission" that have become "the fundamental sources of productivity and power" (Castells, 2000, p. 21). Christian Fuchs (2007) also writes of an informational capitalism of *self-regulation* and sometimes also referred to as the networked model of capitalism.

Another strand emphasizes *cultural capitalism* associated with the change of culture. This strand emerges from work in the 'new geography' and sociology and is epitomized by Richard Sennett's (2007) *The Culture of New Capitalism*, Nigel Thrift's (2006) *Knowing Capitalism*, Boltanskiand Chiapello's (2005) *The New Spirit of Capitalism*, and Paul du Gay and Michael Pryke's (2002) *Cultural Economy*. (See Peters, Britez, & Bulut, 2009.)

With *biocapitalism* (Rose, 2007, p. 6) 'A new economic space has been delineated—the bioeconomy—and a new form of capital—biocapital' (Rose, 2007, p. 6). The term 'biocapitalism' recently has emerged to map the growing significance of the life sciences and biotechnology as an innovation within late capitalism that controls, changes and experiments with the material basis of life. Biocapitalism or 'genomic capitalism' has it has sometimes been called (Rajan, 2003) increasingly is seen as the new funding priority for public good science and the basis of the new genetic revolution symbolized by the significance and 'success' of the Human Genome Project.

Cognitive Capitalism is a theory that has become significant in the last few years for analyzing a new form of capitalism, sometimes referred to as 'third capitalism' *after* mercantilism and industrial capitalism. It is a term that focuses on the socio-economic changes ushered in with the Internet as platform and new Web 2.0 technologies that have transformed the mode of production and the nature of labor. The theory of cognitive capitalism has its origins in French and Italian thinkers, particularly Gilles Deleuze and Felix Guattari's *Capitalism and Schizophrenia*, the work of Michel Foucault on the birth of biopower, and Michael Hardt and Antonio Negri's *Empire* and *Multitude*, as well as the Italian 'Autonomst' Marxist movement that had its origins in the Italian 'Operaismo' ('workerism') in the 1960s.

Finally, the term *finance capitalism* associated with the dominance of neoliberalism and the deregulation of finance markets. Financialization describes the development over several decades of a form of capitalism leading up to the 2007–10 financial crisis where accumulation strategy is based on profit making that occurs increasingly through financial instruments and derivatives rather than trade and commodity production, and financial markets dominate over traditional industrial economy.

Financialization and the Economic Crisis

Financialization is a term that describes an economic system or process that attempts to reduce all value that is exchanged (whether tangible, intangible, future or present promises, etc.) either into a financial instrument or a derivative of a financial instrument. The original intent of financialization is to be able to reduce any work-product or service to an exchangeable financial instrument. An aspect of increased symbolization, mathematization and computerization of financial markets.

It is the first systemic and global crisis of neo-liberal financial capitalism that began with the crisis of the Fordist model of accumulation and the consequent deregulation of the banking system during the 1970s. As the OECD (2009, p. 3) acknowledges:

> The current crisis is the first of this severity to hit OECD countries, since they have shifted to knowledge-based service economies where investment in intangible assets is of equal importance as investment in machinery, equipment and buildings.

Stephanie Blankenburg and José Gabriel Palma (2009, p. 531) writing for the *Cambridge Journal of Economics* suggest 'The current financial and economic crisis that has forced the likes of Alan Greenspan to question the coherence of dominant conceptual frameworks is unprecedented in global reach and systemic gravity' and they go on to plot the dimensions of the crisis in the following terms:

> According to McKinsey's *Mapping Global Financial Markets* (October 2008), global financial assets rose from US$12 trillion in 1980 to US$196 trillion in 2007. The International Monetary Fund's *Global Financial Stability Report* (IMF, 2009) estimate for the latter figure is considerably higher, at US$241 trillion. Global cross-border capital flows more than doubled between 2002 and 2007, with foreign investors holding one in four debt securities and one in five equities. While in 2000 only 11 countries had financial assets of more than 350% of gross domestic product (GDP), 25 countries had deepened their financial markets to the same extent by 2007. As early as 1990, money managers had increased their control of US corporate equities from 8% in 1950 to 60% (Porter, 1992, p. 6; Whalen, 2002, p. 402). Similarly, pension funds had extended their share of total business equities from less than 1% to just short of 39%, and their fraction of corporate debt from 13% to 50% (Ghilarducci, 1992, p. 117; Whalen, 2002, p. 402). In the period from 1986 to 2006, the US financial sector as a whole increased its share of corporate profits from 10% to

30%, while its outstanding debts grew from 20% of GDP in 1980 to 116% in 2007 (FED, 2009). According to Gillian Tett from the *Financial Times*, outstanding credit defaults swaps (CDS) today amount to no less than US$60 trillion, with the risk embodied after discounting mutually off-setting contracts still as high as US$14 trillion (Tett, 2009, p. 264).

They also indicate that US financial institutions have already written off US$1 trillion and are expected to write down at least another US$3–5 trillion. Predictions on the basis of this financial crisis and recover suggest that a decline especially in the Western world is unavoidable with high and sustained levels of unemployment and rapid growth of inequalities.

Financialization and the Roll-Back of Public Education

Neoliberalism is an expression of the power of finance that gathered pace with the internationalization of capital and the globalization of markets. Some scholars suggest that neoliberalism and globalization are themselves expressions of finance, closely tied to the development of derivatives markets and the evolution of an international financial system where the international rentiers have managed to significantly increase their share of national income. The inherent nature of financial markets has a tendency to lead to speculation and the privatization of individual savings in the US economy with investors seeking higher returns from riskier investments. The increasing role of institutional investors, the role of mutual funds, and the rise to power of large Wall Street firms has made the markets susceptible to misinformation, and lobbying of financial agency design to regulate the system.

The advent of financial crisis and apparent collapse of financial capitalism had a large role to play in making Barack Obama's election possible and at the same time signaled a dramatic shift in US federal government policies toward intervention and policies designed to stimulate the economy. Obama in his first term tried to take the initiative on restructuring the health system reforming to provide better public health. The conservative lead by the Tea Party movement has managed to displace job creation as a top priority and made reducing the debt and tax increases for the rich almost an unshakeable article of faith leading up to the next presidential election. The effect has been to popularize a debate on budget cuts across the board for public services provided at the state level with massive cuts to education in all aspects, attacks on collective bargaining, and the sacking of thousands of teachers. The extent of these cuts and their impacts on economic recovery have yet to be assessed but the conservative-led UK government under Cameron has made huge cuts to public universities in the order of 25 percent. Public sector works and public institutions are struggling to remain viable.

Yet these budget cuts come upon long-term changes in education including the wholesale adoption of the human capital policies and the shift from state and publicly funded human capital strategies to the encouragement of private funded investment in human capital especially at the university level. Starting with Gary Becker's (1964, 2004) seminal work *Human Capital: A Theoretical and Empirical Analysis, with Special Emphasis on Education* (1964/2004) human capital theory comes to characterize American neoliberal discourse in the form of Chicago school economics as one that transforms the classical function of labor and *homo economicus* into an 'entrepreneur of himself' (Foucault, 2008) where in the individual takes the risks, makes the investment in themselves through a form of actuarial rationality that in effect is forced upon university students (Peters, 2011; Peters et al., 2008). The effect of many years of neoliberal discourse and policies has been to 'win' the argument concerning whether university is a public good and to force students into increase debt accumulation to finance their studies. Other forms of parallel privatization have accelerating the budget erosion of public universities reducing forms of public and state support and forcing universities to increase tuition fees and to focus on research that wins funds or activities that provide a commercial return (Peters & Roberts, 1999; Roberts & Peters, 2008).

In an editorial entitled 'The University of Finance' the editors of *Ephemera* Armin Beverungen, Stephen Dunne and Casper Hoedemaekers (2009, p. 264) focus on the rise of the business school and turn to finances of the university, writing:

> Once we shift the focus of analysis in the direction of the university and financialisation, we move beyond the content of university teaching, its curricula and pedagogies, and look at the form which university education takes today. In so doing, we proceed to ask how this very form is itself shaped by finance. And so we come to question why there is hardly a university left without a private equity club, a hedge fund society, or a trading room. While some insist on the learning experience and ethical aspects of trading, others note the ways in

which these activities imbue a particular conservatism and opportunism, which deny the call for a critical engagement with finance (Jacobs, 2009).... Apart from finance as a subject of study, on the side of the students, there is student debt, which is rocketing so much so that in the US there is now talk of student debt as the next big bubble (Samuels, 2010b).

They plot 'the transformation of the University of Excellence (Readings, 1996) into the University of Finance, where it is the entrepreneurship of students and faculty, and their financial gravitas that seems to count most.'

After Nietzsche, philosophical critique of the Western university has developed along two interrelated lines: the first, pursued by Weber and continued by Heidegger, Jaspers, Lyotard and Bourdieu, emphasized the dangers of economic interest vested in the university through the dominance of *technical reason*; the second, initiated by members of the Frankfurt School and developed differently by Foucault, traces the imprint and controlling influence of the state in the academy through the apparatus of *administrative reason*. With the rise of the 'neoliberal university' these two forms of reason come together in a new way, first, through capitulation of norms of liberal humanism and the Kantian ethical subject to the main articles of faith underlying the revitalization of economic rationalism and *homo economicus*, and, second, through the imposition of structural adjustments policies of the IMF during the 1980s with devastating impacts of universities in the developing world. Neoliberal universities, with little self-reflection, have been harnessed in service to the 'new economy' under conditions of *knowledge capitalism* that raises issues of intellectual capital, the ownership of the means of knowledge production, and depends upon the encouragement of all forms of capitalization of the self. In the age of global terrorism, when traditional rights are being curtailed and eroded, the neoliberal university is content to pursue business as usual.

'Crisis' and Transformation

The concept of 'crisis' comes from the Greek noun *krisis* (choice, decision, judgment), deriving from the Greek verb *krinein* (to decide) and popular in Greek historical writing as the turning point in a decisionor argument. It reappears in the late eighteenth century as a catchall term for a crucial or decisive stage with reference to historical events, periods, or processes. Jacob Burckhardt developed the concept of crisis in relation to world history, especially the French Revolution and the European revolutions of 1848, and later conservative anxieties over the stage of European modernity. As a historian of the Renaissance and the rise of Christianity, Burckhardt was concerned with periods of rapid social, political, and cultural transformation accompanying the rise of industrial capitalism and mass politics which he viewed with suspicion. Karl Marx developed a different emphasis in his reflections on crisis articulating a theory of economic crisis centered on the economics of overproduction, specifically on the chronic disequilibrium between production and consumption under capitalism. Each crisis would be more severe than the last until a 'general crisis' occurred wherein the working class would rise against their exploiters. As

Reinhart Koselleck (2006, p. 394), the German historian, notes:

> Marx and Engels integrate the economic concept of crisis into their political and historical analysis. This is illustrated in the *Communist Manifesto:* 'For decades, the history of industry and commerce is but a history of the revolt of modern productive forces pitted against modern conditions of production, property relations that are the condition for the existence of the bourgeoisie and its domination.... In these crises there breaks out an epidemic that in all earlier epochs would have seemed an absurdity—an epidemic of overproduction.... How does the bourgeoisie overcome these crises? On the one hand, by enforced destruction of mass productive forces; on the other, by the conquest of new markets and by a more thorough exploitation of old ones. But how then does it do this. By paving the way for ever more extensive and devastating crises and by diminishing the means whereby crises are prevented.' On the basis of this economic interpretation, Marx and Engels could finally predict the foreseeable demise of capitalism. But this requires simultaneous political action by the proletariat, that 'death-bearing' class which the bourgeoisie itself had created. Incorporated into their social and political analysis, is the expectation of a final economic collapse, a 'global crash' as well as the certainty of revolution—or whatever other circumlocution Marx and Engels chose instead: 'A new revolution is possible only in the wake of a new crisis. But the one is as certain as the other' Yet for Marx and Engels 'crisis' retained an essentially positive connotation, though on political rather than economic grounds. As Engels exults in 1857: 'The crisis will make me feel as good as a swim in the ocean.'

The widespread interest in and development of crisis studies that peaked by the early 1970s has in the wake of the current financial crisis experienced increasing use even although the term is often used without precise definition. The concept of 'crisis' has a long and complex genealogy employment to understand issues of order and change since at least the eighteenth century following Marx's notion on the evolution of macro-social developing as an object of inquiry in its own right to indicate transformative and structural change. Koselleck (2006) concludes his inquiry with the following assertion:

> From the nineteenth century on, there has been an enormous quantitative expansion in the variety of meanings attached to the concept of crisis, but few corresponding gains in either clarity or precision. "Crisis" remains a catchword, used rigorously in only a few scholarly or scientific contexts....
> In all the human and social sciences, crisis appears as a key concept; in history, of course, to characterize epochs or 'structures.' Political science tries to operationalize the term and distinguish it from 'conflict.' From medicine the concept has spread to psychology and anthropology, ethnology, and the sociology of culture. Above all, it is the media which have inflated the use of the term. On the basis of current headlines, a list of 200 different contexts was compiled in which the term crisis appears as adjective (crisis-torn), as subject (mini-crisis, crisis of self-confidence) or as defining word (crisis expert, crisis bungler). Not only can 'crisis' be conjoined with other terms, it is easy to do so. While it can be used to clarify, all such coinages then require clarification. 'Crisis' is often used interchangeably with 'unrest,' 'conflict,' 'revolution,' and to describe vaguely disturbing moods or situations (397–8).

In the tradition of Marxian radical political economy Christian Marazzi (2010) in *The Violence of Financial Capitalism* argues that the current financial crisis is a systemic crisis of the entire capitalistic system, which is today a 'cognitive capitalism', based on interconnected global financial markets. This is a fundamental shift that represents the financialization of the reproductive sphere of life itself. Under this regime the monopolization and privatization of knowledge and education has proceeded rapidly. He suggests it is time to redress the balance between private and public knowledge goods at national and global levels through the promotion of 'super-multiplier' investments in global public knowledge infrastructures and the regulation of global knowledge intellectual monopolies and private science. As the blurb clarifies: 'He argues that the processes of financialization are not simply irregularities between the traditional categories of wages, rent, and profit, but rather a new type of accumulation adapted to the processes of social and cognitive production today. The financial crisis, he contends, is a fundamental component of contemporary accumulation and not a classic lack of economic growth'.[2] Marazzi is an Italian economist who works in the tradition of Italian Autonomous Marxism coming from the tradition of *Operaismo* (Workerism) to theorize financialization as a crsis of accumulation of the new 'cognitive capitalism'.

As Francesca Bria (2009, p. 388) remarks 'It is the first systemic and global crisis of neo-liberal financial capitalism that began with the crisis of the Fordist model of accumulation and the consequent deregulation of the banking system during the 1970s' and goes on to provide the following brief account of Marazzi's argument:

> The central thesis of Marazzi's book is that the dualism between the real economy (real money for tangible production) and the financial economy (production of money by means of money) no longer exists. Financialisation now has taken over and it encompasses the whole business cycle; what is really at stake in Marazzi's perspective is the very concept of capital accumulation.

In this context Marazzi argues for a project of *reappropriation* of the commons. Bria (2009, p. 393) expresses the point: 'The central issue is to recognize the question of *the right to social ownership of a common good* or in other words a *social rent*, as opposed to the only right recognized today, which is the right to private ownership.' She goes on to make the assertion:

> If the boundaries between education and production are porous and tend to be more blurred, when we criticised this socio-economic and financial system we are also criticising the educational system and thinking about alternative organisational and pedagogical models that can help us to move beyond this crisis (p. 394).... His analysis clearly shows that this crisis can be used as an opportunity to pursue radical changes and to open new terrains of conflict and sites of struggles, and it is only through struggles that we can identify common perspectives outside and beyond the crisis. This is an invitation to further enquiries into the role of knowledge in the production systems and its relationship with transformations in the capital/labour relation and the collective self-management of common goods (p. 394).

Contemporary forms of knowledge capitalism that have the arts and the sciences as their basis. They emphasize the role of creativity and designing intelligence in intellectual capital modes of production and promote informatization of subjectivity of workers through networks including flexibilization, part-time, competency-based, performance-related, continuous, contract work ('digital labor').

Cognitive Capitalism and Immaterial Labor

Knowledge capitalism involves an increasing and infinite substitution of capital for labor with the automation of secondary (e.g., fully automated factory) and tertiary knowledge activities. The discourse of the knowledge economy has largely ignored the concept of class the labor or recommended their replacement by specialized 'new class' of scientists or students as a new social movement. This new symbolic development involves a clear mathematization of knowledge with the new search algorithms and the development of an algorithmic capitalism (Peters, 2011a) with the attendant 'googlization of higher education'. Siva Vaidhyanathan (2011) asks how Google's ubiquity is affecting the production and dissemination of knowledge.

Cognitive capitalism emerges as a global economic system based on the development of virtual (immaterial) economy ('third capitalism') focused on the increasing informatization (digitization) of production,[3] with increasing formalization, mathematicization and digitization of language, communication, and knowledge (especially journal systems). At the same time, and as a response to the same forces, there is the emergence of social media, social networking and social mode of production enhanced by Web 2.0 technologies and distributed knowledge and learning systems including online publication and archives leading to *open knowledge production* systems including open science economy. The decreasing cost of network access, knowledge-sharing and transmission, and greater 'borderless' interconnectedness of knowledge spaces (emergence of 'world brain').

Distributive knowledge systems under cognitive capitalism lead to the eventual displacement of material production as core of the system with an emphasis on interactive and dynamical relations between material and immaterial sectors, and the digitization and systematization of value (rather than chains) where collective intelligence represents the core of exchange value and profit-making. Co-production exists through 'just-in-time production' where the market precedes production and increasing through processes intellectual property private appropriation of global public knowledge goods takes place through the enforcement of patents, copyright, and trademark. Further, the increasing capacity of computing, copying, file-sharing and storage to help enforcement of intellectual property rights. Externalities in complex systems now determine the general conditions of growth, investment and redistribution of revenue.

There is accorded a central role of innovation with a new sociotechnical 'cybernetic' paradigm of innovation based on 'hothouse' social networking and social media. Continuous endogenous innovation is increasingly focused on science as a leading part of the accumulation regime together with the promotion of new models of social and public entrepreneurship

Fuchs (2010) provides an emerging typology of approaches from theorizations of cognitive capitalism on knowledge labor and class reveal a variety of characterizations that serve as models for understanding intellectual labor within the school and the university:

- *Internet users as a new class*: Terranova (2000) Internet users constitute a kind of free labor that is exploited by capital. Margonelli (1999) talks of 'cybersweatshops.'
- *Knowledge labor as a new class*: Ursula Huws (2003) deskilling and delocalization lead to a new class of information processing workers—'the cybertariat.' McKenzie Wark (2004) antagonism between the hacker class that produces information and the vectoral class that dispossesses the hacker class of its intellectual property by patents and copyrights. Franco Berardi speaks of the emergence of the 'cognitariat'— a "new consciousness of cognitive workers" (Berardi 2003, 4).
- *Knowledge labor as revolutionary class:* The multitude is a new class that is "embedded in cooperative and communicative networks" (Hardt and Negri 2004, xv). Its labor is "immaterial labour" "that creates immaterial products, such as knowledge, information, communication, a relationship, or an emotional response" (Hardt and Negri 2004, 108). Immaterial labor is collective and cooperative and that capital exploits the commons of society for accumulating "revolutionary processes of liberation determined by the multitude" (Hardt and Negri 2000, 249).
- *Precarious knowledge labor as new class*: Nick Dyer-Witheford "poorly paid, insecure, untrained, deskilled" (Dyer-Witheford 1999, 88) service workers constitute the "new high-technology proletariat" (Dyer-Witheford 1999, 96), the "virtual proletariat" (123). AndreGorz sees those expelled from production by automation and computerisation, the underemployed, probationary, contracted, casual, temporary, and parttime labor as "post-industrial neo-proletariat" (Gorz 1980, 69).
- *Knowledge labor as unproductive subsumed labor class*: Resnick andWolff (1987) distinguish between fundamental class processes, in which surplus value is directly produced, and appropriated and subsumed class processes, in which already appropriated surplus value or its products are distributed.

- *Knowledge labor and knowledge capital as one new class*: Florida (2002, 8)—the rise of a "creative class" that is made up of a super-creative core
- *Knowledge labor as petty bourgeoisie*: For Nicos Poulantzas, knowledge workers are part of "the 'new' petty bourgeoisie composed of nonproductive wage earners" (Poulantzas 1973, 106).

The discourse point to the question of 'immaterial labor'. Networks and flows of immaterial labor based on mass participation and collaboration rather than traditional Smithian division of labor that is non-linear and comprise dynamical systems of labor. Learning economies reinforce autonomy and collective intelligence as the main source of value in the market with emphasis on codification and contextualization of practical and implicit knowledge. Situated, personal and implicit knowledge not easily reduced to machine or to mere information (codified software or data). Creative learning economies emphasize 'right brain' ascendancy with an accent on a psychology of openness, meta-cognition and 'learning by doing'. Infinite substitution of capital for labor for 'left brain' logical and sequential tasks releasing creative energies (Pinker, 2010). Fundamental what characterizes cognitive capitalism is the emergence of team or network as fundamental labor units in a new political economy of peer production ('interneting') based on cooperation and collaboration rather than competition. There is an increasing importance of post-human network knowledge and learning practices based on mega-data bases and global portals.

The Promise of Open Science: Reappropriating the Knowledge Commons

Public education is in a state of crisis. After years of neoliberal policies that have reduced levels of public funding, school and university systems, now are being forced to manage with less. At the same time, managerialist ideologies have impacted the administration of education. Public universities in view of funding deficits have been forced to increase student fees and neoliberal policies have overridden the idea that knowledge is a public good to promote the wholesale commercialization of the production of knowledge and/or to develop a regulatory system that closely audit outcomes in the name of efficiency, productivity and accountability.[4] There are alternatives for the restoration of the public university based upon a model of deliberative democracy and empowered participatory governance which promotes a greater reflexivity and a new vision of the public university (Burowoy, 2010; Calhoun & Rhoten, 2011).

There have been many attempts to elaborate the crucial importance of the close relationship between universities and the public good, emphasizing links between civil society, public discourses and deliberation, public culture, and the health of democracy. The notion of the public sphere lies at the heart of the liberal theory of civil society distinguished by an institutional setting characterized by openness in communication and the production of public goods (Calhoun, 2001, 2006). Habermas's (1989 [1962]) *The Structural Transformation of the Public Sphere* serves as the point of departure for the analysis of the formation of the bourgeois public sphere that depended upon the principle of universal access to constitute a realm characterized by critical-rational debate. The institutionalization of a fully political public sphere took place first in Britain during the eighteenth century and was preceded by a literary public culture that revealed the interiority of the self and emphasized an communicative rational subjectivity that created a new phenomenon of public opinion and the basis for a new liberal constitutional social order. There have been critiques of Habermas's conception in terms of marginalized groups excluded from a universal public sphere (Fraser, 1990) and the way in which Habermas draws the distinction between public and private (Benhabib, 1992). Other scholars have sought to develop the concept of the public sphere emphasizing its discursive or rhetorical nature (Hauser, 1998). Habermas's work of the public sphere was written well before the age of the Internet and some followers have developed his theories within the new public space of electronic and social media that, unlike traditional industrial one-way broadcast media, are open, interactive and characterized by a plurality of voices and the absence of a central control or authority (Bohman, 2004; Bohman & Roberts, 2007). Against neoliberal theories that seek to privatize the public sphere, Hardt and Negri (2004, 2009), following Michael Foucault's (2008) biopolitics, suggest that in liberal political economy the very distinction between public and private spheres is founded upon a concept of private property in an economy of scarcity. With the postmodernization of the production of knowledge and a shift to the knowledge economy, Hardt and Negri (2009) see open source and open access as encouraging new forms of collaboration that no longer hold that economic value is founded upon exclusive possession, but rather increasing depends upon new collectives based on the logic of networking that has the power to reconstitute the public sphere.

The global knowledge economy represents a set of deep structural transformations in the transition to a networked information economy that has the power to alter not only modes of economic organization and social practices of knowledge production but also the very fabric of liberal economy and society. As Yochai Benkler (2006, p. 2) expresses the point: 'Information, knowledge, and culture are central to human freedom and human development' and changes to the 'information environment' in advanced economies heralding new freedoms and a more active role for individuals than was possible in the industrial economy. Benkler focuses on the effects of laws that regulate information production and exchange on the distribution of control over information flows, knowledge, and culture in the digital environment.[5] He is talking about *freedom* in a practical sense:

> as a platform for better democratic participation; as a medium to foster a more critical and self-reflective culture; and, in an increasingly information dependent global economy, as a mechanism to achieve improvements in human development everywhere.

The new open communications environment has the power to reshape the university as a networked environment, allowing the emergence of radically decentred forms of social nonproprietarian and nonmarket models of academic production and exchange, alongside market and property forms, that will transform cultural production in general and the concepts of readership, scholarship and authorship that have ruled the academic economy. In the process, these changes will also alter the concept of the disciplines, disciplinarity and its cognate concepts of inter- and multidisciplinarity. The university is caught in an epic struggle between a neoliberal construction of knowledge capitalism as the latest phase of globalization based on what I have called the 'capitalization of knowledge', the 'deterritorialization of information' and the 'technologization of education' and 'knowledge socialism' based on the effective and large-scale collegial and peer production of information, knowledge and culture exemplified in the convergence of open source, open access and free science movements.

The debate concerning knowledge capitalism becomes one that increasingly turns on the economics of knowledge, the communicative turn, and the emerging international knowledge system where the politics of knowledge and information dominates. One issue concerns intellectual property, not only copyright, patents and trademarks, but also the emergence of international regimes of intellectual property rights, and the accompanying emphasis on human capital and embedded knowledge processes that now drive university management. In these debates, issues of freedom and control reassert themselves at the levels of content, code and infrastructure. The issue of freedom/control concerns the ideation and codification of knowledge and the new 'soft' technologies that take the notion of 'practice' as the new desideratum: practitioner knowledge, communities of practice, and different forms of organizational learning adopted and adapted as part of corporate practice.

Since Boyle's 'invisible college' and the birth of learned societies in the late seventeenth century modern science has always been the prototype of open scientific communication based on peer governance and review. There are some signs that the globalized privatization regime in science funding representing the end of 'big science', shrinking budgets and the breakdown of scientific nationalism that define the Bush years has begun to recognize the new model of open science as an aspect of an emergent global science system structured by the forces of *networks, emergence, circulation, stickiness (place),* and *distribution (virtual).*[6] The decline of the U.S. economy relative to those of the rest of the world is facilitating the strengthening of science elsewhere with an evolving multi-polar world economy leading to multiple centers of science. The increasing wealth of China, India and South Korea is enabling them to lure back many younger scientists trained abroad in the world's leading institutions. In this changing environment there has been a shift to international collaborative research with an accent on the virtual organization of global science teams.

Truly transnational open science alternatives are emerging in new research cultures that are no longer solely state and university-oriented although there is concomitantly rapid growth of corporate multinational research especially in new materials, biotechnology (genetics), pharmaceutics, information technology—growth of private science. This shift is accompanied by a change in funding regimes from public to private, state to global, and big science to applied science, science to technology. There is also a new role for humanities, performing arts and social sciences as 'soft' sciences and technologies concerned with new international values, legalities, global civic cultures, knowledge measurement, and knowledge management, together with recognition of the increasing importance of internationalization in education and research training and new forms of technology-led education on the basis of new architectures of participation and collaboration. Global science and research organization and cultures are emerging, extra-national organizations, NGOs, UN, UNESCO, ESF and other international science-based organizations and science portals that aim as addressing corss-border problems beyond the resources of a single country.

The struggle is between new models of open science versus expanded protection of IP. Open source initiatives have facilitated the development of new models of production and innovation.

The public and nonprofit sectors have called for alternative approaches dedicated to public knowledge redistribution and dissemination. Distributed peer-to-peer knowledge systems rival, the scope and quality of similar products produced by proprietary efforts. The speed of diffusion of open source projects is a huge advantage and there have been many successful projects in software and open source biology.

Open access science has focused on making peer-reviewed, online research and scholarship freely accessible to a broader population (incl. digitized back issues). Open science demonstrates an "exemplar of a compound of 'private-collective' model of innovation" that contains elements of both proprietary and public models of knowledge production (Von Hippel & von Krogh, 2003). Science 2.0 sites are beginning to proliferate; one notable example is the OpenWetWare project started by biological engineers at the Massachusetts Institute of Technology. Rich text, highly interactive, user generated and socially active Internet (Web 2.0) has seen linear models of knowledge production giving way to more diffuse open ended and serendipitous knowledge processes.

There have been dramatic changes in creation, production and consumption of scholarly resources—'creation of new formats made possible by digital technologies, ultimately allowing scholars to work in deeply integrated electronic research and publishing environments that will enable real-time dissemination, collaboration, dynamically-updated content, and usage of new media' (Brown et al., 2007, p. 4). Alternative distribution models (institutional repositories, pre-print servers, open access journals) have also arisen with the aim to broaden access, reduce costs, and enable open sharing of content' (Brown et al., 2007).

One might argue that the open science economy plays a *complementary* rather than an oppositional role with corporate and transnational science and implies strong role for governments. Increasingly, portal-based knowledge environments and global science gateways support collaborative science (Schuchardt et al., 2007).[7] Cyber-mashups of very large data sets let users explore, analyze, and comprehend the science behind the information being streamed. The new Web 2.0 technologies and development of data sharing with cloud computing has revolutionized how researchers from various disciplines collaborate over long distances especially in the Life Sciences, where interdisciplinary approaches are becoming increasingly powerful as a driver of both integration and discovery (with regard to data access, data quality, identity, and provenance).

The economic crisis of Western neoliberal capitalism brought about through the Great Recession has impacted on the nature of public knowledge and education institutions, privatization education and monopolizing knowledge flows. Education and science have always been wedded to principles of free inquiry and to the academic freedoms that are necessary to sustain the open society and social democracy. The project for revitalizing and restoring the publicness of science and education is enhanced especially in an era of severe budget cuts to public services through the utilization of new platforms of openness based on Web 2.0 technologies that promotes universal access to knowledge and economical forms of collaboration through file-sharing and the nested convergences in open access, open archiving, open publishing (open journals systems) that have the potential to reconstitute science and education as open and public institutions in the years to come.

Notes

1   For work on the knowledge economy and its different modes, see Peters & Besley (2006), Peters (2007), Peters, Marginson & Murphy (2009), Marginson, Murphy & Peters (2010), Murphy, Peters & Marginson (2010), Araya & Peters (2010).

2   See http://mitpress.mit.edu/catalog/item/default.asp?ttype=2&tid=12084.

3   This is my compilation adapted and developed from Moulier Boutang (2007) with allusions to the work of Lyotard, Deleuze & Guattari, Foucault, Hardt & Negri, Cas-

tells, Benkler, Lessig, Bauwens, Tapscott, Fuchs, Howkins, Florida, Gorz, Pink, Lundvall, and others.

4   See the 'Universities in Crisis' Blog of the International Sociological Association with some over 50 reports from some 35 countries. See also the UK based 'Campaign for the Public University' at http://publicuniversity.org.uk/; 'University Politics – Universities as Public Goods' at http://universitypolitics.blogspot.com/; and the excellent website Transformations of the Public Sphere' at http://publicsphere.ssrc.org/.

5   See Benkler's webpage at http://www.benkler.org/. The site contains a statement of his research interests as well as selected online papers on themes of the intellectual commons, intellectual property, open spectrum, democracy and information, and regulation of the Internet.

6   For my work on openness, see Peters & Britez (2008), Peters (2009a; 2010a,b,c,d; 2011b), Peters & Roberts (2011).

7   See, for example, http://www.science.gov/.

References

Araya, D., & Peters, M. A. (Eds.). (2010). *Education in the creative economy*. New York, NY: Peter Lang.

Bell, D. (1973). *The coming of post-industrial society: A venture in social forecasting*. New York, NY: Basic Books.

Benhabib, S. (1992). Models of public space. In C. Calhoun (Ed.), *Habermas, and the public sphere* (pp. 73–98). Cambridge, MA: MIT Press.

Benkler, Y. (2006). *The wealth of networks: How social production transforms markets and freedom*. New Haven, CT: Yale University Press.

Benkler, Y., & Nissenbaum, H. (2006). Commons-based peer production and virtue. *The Journal of Political Philosophy, 14*(4), 394–419.

Beverungen, A., Dunne, S., & Hoedemaekers, C. (2009). The university of finance. *ephemera, 9*(4), 261–270. Retrieved from http://www.ephemeraweb.org/journal/9-4/9-4ephemera-nov09.pdf.

Blankenburg, S., & Palma, J. G. l. (2009). Introduction: The global financial crisis. *Cambridge Journal of Economics, 33*(4), 531–538.

Bohman, J. (2007). *Democracy across borders, From Dêmos to Dêmoi*. Cambridge, MA: MIT Press.

Bohman, J., & Roberts, J. M. (2004). Expanding dialogue: The internet, the public sphere and prospects for transnational democracy. In N. Crossley (Ed.), *After Habermas: New perspectives on the public sphere* (pp. 131–155). Oxford, United Kingdom: Blackwell.

Boltanski, L., & Chiapello, E. (2005). *The new spirit of capitalism* (G. Elliott, Trans.). London, United Kingdom: Verso.

Boutang, Y. M. (2007). *Cognitive capitalism and entrepreneurship decline in industrial entrepreneurship and the rising of collective intelligence*. Paper presented the Capitalism and Entrepreneurship Conference, Cornell University, Ithaca, NY. Retrieved from http://www.economyandsociety.org/events/YMoulier_Boutang.pdf

Bria, F. (2009) A crisis of finance: *Financialisation* as a crisis of accumulation of new capitalism. *ephemera, 9*(4), 388–395.

Brown, L., Griffiths, R., & Rascoff, M. (2007). University publishing in a digital age (The Ithaka Report). *Journal of Electronic Publishing, 10*(3). doi: http://dx.doi.org/10.3998/3336451.0010.301

Buroway, M. (2010). *A new vision of the public university*. Retrieved from http://publicsphere.ssrc.org/burawoy-redefining-the-public-university/

Calhoun, C. (2001). Civil society/public sphere: History of the concept(s). In *International encyclopedia of the social and behavioral sciences* (pp. 1897–1903). Amsterdam, the Netherlands: Elsevier.

Calhoun, C. (2006). The university and the public good. *Thesis Eleven, 84*, 7–43.

Calhoun, C., & Rhoten, D. (Eds.) (2011). *Knowledge matters: The public mission of the research university*. New York, NY: Columbia University Press/SSRC Books.

Castells, M. (2000). *The rise of the network society* (2nd ed.). Malden, MA: Blackwell.

Coleman, D. C. (Ed.). (1969). *Revisions in mercantilism: Debates in economic history*. London, United Kingdom: Methuen.

Deleuze, G., & Guattari, F. (2004). *Capitalism and schizophrenia* (B. Massumi, Trans.) (Vols. 1–2). London, United Kingdom: Continuum.

Du Gay, P. L. J, & Pryke, M. (Eds.). (2002). *Cultural economy: Cultural analysis and commercial life*. London, United Kingdom: Sage.

Dyer-Witheford, N. (1999). *Cyber-Marx. Cycles and circuits of struggle in high-technology capitalism*. Urbana, IL: University of Illinois Press.

Farrell, D., Lund, S., Skau, O., Atkins, C., Mengeringhaus, J. P., & Pierce, M. S. (2008). *Mapping global financial markets: Fifth annual report*. Retrieved from http://www.mckinsey.com/insights/mgi/research/financial_markets/mapping_global_capital_markets_fifth_annual_report

FED (Federal Reserve Board). (2009). *Flow of funds accounts of the United States*. Retrieved from http://www.federalreservebank.gov/datadownload

Florida, R. (2002). *The rise of the creative class*. New York, NY: Basic Books.

Foray, D. (2000). *The economics of knowledge*. Cambridge, MA: MIT Press.

Foucault, M. (2008). *The birth of biopolitics: Lectures at the Collège de France, 1978–1979*. Maidenhead, United Kingdom: Palgrave Macmillan.

Fraser, N. (1990). Rethinking the public sphere: A contribution to the critique of actually existing democracy. *Social Text, 25*(26), 56–80.

Fuchs, C. (2007). Transnational space and the network society. *21st Century Society, 2*(1), 49–78.

Fuchs, C. (2010). Labor in informational capitalism and on the internet. *The Information Society, 26*(3), 179–196.

Ghilarducci, T. (1992). *Labor's capital: The economics and politics of private pensions.* Cambridge, MA: MIT Press.

Gorz, A. (1980). *Farewell to the working class.* London, United Kingdom: Pluto.

Granovetter, M. (1973). The strength of weak ties. *American Journal of Sociology, 78*(6), 1360-1380.

Habermas, J. (1989). *The structural transformation of the public sphere: An inquiry into a category of bourgeois society* (T. Burger, Trans.). Cambridge, MA: MIT Press. (Original work published 1962)

Hardt, M., & Negri, A. (2004). *Multitude: War and democracy in the age of empire.* New York, NY: Penguin.

Hardt, M., & Negri, A. (2009). *Commonwealth.* Cambridge, MA: Belknap Press of Harvard University Press.

Hauser, G. (1998). Vernacular dialogue and the rhetoricality of public opinion. *Communication Monographs, 65*(2), 83-107.

Hearn, G., & Rooney, D. (Eds.). (2008). *Knowledge policy: Challenges for the twenty first century.* Cheltenham, United Kingdom: Edward Elgar.

Howkins, J. (2001). *The creative economy: How people make money from ideas.* London, United Kingdom: Allen Lane.

Huws, U. (2003). *The making of a cybertariat.* New York, NY: Monthly Review Press.

International Monetary Fund. (2009). *Global financial stability report: The quest for lasting stability.* Retrieved from http://www.imf.org/external/pubs/ft/gfsr/2012/01/index.htm

Jacobs, E. (2009). Business class. *Financial Times,* December 3. Retrieved from http://www.ft.com/cms/s/0/ee8af4ae-d960-11de-b2d5-00144feabdc0.html#axzz205JDgqzE

Jain, A. K. (2010). Fool's gold: How unrestrained greed corrupted a dream, shattered global markets and unleashed a catastrophe. *Critical Perspectives on International Business, 6*(1), 72-75.

Jameson, F. (1991). *Postmodernism or the cultural logic of late capitalism.* London, United Kingdom: Verso.

Koselleck, R. (2006) Crisis. Trans. Richter, Michaela. *Journal of the History of Ideas, 67*(2), April, 357-400.

Landry, C. (2000). *The creative city: A toolkit for urban innovators.* Oxford, United Kingdom: Earthscan (Routledge).

Lorenz, E., & Lundvall, B.-Å. (Eds.). (2006). *How Europe's economies learn.* Oxford, United Kingdom: Oxford University Press.

Lundvall, B.-A. (1996). The social dimension of the learning economy. *Druid Working Paper 96-1.* Retrieved from http://www3.druid.dk/wp/19960001.pdf

Lundvall, B.-Å., & Johnson, B. (1994). The learning economy. *Journal of Industry Studies, 1*(2), 23-42.

Lyotard, J.-F. (1984). *The postmodern condition: A report on knowledge* (G. Bennington & B. Massumi, Trans.). Manchester, United Kingdom: Manchester University Press.

Machlup, F. (1962). *The production and distribution of knowledge in the United States*, Princeton, NJ: Princeton University Press.

Marazzi, C. (2010). *The violence of financial capitalism* (K. Lebedeva, Trans.). New York, NY: Semiotext(e).

Marginson, S., Murphy, P., & Peters, M. A. (2010). *Global creation: Space, connection and synchrony in the age of the knowledge economy*. New York, NY: Peter Lang.

Margonelli, L. (1999). Inside AOL's 'cyber-sweatshop.' *Wired* 7(10). Retrieved from http://www.wired.com/wired/archive/7.10/volunteers.html

Miller, J. C. (1988). *Way of death: Merchant capitalism and the Angolan slave trade 1730–1830*. Madison, WI: University of Wisconsin Press.

Murphy, P., Peters, M. A., & Marginson, S. (2010). *Imagination: Three models of imagination in the age of the knowledge economy*. New York, NY: Peter Lang.

Negri, A., & Hardt, M. (2001). *Empire*. Cambridge, MA: Harvard University Press.

Negri, A., & Hardt, M. (2004). *Multitude: War and democracy in the age of empire*. New York, NY: Penguin.

OECD. (1996). *The knowledge-based economy*. Paris, France: OECD.

OECD. (2009). *Policy responses to the economic crisis: Investing in innovation for long-term growth*. Paris, France: OECD.

Peters, M. A. (2003). Education policy in the age of knowledge capitalism. *Policy Futures in Education*, 1(2), 361–380.

Peters, M. A. (2007). *Knowledge economy, development and the future of higher education*. Rotterdam, the Netherlands: Sense.

Peters, M. A. (2008). Education and the knowledge economy. In G. Hearn, D Rooney, & D. Wright (Eds.), *Knowledge policy: Challenges for the 21st century* (pp. 27–44). London, United Kingdom: Edward Elgar.

Peters, M. A. (2009a). On the philosophy of open science. *The International Journal of Science in Society*, 1(1), 1–27.

Peters, M. A. (2009b). Education, creativity and the economy of passions: New forms of educational capitalism. *Thesis Eleven*, 96, 40–63.

Peters, M. A. (2010a). Three forms of knowledge economy: Learning, creativity, openness. *British Journal of Educational Studies*, 58(1), 67–88.

Peters, M. A. (2010b). Knowledge economy and scientific communication: Emerging paradigms of 'open knowledge production' and 'open education'. In M. Simons, M. Olssen, & M. A. Peters (Eds.), *Re-reading education policies: A handbook studying the policy agenda of the twenty-first century* (pp. 293–318). Rotterdam, the Netherlands: Sense.

Peters, M. A. (2010c). Open education and the open science economy. *Yearbook of the National Society for the Study of Education*, 108(2), 203–225.

Peters, M. A. (2010d). Open works, open cultures, and open learning systems. In T. W. Lukes & J. Hunsinger (Eds.), *Putting knowledge to work and letting information play: The Center for Digital Discourse and Culture*. (pp. 75-99). Blacksburg, VA: Virginia Tech, Center for Digital Discourse and Culture.

Peters, M. A. (2011a). *Neoliberalism and after? Education, social policy and the crisis of capitalism*. New York, NY: Peter Lang.

Peters, M. A. (2011b). Manifesto for education in the age of cognitive capitalism: Freedom, creativity and culture. In C. McCarthy (Ed.), *New times: Making sense of critical/cultural theory in a digital age* (pp. 349–364). New York, NY: Peter Lang.

Peters, M. A., & Besley, T. (A.C.). (2006). *Building knowledge cultures: Education and development in the age of knowledge capitalism*. Oxford, United Kingdom: Rowman & Littlefield.

Peters, M. A., Besley, T. (A. C.), Olssen, M., Maurer, S., & Weber, S. (Eds.). (2009). *Governmentality studies in education*. Rotterdam, the Netherlands: Sense Publishers.

Peters, M. A., & Britez, R. (Eds.). (2008). *Open education and education for openness*. Rotterdam, the Netherlands: Sense Publishers.

Peters, M. A., Britez, R., & Bulut, E. (2010). Cybernetic capitalism, informationalism, and cognitive labor. *Geopolitics, History and International Relations, 1*(2), 11–40.

Peters, M., Marginson, S., & Murphy, P. (2009). *Creativity and the global knowledge economy*. New York, NY: Peter Lang.

Peters, M. A., & Roberts, P. (1999). *University futures and the politics of reform*. Palmerston North, New Zealand: Dunmore Press.

Peters, M. A., & Roberts, P. (2011). *The virtues of openness: Education, science and scholarship in a digital age*. Boulder, CO: Paradigm.

Pinker, S. (2010). *The cognitive niche: Coevolution of intelligence, sociality, and language*. Proceedings of the National Academy of Sciences. 107, 8893–8999.

Porat, M. (1977). *The information economy*. Washington, DC: US Department of Commerce.

Porter, M. E. (1992). Capital disadvantage: America's failing capital investment system. *Harvard Business Review*, September–October, 65–82.

Poulantzas, N. (1982). On social classes. In A. Giddens, & D. Held (Eds.), *Classes, power, and conflict* (pp. 101–111). Berkeley, CA: University of California Press. (Original work published 1973).

Rajan, K. S. (2003). Genomic capital: Public cultures and market logics of corporate biotechnology. *Science as Culture, 12*(1), 87–121.

Readings, B. (1996). *The university in ruins*. Cambridge, MA: Harvard University Press.

Resnick, S. A., & Wolff, R. D. (1987). *Knowledge and class. A Marxian critique of political economy*. Chicago, IL: University of Chicago Press.

Roberts, P., & Peters, M.A. (2008). *Neoliberalism, scholarship and intellectual life*. Rotterdam, the Netherlands: Sense Publishers.

Rose, N. (2007). *The politics of life itself: Biomedicine, power, and subjectivity in the twenty-first century*. Princeton, NJ: Princeton University Press.

Samuels, B. (2010b). Student loans: the new big bubble. *The Huffington Post*, February 24. Retrieved from http://www.huffingtonpost.com/bob-samuels/student-loans-the-new-big_b_475125.html

Schuchardt, K., Pancerella, C., Rahn, L., Didier, B., Kodeboyina, D., Leahy, D., et al. (2007). Portal-based knowledge environment for collaborative science. *Concurrency Computation Practice and Experience, 19*(12), 1703–1716.

Sennett, R. (2006). *The culture of new capitalism.* New Haven, CT: Yale University Press.

Slevin, J. (2000). *The internet and society.* Malden, MA: Polity Press.

Susi, T., & Ziemke, T. (2001). Social cognition, artefacts, and stigmergy: A comparative analysis of theoretical frameworks for the understanding of artefact-mediated collaborative activity. *Cognitive Systems Research, 2*(4), 273–290.

Terranova, T. (2000). Free labour: Producing culture for the digital economy. *Social Text, 18*(2), 33–57.

Tett, G. (2009). *Fool's gold: How unrestrained freed corrupted a dream, shattered global markets and unleashed a catastrophe.* London, United Kingdom: Little, Brown.

Thrift, N. (2005). *Knowing capitalism: Theory, culture and society.* London, United Kingdom: Sage.

Toffler, A. (1980). *The third wave.* New York, NY: Bantam Books.

United Nations. (2008). *The creative economy report.* Retrieved from http://www.unctad.org/en/docs/ditc20082cer_en.pdf

von Hippel, E., & von Krogh, G. (2003). Open source software and the "private-collective" innovation model: Issues for organization science. *Organization Science, 14*(2), 209–223.

Wagner, C. (2008), *The new invisible college: Science for development.* Washington, DC: The Brookings Press.

Wark, M. (2004). *A hacker manifesto. Version 4.0. subsol.* Retrieved from http://subsol.c3.hu/subsol 2/contributors0/warktext.html

Whalen, C. J. (2002). Money-manager capitalism: Still here, but not quite as expected. *Economic Issues, 36*(2), 401–406.

World Bank, The. (1998). *World development report: Knowledge for development.* Oxford, United Kingdom: Oxford University Press.

Chapter 10

'Openness' and the Global Knowledge Commons
An Emerging Mode of Social Production for Education and Science

Michael A. Peters

Introduction

This chapter documents the potential for the open access (OA) of knowledge, information and debate to create a new public space and culture that could underpin education, democracy and the economy. The implication of this discussion of OA is that it could release the knowledge, creativity and research to develop highly skilled productive economies to the benefit of the many rather than the few. However, the developments in OA, which are documented below need to be balanced against the possibilities that the same technologies that enable OA can be used to generate economic crises, arbitrage the cost of skilled labour and de-skill knowledge based jobs across the globe. We are at point in history where the liberating potential of OA is finely balanced against a set of opposing forces.

On February 14, 2008, Harvard University's Faculty of Arts and Sciences adopted a policy that required faculty members to allow the university to make their scholarly articles available free online.[1] The new policy made Harvard the first university in the United States to mandate open access to its faculty members' research publications and marked the beginning of a new era that will encourage other U.S. universities and universities around the world to do the same. Open access means putting peer-reviewed scientific and scholarly literature on the internet, making it available free of charge and free of most copyright and licensing restrictions, and removing the barriers to serious research. Open access has already transformed the world of scholarship and its pace continues with major accord, statements and manifestos that record the commitment worldwide to the possibilities of open access to establish a global science and education commons, reinventing and reinvigorating the notion of the public sphere. Since the early 2000s major OA statements including Budapest in 2002 have multiplied and the movement has picked up momentum developing a clear political ethos. Harvard's adoption of the new policy follows hard on the heels of open access mandates passed by the National Institutes of Health (NIH) and the European Research Council (ERC). Open access, open publishing and open archiving of peer-reviewed journal articles, reports and shared scientific data bases is now building into an irreversible worldwide movement to establish a scientific and educational global public sphere. As universities around the world follow Harvard's lead and also innovate to make freely available learning materials through open archiving to anyone including students and faculty from developing and transition countries the movement also at the philosophical and political levels begins to extend and develop through technological affordances and political will the original concepts of freedom, self organization and public good that characterized civil society. Harvard's adoption of the open archiving mandate is similar in scope to the step taken by MIT to adopt OpenCourseWare (OCW) in 2001 and establish the institutional means to begin global sharing of open learning resources. These initiatives are emblematic of a myriad of new arrangements, foundations, and institutions that utilize Web 2.0 technologies and principles of new social media. They are part of emergent interlocking and overlapping *knowledge ecologies* that will determine the shape of learning, scholarly publishing, scientific collaboration and the future of the university challenging commercial publishing business models and raising deeper questions about learning, scientific and content development processes as well as practical questions of resourcing and sustainability.

The Ithaka Report, *University Publishing in a Digital Age* (2007) indicates that there have been massive changes in the creation, production and consumption of scholarly resources with the "creation of new formats made possible by digital technologies, ultimately allowing scholars to work in deeply integrated electronic research and publishing environments that will enable real-time dissemination, collaboration, dynamically-updated content, and usage of new media" (p. 4). These changes in content creation and publication "alternative distribution models (Institutional repositories, pre-print servers, open access journals) have also arisen with the aim to broaden access, reduce costs, and enable open sharing of content" (p. 4).[2]

Open publishing, open archiving, open education are essential parts of the wider movement of Open Access (OA) that builds on the nested and evolving convergences of open source, open access and open science, and also emblematic of a set of still wider political and economic changes that ushers in a mode of social production as a resistant and alternative to the neoliberal global economy that has proved both fragile and volatile as the ongoing effects of 2007-8 world recession, credit and banking crisis demonstrates so well.

The present era can be called the 'open' era (open source, open systems, open standards, open archives, open everything) just as the 1990s were called the 'electronic' decade (e-text, e-learning, e-commerce, e-governance) (Materu, 2004). And yet it is more than just a 'decade' that follows the electronic innovations of the 1990s: it is a change of philosophy, ethos and practices, a set of interrelated and complex changes that transforms markets and the mode of production, issuing in a new collection of values based on openness, an ethic of participation and deepening of peer-to-peer collaboration. In the 'Postscript' to *Building Knowledge Cultures: Education and Development in the Age of Knowledge Capitalism* we made the argument that

> there has been a shift from an underlying metaphysics of production—a 'productionist' metaphysics—to a metaphysics of consumption and we must now come to understand the new logics and different patterns of cultural consumption in the areas of new media where symbolic analysis becomes a habitual and daily activity. Here the interlocking sets of enhanced mobility of capital, services, and ideas, and the new logics of consumption become all important. These new communicational practices and cross-border flows cannot be effectively policed. More provocatively we might argue, the global informational commons is an emerging infrastructure for the emergence of a civil society still yet unborn. (Peters & Besley, 2006, p. 186)

In the Postscript we also emphasized the link of this new logic of consumption to a classical concept of freedom as an essential aspect for transforming digital network practices into knowledge cultures and we commented upon the political economy of information and its eco-cybernetic rationalities that accompany an informational global capitalism comprised of new multinational information utilities that threaten to privatize and commercialize knowledge and monopolize the new knowledge spaces. These info-utilities based on systems-scale economies are more dangerous than the economies of scale that characterized industrial capitalism and are clearly capable of colonizing the emergent ecology of info-social networks preventing the development of knowledge cultures based on non-proprietary modes of knowledge production and exchange.

This chapter builds on these insights and makes the argument for the emergent paradigm of open education (OE) and open science (OS). The first term was used in the phrase "open educational resources" and came into use at a conference hosted by UNESCO in 2002 that defined as "the open provision of educational resources, enabled by information and communication technologies, for consultation, use and adaptation by a community of users for noncommercial purposes." As the OECD report (2007, pp. 30–31) comments "open educational resources are digitised materials offered freely and openly for educators, students and self-learners to use and reuse for teaching, learning and research".

While this is a useful definition I prefer to systematically relate the notion of open education to "open knowledge production systems" as a basis for creating, building and nurturing "knowledge cultures," a term that serves as a critique of the knowledge economy/knowledge society distinction (Peters & Besley, 2006). This kind of analysis allows a better analysis of the new political economy and emerging paradigm of "social production" of which open education and open science is a part.

This chapter first plots the dimensions of the emerging paradigm of *open education* by discussing the idea of open science in relation to an emerging global knowledge commons. It then explores the relationship between open science, the public domain and an emerging global knowledge commons, before making some concluding observations.

Open Courseware

The Cape Town Open Education Declaration subtitled 'Unlocking the promise of open educational resources' arose from a meeting convened in September 2007 declaring: "We are on the cusp of a global revolution in teaching and learning. Educators worldwide are developing a vast pool of educational resources on the Internet, open and free for all to use." The declaration goes on to argue:

'OPENNESS' AND THE GLOBAL KNOWLEDGE COMMONS

> This emerging open education movement combines the established tradition of sharing good ideas with fellow educators and the collaborative, interactive culture of the Internet. It is built on the belief that everyone should have the freedom to use, customize, improve and redistribute educational resources without constraint. Educators, learners and others who share this belief are gathering together as part of a worldwide effort to make education both more accessible and more effective.

The Declaration states that open education "is not limited to just open educational resources...[but] also draws upon open technologies that facilitate collaborative, flexible learning and the open sharing of teaching practices that empower educators to benefit from the best ideas of their colleagues." It goes on to provides a statement based on a three-pronged strategy designed to support "open educational technology, open sharing of teaching practices and other approaches that promote the broader cause of open education".[3]

'Open education' has emerged strongly as a new mode of social production in the global knowledge commons. Several major reports have documented existing developments and new tools and technologies, heralded the utopian promise of "openness" in global education extolling its virtues of shared commons-based peer-production and analyzed the ways in which it contributes to skill formation, innovation and economic development. In 2007 three substantial reports were released that reviewed open education as a movement and assessed its benefits: The OECD's (2007) *Giving Knowledge for Free: The Emergence Of Open Educational Resources*;[4] Open e-Learning Content Observatory Services (OLCOS) project and report entitled *Open Educational Practices and Resources*;[5] *A Review of the Open Educational Resources (OER) Movement: Achievements, Challenges, and New Opportunities* (Eds. Atkins, Brown, & Hammond, 2007), a report to The William and Flora Hewlett Foundation.[6] These three reports share similar emphases each focusing on 'openness' and the promise of the new technologies and their educational benefits.

The Executive Summary gives us a flavor of the potential of OE[7] and the utopian educational promise that graces these three reports:

> An apparently extraordinary trend is emerging. Although learning resources are often considered as key intellectual property in a competitive higher education world, more and more institutions and individuals are sharing digital learning resources over the Internet openly and without cost, as open educational resources (OER). (p. 9)

The report then concerns itself with the following questions: What are open educational resources? Who is using and producing OER and how much? Why are people sharing for free? What are the provisions for copyright and open licences? How can OER projects be sustained in the long run?

In asking this question, we should consider not only the possibilities for collaborative interaction and learning that the technology now affords but also the downsides. The reports, it might be argued, are too wedded to a technological account of open education and to an engineering notion of information that blind them to the criticisms that have been and can be mounted against various conceptions of "openness," "information" and the cybernetic society based upon it. Thy also might be criticized for not recognizing the problem of *structured ignorance* "information overload," "misinformation," and "disinformation" that accompanies the commercial exploitation of edutainment technologies (Goodman, 1986), the lack of context for entertaining claims for open education in order to understand of fundamental changes to liberal political economy; and the relation of OE to traditional goals of education policy to notions of freedom, equality, access and distribution of public goods.

Open Science, the Public Domain and the Global Knowledge Commons: Declarations and Manifestos

Open science and open education, then, are part of the world wide open access (OA) movement that makes digital content freely available and focuses on peer reviewed academic journals extending the historic principles of peer review as the basis of the global knowledge commons.[8] Increasingly public funding agencies require open access to publicly funded research and universities and other knowledge institutions are encouraged to deposit all journal article, dissertations and theses in their own OA repository. Peter Suber, the philosopher, commentator and archivist for open access provides a comprehensive timeline defines OA as "Open-access (OA) literature is digital, online, free of charge, and free of most copyright and licensing restrictions".[9] Clearly, OA is bigger than *access* including *grey literature, open data, social software, free culture,* and *digital libraries and repositories.* In fact, one could argue that open science is a direct descendant of the enterprise of peer reviewed science strongly wedded to concepts of civil society as it developed institutionally in the late seventeenth and eighteenth centuries.

Open Access, the Public Sphere and Civil Society

The concept of the public sphere is closely related to the emergence of the concept of "civil society" as a space of open communication and social self-organization oriented to the public good. The modern form took shape in the seventeenth century largely through the development of a series of interrelated knowledge institutions including the birth of learned societies, the development of the modern research university, the research library, the museum of natural history, and the research laboratory that formed a knowledge network. While the earliest societies, some thirty of them, were established in the period 1323–1599 overwhelmingly in Italy (19 of 30), but also in France, England, Ireland, Scotland and Spain, a further forty-three societies were established in the period 1600 to 1699 again predominantly in Europe (mostly Italy) with some societies being founded in Germany. It was during this period the Royal Society of London was established in 1660 strongly influenced by the philosophy of Francis Bacon especially "experimentall learning" developed in his *The New Atlantis*. This was the birth of experimental science in England. Elias Ashmole established the Ashmolean Museum as a scientific institution at the University of Oxford during the period 1679 and 1683 housed the first chemical laboratory in the UK. The Royal Society known as the "invisible college" started as a group of some twelve "scientists" including John Wilkins, Robert Hooke, Christopher Wren, William Petty and Robert Boyle who met regularly in London from 1645 onwards, forming a "College for the Promoting of Physico-Mathematical Experimental Learning," and was later granted a Royal charter by King Charles II in 1662 for "the improvement of natural knowledge." Early meetings were almost always devoted to experiments.

The history of civil society as related to a public sphere develops from diverse sources in works of Locke, Ferguson, Rousseau and Hegel that harked back to the idea of open communication among free citizens in the medieval city as a basis for decisions about how to pursue the public good. In the pragmatist tradition Dewey (1927) argued for the potential of reason through industrial media defending a version of his open inquiry based on the scientific community and Peirce (1878) argued that the formation of consensus on the basis of openness was the best guarantee of scientific truth, a position not entirely different from Habermas's (1962) use of the public sphere as a means to theorize democracy and the emancipatory potential of a meta-discourse ("the ideal speech community") where claims can be discussed rationally in the absence of force or any form of coercion and where only the force of argumentation alone is compelling. This is to draw a strong connection between civil society and the use of public reason which critically depends on access to education as a means of equalizing speaking and acting chances within a democracy (Calhoun, 1992). As Habermas (1992, p. 367): 'The core of civil society comprises a network of associations that institutionalizes problem-solving discourses on questions of general interest inside the framework of organized public spheres.' This model is best exemplified I would argue in the notion of the scientific community that is based on free and open inquiry and norms of peer review, collaboration, and cooperation in the name of knowledge as a public good and public good science.

The notion of open science is relatively recent nomenclature. As I have previously argued (Peters, 2010d, p. 15):

> 'Open science' is a term that is being used in the literature to designate a form of science based on open source models or that utilizes principles of open access, open archiving and open publishing to promote scientific communication. Open science increasingly also refers to the open governance and more democratized engagement and control of science by scientists and other users and stakeholders. Sometimes other terms are used to refer to the same or similar conceptions of science—'wiki science' and 'science 2.0'—that focus on 'technologies of openness' that not only promote more effective forms of scientific communication but also increasingly the sharing of large data bases ('linked data') and 'cloud computing'.

The Science Commons dedicated to making the Web work for science made the following recommendations on Open Science in 2008:

> *Open Access to Literature from Funded Research* By "open access" to this literature, we mean that it should be on the internet in digital form, with permission granted in advance to users to "read, download, copy, distribute, print, search, or link to the full texts of articles, crawl them for indexing, pass them as data to software, or use them for any other lawful purpose, without financial, legal, or technical barriers other than those inseparable from gaining access to the internet itself."
>
> *Data from Funded Research in the Public Domain* Research data, data sets, databases, and protocols should be in the public domain. This status ensures the ability to freely distribute, copy, re-format, and integrate data from research into new

research, ensuring that as new technologies are developed that researchers can apply those technologies without legal barriers. Scientific traditions of citation, attribution, and acknowledgment should be cultivated in norms.

Access to Research Tools from Funded Research By "access" to research tools, we mean that the materials necessary to replicate funded research—cell lines, model animals, DNA tools, reagents, and more, should be described in digital formats, made available under standard terms of use or contracts, with infrastructure or resources to fulfill requests to qualified scientists, and with full credit provided to the scientist who created the tools.

Invest in Open Cyberinfrastructure Data without structure and annotation is a lost opportunity. Research data should flow into an open, public, and extensible infrastructure that supports its recombination and reconfiguration into computer models, its searchability by search engines, and its use by both scientists and the taxpaying public. This infrastructure should be treated as an essential public good.[10]

The growing interconnectedness of the Web has also passed into a new phase that Tim Berners-Lee calls 'linked data', an aspect of the 'semantic web' used to describe a method of exposing, sharing, and connecting data.[11] Science is traditionally an open endeavor where the system of peer review is the core practice that anticipates the mode of social production.

Benkler and Nissenbaum (2006, p. 394) emphasize a form of social production that is facilitated by an infrastructure to provide collective knowledge goods:

> Commons-based peer production is a socio-economic system of production that is emerging in the digitally networked environment. Facilitated by the technical infrastructure of the Internet, the hallmark of this socio-technical system is collaboration among large groups of individuals, sometimes in the order of tens or even hundreds of thousands, who cooperate effectively to provide information, knowledge or cultural goods without relying on either market pricing or managerial hierarchies to coordinate their common enterprise.

Benkler (2006) indicates that a set of related changes in the information technologies entailing new social practices of production has fundamentally changed how we make and exchange information, knowledge, and culture, and he envisages these newly emerging social practices as constituting a new information environment that gives individuals the freedom to take a more active role in the construction of public information and culture.

Benkler's view can be seen to belong to the broader tradition of thought that theorizes the co-production of public goods through newly enabled forms of "community" that are non-constraining and occur without central planning or the agency of the State.

The potential for Open Access to bring out a new educational political and economic culture is clearly articulated in the Public Domain Manifesto (2010) begins with a reference to James Boyle:

> Our markets, our democracy, our science, our traditions of free speech, and our art all depend more heavily on a Public Domain of freely available material than they do on the informational material that is covered by property rights. The Public Domain is not some gummy residue left behind when all the good stuff has been covered by property law. The Public Domain is the place we quarry the building blocks of our culture. It is, in fact, the majority of our culture. (James Boyle, *The Public Domain*, p. 40f, 2008)

The manifesto defines the public domain "the wealth of information that is free from the barriers to access or reuse usually associated with copyright protection, either because it is free from any copyright protection or because the right holders have decided to remove these barriers." It goes on to describe the role and social and economic advantages of the public domain insisting on its status as a cultural right:

> It is the basis of our self-understanding as expressed by our shared knowledge and culture. It is the raw material from which new knowledge is derived and new cultural works are created. The Public Domain acts as a protective mechanism that ensures that this raw material is available at its cost of reproduction—close to zero—and that all members of society can build upon it. Having a healthy and thriving Public Domain is essential to the social and economic well-being of our societies. The Public Domain plays a capital role in the fields of education, science, cultural heritage and public sector information. A healthy and thriving Public Domain is one of the prerequisites for ensuring that the principles of Article 27 (1) of the Universal Declaration of Human Rights ('Everyone has the right freely to participate in the cultural life of the community, to enjoy the arts and to share in scientific advancement and its benefits.') can be enjoyed by everyone around the world.[12]

Concluding Observations

In this chapter I have analyzed and argued for the "openness" that characterizes emergent global knowledge commons exemplified in the establishment and rapid growth of open education and open science. I have been more concerned to make the case for open education and open science and I have not had the space to relate these issues to the wider historical context and political economy in any systematic way. It is clear that openness has played central role in the history and philosophy of the public good in the developing tradition in liberal politics of the civil society. I have tried to make this line of argument credible and sketched aspects of its history but a more comprehensive approach would require a critical review of the defense of liberal society and of the ideological nature of the "open society" as proposed by Karl Popper, Friedrich von Hayek and George Soros—the dominant view that prevailed in the post-War period. Such a review would need to contextualize Popper in era of the Cold War against the background of state phobia of late 1940s, the rise of neoliberalism in Germany, France and the US, and focus on Popper's links to Hayek and the Mont Perelin Society. This kind of critical intellectual history would bring out both the differences and dangers of different conceptions of "openness", the distinction between open society and open democracy on the one hand versus open markets on the other. It would also plot the rise of the "information utility" and new forms of "information imperialism" within knowledge capitalism. Clearly, there is a sense where criticisms of the liberal defense of openness also point to the limitations of liberal political economy in regard to questions of "open governance" in an era of globalization, the state's and the corporation's massive new powers of surveillance and problems of numerical identity and the digital self. Perhaps most importantly, the production and consumption of global public knowledge goods are engaged in a fierce struggle against the imposition of intellectual property rights, the privatization of education and the monopolization of information and knowledge.

Notes

1   This chapter is based on a paper originally presented at the Economic and Social Research Council (ERSC, UK) Seminar Series on 'Education and the Knowledge Economy', University of Bath, March 6–7, 2008.

2   The Association of College and Research Libraries (ACRL) recently released their research agenda for scholarly publishing around eight themes: The impact and implications of cyberinfrastructure; Changing organizational models; How scholars work; Authorship and scholarly publishing; Value and value metrics of scholarly communications; Adoptions of successful innovations; Preservation of critical mate-

rial Public policy and legal matters. See http://www.acrl.ala.org/scresearch agenda/index.php?title=Main_Page.
3   The full declaration can be found at http://www.capetowndeclaration.org/read-the-declaration.
4   Available electronically at http://www.oecd.org/document/41/0,3343,en_2649_201185_38659497_1_1_1_1,00.html.
5   Available at http://www.olcos.org/cms/upload/docs/olcos_roadmap.pdf.
6   Available at http://www.oerderves.org/wp-content/uploads/2007/03/a-review-of-the-open-educational-resources-oer-movement_final.pdf.
7   I prefer the term OE to OER because it embraces the notion of *practices* as well as the notion of sharing educational resources and also because it gels with open source, open access, and open science (as well as open innovation).
8   The world of freely accessible, open and collaborative digital knowledge continues to expand. See for instance, Scientific Commons: http://en.scientificcommons.org/
9   See http://www.earlham.edu/~peters/fos/overview.htm.
10 See http://sciencecommons.org/wpcontent/uploads/esof_recommendations_one page _medres.pdf.
11 See the Web Design Issues Note by Berners-Lee at http://www.w3.org/ DesignIssues/LinkedData.html; see the whitepaper at http://virtuoso.openlinksw.com/ Whitepapers/html/VirtLinkedDataDeployment.html; and Berners-Lee on the next Web at TED (video) at http://www.ted.com/index. php/talks/tim_berners_lee_on_ the_next_web.html.
12 See http://www.publicdomainmanifesto.org/manifesto.

References

Benkler, Y. (2003). *Freedom in the commons: Towards a political economy of information.* Retrieved from http://www.law.duke.edu/shell/cite.pl?52+Duke+L.+J.+1245.

Benkler, Y. (2006). *The wealth of networks: How social production transforms markets and freedom.* New Haven, CT: Yale University Press.

Benkler, Y. (2008). Educating for participation in the networked environment: Symposium: The wealth of networks. *Policy Futures in Education, 6*(2), 152–175.

Benkler, Y., & Nissenbaum, H. (2006). Commons-based peer production and virtue. *The Journal of Political Philosophy, 14*(4), 394–419.

Boyle, J. (1997). *A politics of intellectual property: Environmentalism for the net?* Retrieved from http://www.james-boyle.com/

Calhoun, C. (Ed.). (1992). *Habermas and the public sphere.* Cambridge, MA: MIT Press.

Dewey, J. (1927). *The public and its problems.* Columbus, OH: Ohio State University Press.

Easthope, G. (1975). *Community, hierarchy and open education.* London, United Kingdom: Routledge.

Flanagan, H., & Nissenbaum, H. (2005). *Embodying values in technology: Theory and practice* (Draft). Retrieved from http://www.nyu.edu/projects/nissenbaum/papers/Nissenbaum-VID.4-25.pdf.

Goodman, P. (1986). *Amusing ourselves to death: Public discourse in the age of show business.* Harmondsworth, United Kingdom: Penguin.

Habermas, J. (1991). *The structural transformation of the bourgeois public sphere: An inquiry into a category of bourgeois society* (T. Burger, Trans.). Cambridge, MA: MIT Press. (Original work published 1962)

Habermas, J. (1992). *Between facts and norms.* Cambridge, MA: MIT Press.

Kapitkze, C., & Peters, M. A. (2007). *Global knowledge cultures.* Rotterdam, the Netherlands: Sense Publishers.

Lessig, L. (2001). *Code: And other laws of cyberspace.* New York, NY: Basic Books.

Lessig, L. (2002). *The future of ideas: The fate of the commons in a connected world.* New York, NY: Random House.

Lessig, L. (2004). *Free culture: How big media uses technology and the law to lock down culture and control creativity.* New York, NY: Penguin.

Materu, P. (2004). *Open source courseware: A baseline study.* Washington, DC: The World Bank.

Nyberg, D. (Ed.). (1975). *The philosophy of open education.* London, United Kingdom: Routledge.

Peirce, C. S. (1992). *The essential Peirce: Selected philosophical writings, 1867–1893.* Bloomington, IL: Indiana University Press. (Original work published 1878)

Peltonen, M. (Ed.). (1996). *The Cambridge companion to Bacon.* Cambridge, United Kingdom: Cambridge University Press.

Peters, M. A. (1994). The new science policy regime in New Zealand: A review and critique. *New Zealand Sociology, 9*(2), 317–348.

Peters, M. A. (2004). Towards philosophy of technology in education: Mapping the field. In J. Weiss, J. Nolan, J. Hunsinger, & P. Trifonas (Eds.), *The international handbook of virtual learning environments* (pp. 95–116). Dordrecht, the Netherlands: Springer.

Peters, M. A. (2006). The rise of global science and the emerging political economy of international research collaborations. *European Journal of Education: Research, Development and Policies 41*(2), 225-244. doi:10.1111/j.1465-3435.2006.00257.x

Peters, M. A. (2007a). *Knowledge economy, development and the future of higher education: Reclaiming the cultural mission.* Rotterdam, the Netherlands: Sense Publishers.

Peters, M. A. (2007b). Opening the book: From the closed to the open text. *The International Journal of the Book, 5*(1), 77–84. Retrieved from http://ijb.cgpublisher.com/product/pub.27/prod.199

Peters, M. A. (2010a). On the philosophy of open science. *Review of Contemporary Philosophy, 9*, 15–53.

Peters, M. A. (2010b). Knowledge economy and scientific communication: Emerging paradigms of 'open knowledge production' and 'open education'. In M. Simons, M.

Olssen, & M. A. Peters (Eds.), *Re-reading education policies: A handbook studying the policy agenda of the twenty-first century* (pp. 293–318). Rotterdam, the Netherlands: Sense.

Peters, M. A. (2010c). Open education and the open science economy. *Yearbook of the National Society for the Study of Education, 108*(2), 203–225.

Peters, M. A. (2010d). Open works, open cultures, and open learning systems. In T. W. Lukes & J. Hunsinger (Eds.), *Putting knowledge to work and letting information play: The center for digital discourse and culture*, (pp. 75–99). Blacksburg, VA: Virginia Tech, Center for Digital Discourse and Culture.

Peters, M. A. (2011). Manifesto for education in the age of cognitive capitalism: Freedom, creativity and culture. In C. McCarthy (Ed.), *New times: Making sense of critical/cultural theory in a digital age* (pp. 349-3
64). New York, NY: Peter Lang.

Peters, M. A., & Besley, T. (A.C.). (2006). *Building knowledge cultures: Education and development in the age of knowledge capitalism*. Lanham, MD: Rowman & Littlefield.

Peters, M. A., & Britez, R. (Eds.). (2008). *Open education and education for openness*. Rotterdam, the Netherlands: Sense Publishers.

Brown, L., Griffiths, R., & Rascoff, M. (2007). University publishing in a digital age (The Ithaka Report). *Journal of Electronic Publishing, 10*(3). doi: http://dx.doi.org/10.3998/3336451.0010.301

Settle, T., Javie, I. C., & Agassi, J. (1974). Towards a theory of openness to criticism. *Philosophy of the Social Sciences, 4,* 83—90. Retrieved from http://pos.sagepub.com/content/32/2/240.full.pdf+html

Willenski, J. (2006). *The access principle: The case for open access to research and scholarship*. Cambridge, MA: MIT Press.

Chapter 11

Open Education and the Open Science Economy

Michael A. Peters

Introduction

Openness as a complex code word for a variety of digital trends and movements has emerged as an alternative mode of 'social production' based on the growing and overlapping complexities of open source, open access, open archiving, open publishing and open science.[1] Openness in this sense refers to open source models of scientific communication, knowledge distribution and educational development although it has a number of deeper registers that refer more widely to government ('open government'), society ('open society'), economy (open economy') and even psychology (openness as one of the five traits of personality theory). The concept and evolving set of practices has profound consequences for education at all levels. 'Openness' has become a leading source of innovation in the world global digital economy increasingly adopted by world governments, international agencies and multinationals as well as leading educational institutions as a means of promoting scientific inquiry and international collaboration. It is clear that the Free Software and 'open source' movements constitute a radical non-propertarian (i.e., social) alternative to traditional methods of text and symbolic production, distribution, archiving, access and dissemination. This alternative non-proprietary model of cultural production and exchange threatens traditional models of intellectual property and it challenges the major legal and institutional means such as copyright currently used to restrict creativity, innovation and the free exchange of ideas.

It is the argument of the chapter that the openness movement with its reinforcing structure of overlapping networks of production, access, publishing, archiving, and distribution provide an emerging architecture of alterative educational globalization not wedded to existing neoliberal forms. The open education movement and paradigm has arrived: it emerges from a complex historical background and its futures are intimately tied not only to open source, open access and open publishing movements but also to the concept of the 'open society' itself which has multiple, contradictory and contested meanings. This chapter first theorizes the development and significance of 'open education' by reference to the Open University, OpenCourseWare (OCW) and open access movements. The chapter takes this line of argument further arguing for a conception of 'open science economy' which involves strategic international research collaborations and provides an empirical and conceptual link between university science and the global knowledge economy.

MIT was one of the first universities to introduce OCW, announcing its intention in the *New York Times* in 2001. It formed the OpenCourseWare Consortium in 2005 and by 2007 published virtually all its courses online.[2] The OCW Consortium advertises itself in the following terms emphasizing one aspect of alternative educational globalization—the distribution and free exchange of course content and also potentially a major source for the internationalization of curriculum:

> An OpenCourseWare is a free and open digital publication of high quality educational materials, organized as courses. The OpenCourseWare Consortium is a collaboration of more than 200 higher education institutions and associated organizations from around the world creating a broad and deep body of open educational content using a shared model. The mission of the OpenCourseWare Consortium is to advance education and empower people worldwide through opencourseware. (http://videolectures.net/ocwc/)

On February 14, 2008, Harvard University adopted a policy that requires faculty members to allow the university to make their scholarly articles available free online. The new policy makes Harvard the first university in the United States to *mandate* open access to its faculty members' research publications and marks the beginning of a new era that will encourage other U.S. universities to do the same. The Harvard policy is a move to disseminate faculty research and scholarship and to give the University a worldwide license to make each faculty member's scholarly articles available globally. In effect the new policy establishes a global scholarly publishing system that allows scholars to use and distribute their own work giving them greater control over these aspects of scholarly production. Harvard's open-access repository makes scholarly research available worldwide for free while the faculty member retains the copyright of the article.

Harvard University is not alone, both the National Institutes of Health (NIH) and the European Research Council have recently adopted similar open access mandates putting pressure on other government agencies in the US and governments abroad to do the same. In a clear sense this is the beginning of a mega-trend that will make intellectual research and teaching resources freely available worldwide and to encourage forms of education based on open source, open access, open archiving and open publishing models as well as support for burgeoning initiatives like the Creative Commons project,[3] the P2P Foundation,[4] the Public Knowledge Project[5] that supports Open Journal Systems, and the Open Knowledge Foundation,[6] to mention only a few.

While I focus on higher education in this context it does not take much imagination to see the ramifications for the extension of the principles and architectures to K–12 and, indeed, to all levels of education from pre-school to university. What I call the 'open education' paradigm (Peters & Britez, 2009) has strong connections to and is reinforced by what I call the 'open science economy', a concept I tentatively and experimentally seek both to develop and explain in the second part of the chapter by investigating the political economy of global science and the global economics of science. The chapter begins with an account of the emergence of the paradigm of open education by reference to four major reports.

The Emergence of the *Open Education* Paradigm

What I now called simply 'open education' has emerged strongly as a new paradigm of social production in the global knowledge economy. In the last year or so four major reports have documented existing developments and new tools and technologies, heralded the utopian promise of 'openness' in global education extolling its virtues of shared commons-based peer-production and analyzed the ways in which it contributes to skill formation, innovation and economic development.

The powerful Washington-based Committee for Economic Development[7] released its report *Open Standards, Open Source, and Open Innovation: Harnessing the Benefits of Openness*[8] in April 2006 examining the phenomenon of 'openness' in the context of today's digital economy highlighting the key attributes of accessibility, responsiveness, and creativity and commenting on the relevance of three areas of open standards, open-source software, and open innovation. The report by the Digital Connections Council of the Committee for Economic Development built on three earlier reports dating from 2001: *The Digital Economy and Economic Growth* (2001), *Digital Economy: Promoting Competition, Innovation, and Opportunity* (2001) and *Promoting Innovation and Economic Growth: The Special Problem of Digital Intellectual Property* (2004).[9] These reports emphasized intellectual property issues involved with file-sharing and peer-to-peer networks and the way that 'heavy-handed enforcement of intellectual property rules and reliance on business practices designed for the trade of physical goods can stifle the collaboration and innovation that is vital to the growth of the digital economy'. What is perhaps of greatest interest in the present context is the emphasis in the new report on what they call 'open innovation'— new collaborative models of open innovation, originating outside the firm, that results in an 'architecture of participation'[10] and to a lesser extent their definition of 'openness'. This is what the report says about 'open innovation':

> Open innovation can be seen in the growing use of digital software tools tied to computer-controlled fabrication devices that allow users to design an object and then produce it physically. As the costs of these digital design tools decrease, users are able to innovate, breaking the model of manufacturers being the source of innovation and customers simply consuming them. The openness model, the antithesis of a "not invented here" attitude, encompasses not only manufacturers and users, but suppliers whose innovations should be welcomed by the companies they supply. (Executive Summary)

The report goes on to mention 'the extraordinary increase in "peer production" of digital information products' which are produced by individuals without any expectation of monetary gain and commenting that 'sophisticated commercial firms are harvesting the benefits of openness'. In this same context they mention the movement of 'open science' promoted by the National Institutes of Health (NIH) and the model of open courseware on which they comment:

> Advocates for more openness contend that openness will result in greater innovation than would be achieved by restricting access to information or allowing first creators to exert greater control over it. Such a belief in the value of tapping the collective wisdom is profoundly democratic.

As one can see this set of statements makes a string connection between firm innovation, open education and the emergence of the social mode of production (Benkler, 2006) which is based on the employment of social media and social networking as a means of freely exchanging ideas. In effect, the social mode of production names a new, third mode of production in the digitally networked environment that Benkler (2006) calls 'commons-based peer-production', to distinguish it from the property- and contract-based models of firms and markets. As he says, 'Its central characteristic is that groups of individuals successfully collaborate on large-scale projects following a diverse cluster of motivational drives and social signals, rather than either market prices or managerial commands' (Benkler, 2002, n.p.). Benkler explains 'why this mode has systematic advantages over markets and managerial hierarchies when the object of production is information or culture': first, it is better at identifying and assigning human capital to information and cultural production processes ('information opportunity cost') and second, 'there are substantial increasing returns to allow very larger clusters of potential contributors to interact with very large clusters of information resources in search of new projects and collaboration enterprises' (Benkler, 2002, n.p.).

In 2007 three substantial reports were released that reviewed open education as a movement and assessed its benefits: the OECD's (2007) *Giving Knowledge for Free: The Emergence of Open Educational Resources*;[11] Open e-Learning Content Observatory Services (OLCOS) project and report entitled *Open Educational Practices and Resources*;[12] *A Review of the Open Educational Resources (OER) Movement: Achievements, Challenges, and New Opportunities* (Eds. Atkins, Brown, & Hammond, 2007), a report to the William and Flora Hewlett Foundation.[13] These three reports share similar emphases each focusing on 'openness' and the promise of the new technologies and their educational benefits. The OECD report focuses on four questions:

- How can sustainable cost/benefit models for OER initiatives be developed?
- What are the intellectual property rights issues linked to OER initiatives?
- What are the incentives and barriers for universities and faculty staff to deliver their materials to OER initiatives?

- How can access and usefulness for the users of OER initiatives be improved? (pp. 3-4, Foreword)

The Executive Summary gives us a flavor of the potential of OE[14] and the utopian educational promise that graces these three reports:

> An apparently extraordinary trend is emerging. Although learning resources are often considered as key intellectual property in a competitive higher education world, more and more institutions and individuals are sharing digital learning resources over the Internet openly and without cost, as open educational resources (OER). (p. 9)

The report then concerns itself with the following questions: What are open educational resources? Who is using and producing OER and how much? Why are people sharing for free? What are the provisions for copyright and open licences? How can OER projects be sustained in the long run? Alongside a set of policy implications and recommendations.

The OLCOS report, by comparison, focuses on: Policies, institutional frameworks and business models; Open Access and open content repositories; and Laboratories of open educational practices and resources, warning against instituting open education within the dominant model:

> OER are understood to be an important element of policies that want to leverage education and lifelong learning for the knowledge economy and society. However, OLCOS emphasizes that it is crucial to also promote innovation and change in educational practices. In particular, OLCOS warns that delivering OER to the still dominant model of teacher centred knowledge transfer will have little effect on equipping teachers, students and workers with the competences, knowledge and skills to participate successfully in the knowledge economy and society. This report emphasises the need to foster open practices of teaching and learning that are informed by a competency-based educational framework. However, it is understood that a shift towards such practices will only happen in the longer term in a step-by-step process. Bringing about this shift will require targeted and sustained efforts by educational leaders at all levels. (p. 12)

In Chapter 4 'Competences for the Knowledge Society' the report opines 'priority must be given to open educational practices that involve students in active, constructive engagement with content, tools and services in the learning process, and promote learners' self-management, creativity and working in teams' (p. 37) and 'introduces the idea of value chains of open educational content which emerge when teachers and students re-use available content and make enriched and/or additional material (e.g., use cases, experiences, lessons learned, etc.) available again to a larger community of practice' (p. 37). The report defines a competency-focused, collaborative paradigm of learning and knowledge acquisition where 'priority is given to learning communities and development of knowledge and skills required for tackling and solving problems instead of subject-centred knowledge transfer'. For the purposes of this chapter and audience I quote further from the report:

> We believe that, to acquire the competences and skills for personal and professional achievement in the knowledge-based society, the learner's autonomy, personal mastery and self-direction must be acknowledged and innovative approaches implemented that foster self management, communication and team skills, and analytical, conceptual, creative and problem solving skills. However, there is of course a huge difference between identifying required competences and operationalising them for inclusion in the concrete practices of teaching and learning at different educational levels. (p. 39)

The report then lists the following skills of 'digital competence':

- Ability to search, collect and process (create, organise, distinguish relevant from irrelevant, subjective from objective, real from virtual) electronic information, data and concepts and to use them in a systematic way;
- Ability to use appropriate aids (presentations, graphs, charts, maps) to produce, present or understand complex information;
- Ability to access and search a website and to use internet-based services such as discussion fora and e-mail;
- Ability to use ICT to support critical thinking, creativity and innovation in different contexts at home, leisure and work. (p. 39)

The report to the William and Flora Hewlett Foundation is perhaps, the most comprehensive even although it follows similar lines of investigation to the others but frames the report in terms of Amartya Sen's work with the plan to develop 'a strategic international development initiative to expand people's substantive freedoms through the removal of "unfreedoms"'. What is impressive about this report is not only the inventory of open education projects (the incubation of high-quality specialized open resources) but also its attempt to conceptualize the issues and to move to a new understanding of openness in terms of an ethic of participation (and the design of 'open participatory learning infrastructure') that supports the role of technology in emphasizing the social nature of learning and its potential to address questions of the digital divide in developing countries.

There is much else that deserves attention in these reports. While they touch on conceptual issues to do with openness and document aspects of the contemporary movement of open educational resources they do not provide a history of 'openness' in education—it has a long, complex and significant history that influences conceptions of its wider purposes—or make the necessary theoretical links to the wider political literature (see Peters & Britez, 2009). The reports, it might be argued, are too wedded to a technological account of open education and to an engineering notion of information that blind them to the criticisms that have been and can be mounted against various conceptions of 'openness,' 'information' and the 'cybernetic society' based upon it. To see the force of these criticisms we need to understand something about the emerging political economy of global science and the economics of science.

The Political Economy of Global Science

The emerging political economy of global science is a significant factor influencing development of national systems of innovation, and economic, social and cultural development, with the rise of multinational actors and a new mix of corporate, private/public and community involvement. It is only since the 1960s with the development of research evaluation and increasing sophistication of bibliometrics that it has been possible to map the emerging economy of global science, at least on a comparative national and continental basis. The Science Citation Index provides bibliographic and citational information from 3,700 of the world's scientific and technical journals covering over one hundred disciplines. The expanded index available in an online version covers more than 5,800 journals. Comparable 'products' in the social sciences (SSCI) and humanities (A&HCI) cover, respectively, bibliographic information from 1,700 journals in fifty disciplines and 1,130 journals.

On a world scale it is now possible to get some idea of science distributions in terms of academic papers for the first time. An issue of the UIS Bulletin on Science and Technology Statistics (UNESCO 2005), published in collaboration with the *Institut National de la Recherche Scientifique*

(INRS) (Montréal, Canada), presents a bibliometric analysis of 20 years of world scientific production (1981-2000), as reflected by the publications indexed in the Science Citation Index (SCI). It indicates that

> In 2000 the SCI included a total of 584,982 papers, representing a 57.5% increase from 1981, when 371,346 papers were published worldwide. Authors with addresses in developed countries wrote 87.9% of the papers in 2000, a decrease from 93.6% in 1981. Developing countries, on the other hand, saw a steady increase in their share of scientific production: from 7.5% of world papers in 1981 to 17.1% in 2000.... Since 1981 the world map of publications changed significantly. North America lost the lead it had in 1996, and in 2000 produced 36.8% of the world total, a decrease from 41.4% in 1981. The opposite trend can be found in the European Union, which in 2000 published 40.2% of the world total, up from 32.8% in 1981. Japan went up from 6.9% to 10.7% in 2000. Collectively this 'triad' has therefore maintained its dominance, accounting for 81% of the world total of scientific publications in 2000, up from 72% in 1981.

While sub-Saharan African publications remained stable at around 1% of the world total, and the share of publications from the Arab States increased from 0.6% in 1981 to 0.9% in 2000, and the Central Eastern European share remained stable around 3% of the world total, both the Newly Industrialised Countries (NIC) in Asia (a group that includes China) and Latin America and the Caribbean (LAC) increased their share significantly, respectively, from 0.6% of the world total in 1981 to 4.2% in 2000 (with China accounting for 85% of the publications an increase from 63% in 1981), and 1.3% to 3.2% in LAC countries. The SCI covers biology, biomedicine, chemistry, clinical medicine, earth and space, engineering and technology, mathematics, and physics.

The UIS Bulletin concludes that the developed world share of publications has declined while developing regions (Asia and Latin America) have expanded and Africa has stagnated. There is also clear evidence that there has been considerable growth in international collaboration. These bibliometric measures present a biased view in the sense that they do not take into account book citations, important for the humanities and social sciences, and they tend to favor English as the global medium of communication. Nevertheless, used with caution, as the UNESCO publication suggests, they can reveal some insights through trends regarding aspects of scientific production at global level.

Britain's Chief Scientist David A. King (2004) provides an analysis of the output and outcomes from research investment over the past decade, to measure the quality of research on national scales and to set it in an international context, reveals the unevenness of world distribution of science and ascendancy of a group of 31 countries[15] that accounted for 'more than 98% of the world's highly cited papers, defined by Thomson ISI as the most cited 1% by field and year of publication. The world's remaining 162 countries contributed less than 2% in total' (p. 311). His analysis reveals the overwhelming dominance of the United States, whose share has declined recently, United Kingdom and Germany, and the fact that 'The nations with the most citations are pulling away from the rest of the world' (p. 311). He provides the following analysis:

> The countries occupying the top eight places in the science citation rank order...produced about 84.5% of the top 1% most cited publications between 1993 and 2001. The next nine countries produced 13%, and the final group share 2.5%. There is a stark disparity between the first and second divisions in the scientific impact of nations. Moreover, although my analysis includes only 31 of the world's 193 countries, these produce 97.5% of the world's most cited papers. (p. 314)

And King goes on to draw the following conclusion:

> The political implications of this last comparison are difficult to exaggerate. South Africa, at 29th place in my rank ordering, is the only African country on the list. The Islamic countries are only represented by Iran at 30th, despite the high GDP of many of them and the prominence of some individuals, such as Nobel prizewinners Abdus Salam (physics, 1979) and Ahmed Zewail (chemistry, 1999). (p. 314)

There are clear igns that architecture of global science is shifting especially with the huge investment in research and the consequent growth of scientific publications in Asia. Adams and Wilsdon (2006) report that China's spending on research has increased by more than 20% per year, reaching 1.3% of GDP in 2005 and making it third in the global league table in research expenditure after U.S. and Japan. Science budgets in India have increased by the same annual percentage, adding some 2.5 million IT, engineering and life sciences graduates, 650,000 postgraduates and 6,000 PhDs every year.

The U.S. National Science Board's (2008) publication *Research and Development: Essential Foundation for U.S. Competiveness in a Global Economy* charts the decline since 2005 of Federal and industry support for basic research which accounted for 18% ($62B) of the $340B U.S. research budget in current dollars in 2006. The report comments:

Federal obligations for academic research (both basic and applied) and especially in the current support for National Institutes of Health (NIH) (whose budget had previously doubled between the years 1998 to 2003) declined in real terms between 2004 and 2005 and are expected to decline further in 2006 and 2007. This is the first multiyear decline in Federal obligations for academic research since 1982.

The report also clearly shows the declining competiveness of U.S. science and technology: patents dropped from 55% in 1996 to 53% in 2005; and, 'Basic research articles published in peer-reviewed journals by authors from U.S. private industry peaked in 1995 and declined by 30% between 1995 and 2005.' The report goes on to say: 'The drop in physics publications was particularly dramatic: decreasing from nearly 1,000 publications in 1988 to 300 in 2005.' The loss in U.S. share and its decline of science and technology 'reflects the rapid rise in share by the East Asia-4 (comprising China, South Korea, Singapore, and Taiwan).'

The architecture of world science is changing rapidly. The U.S. needs a comprehensive strategy based on an understanding of the emergent globalization of science, the promotion of innovation through international collaboration and the global value chain, and the fostering of a world vision of open science that makes maximum use of Web 2.0 technologies, if it is to remain both competitive and responsive in the coming decades. The globalization of science that in part takes place through new global architectures that promote scientific communication and collaboration also in effect constitute one form of the globalization of education especially at the higher levels where PhD study takes place in the sciences as part of a scientific team contributing to a well defined problem. There is a series of connections in this respect between globalization of science and the ways that the new social media promotes and ethic of participation and collaboration, and the globalization of education that utilizes the same soft architectures to encourage learning in distributed environments.

The Economics of Open Science

The Argument Concerning Digital Knowledge Goods

Knowledge as an economic good defies traditional understandings of property and principles of exchange and closely conforms to the criteria for a public good. In this sense it has been described as non-rivalrous, barely excludable, and not transparent:

1. knowledge is non-rivalrous: the stock of knowledge is not depleted by use, and in this sense knowledge is not consumable; sharing with others, use, reuse and modification may indeed add rather than deplete value;
2. knowledge is barely excludable: it is difficult to exclude users and to force them to become buyers; it is difficult, if not impossible, to restrict distribution of goods that can be reproduced with no or little cost;
3. knowledge is not transparent: knowledge requires some experience of it before one discovers whether it is worthwhile, relevant or suited to a particular purpose.

Thus, knowledge at the ideation or immaterial stage (considered as belonging to the realm of pure ideas) operates expansively to defy the law of scarcity. It does not conform to the traditional criteria for an economic good, and the economics of knowledge is therefore not based on an understanding of those features that characterize property or exchange and cannot be based on economics as the science of the allocation of scarce public goods. As soon as knowledge becomes codified or written down or physically embedded in a system or process, then it can be made subject to copyright or patent and then may be treated and behave like other commodities.

In so far as digital information goods approximate pure thought or the ideational stage of knowledge, they conform to knowledge as a global public good and can be considered to escape traditional understandings of property and principles of exchange. This is even more the case when information through experimentation and hypothesis testing (the traditional methods of sciences) can be turned into 'justified true belief,' the three conditions logically necessary for knowledge. The classical account of Western knowledge is the source of traditional epistemology dating from Plato's conceptual investigations in the dialogue the *Theatetus* where Socrates considers a number of theories as to what knowledge is, the last being that knowledge is true belief that has been 'given an account of.' Epistemology normally draws the distinction between 'knowing how' and 'knowing that' (or propositional knowledge, i.e., that expressed in sentence, we would say today). It also considers counterexamples to the classical or three-cornered view of knowledge first suggested by Edmund Gettier in 1963.

In other words, digital information goods also undermine traditional economic assumptions of rivalry, excludability and transparency, as the knowledge economy is about creating intellectual capital rather than accumulating physical capital. Digital information goods differ from traditional goods in a number of ways:

1. Information goods, especially in digital forms, can be copied cheaply, so there is little or no cost in adding new users. Although production costs for information have been high, developments in desktop and just-in-time publishing, together with new forms of copying, archiving and content creation, have substantially lowered fixed costs.
2. Information and knowledge goods typically have an experiential and participatory element that increasingly requires the active co-production of the reader/writer, listener and viewer.
3. Digital information goods can be transported, broadcast or shared at low cost, which may approach free transmission across bulk communication networks.
4. Since digital information can be copied exactly and easily shared, it is never consumed (see Morris-Suzuki, 1997; Davis & Stack, 1997; Kelly, 1998; Varian, 1998).

This analysis summarizes a large and growing body of literature that demonstrates that the traditional law of scarcity that governs supply and demand does not apply to digital information goods in so far as they approach the status of pure thought or the ideation stage of production of science. This analysis provides an understanding of global information and knowledge goods and the way in which ideas do not lose their value (or are not depleted) when used but that sharing may enhance the value of an ideas leading to its refinement and development. Symbolic and cultural goods that take the form of information and knowledge global goods often as digital goods therefore exhibit a different mode of development (see Peters et al., 2009; Marginson et al., 2009; Peters, 2007; Peters & Besley, 2006).

Towards an Open Science Economy

The Mode of Open Production

Openness is a new mode of social production that has become a leading source of innovation in the world global digital economy and constitutes a radical non-propertarian alternative to traditional methods of text production, dissemination and distribution. In terms of a model of communication there has been a gradual shift from content to code in the openness, access, use, reuse and modification reflecting a radical personalization that has made these open characteristics and principles increasingly the basis of the cultural sphere. So open source and open access has been developed and applied in open publishing, open archiving, and open music constituting the hallmarks of 'open culture.' For some theorists, such as law professors Yochai Benkler and Larry Lessig, this symbolizes a new mode of social production and a form of cultural formation that represents an alternative to capitalist forms of globalization. As a number of economists have remarked (see the list above) this marks the emergence of global science and knowledge as a global public good that rest on an ethic of participation and collaboration based on the co-production and co-design of knowledge goods and services.

As one author expresses the point:

> The present decade can be called the 'open' decade (open source, open systems, open standards, open archives, open everything) just as the 1990s were called the 'electronic' decade (e-text, e-learning, e-commerce, e-governance). (Materu, 2004, p. 1)

And yet it is more than just a 'decade' that follows the electronic innovations of the 1990s; it is a change of philosophy and ethos, a set of interrelated and complex changes that transforms markets and the mode of production, ushering in a new collection of values based on openness, the ethic of participation and peer-to-peer collaboration.

New forms of freedom are occurring in the fundamental shift from an underlying metaphysics of production—a 'productionist' metaphysics—to a metaphysics of consumption as use, reuse and modification. New logics and different patterns of cultural consumption are appearing in the areas of new media where symbolic analysis becomes a habitual and daily activity. It is now a truism to argue that information is the vital element in a 'new' politics and economy that links space, knowledge and capital in networked practices. Freedom is an essential ingredient in this equation if these network practices develop or transform themselves into knowledge cultures.

The specific politics and eco-cybernetic rationalities that accompany an informational global capitalism comprised of new multinational edutainment agglomerations are clearly capable of colonizing the emergent ecology of public info-social networks and preventing the development of knowledge cultures based on non-proprietary modes of knowledge production and exchange.

OPEN EDUCATION AND THE OPEN SCIENCE ECONOMY

Complexity as an approach to knowledge and knowledge systems now recognizes both the development of global systems architectures in (tele)communications and information with the development of open knowledge production systems that increasingly rest not only on the establishment of new and better platforms (sometimes called Web 2.0), the semantic web, new search algorithms and processes of digitization. Social processes and policies that foster openness as an overriding value as evidenced in the growth of open source, open access and open education and their convergences that characterize global knowledge communities that transcend borders of the nation-state. I would argue that 'openness' seems also to suggest political transparency and the norms of open inquiry, indeed, even democracy itself as both the basis of the logic of inquiry and the dissemination of its results. In other words, certain institutional forms are required to promote the organization of knowledge which enhance its free flow, the mode of open criticism, testing and validation characteristic of science-based institutions, and the nonideological replication, trial and error ethos that typifies the scientific method consonant with an open community of inquiry.

The role of nonmarket and nonproprietary production promotes the emergence of a new information environment and networked economy that both depends upon and encourages great individual freedom, democratic participation, collaboration and interactivity. This 'promises to enable social production and exchange to play a much larger role, alongside property—and market based production, than they ever have in modern democracies' (Benkler, 2006. p. 3). Peer production of information, knowledge, and culture enabled by the emergence of free and open-source software permits the expansion of the social model production beyond software platform into every domain of information and cultural production.

Open knowledge production is based upon an incremental, decentralized (and asynchronous), and collaborative a development process that transcends the traditional proprietary market model. Commons-based peer production is based on free cooperation, not on the selling of one's labor in exchange of a wage, nor motivated primarily by profit or for the exchange value of the resulting product; it is managed through new modes of peer governance rather than traditional organizational hierarchies and it is an innovative application of copyright which creates an information commons and transcends the limitations attached to both the private (for-profit) and public (state-based) property forms).[16]

As the Ithaka Report *University Publishing in a Digital Age* (2008) reveals these broad initiatives in open source, open access, open publishing and open archiving are part of emerging knowledge ecologies that will determine the future of educational resources and scholarly publishing challenging commercial publishing business models and raising broader and deeper questions about content development processes as well as questions of resourcing and sustainability. The new digital technologies promise changes in creation, production and consumption of scholarly resources including the development of new formats allowing integrated electronic research and publishing environments that will enable real-time dissemination and dynamically updated content as well as alternative distribution models including institutional repositories, pre-print servers, open access journals, that will broaden access, reduce costs, and enable open sharing of content.

On February 14, 2008, Harvard University's Faculty of Arts and Sciences adopted a policy that requires faculty members to allow the university to make their scholarly articles available free online. The new policy makes Harvard the first university in the United States to mandate open access to its faculty members' research publications and marks the beginning of a new era that will encourage other US universities to do the same. Open access means 'putting peer-reviewed scientific and scholarly literature on the internet, making it available free of charge and free of most copyright and licensing restrictions, and removing the barriers to serious research.' As Lila Guterman reports in *The Chronicle of Higher Education News Blog:*

> Stuart M. Shieber, a professor of computer science at Harvard who proposed the new policy, said after the vote in a news release that the decision "should be a very powerful message to the academic community that we want and should have more control over how our work is used and disseminated.[17]

Open access has transformed the world of scholarship and since the early 2000s with major OA statements starting with Budapest in 2002 movement has picked up momentum and developed a clear political ethos. Harvard's adoption of the new policy follows hard on the heels of open access mandates passed within months of each other—the National Institutes of Health (NIH) and the European Research Council (ERC). As one blogger remarked: 'open archiving of peer-reviewed journal literature [is] now on an irreversible course of expansion' not only as US universities follow Harvard's lead but also as open archiving makes available learning material to anyone including students and faculty from developing and transition countries. Harvard's adoption of the open archiving mandate is similar in scope to the step taken by MIT to adopt OpenCourseWare (OCW) in 2001. These initiatives are part of new strategies to establish knowledge cultures that will determine the future of scholarly publishing, the form and content of educational resources, and therefore also the future of innovation and research in the digital global economy.

Open Science Economy

In the emergent science system five forces are structuring the twenty-first century (open) science system: networks, emergence, circulation, stickiness (place), and distribution (virtual).

The decline of the U.S. economy relative to those of the rest of the world is facilitating the strengthening of science elsewhere. An evolving multi-polar world economy is leading to multiple centres of science—the United States, the European Union, Japan, China, Russia and possibly India. The increasing wealth of several of these societies is enabling them to lure back many younger scientists trained abroad in the world's leading institutions. In particular, China is moving towards an integrated system of national innovation replacing state control with more enabling frameworks and focusing on improving the university and research systems. It is also stepping up the internationalization of research with collaborative networks across Europe, Japan and U.S. The predictions are that by the end of 2020 China will achieve more science and technological breakthroughs of great world influence, qualifying it to join the ranks of the world's most innovative countries. Some think that in twenty years global science will be driven by Indian scientists, with new interfaces in science and new rules, where new countries can contribute on an equal footing.

One thing is clear is the emergence of a globalized science system with the increasing globalization of research, science, engineering and technology. The growth of China, India and South Korea are changing the atlas of the world scientific knowledge system.

International research collaboration is becoming an important source of national comparative advantage and nations see the importance of tracking and analyzing global knowledge flows and transfers to determine national and regional collaborations. Increasingly, nation science administrations use of information technologies and bibliometrics in facilitating cross-border knowledge flows and also in analyzing citations, co-authorship, and collaborations and focus on the development of new metrics systems including webometrics for the measurement of research impacts, growth and distributions. What is even more marked is the increasing significance of new social networking and social media for Web 2.0 science and open-access publishing.

In this new 'open science economy' there are significant advantages of smallness both with the shift to international collaborative research and virtual organization of global science teams. Teams produce more papers and receive more citations (see Wuchty et al., 2007). Big science has built in irreversible constraints including bureaucratic, fragmented, communication difficulties, organization rigidities. Now science policy experts argue that excellence in science requires nimble, autonomous organizations—qualities more likely to be found in small research settings. Enhanced performance takes place through creation of several dozen small research organizations in interdisciplinary domains or in emerging fields. Small, flexible, specialized teams are seen to be the answer. Dozens of scientists who made significant advances did so in organizations with fewer than 50 full-time researchers. In the past decade Nobel prizes have been awarded to scientists for work done in relatively small settings: Günter Blobel (physiology or medicine), Ahmed Zewail (chemistry), Paul Greengard (physiology or medicine), Andrew Fire (physiology or medicine), Roderick MacKinnon (chemistry) and Gerhard Ertl (chemistry) (see Hollingsworth et al., 2008). Many economists draw attention to the development of small, flexible, specialized teams in regional centers ('clustering').

Alongside antion science systems a increasingly complex transnational science is occuring. New research partnerships that are no longer solely state and university-oriented are emerging. There is also spectacular growth of corporate multinational research especially in new materials, biotechnology (genetics), pharmaceutics, information technology—growth of private science with shifts in funding regimes from public to private, state to global, and big science to applied science, science to technology and technology transfer. In this context a new role for humanities, performing arts and social sciences as 'soft' sciences and technologies concerned with new international values, legalities, global civic cultures, knowledge measurement, management and PR—the so-called 'soft' programing architectures that encourage new forms of technology-led education on the basis of new architectures of participation and collaboration. There is also an emergence of global science and research organization and cultures—extra-national organizations, NGOs, UN, UNESCO, ESF and other international science-based organizations.

New models of open science are rapidly developing based on mode 2.0 with greater interdisciplinarity and 'flattening' of geocentric science centers and knowledge flows toward global teams. Correspondingly there is a reversal from close conduit peer review to open source public scrutiny and increased use of open source data analysis, management of large data bases, and sharing (bioinformatics). Science publishing has undergone a sea change with 'changes in creation, production and consumption of scholarly resources'—creation of new formats made possible by digital technologies, ultimately allowing scholars to work in deeply integrated electronic research and publishing environments that will enable real-time dissemination, collaboration, dynamically updated content, and usage of new media' and 'alternative distribution models (institutional repositories, pre-print servers, open access journals) have also arisen with the aim to broaden access, reduce costs, and enable open sharing of content' (Ithaka Report, 2007, p. 4).[18] The new models of open science are to some extent in opposition or conflict with expanded protection of IP. Open source initiatives have facilitated the development of new models of production and innovation. The public and nonprofit sectors have called for alternative approaches dedicated to public knowledge redistribution and dissemination. Now distributed peer-to-peer knowledge systems rival, the scope and quality of similar products produced by proprietary efforts where speed of diffusion of open source projects is an obvious advantage.The successful projects occur in both software and open source biology. Open access science has focused on making peer-reviewed, online research and scholarship freely accessible to a broader population (including digitized back issues). Open science demonstrates an "exemplar of a compound of 'private-collective' model of innovation" that contains elements of both proprietary and public models of knowledge production (Von Hippel & von Krogh, 2003). Rhoten & Powell (2007) asks 'does the expansion of a patenting culture undermine the norms of open science? Does the intensification of patenting accelerate or retard the development of basic and commercial research?'

M. Mitchell Waldrop (2008), in *Scientific American*, acknowledges the emergence of Science 2.0:

> generally refers to new practices of scientists who post raw experimental results, nascent theories, claims of discovery and draft papers on the Web for others to see and comment on. Proponents say these "open access" practices make scientific progress more collaborative and therefore more productive. Critics say scientists who put preliminary findings online risk having others copy or exploit the work to gain credit or even patents. Despite pros and cons, Science 2.0 sites are beginning to proliferate; one notable example is the OpenWetWare project started by biological engineers at the Massachusetts Institute of Technology.

Waldrop (2008) demonstrates that rich text, highly interactive, user-generated and socially active Internet (Web 2.0) has seen linear models of knowledge production giving way to more diffuse open-ended and serendipitous knowledge processes.

Open science economy plays a complementary role with corporate and transnational science and implies strong role for governments. Increasingly, portal-based knowledge environments and global science gateways support collaborative science (Schuchardt et al., 2007; see, for instance, Science.gov & Science.world). Cyber-mashups of very large data sets let users explore, analyze, and comprehend the science behind the information being streamed (Leigh & Brown, 2008). The World Wide Web has revolutionized how researchers from various disciplines collaborate over long distances especially in the Life Sciences, where interdisciplinary approaches are becoming increasingly powerful as a driver of both integration and discovery (with regard to data access, data quality, identity, and provenance) (Sagotsky et al., 2008). National science review and assessment to focus on formative role in developing distributed knowledge systems based on quality journal suites in disciplinary clusters with an ever finer mesh of in-built indicators. Meanwhile economists argue that open source software can be an engine of economic growth (see Garzarelli et al., 2008; Etzkowitz, 1997; 2003; 2008; David, 2003) and clearly the notion of open science economy is one of the leading sectors of the knowledge economy.

Concluding Observations

The open science economy constitutes a strong leading-edge development within the science and general knowledge economies that are based on different social and economic principles that can be referred to under the notion of the social mode of production. Paul A. David[19] (2003) has described open science in terms that strongly contrast with industrial or knowledge economy models based on strong institutions of intellectual property

> "Open science" institutions provide an alternative to the intellectual property approach to dealing with difficult problems in the allocation of resources for the production and distribution of information. As a mode of generating reliable knowledge, "open science" depends upon a specific non-market reward system to solve a number of resource allocation problems that have their origins in the particular characteristics of information as an economic good. (Abstract, p. i)

Elsewhere he writes, 'Scientific and technological collaboration is more and more coming to be seen as critically dependent upon effective access to, and sharing of digital research data, and of the information tools that facilitate data being structured for efficient storage, search, retrieval, display and higher level analysis' (David, 2005).

Open science has become an important part of the knowledge economy in advanced industrial societies. In part is has grown out of similar trends in alternative modes of creation, production, and distribution of information through the development of social media that has given rise to the movement of open education. Indeed these two parallel movements have only recently been seen as part of an emerging seamless whole that clearly links school to university and education at these levels to open scientific research that depends on the same or similar norms of sharing and collaboration in open networked environments.[20] Some scholars have already warned how the commercialization of campuses threaten the development of the open science economy. John Willinsky (2005), for instance, writes:

> Are universities currently re-entering the world on the side of a greater openness among intellectual properties or are they getting in on a greater share of knowledge-based property rights? Up to this point, the universities have fostered open science, and advanced open source software, even if both originated off campus in large measure. With the more recent of these open initiatives—open access—it

falls almost entirely to the universities and their faculty to take the lead. Universities "re-entering the world" with the intent to "serve the world" would do well to support faculty participation in open access archives and journals. Open access to research and scholarship would foster a global exchange of public goods. It would extend and sustain an open, alternative economy for intellectual properties. It would strengthen the links between open source software—which is vital to providing open access to research—and the university's long-standing tradition of open science. Given the encroachments, not to mention the temptations, of the knowledge business, this is no time to take the commonwealth of learning for granted. It falls to the members of that commonwealth to recognize and support the current convergence of open initiatives that represent dedicated efforts to ensure the future of that learning. (p. 70)

Notes

1 I would like to thank the editors, Tom Popkewitz and Fazal Rizvi, for a set of useful criticisms on an earlier version of this chapter.
2 See the OCW website at http://www.ocwconsortium.org/.
3 See http://creativecommons.org/.
4 See http://p2pfoundation.net/The_Foundation_for_P2P_Alternatives.
5 See http://pkp.sfu.ca/.
6 See http://www.okfn.org/.
7 See the website http://www.ced.org
8 See http://www.ced.org/docs/report/report_ecom_openstandards.pdf.
9 Digital versions are available on their website at http://www.ced.org/projects/ecom.shtml.
10 See Tim O'Reilly (2005) on Web 2.0 technologies ('Design Patterns and Business Models for the Next Generation of Software') at http://www. oreillynet.com/pub/a/oreilly/tim/news/2005/09/30/what-is-web-20.html , including 'harnessing collective intelligence', 'blogging and the wisdom of crowds', and 'architectures of participation'. As O'Reilly mentions: 'Mitch Kapor once noted that "architecture is politics." Participation is intrinsic to Napster, part of its fundamental architecture.
11 Available electronically at http://www.oecd.org/document/41/0,3343,en_2649_201185_38659497_1_1_1_1,00.html.
12 Available at http://www.olcos.org/cms/upload/docs/olcos_roadmap.pdf.
13 Available at http://www.oerderves.org/wp-content/uploads/2007/03/a-review-of-the-open-educational-resources-oer-movement_final.pdf.
14 I prefer the term OE to OER because it embraces the notion of *practices* as well as the notion of sharing educational resources and also because it gels with open source, open access, and open science (as well as open innovation).
15 The countries are Australia, Austria, Belgium, Brazil, *Canada*, China, Denmark, Finland, *France, Germany*, Greece, India, Iran, Ireland, Israel, *Italy, Japan*, Luxem-

bourg, the Netherlands, Poland, Portugal, *Russia*, Singapore, Spain, South Africa, South Korea, Sweden, Switzerland, Taiwan, the *United Kingdom* and the *United States* (with G8 countries in italics).

16 See, for instance, Michel Bauwens's P2P Foundation work at the P2P Foundation at http://p2pfoundation.net/3._P2P_in_the_Economic_Sphere.

17 See http://chronicle.com/news/article/3943/harvard-faculty-adopts-open-access-requirement.

18 See, for instance, the *Journal of Visualized Experiments* at http://www.jove.com/.

19 See David's recent papers on the relationship between open software and economic growth at http://ideas.repec.org/e/pda76.html. On 'The Historical Origins and Economic Logic of 'Open Science', see http://videolectures.net/cern_david_openscience/.

20 See, for example, the Prague-based Project of Open Science at http://www.otevrena-veda.cz/ov/index.php?p=o_projektu&site=ov_en designed to increase the competitiveness of the Czech economy.

References

Adams, J., & Wilsdon, J. (2006). *The new geography of science: UK research and international collaboration.* London, United Kingdom: Demos.

Benkler, Y. (2002). Coase's Penguin, or Linux and the nature of the firm. *The Yale Law Journal, 112.* Retrieved from http://www.yale.edu/yalelj/112/BenklerWEB.pdf

Benkler, Y. (2006). *The wealth of networks.* New Haven, CT: Yale University Press.

Brown, L., Griffiths, R., & Rascoff, M. (2007). University publishing in a digital age (The Ithaka Report). *Journal of Electronic Publishing, 10*(3). doi: http://dx.doi.org/10.3998/3336451.0010.301

David, P. A. (2003). *The economic logic of "open science" and the balance between private property rights and the public domain in scientific data and information: A primer.* Retrieved from http://129.3.20.41/eps/dev/papers/0502/0502006.pdf

David, P. A. (2005). *Towards a cyber-infrastructure for enhanced scientific collaboration: Providing its 'soft' foundations may be the hardest part.* Retrieved from http://129.3.20.41/eps/le/papers/0502/0502004.pdf

Davis, J., & Stack, M. (1997). The digital advantage. In J. Davis, T. A. Hirschl, & M. Stack (Eds.), *Cutting edge: Technology, information capitalism and social revolution* (pp. 121–144). London, United Kingdom: Verso.

Etzkowitz, H. (1997). The entrepreneurial university and the emergence of democratic corporatism. In H. Etzkowitz & L. Leydesdorff (Eds.), *Universities and the Global Knowledge Economy: A triple helix of university-industry-government relations* (pp. 141–154). London, United Kingdom: Continuum.

Etzkowitz, H. (2003). Innovation in innovation: The triple helix of university-industry-government relations. *Social Science Information, 42*(3), 293–337.

Etzkowitz, H. (2008). *The triple helix: University-industry-government innovation in action.* London, United Kingdom: Routledge.

Etzkowitz, H., Carvalho de Mello, J. S., & Almeida, M. (2005). Towards "meta-innovation" in Brazil: The evolution of the incubator and the emergence of a triple helix. *Research Policy, 34*, 411–424.

Garvey, R., & Williamson, W. (2002). *Beyond knowledge management: dialogue, creativity, and the corporate curriculum.* Harlow, United Kingdom: Pearson Education Limited.

Garvin, D. (1993). Building learning organizations. *Harvard Business Review, 71*(4), 78–91.

Garzarelli, G., Limam, Y. R., & Thomassen, B. (2008). Open source software and economic growth: A classical division of labor perspective. *Information Technology for Development 14*(2), 116-135.

Hollingsworth, J. S., Müller. K. H., & Hollingsworth, E. J. (2008). China: The end of the science superpowers. *Nature, 454*, 412–413.

Jones, B. F., Wuchty, S., & Uzzi, B. (2008). Multi-university research teams: Shifting impact, geography, and stratification. *Science, 322*, 1259-1262.

Kapitzke, C., & Peters, M. A. (Eds.). (2007). *Global knowledge cultures.* Rotterdam, the Netherlands: Sense Publishers.

Kelly, K. (1998). *New rules for the new economy.* London, United Kingdom: Fourth Estate.

King, D. A. (2004). The scientific impact of nations: What different countries get for their research spending. *Nature, 430*, 311–316. Retrieved from www.nature.com/nature

Leigh, J., & Brown, M. (2008). Cyber-commons: Merging real and virtual worlds. *Communications of the ACM, 51*(1): 82–85.

Marginson, S., Murphy, P., & Peters, M. A. (2009). *Global creation: Space, connection and universities in the age of the knowledge economy.* New York, NY: Peter Lang.

Materu, P. N. (2004). *Open Source Courseware: A Baseline Study.* The World Bank, November. Retrieved from siteresources.worldbank.org/.../open_source_courseware.pdf.

Morris-Suzuki, T. (1997). Capitalism in the computer age and afterward. In J. Davis, T. A. Hirschl, & M. Stack (Eds.), *Cutting edge: Technology, information capitalism and social revolution* (pp. 13–28). London, United Kingdom: Verso.

National Science Board. (2008). *Research and development: Essential foundation for U.S. competiveness in a global economy.* Retrieved from http://www.nsf.gov/statistics/nsb0803/start.htm

Peters, M. A. (2007). *Knowledge economy, development and the future of higher education.* Rotterdam, the Netherlands: Sense Publishers.

Peters, M. A., & Besley, T. (A. C.). (2006). *Building knowledge cultures: Education and development in the age of knowledge capitalism.* Lanham, MD: Rowman & Littlefield.

Peters, M. A., & Britez, R. (Eds.). (2009). *Open education and education for openness.* Rotterdam, the Netherlands: Sense Publishers.

Peters, M. A., Marginson, S., & Murphy, P. (2009). *Creativity and the global knowledge economy.* New York, NY: Peter Lang.

Rhoten, D., & Powell, W. W. (2007). The frontiers of intellectual property: Expanded protection versus new models of open science. *Annu. Rev. Law Soc. Sci. 2007. 3*: 345–73.

Sagotsky J. A., et al. (2008). Life sciences and the web: a new era for collaboration. *Mol. Syst. Biol, 4,* 201.

Schuchardt, K., Pancerella, C., Rahn, L.A., Didier, B, Kodeboyina, D., Leahy, D., et al. (2007). Portal-based knowledge environment for collaborative science. *Concurrency Computation Practice and Experience. 19*(12), 1703-1716.

Stiglitz, J. (1999). *Knowledge as a global public good.* Retrieved from http://www.worldbank.org/knowledge/chiefecon/articles/undpk2/

UNESCO. (2005, September). What do bibliometric indicators tell us about world scientific output? *UIS Bulletin on Science and Technology Statistics, 2.* Retrieved from http://www.csiic.ca/PDF/UIS_bulletin_sept2005_EN.pdf

Varian, H. R. (1998). *Markets for information goods* (Draft). Retrieved from http://people.ischool.berkeley.edu/~hal/Papers/japan/japan.pdf

von Hippel, E., & von Krogh, G. (2003). Open source software and the 'private-collective' innovation model: Issues for organization science. *Organization Science, 14*(2), 209-223.

Waldrop, M. M. (2008). Science 2.0: Great new tool, or great risk? *Scientific American, 298*(5). Retrieved from http://www.scientificamerican.com/article.cfm?id=science-2-point-0-great-new-tool-or-great-risk

Wessner, C. (2007). *Innovation policies for the 21st century.* Washington, DC: National Academy Press.

Willinsky, J. (2005). The unacknowledged convergence of open source, open access, and open science. *First Monday, 10*(8). Retrieved from http://firstmonday.org/htbin/cgiwrap/bin/ojs/index.php/fm/rt/printerFriendly/1265/1185

Wuchty, S., Jones, B. F., & Uzzi, B. (2007). The increasing dominance of teams in production of knowledge. *Science, 316,* 1036-1039.

CHAPTER 12

Digital Technologies in the Age of YouTube
Electronic Textualities, the Virtual Revolution and the Democratization of Knowledge

Michael A. Peters and Peter Fitzsimons

> Our current revolution is obviously more extensive than Gutenberg's. It modifies not only the technology for reproduction of the text, but even the materiality of the object that communicates the text to the readers. Until now, the printed book has been heir to the manuscript in its organization of leaves and pages [...] and its aids to reading (concordances, indices, tables). The substitution of screen for codex is a far more radical transformation because it changes methods of organization, structure, consultation, even the appearance of the written word.
>
> —Roger Chartier (1995, p. 15), *Forms and meanings: Texts, performances, and audiences from codex to computer*

> New media are less points of epistemic rupture than they are socially embedded sites for the ongoing negotiation of meaning as such. Comparing and contrasting new media thus stand to offer a view of negotiability in itself—a view, that is, of the contested relations of force that determine the pathways by which new media may eventually become old hat.
> —Lisa Gitelman (2006, p. 6), *Always Already New: Media, History, and the Data of Culture*

Introduction: Electronic Textuality

Writing seventeen long techno-years ago, Roger Chartier (1995) argued that the current shift from print to digital technology entails a change greater than the one from manuscript to print. This shift was a fundamental watershed in our culture that changed the topography, the shape and time of media—from an industrial one-way broadcast media regime to the radical interactivity of social media and user-generated creativity. The significance of this set of changes is not easily captured or understood and its knock-on effects or remediation of economy and society required a rethinking of our most cherished institutions from the operations of government and its departments to scientific communication, scholarship and pedagogy. In particular, the *network* of knowledge institutions that grew up during the Enlightenment—the research university, the modern research library, learned societies, the laboratory, the museum—were transformed as the norms of peer review and governance became even more internally related to the scientific enterprise and the technical platform for scholarly communication enabled greater intensities of global collaboration and knowledge sharing.

From the point where Chartier and others identified the contours of change scholars tried to understand how the computer began to restructure the economy of writing altering the cultural status of writing and the relationships of author to text, and author and text to reader. Jay Bolter (1991) approaching new digital media from the history of technical culture talked of writing space and "remediation" as a central concept to understand the new aesthetic and cultural principles of digital media, suggesting that new visual media refashion rather than rival earlier media such as perspective painting, photography, film, and television (Bolter & Grusin, 2000). George Landow (1994, 2005) examining text-based computing in the humanities and electronic literature used the notion of hypermedia to describe and analyze the epistemological passage from closed authorial systems to open hypertextual systems. Some like Michael Heim adopted the term "virtual reality" and tried to describe its metaphysical properties, drawing on the work of Heidegger. Others programmatically followed the work of Jean Baudrillard on simulation, Deleuze on film, or Derrida on grammatology.

Lev Manovich (2000) focused pragmatically on mapping the language of new media as signaling a broader shift of symbolic representation to a global digital network stating five intrinsic principles of new media.

1. Numerical representation can describe new objects in a formal mathematical language which is subject to algorithmic manipulation that implies that "media becomes programmable" (p. 27);
2. New media objects (e.g., digital film, or web page) have modularity at the level of both representation and code and thus are "composable" from an assemblage of elements (images, sounds, shapes) that sustain their separate identity and can be operated upon separately, without rendering the rest of the assemblage unusable.
3. Numerical coding and modularity "allow for the automation of many operations involved in media creation, manipulation, and access" (p. 32).
4. New media are characterized by variability allowing users to define parameters, branching-type interactivity, periodic updates, and scalability as to size or detail (pp. 37-38)
5. New media find themselves at the center of the "transcoding" between the layers of the computer and the layers of culture (p. 46) allowing translations into different formats.

Chartier, a French historian and member of the Annales school who works on the history of books, publishing and reading,[1] deliberated over *electronic textuality* suggesting that the screen is "a three-dimensional space, possessing width, height, and depth, as if texts arrived on the surface of the screen from deep within the monitor" the folds the text itself with the consequence that "reading therefore consists of unfolding this moving and infinite textuality" (Chartier, 2004). He argues:

> Such a reading brings up ephemeral, multiple, and unique textual units onto the screen, units that are created following the will of the reader, and they are in no respect pages set down once and for all. The image that has become so familiar, that of surfing the web, clearly indicates the characteristics of a new way of reading: segmented, fragmented, discontinuous.... One of the great questions of the future is whether or not digital textuality will be able to overcome the ten-

dency toward fragmentation that characterizes both the structure of texts and the modes of reading that it proposes.[2]

Emphasizing the fundamental nature of change he argues "Regarding the order of discourse, the electronic world thus creates a triple rupture: it provides a new technique for inscribing and disseminating the written word; it inspires a new relationship with texts; and it imposes a new form of organization on texts." Regarding the first set of changes he suggests that this new form of textuality" combines a revolution in the technical means for reproducing the written word" with "a revolution in the medium of the written word..., and a revolution in the use of and the perception of texts." The second set of changes concerns the order of reasoning "electronic textuality enables the development of theses following a logic that is no longer necessarily linear or deductive" enabling "an open, fragmented, relational articulation of the reasoning, made possible by a greater number of hypertextual connections" representing "a fundamental epistemological mutation that profoundly transforms the techniques of a proof and the modalities of the construction and validation of the discourse of knowledge".[3] The third set of changes reorders the concept of property in both a juridical sense and a textual sense for the reader "can intervene not only in its margins, but in its very content, by removing, reducing, adding, or reworking the textual units that he or she has obtained." It is this last issue concerning the mobility of the open and malleable text that impinges on the unique identification of texts and the battle over intellectual property generated by electronic publishing and open access of scientific communication. As he says there are two different logics operating: "the logic of free communication, which is associated with the ideal of the Enlightenment that upheld the sharing of knowledge, and the logic of publishing based on the notions of an author's rights and of commercial gain."

Chartier quotes D. F. McKenzie[4] (1986, p. 9), the New Zealand bibliographer and critic, "forms affect sense" arguing:

> A text is always conveyed by a specific materiality; the written object upon which it is copied or printed, the voice that reads, recites, or otherwise utters it, the performance that allows it to be heard. Each of these forms of publication is arranged in its own unique fashion, and each form, in different ways, influences how meaning is produced. Thus, looking only at the printed text, the format of

the book, the layout, the division of the text, typographic conventions, punctuation, all are invested with an expressive function.

Alan Liu (2008) in "Imagining the New Media Encounter" suggests "the boundary between codex-based literature and digital information has now been so breached by shared technological, communicational, and computational protocols that we might best think in terms of an encounter rather than a border".[5] Liu (2008) approaches the embedded complexity through what he calls "narratives of new media encounter" in the form of first contact with the Word, Book, Law, Image, Music, and (more recently) Code are deeply embedded in the entire historiography of Early Modern religious or imperial conquest, Enlightenment and industrial "modernization," twentieth-century "control through communication" (coupled with "mass entertainment"), and postindustrial "informating" or "knowledge work." At once descriptive and interpretive, speculative and wary, proselytizing and critical, and visionary and regulatory, narratives of new media encounter are the elementary form of media theory—the place from which all meta-discourse about media starts. Or again, they are *intra*-discursive: part of the self-mediating discourse or feedback by which media "ecologies," as they have recently been called, adapt systemically when new forces swarm across the border.

He details the narratives of new media in terms of four organizers:

1. *Narratives of new media encounter are identity tales in which media at once projects and introjects "otherness."*
2. *Narratives of new media encounter emplot their identity tale as a life cycle of media change.*
3. *The life story of the new media encounter plays out in the key registers of human significance: Historical. The very phrase "new media," of course, stages an exaggerated encounter between old and new.*
4. *When fully realized in their historical, socio-political, and personal entanglements, the identity tales created by narratives of new media encounter are unpredictable*

    (italics in original). (At http://www.digitalhumanities.org/companion/view?docId=blackwell/9781405148641/9781405148641.xml&chunk.id=ss1-3-1&toc.depth=1&toc.id=ss1-3-1&brand=9781405148641_brand)

New digital media are potentially transformative for the future of pedagogy and scholarly communication; perhaps more for the latter than the former and in different ways, which may say about educators' refusal to engage with new digital media, rather than its lack of transformative potential for pedagogy.

Digital publishing, archiving, data-sharing as well as models and formats for scholarship including blogging, podcasting, etc., are all well advanced whereas the institutional effects of new digital media in schools seem somewhat retarded by comparison, except for the huge investment in online learning that has strong front-end preparation but promises to make efficiencies in the delivery of programs especially through forms of digital Taylorism that offers easy cuts to academic labor costs. The potential of digital media is related to a number of features that distinguish these resources from its industrial predecessor:

1. they can be delivered to any point on the earth and at any time;
2. they can be fundamentally hypertextual, supporting comprehensive links between assertions and their evidence;
3. they dynamically recombine small, well-defined units of information to serve particular people at particular times;
4. they learn on their own and apply as many automated processes as possible, not only automatic indexing but morphological and syntactic analysis, named entity recognition, knowledge extraction, machine translation, etc., with changes in automatically generated results tracked over time;
5. they learn from their human readers and can make effective use of contributions, explicit and implicit, from a range of users in real time;
6. they automatically adapt themselves to the general background and current purposes of their users (adapted from Crane, Bamman, & Jones, 2008).

In addition we can also mention a number of other features that spring from the nature of digital systems:

7. digital resources are easy-to-make assemblages because of their modularity;
8. they provide the basis for "remediation" embedding media within media (e.g., the video clip);
9. they provide the basis for algorithmic search functions and the prospect of the integration of "ready-mades";
10. they invite interactivity, collaboration, networking and knowledge sharing as deep structural features of digital media;
11. through their system scalability they also present risks of "knowledge totalities" and encyclopedic universal information systems that have inherent dangers of knowledge privatization and monopologization;

12. they provide the prospect of "open textual environments" that perform as extended and dynamic sites for backstories, side bars, case studies, interviews, and new forms of visualization.

The list could be added to further contrasting in more detail the differences between industrial and social media with accompanying effects on modes of inquiry, the coproductive and creative possibilities of user-generated cultures (Peters, 2011a), the logic of new forms of openness in pedagogy and scholarly communication (Peters & Roberts, 2011; Peters, Ondercin & Liu, 2010a,b,c), and innovations in both digital production and dissemination of scholarly work with electronic scholarly editions (Price, 2008), digital repositories and collections, digital books, e-readers and iPads.

The Virtual Revolution and the Democratization of Knowledge

At one level, it is possible to describe the move to electronic textuality as a set of technological changes, albeit with some changes in the way we think about technology and some adaptation required in our interaction within a digital world. But the shifts are much further reaching than the mode of transmission or even what might be transmitted through the new media. A shift is occurring in the fundamental nature of what we mean by knowledge, and more specifically for our purpose, its impact on pedagogy—and therefore our very subjectivity.

Attempts by educators to define knowledge as a commodity with pre-specified characteristics and recognizable qualities such as truth, belief, and justification—something to be processed (developed, categorized, standardized transmitted and tested) as part of schooling—provide closed systems and tidy packages for analysis (e.g., Hirst's seven discrete forms of knowledge, a school curriculum segmented into discrete 'subjects', or step-by-step grade assessments). Higher status is traditionally ascribed to knowledge than to mere 'information'. But tradition is of limited value in coping with what a recent BBC documentary calls *The Virtual Revolution*—the story of how the web is overturning centuries of authority structures and models of ownership, remaking our world and our cultural reality, and evolving a new virtual 'species'—Homo Interneticus.[6]

The virtual revolution has been likened to the industrial revolution—supercharging information in much the same way that steam did for mechanical force, accelerating the development and transmission of information, allowing anyone to publish and distribute words, images, videos and software globally, instantly and virtually for free. According to the documentary, a quarter of the people on our planet now uses the internet, with Wikipedia attracting 65 million users each month. As well as accessing knowledge, anybody in the world with access to a computer can edit the information. The idea is that instead of truth, knowledge and accuracy being agreed on by experts, and handed down by an elite from above, it will slowly emerge from the masses and come up from below. Centuries of scholarship have maintained knowledge as the preserve of the learned few, a preserve that is now under siege.

Jimmy Wales, creator of Wikipedia, talks about wanting to unleash the power of the crowd to break down hierarchical assumptions and democratize human knowledge—even to the point of how we might evaluate that knowledge. In a form of anti-elitism, he claims that it is easier to get quality when you have a lot of people participating, and that we should judge the quality of someone's work on its own merits rather than paying too much attention to their credentials. Such populist perspectives remind us that knowledge has been historically grounded in social traditions, and so represent a significant philosophical and economic threat to universities and other institutions whose eminence and authority depends on the rationing of credentials, and the centralizing of knowledge within their own disciplinary structures.

The Wikipedia project has been criticized severely for its anarchic approach to authoritative definitions and scholarly writing. Wales admits that open access leaves projects like Wikipedia vulnerable to being hijacked, and has recently toughened up the rules, so that instead of truth emerging purely by consensus, increasingly it has to be policed. Thus a whole system has evolved to reconcile open access with the need for accuracy and authority. Editors lock pages, administrators can delete them, a small arbitration committee adjudicates on disputes, and ultimately in charge is Jimmy Wales himself—an interesting mix of democracy and aristocracy. In relation to Wikipedia, Wales avoids talk of elites and hierarchies, as such terms are associated with top-down authoritarian structures. He prefers to talk about communities coming together to create norms, standards and institutions, but also having some limits in place to ensure that participation is constructive. He says, 'We used to be criticized for being too egalitarian; now we are criticized for being too elitist, but somewhere in the middle we passed the day when everything was fine and no one noticed.'[7]

In his now dated but still relevant 'banking' metaphor for what often passes as education, Freire (1993) criticized teachers for talking about reality as though it were motionless, static, compartmentalized and predictable. He called instead for students to be actively engaged in critical thinking, for a profound trust in people and their creative power. Authentic thinking, he argued, does not take place in ivory tower isolation, but only in communication, engaging with and reflecting on reality. We are, he says, beings in the process of becoming—unfinished, incomplete beings in an unfinished reality, so education is necessarily an ongoing and dialogical activity. Freire's call for education as a dynamic, integrative and creative process predated the social media that today makes his vision possible. Yet, despite the technology now being available, we as educators (as government emissaries perhaps?) are reluctant to move away from the familiar, the grounded and the predictable. We objectivize and categorize knowledge within traditional subject boundaries, and sequentialize what we believe can be known at various stages of development. We pre-specify outcomes, standardize learning, quantify assessments, and moderate our assessments to ensure uniformity. Some of us then scale marks to suit preconceived ideas about the status of different school or academic subjects. We grade and classify various pieces of work as successes or failures, and attribute such grades to the person of our students as a measure of their intellectual capability or academic potential. We then compete with one another to see who can do all this the most efficiently and effectively as we strive for promotion and for various awards in teaching excellence.

Whereas knowledge has traditionally been the preserve of the educated few, documented in the learned texts, and locked down for sale either in encyclopaedia or as part of packaged credentials (university degrees), the web has democratized knowledge in the promise of leveling out the playing field, and overturning long held notions of ownership, value and institutionalised expertise. The dream is of equal access and equal voice. The web is thus a rebellion, mirroring the politics of its early developers—people opposed to hierarchy and authority. John Perry Barlow, from the old American supergroup the Grateful Dead, talks of the Internet as a challenge to traditional authority—setting information free will set us all free. His criticism of authority is that you don't have to control people much if you can control what they believe, and that you can control what they believe if you control what they have access to. Barlow helped start the influential Electronic Frontier Foundation, that campaigns for freedom online. It is based on beliefs distilled in his *Declaration of the Independence of Cyberspace:*

> Governments of the Industrial World, you weary giants of flesh and steel, I come from Cyberspace, the new home of Mind. On behalf of the future, I ask you of the past to leave us alone. You are not welcome among us. You have no sovereignty where we gather.... Your legal concepts of property, expression, identity, movement, and context do not apply to us. They are all based on matter, and there is no matter here....Your increasingly obsolete information industries would perpetuate themselves by proposing laws, in America and elsewhere, that claim to own speech itself throughout the world. These laws would declare ideas to be another industrial product, no more noble than pig iron. In our world, whatever the human mind may create can be reproduced and distributed infinitely at no cost. The global conveyance of thought no longer requires your factories to accomplish.... We will create a civilization of the Mind in Cyberspace. May it be more humane and fair than the world your governments have made before. (Barlow, 1996)

With a free flow of information, knowledge is clearly on a collision course with authority and traditional notions of intellectual property. The ability we now have to share information globally and at minimal cost means we no longer need agents, publishers, newspaper editors. People can now connect directly with one another and exchange ideas freely, undermining centuries old notions of private property and copyright. Music piracy is now a global phenomenon, and copyright laws are being ramped up to cope. New Zealand has recently enacted the Copyright (Infringing File Sharing) Amendment Act 2011 that focuses specifically on file sharing infringements, imposing tight restrictions on internet service providers as well as end users, resulting in eventual exclusion from the Internet for ongoing infringements. In a digital world where one's identity is increasingly dependent on participation in online community, such exclusion might be considered a form of digital death penalty.

As a measure of how connected the digital world now is, at last look (September 10, 2011) Facebook boasted over 750 million users, each with an average of 130 friends. 700 billion hours are spent on Facebook each month, and more than 30 billion pieces of content (web links, news stories, blog posts, notes, photo albums, etc.) are shared each month (Facebook Statistics, 2011). YouTube statistics in August this year report that 48 hours of video are uploaded every minute, with over 3 billion videos viewed each day, and more than 50% of videos on YouTube have been rated or include comments from the community (Digital Stats, 2011). An even more staggering statistic is from January this year, when Google was reported as having a 48% share of the daily web traffic of all internet users worldwide. Aside from specific projects like Wikipedia and Facebook, the internet abounds with blogs, online diaries and opinionated commentary on the news—a kind of global conversation, in which people express their ideas, reflect on what other people are contributing, and then develop better ideas—an evolutionary (if not revolutionary) prospect and one that accords well with the better aspects of belonging to a democratic educational community.

Anti-Democratizing Trends

Despite the exponential growth in our technological capacity and the groundswell of engagement with social networking, it would be something of an overstatement to claim that we have achieved some kind of online freedom or guarantee of a new democracy. We have, in many respects, established an environment for user-generated, self-promoting contributions within a shared community—but within considerable and real (anti-democratic) constraints. There is increasing control by commercial and other interests over what is allowed to be generated and transmitted within and across such communities. At one level, surveillance is justified on the grounds of public safety in an age of terrorism, so that certain points of view are not able to be shared (or even held) in public. More insidious though is the degree to which creativity is defined by and subject to the provisions of copyright law, and the way that the building blocks for future creativity are being shepherded into the private domain where they can be harnessed as part of the multinational profit-making enterprise of royalties and copyright infringement.

This latter point was explored in a recent open source documentary film about the changing concept of copyright. Brett Gaylor's (2008) *RiP!: A Remix Manifesto* argues that cultural knowledge should not be commodified, segregated or privately owned, as culture builds upon culture and is thus a communal project. Gaylor's manifesto is built on four assertions:

(1) Culture always builds on the past
(2) The past always tries to control the future
(3) Our future is becoming less free
(4) To build free societies, you must limit the control of the past

Gaylor's film explores and promotes a very different concept—that of 'copyleft', indicated by a backward 'c' symbol, referring to a method for making a work free to distribute while insisting that any future modification of that work has to remain free as well. In other words, it intentionally and explicitly preserves the creative commons aspect of a work that is put in the public domain.

Gaylor 'remix' draws on the work of Lawrence Lessig, founder of the Creative Commons project, who sees creativity as a communal project, a kind of conversation, each participant taking what the other has done and adding to it, mixing it and changing it. Lessig argues in favor of abolishing the anti-piracy laws that corporations champion, because the function of copyright is to ascribes ownership of various aspects of culture to selected parties who might best be considered *contributors* to creative works than their *originators*. They have developed ideas, thoughts and motifs that have gone before and so have no moral grounds for claiming ownership—even if legally entitled to do so because of copyright or patent law. Sharing ideas, remixing, and generating variations on what has gone before amount to what Lessig sees as 'writing in the 21st century'. It is, he says in the film, 'literacy for a new generation; it is building a different democracy, a different culture where people participate in the creation and recreation of the culture around them'. This is what Lessig refers to elsewhere as a 'read/write culture' (Lessig, 2007), in contrast to the 'read only' culture we are left with after decades of one way *broadcast* transmission technology—a 'culture which is top-down owned where the vocal chords of the millions have been lost. It is technology, says Lessig, that has generated the new creativity and undermined our anti-piracy laws:

> We need to recognize you can't kill the instinct that technology produces; we can only criminalize it. We can't stop our kids from using it; we can only drive it underground. We can't make our kids passive again; we can only make them,

quote, 'pirates'.... Ordinary people live life against the law... that's what I/we are doing to our kids. (Lessig, 2007)

Beyond the territory of ownership and property rights, as a further block to the idea of online community as some kind of egalitarian nirvana, is the way power and influence shape communal spaces and public opinion, and therefore private realities. The hope is that in the new world of media we might come across a new order, especially in terms of open access to information no longer bound up as commercial property. And yet in this hybrid future, we see the new media frequently criticized for filtering and shaping opinion. Arianna Huffington, co-founder of *Huffington Post*, talks about the future of journalism as a *hybrid* future where "traditional media players embrace the ways of new media (including transparency, interactivity, and immediacy) and new media companies adopt the best practices of old media (including fairness, accuracy, and high-impact investigative journalism)" (Huffington, 2009). Rupert Murdoch may have fallen, but the new gatekeepers (and here Huffington is included) are re-establishing the old hierarchy, so that an elite few may still colonize the web, mirroring the inequalities and the hierarchies in the old world of industrial media.

Of course the internet holds potential for democratization, but as Guattari points out, the expansion in communications technology, and, in particular, the development of world telecommunications, has served to shape a new type of passive subjectivity, saturating the unconscious in conformity with global market forces. The phenomenon he calls 'Integrated World Capitalism' poses a direct threat to the environment in ways that are now all too familiar to us—pollution of all forms, extinction and depletion of species with the consequent reduction of biodiversity etc. But he also alerts us to the dimension of social ecology and its practical politics—in particular what he calls mental ecology: how the structures of human subjectivity are, like a rare species, under threat of extinction. He calls for new systems of value that incorporate and strengthen the not-for-profit sector:

> A market system which regulates the distribution of financial and social rewards for human social activities on the basis of profit alone, is becoming less and less legitimate. The time has come to take serious account of other value systems: of 'profitability' in the social and aesthetic sense, of the values of desire, etc. Until now, of course, domains of value not governed by capitalist profit

have been dominated by the state: viz. the state-fostered appreciation of the national heritage. We have, however, reached a point where new social associations—with charitable foundations, for example—should be drawn upon to expand the financing of a more flexible third sector which is neither private nor public. (Guattari, 1989, p. 147)

A Reconciliation?

We have, then, on the one hand, the private profit-driven imperative of international capitalism to develop, control and harness the power of technology and the online market for its own commercial ends. On the other hand are the dedicated millions in search of meaning through their engagement with others in online community, using the Internet as the new social fabric to facilitate communication among various networks. Some reconciliation between these two apparently opposed images might be found in the work of Michel Bauwens, a Belgian researcher in the field of technology, culture and business innovation. In his seminal work *The Political Economy of Peer Production*, he explores some of the characteristics of peer to peer networks (P2P): they operate in distributed networks with distributed power and distributed resources, they focus on communal benefit, they feature open access to information among participants, they are governed by the community of users themselves, and are open to participation on the basis of willingness to contribute. Such features locate P2P networks very much within the scope of the third sector (Bauwens, 2005a).

Bauwens regards P2P phenomena as an emerging alternative to capitalist society, although he acknowledges their mutual interdependence. Peer production is highly dependent on the income provided by the market. But the market and the capitalist system also rely on distributed networks, in particular on the P2P infrastructure in computing and communication. Case in point is the marriage between open source software and IT companies who eagerly provide venture capital for development of open source software that will drastically undercut their monopolistic competitors. Such mutual interest has resulted in a new subclass that Bauwens refers to as the 'netarchical class' who prosper from the enablement and exploitation of the participatory networks.

> It is significant that Amazon built itself around user reviews, eBay lives on a platform of worldwide distributed auctions, and Google is constituted by user-generated content. However, although these companies may rely on IP rights

for the occasional extra buck, it is not in any sense the core of their power. Their power relies on their ownership of the platform. (Bauwens, 2005a)

In another essay "Peer to Peer and Human Evolution" Bauwens expands the P2P theme beyond computer technology. In its more generic form, he argues that egalitarian networking is a relational dynamic that is emerging throughout the social field, not only within computer and internet technology as a general mode of knowledge exchange and collective learning, but in all areas of social and cultural life, profoundly transforming the way in which society and human civilization is organised. He sees P2P as a revolt against the total functionalization of our society, about its near-total and growing determination by instrumental reason and efficiency thinking, that is now even infecting our social and personal lives.

> It is a vivid protest, a longing for a different life, not solely dictated by calculation and the overriding concern for profit and productivity. It is not just protest against the intolerable facets of postmodern life, but always already also a construction of alternatives. Not an utopia, but really existing social practice. And a practice founded on a still unconscious, but coherent set of principles, i.e. a new social imaginary. (Bauwens, 2005b)

So it would be wrong to close the door on revolutionary possibilities for the new media. It was Victor Hugo that maintained one thing stronger than all the armies in the world, is an idea whose time has come. Judging by the whirlwind speed with which digital gossip zips through pages of Facebook and Twitter, the apparent immediacy of digitally inspired phenomena like flash mobs, and the radical interactivity of social media and the user-generated creativity of YouTube, a transformation may be quick in the making and one which turns our familiar ways of knowing on their respective ears.

> The web is more than a simple reflection of our world. It is endlessly reinventing itself. By placing so much power in the hands of the people who use it, whenever one part of the web is closed down, colonised or controlled, the technology opens up new frontiers. It is a face of perpetual innovation. No one can stop it but we do need to take care of it. This virtual revolution is an extraordinary challenge and responsibility, but at the same time, an extraordinary opportunity. (The Great Levelling?, 2010)

Educational and Political Significance of New Social Media

The year 2010 was named the 'Year of Social Media'. Social media are a technology of communication and for creating and exchanging 'user-generated content'. Together, these functions transform traditional broadcast media monologues into social media dialogues that spread ideas, news and information faster and wider than television, radio or print. *Time* magazine names Facebook founder Mark Zuckerberg "Person of the Year" and Hollywood releases a movie entitled *The Social Network*. Young Egyptians use Facebook and Twitter to organize protests in Liberation Square to topple an authoritarian regime and 'open up' the Middle East. WikiLeaks releases masses of classified documents on the Internet. Over the past 10 years, English Internet content grew by only 281%, while Chinese Internet content grew by 1,277%.

Nine core principles underlie the value of social media, serving to define characteristics that set them apart from other forms of communication and collaboration:

1. *Participation*: user participation taps mass collaboration.
2. *Collective wisdom*: users 'collect', share and modify user-generated content.
3. *Transparency*: each participant gets to see, use, reuse, augment, validate, critique and evaluate others' contributions, leading to collective self-improvement.
4. *Decentralization*: from 'one to many' to 'many to many'—interactive anytime, anyplace collaboration independently of other contributors.
5. *Virtual community*: sociality based on 'conversations' that are relationship-seeking.
6. *"Design is politics"*: how a social media site is designed determines how people will use it.
7. *Emergence*: self-organizing social structures, expertise, work processes, content organization and information taxonomies that are not a product of any one person.
8. *Revisability*: social media can be altered, unlike industrial media.
9. *Ownership*: social media are accessible and available at little cost, unlike industrial media that are government or privately owned.

These are the new social media principles of education that will define the shape of education inb the future.

Notes

1 See his Stanford Presidential Lectures in the Humanities and Arts at http://prelectur.stanford.edu/lecturers/chartier/.

2   See "Languages, Books, and Reading from the Printed Word to the Digital Text" at http://criticalinquiry.uchicago.edu/features/artsstatements/arts.chartier.htm.
3   In "History, Time, and Space" Chartier (2011) argues: "electronic textuality transforms the way in which arguments, historical or not, can be organized and the criteria that a reader might mobilize to accept or reject them. For the historian, it enables the development of demonstrations according to a logic that is no longer necessarily linear or deductive like that imposed by the inscription, whatever its technique may be, of a text on to a page. It enables an open, fragmented, and relational articulation of reasoning made possible by hypertextual links. For the reader, the validation or refutation of an argument can henceforth be based on the consultation of texts (as well as fixed or moving images, recorded speech, or musical compositions) that are the very object of study—provided, of course, that they are accessible in digital format. If such is the case, the reader is no longer merely obliged to trust the author; if he or she has the will or the time, he or she can in turn reproduce all or part of the research."
4   See the "Unofficial" homepage set up in his honor at http://users.ox.ac.uk/~hobo/dfm/dfmhome2.html. McKenzie set up Wai-te-ata Press at Victoria University of Wellington and contributed to the development of the Alexander Turnbull and National Libraries, and of Downstage Theatre before taking up a position at Oxford, completing *The Complete Works of William Congreve* and playing an instrumental role in the British Library's scholarly project *A History of the Book in Britain*.
5   See the full text of *A Companion to Digital Literary Studies*, including Liu's introduction at http://www.digitalhumanities.org/companion/view?docId=blackwell/9781405148641/9781405148641.xml&chunk.id=ss1-3-1&toc.depth=1&toc.id=ss1-3-1&brand=9781405148641_brand.
6   Homo Interneticus is an episode of a BBC/Open University collaboration that went to air in 2010. The documentary series entitled *The Virtual Revolution* was presented by Aliks Krotoski. See http://www.bbc.co.uk/programmes/b00n4j0r.
7   See the first program of *The Virtual Revolution* at http://alekskrotoski.com/post/digital-revolution-the-great-levelling-saturday-30-january-2010.

References

Barlow, J. P. (1996). *A declaration of the independence of cyberspace*. Retrieved from https://projects.eff.org/~barlow/Declaration-Final.html

Bauwens, M. (2005a). The political economy of peer production. *1000 Days of Theory* [online journal]. Retrieved from www.ctheory.net/

Bauwens, M. (2005b). *P2P and human evolution: Placing peer to peer theory in an integral framework*. Retrieved from http://www.integralworld.net/bauwens2.html

BBC and The Open University (Producer)., & Krotoski, A. (Director). (2010). *The great levelling (episode 1): Homo Interneticus*. Retrieved from http://topdocumentaryfilms.com/virtual-revolution/

BBC and The Open University (Producer)., & Krotoski, A. (Director). (2010). *The virtual revolution (episode 4): Homo Interneticus*. Retrieved from http://topdocumentary films.com/virtual-revolution/

Bolter, J. D. (1991). *Writing space: The computer, hypertext, and the history of writing*. Hillsdale, NJ: Lawrence Erlbaum.

Bolter, J. D., & Grusin, R. (2000). *Remediation: Understanding new media*. Cambridge, MA: MIT Press.

Chartier, R. (1995). *Forms and meanings: Text, performances, and audiences from codex to computer*. Philadelphia, PA: University of Pennsylvania Press.

Chartier, R. (2004). Languages, books, and reading from printed word to digital text (T. L. Fagan, Trans.). *Critical Inquiry, 31*,133–152. Retrieved from http://criticalinquiry.uchicago.edu/features/artsstatements/arts.chartier.htm

Chartier, R. (2011). History, time, and space. *Republics of Letters: A Journal for the Study of Knowledge, Politics, and the Arts, 2*(2). Retrieved from http://rofl.stanford.edu/node/100

Crane, G., Bamman, D., & Jones, A. (2008). ePhilology: When the books talk to their readers. In R. Seimens & S. Schreibman (Eds.), *A companion to digital literary studies*. Oxford: Blackwell.

Digital Stats. (2011) *Official YouTube statistics*. Retrieved from http://digital-stats.blogspot.com/2011/08/official-youtube-statistics.html

Facebook Statistics. (2012, March). Retrieved from http://newsroom.fb.com/Key-Facts/Statistics-8b.aspx

Freire, P. (1993). *Pedagogy of the oppressed: Revisited 20th anniversary edition*. New York, NY: Continuum.

Gaylor, B. (2008). *RiP! A remix manifesto*. Retrieved from http://www.nfb.ca/film/rip_a_remix_manifesto/

Gitelman, L. (2006). *Always already new: Media, history, and the data of culture*. Cambridge, MA: MIT Press.

Guattari, F. (1989). The three ecologies (C. Turner, Trans.). *New Formations, 8*, 131–147. Retrieved from http://www.amielandmelburn.org.uk/collections/newformations/08_131.pdf

Huffington, A. (2009, January 12). Journalism 2009: Desperate metaphors, desperate revenue models, and the desperate need for better journalism. *Huffington Post*. Retrieved from http://www.huffingtonpost.com/arianna-huffington/journalism-2009-desperate_b_374642.html

Landow, G. (Ed.). (1994). *Hyper/text/theory*. Baltimore, MD: Johns Hopkins University Press.

Landow, G. (2005). *Hypertext 3.0: Critical theory and new media in an era of globalization*. Baltimore, MD: Johns Hopkins University Press.

Lessig, L. (2007). *The laws that choke creativity* [Ted Talk]. Retrieved from http://www.ted.com/talks/larry_lessig_says_the_law_is_strangling_creativity.html

Liu, A. (2008). Imagining the new media encounter. In R. Seimens & S. Schreibman (Eds.), *A companion to digital literary studies.* Oxford: Blackwell.

Manovich, L. (2000). *The language of new media.* Cambridge, MA: MIT Press.

McKenzie, D. F. (1986). *Bibliography and the sociology of texts.* London, United Kingdom: Cambridge University Press. Retrieved from http://catdir.loc.gov/catdir/samples/cam032/98031000.pdf

Peters, M. A. (2011a). Creativity, openness and the global knowledge economy: The advent of user generated cultures. *Economics, Management, and Financial Markets, 5*(3), 15–36.

Peters, M. A. (2011b). Manifesto for education in the age of cognitive capitalism: Freedom, creativity and culture. *Economics, Management, and Financial Markets, 6*(1), 63–92.

Peters, M. A., & Herrera, L. (2011). The educational and political significance of the new social media: A dialogue with Linda Herrera and Michael A. Peters. *Policy Futures in Education, 8*(4), 364–374.

Peters, M. A., & Roberts, P. (2011). *The virtues of openness: Education, science and scholarship in a digital age.* Boulder, CO: Paradigm Publishers.

Peters, M. A., Ondercin, D., & Liu, T.-C. (2011a). Open learning systems: The next evolution for education. *Review of Contemporary Philosophy, 10,* 9–24.

Peters, M. A., Ondercin, D., & Liu, T.-C. (2011b). Esoteric and open pedagogies. *Contemporary Readings in Law and Social Justice, 3*(2), 23–47.

Peters, M. A., Ondercin, D., & Liu, T.-C. (n.d.). Learned societies, public good science and openness in the digital age. *Educational Philosophy and Theory* (forthcoming).

Price, K. M. (2008). Electronic scholarly editions. In R. Seimens & D. Schreibman, *A companion to digital literary studies.* Oxford, United Kingdom: Blackwell. Retrieved from http//:www.digitalhumanities.org/companionDLS

Seimens, R., & Schreibman, S. (Eds.). (2008). *A companion to digital literary studies.* Oxford, United Kingdom: Blackwell. Retrieved from http//:www.digitalhumanities.org/companionDLS.alhumanitieshttp://www.digitalhumanities.org/compan

Chapter 13

Manifesto for Education in the Age of Cognitive Capitalism
Freedom, Creativity and Culture

Michael A. Peters

> Transform the world, said Marx, change life, said Rimbaud. These two watchwords for us one only.
> —André Breton

> The social revolution of the nineteenth century cannot derive its poetry from the past, but only from the future. It cannot begin with itself, before it has shed all superstitious belief in the past. Earlier revolutions needed to remember previous moments in world history in order to numb themselves with regard to their own content. The revolution of the nineteenth century must let the dead bury the dead in order to arrive at its own content. There, the phrase exceeded the content. Here the content exceeds the phrase.
> —Karl Marx, *The 18th Brumaire of Louis Bonaparte*

Manifestos, Art and Politics

In the *Manifeste du Surréalisme*, Breton defines Surrealism as 'pure psychic automatism with which one proposes to express, either orally or in any other manner, the real process of thought, in the absence of any control exercised by reason, outside any aesthetic or moral concerns'.[1] Surrealist poetics revalues and reconsiders the irrational element in human creativity and the will to express itself through art at a subconscious level. Freud, Marx and Rimbaud are the guiding lights for Breton as he derives a form of ('fleeting') modernity after Baudelaire that is truly revolutionary and which is based upon total freedom of expression that goes beyond (bourgeois) reality to uncover the super real. In this revolutionary overthrow Breton and his surrealist compatriots utilize all the aspects of the unthought and unconscious including dream, madness, hallucination and irrationality all of which allegedly bring us closer to *life*.

In *Poetry of the Revolution* Martin Puchner (2005, p. 2) argues that Marx had invented a poetry of the future revolution in the *Communist Manifesto* which 'seeks to produce the arrival of the "modern revolution" through an act of self-foundation and self-creation: we, standing here and now, must act!' As Puchner notes 'manifestos weave together social theory, political acts, and poetic expression' (p. 2). The manifesto itself is an act of creation, a creative practice that seeks to prefigure and realize the future. The interesting fact is that the *Manifesto* became part of "world literature" and entered the world of art in the twentieth century through its acts of reception, transportation and translation. In this sense Puchner (2005) argues that in the twentieth century we should read avant-garde manifestos alongside political manifestos because they were intimately self-referencing and involved: Italian and Russian Futurists, Dadaism, Surrealism, Debord's revolt against the spectacle. Thus, the study of manifestos requires not only a poetics of the form but also the politics of speech acts. Puchner argues that the *Communist Manifesto* forms the genre and then undergoes a process of temporal, linguistic and geographical diffusion drifting into the realm of aesthetics as well as politics with the appearance of the avant-garde manifesto.

Manifesto, from the Italian, means to 'make clear'. Manifestos are declarations. They often shape intentions and political actions. It is nor remarkable that politics and art should be expressed in a kind of poetry that constitutes a kind of speech act or performance. Resistance often first registers in a form of poetics that expresses the emotions and feelings associated with exploitation and other forms of oppression (Peters & Besley, 2006).

In *The Theory of the Avant-Garde* (first published in Italian in 1962) Renato Poggioli (1981) attempted to demonstrate that avant-garde artists existed in a critical relationship to tradition, fashion and the public, united across the arts in their alienation and opposition to the bourgeoisie. Clement Greenberg (1939) in his famous article argued that the avant-garde, distinctively bohemian, repudiated both bourgeois ('high art') and revolutionary politics and developed in opposition to the mass produced culture of kitsch to preserve the living culture we still have. This avant-garde opposition to mass consumerism and its kitsch culture has been taken up by leading members of the Frankfurt school. Peter Bürger (1984) in his *Theory of the Avant-garde* distinguishes the historical avant-garde—Dada, Surrealism, Russian avant-garde after October revolution—from the 'neo' avant-garde (Abstract Expressionism, Pop Art, Noveau Réalism, Fluxus) which simply recycles earlier strategies. The historical avant-garde involves a radical break with tradition and opposition to art as an institution such as it has developed in bourgeois society with its insistence on the autonomy of the aesthetic. Its main tendency is the sublation of art in everyday praxis and it reacts against aestheticism which is detached from the praxis of life. Bürger also engages in an extended discussion of Bertolt Brecht (1898–1956) who experimented with dada and expressionism, but developed a style more suited his own unique vision in his later work that rejected the commodification of the world.

One of the major questions is whether the avant-garde is still possible —whether its energy, opposition to mainstream culture, and its formal innovation has been totally recuperated by capitalist culture (Habermas)—or whether the avant-garde still has the spirit of criticism that enables it to break the rules of art and go beyond what is accepted (Lyotard). Irmelia Hautamaki (2003) indicates the concept of the avant-garde has both a political and a cultural dimension which are closely intertwined: the concept applied to art was first mentioned in the political programs of French utopian socialists and later used to describe the 'most advanced and stylistically innovative art' based on the work the poets Arthur Rimbaud, Paul Verlaine, Stephane Mallarmé and Charles Baudelaire. As Matei Calinescu (1987, p. 114) indicates Marxists used avant-garde as political term in the 1880s—the party is the avant-garde of the working class. Yet Marxist critics also referred to avant-garde literature as 'modernist' or 'decadent' in contrast to 'socialist realism', a discussion reflected in the so-called realism (expressionism) debate that took place between György Lukács (1885–1971) and Bertolt Brecht (1898–1924), characterized by Bela Kiralyfalvi (1990) as 'primarily a broad discussion of disagreements among Marxist artists and theorists about the values and characteristics of classical, bourgeois and socialist art'.[2]

The idea that the classical realist tradition should be followed by modern writers is a problem that arose out of Lukács' attempt to remain faithful to Marxist aesthetics but in view of the development of modernist fiction, art or theatre ultimate unsatisfactory and a kind of assertion that totalizes realism as the objective perspective on the world. Pike (1985) intelligently suggests that 'their commitment to a dogmatized and dogmatic political credo was the prime source of their artistic and philosophical inspiration; the dogma inspired them in their quest for aesthetic solutions appropriate to the contemporary political age, the transition from capitalism to socialism, and they both used it to claim exclusivity for their respective theoretical approaches' (p. xi).

This debate is part of the wider canvas meeting of Marxism and Modernism that took place in Germany and elsewhere in Europe that provide a struggle over the very meaning of the avant-garde and its relation to capitalist society. Marxism provides a trenchant critique of capitalist economy and yet its attempt to provide an aesthetics based on the dogma of a 'copy' theory of consciousness as a straightforward reflection of objective processes impugns its usefulness and consigns most of the intelligent thought-provoking, challenging and experimental art, theatre and music to the dustbin of history while aggrandizing the palpably meagre achievements of 'socialist realism'. It is also to rob Marxist aesthetics of its vitality and openness.

In this chapter I want to run together art, politics and education. In particular, I want to argue that the future of education is a matter of aesthetics, of the design of systems. Insofar as the future of education is a question of the *design* of knowledge and learning systems—communication and data networks that promote participation and collaboration—then design is also a matter of politics for who owns and designs education and new media systems are critical to what kinds of systems architectures and platforms are promoted and what kind of knowledge and learning cultures are possible.

Designing Educational Futures and Knowledge Cultures[3]

It was Nietzsche who said 'The future influences the present just as much as the past' and Paul Valery, the French poet and critic, who said 'The future isn't what it used to be.' In the past philosophers have attempted to lay down principles for a philosophy of the future: I am thinking not only of Nietzsche but also Feuerbach's (1843) *Principles of Philosophy of the Future* and Bloch's (1970) *A Philosophy of the Future*.[5] My starting point is Nietzsche, Wittgenstein and Heidegger—'prophets of postmodernity' (as I call them)—who provide some ground on which to stand. Nietzsche, of the three, perhaps most explicitly addressed questions of the future. In a work that was to have been his second book, *On the Future of Our Educational Institutions*,[6] portions of which appear in *Un-*

timely Meditations,[7] he called for radical educational reform presented in the form of a prolonged narrative dialogue. *Beyond Good and Evil* was subtitled *A Prelude to a Philosophy of the Future* and he often talked of 'philosophers of the future' who have a specific task:

> All sciences are now under the obligation to prepare the ground for the future task of the philosopher, which is to solve the problem of value, to determine the true hierarchy of values.

In the Preface to *The Will to Power*, Nietzsche describes himself as the 'perfect nihilist of Europe' but one, at the same time, who had 'lived through the whole of nihilism, to the end, leaving it behind, outside himself' (p. 3). As he writes, again in the Preface, the title—*The Will to Power: Attempt at a Revaluation of All Values*—is formulated as a *countermovement* that will take the place of nihilism, but which at the same time logically and psychologically presupposes it in the sense that only after the advent of nihilism can we realize that nihilism is the logical extension of our values. Only after our experience of nihilism can we discover for the first time what these values really meant, and what real value they had. Only at that point, will we realize that we require new values.

Knowledge cultures is an approach to philosophy of education that ties it to contemporary debates about knowledge and the value of knowledge, especially those accounts that draw on the concepts of 'post-industrialism', 'post-Fordism', 'knowledge economy', 'creative economy' and open source models of scientific communication, scholarship and science. In this chapter I do not have the space to defend this broad approach to the philosophy of education[10] as I need to be programmatic in setting out an agenda which is concerned not only with the idea of creating or designing futures but also that is critical in an accepted sense. Such an approach needs to be non-deterministic especially in relation to technology, sensitive to cultural difference, and radically interdisciplinary. Most importantly, it needs to accept there is a logical as well as temporal asymmetry between the future and the past.[11]

Philosophy of the future is a platform for rethinking the philosophy of education and policy futures in education. While policy futures may draw on the techniques and methodologies of futures studies it is not reducible to this field, or to its siblings—futurology, scenario planning, foresight, or science fiction. I am much more inclined to see futures in an applied philosophical framework that is akin to what Foucault, after Nietzsche, calls 'histories of the present' which is driven by a genealogical investigation of value and guided by the epistemological question of how the historical awareness of our present circumstances affect what and how we know and can know.[12] Consider 'histories of the future' a separate but parallel critical activity. It is an approach that I have attempted to develop and exemplify over the past few years through the establishment of journals and books series, and through various books and courses.[13]

In this chapter I want to draw attention to one aspect of this program that I have called 'Knowledge Cultures' which I have addressed in terms of three specific aspects: 'Open source, open access, and free science' (Peters & Besley, 2006). In Nietzsche's terms I am trying to determine the true hierarchy of values in relation to knowledge futures, and, on some indicative evidence I want to assert the value of *freedom* to relation to the future of knowledge.[14] 'Freedom' on the standard account has been defined as *freedom from the dependence on the will of others*—which is the classic statement by the tradition of nineteenth British liberalism stated first by Locke, then elaborated by Mill, Bentham, Green and others, and later adopted in the twentieth century by Hayek (1960) in his influential *The Constitution of Liberty*. This notion of liberty, which is at the heart of liberalism in both its Protestant and Catholic forms, is also historically tied to democracy and to the development free intellectual inquiry, the modern university and the value of openness. Academic freedoms, stemming from freedom of speech, refer to alleged rights of students, teachers and institutions to pursue the truth or persuade, without political suppression.[15] The U.S. Supreme Court in *Regents of the University of California v. Bakke*, 438 U.S. 265, 312; 1978 states that academic freedom means a university can 'determine for itself on academic grounds: who may teach; what may be taught; how it should be taught; and who may be admitted to study.'

This is not the place to pursue the full genealogy of freedom in its educational forms but let us state some significant aspects of its continuing importance:

Freedom

1. Today the value of freedom in relation to the distribution, access and exchange of knowledge is under threat at an historical moment that also provides unparalleled

opportunities for the establishment of open global architectures for knowledge, science, learning and education.

2. The study of education should concern itself in a critical way with the historical forms of freedom and their uneven development—freedom of expression and of speech, of freedom to learn, of freedom to teach, and of freedom to publish.

3. The assertion and establishment of these freedoms take different historical forms and pose different technical, political and ethical problems for knowledge and learning futures, including those of copyright, intellectual property, and plagiarism.

4. The lesson I take from Marx, and from Nietzsche, Wittgenstein and Heidegger based on a materialist and historicist approach is that *knowledge and the value of knowledge is rooted in social relations*. In order to investigate the genealogy of the value of knowledge in relation to its freedoms, its freedoms-to-come, and their educational significance we must critically examine its various emergent institutional and networked forms as well as the obstacles to them.

5. In the practical context this program means an investigation of the value of openness and the mode of open production. Openness has emerged as an alternative mode of *social production* based on the growing and overlapping complexities of open source, open access, open archiving, open publishing and open science. It has become a leading medium and source of creativity and innovation in the world global digital economy.

6. The Free Software and 'open source' movements constitute a radical non-propretarian alternative to traditional methods of text production, distribution and reception and we need to develop a radical political economy of distributive knowledge and learning to promote intercultural exchanges between and among the North and South so that knowledge and access to knowledge is evenly shared.

7. This alternative non-proprietary method of cultural and knowledge exchange threatens traditional models and the legal and institutional means used to restrict creativity, innovation and the free exchange of ideas. In terms of a model of communication there has been a gradual shift from content to code in the openness, access, use, reuse and modification reflecting a radical personalization that has made these open characteristics and principles increasingly the basis of the cultural sphere. So open source and open access has been developed and applied in open publishing, open archiving, and open music constituting the hallmarks of 'open culture.'

8. The values of freedom and openness are the metavalues that will determine knowledge cultures in the future and, therefore, also the production of knowledge and the design of knowledge and learning systems.

9. Today increasingly we must talk of the freedom to use, to make and distribute copies, and to makes changes and improvements; that is, anything represented in digital form permits the growing globalization of *open works* and for a growing part of humanity to *access, create, modify, publish and distribute* various kinds of works.[4]

Freedom, Openness and Creativity[5]

Every aspect of culture and economy is becoming transformed through the process of digitization that creates new systems of archives, representation and reproduction technologies that portend Web 3.0 and Web 4.0 where all production, material and immaterial, is digitally designed and coordinated through distributed information systems.

Digitization transforms all aspects of cultural production and consumption favouring the networked peer community over the individual author and blurring the distinction between artists and their audiences. These new digital logics alter the logic of the organization of knowledge, education and culture spawning new technologies as a condition of the openness of the system. Now the production of texts, sounds and images are open to new rounds of experimentation and development providing what Felix Stalder (2004) calls 'a new grammar of digital culture' and transforming the processes of creativity which are no longer controlled by traditional knowledge institutions and organizations but rather permitted by enabling platforms and infrastructures that encourage large-scale participation and challenge old hierarchies.

The shift to networked media cultures based on the ethics of participation, sharing and collaboration, involving a volunteer, peer-to-peer gift economy has its early beginnings in the right to freedom of speech that depended upon the flow and exchange of ideas essential to political democracy, including the notion of a 'free press', the market and the academy. Perhaps, even more fundamentally free speech is a significant personal, psychological and educational good that promotes self-expression and creativity and also the autonomy and development of the self-necessary for representation in a linguistic and political sense and the formation of identity.

Openness has emerged as a global logic based on free and open source software constituting a generalized response to knowledge capitalism and the attempt of the new mega-information utilities such as Google, Microsoft, and Amazon.com to control knowledge assets through the process of large-scale digitization, of information often in the public domain, the deployment of digital rights management regimes and strong government lobbying to enforce intellectual property law in the international context.

The Internet is a dynamic changing open ecosystem that progressively changes its nature towards greater computing power, interactivity, inclusiveness, mobility, scale, and peer governance. In this regard and as the overall system develops it begins to approximate the complexity of the architectures of natural ecosystems. The more it develops, one might be led to hypothesize, the greater the likelihood of not merely emulating Earth as a global ecosystem but becoming an integrated organic whole. Open cultures become the necessary condition for the systems as a whole, for the design of open progressive technological improvements and their political, epistemic and ontological foundations.

The other side of the state and corporate digital reproduction of identity is a tendency that emphasizes the relation between openness and creativity as part of a networked group. The "open self" is self-organizing and is formed at the interstices of a series of membership of online communities that shaped spontaneous self-concept and self-image.

Openness to experience is one of the five major traits that has shaped personality theory since its early development by L. L. Thurstone in the 1930s and is strongly correlated with both creativity and divergent thinking (McCrae, 1987). Sometimes referred to as the "big five" personality traits or "the five factor model" trait theory emerged as a descriptive, data-driven model of personality based on openness, conscientiousness, extraversion, agreeableness, and neuroticism. Openness is associated with creativity and the appreciation of art, emotionality, curiosity, self- expression and originality. Meta-analysis reviewing research that examines the relationships between each of the five-factor model personality dimensions and each of the 10 personality disorder diagnostic categories of the *Diagnostic and Statistical Manual of Mental Disorders* (4th ed. DSM-IV) reveal strongly positive (with neuroticism) and negative associations (with the other factors) (Saulsman & Page, 2004). One of the limitations of personality theory is its focus on the individual and in the age of networks this centeredness might seem somewhat misplaced. There are close links between open content, open science and open collaboration that makes collaborative creativity sustainable.

Openness to experience is probably the single most significant variable in explaining creativity and there is some evidence for the relationship between brain chemistry and creative cognition as measured with divergent thinking (Jung et al., 2009). Openness also can be defined in terms of the number, frequency, and quality of links within a network. Indeed, the mutual reinforcement of openness and creativity gels with Daniel Pink's (2005) contention that right-brainers will rule the future. According to Pink, we are in the transition from an 'Information Age' that valued knowledge workers to a 'Conceptual Age' that values creativity and right-brain-directed aptitudes such as design, story, symphony, empathy, play, and meaning.

Creativity as the New Development Paradigm

The contemporary politics of creativity rests on the intersection between art and politics tracing the influence between art and labor in the form of co-creativity and peer collaboration and within the new mode of social production. This much, at least in its nascent form, has been recognized now by the United Nations (2008) that there is another reality and narrative emerging that provides an interpretation of 'globalization as connectivity' rather than economic integration or free trade and is 'reshaping the overall pattern of cultural production, consumption and trade in a world increasingly filled with images, sounds, texts and symbols' (p. iii).[6] As the 'Overview' of the UN *Creative Economy Report 2008* clarifies:

> In the contemporary world, a new development paradigm is emerging that links the economy and culture, embracing economic, cultural, technological and social aspects of development at both the macro and micro levels. Central to the new paradigm is the fact that creativity, knowledge and access to information are increasingly recognized as powerful engines driving economic growth and promoting development in a globalizing world. "Creativity" in this context refers to the formulation of new ideas and to the application of these ideas to produce original works of art and cultural products, functional creations, scientific inventions and technological innovations. (p. 3)

Rather than accept this mainstream neoclassical economic orientation that endeavors to understand the economic aspect of creativity through its contributions to entrepreneurship, and the ways in which it fosters innovation, enhances productivity and promotes economic growth, one might follow the debates in the literature on 'cognitive capitalism' to focus on labor struggles and begin to interpret this in the light of 'biopolitics' and see it signaling 'the moment that the traditional nation/State dichotomy is overtaken by a political economy of life in general' where 'power has invested life' to create 'sites of the production of subjectivity' privileging the 'the transformation of work in the organization of labor'(Negri, 2008, pp. 13-14). Antonio Negri, drawing on both Foucault and Deleuze, investigates the organization of labor under neoliberal globalization and the radical transformation of the production process though new processes of self-regulation and expressive creativity unleashed by information and communication technology that facilitates the rise of what Negri and other call 'immaterial labor' (after Marx's 'general intellect') as the dominant productive force that take places with the development and cultivation of new laboring subjectivities.

A manifesto for education in the age of cognitive capitalism must address the question of new laboring subjectivites and their cultivation, socialization and education. In this case we can take our as our starting point the 'creative energy of labor'—as Negri (2008, p. 20) argues:

> In the Fordist era, temporality was measured according to the law of labor value: consequently it concerned an abstract, quantitative, analytic temporality, which, because it was opposed to living labor time, arrived at the composition of the productive value of capital. As it is described by Marx, capitalist production represents the synthesis of the living creativity of labor and of the exploitive structures organized by fixed capital and its temporal laws of productivity. In the era of post-Fordism, on the contrary, temporality is no longer—nor totally—enclosed within the structures of constant capital: as we have seen, intellectual, immaterial, and affective production (which characterizes post-Fordist labor) reveals a surplus. An abstract temporality—that is to say, the temporal *measure* of labor—is incapable of understanding the *creative energy of labor itself.* (My emphasis)

Notes

1 I would like to acknowledge the PhD students in my advanced seminar at the University of Illinois, 'Contemporary Marxisms and Education: Marxisms after Marx' (Spring 2009) and especially my grad assistant Ergin Bulut. The course helped me to rethink Marxist aesthetics in relation to the question of design of educational knowledge and learning systems. This chapter is in part the result of the readings discussed in the course and reflects the nature of class discussions.

2 Kiralyfalvi (1990) provides the following genealogical and bibliographical footnote: 'The debate originated with Lukacs's critique of the work of Willi Bredel in *Linkskurve* (1931) and his comments on Ernst Ottwalt's documentary novel (*Denn sie wissen, was sie tun*) in 1932. Lukacs's 1934 essay, "Expressionism: Its Significance

and Decline," published in *Internationale Literatur*, sparked a long debate conducted mostly in *Das Wort* until 1939. Those participating in the early debate included Klaus Mann, Alfred Kurella, Klaus Berger, Bêla Balazs, Ernst Bloch, Anna Seghers, Bertolt Brecht and Walter Benjamin. Contributions to the debate by Theodor Adorno, Walter Benjamin, Ernst Bloch and Frederic Jameson can be found in *Aesthetics and Politics* (London: NLB, 1977).'

3   This draws on my paper 'Futures of Philosophy of Education' (Peters, 2009).
4   See http://freedomdefined.org/Definition.
5   This section draws on 'Open Works, Open Cultures, and Open Learning Systems' (Peters, 2010).
6   See *Creative Economy Report 2008* at http://www.unctad.org/en/docs/ditc20082cer_en.pdf.
7   This volume also contains *Assorted Opinions and Maxims*, Trans. R.J. Hollingdale, and *The Wanderer and His Shadow*, Trans. R.J. Hollingdale.

References

Bloch, E. (1970). *A philosophy of the future* (J. Cumming, Trans.). New York, NY: Herder & Herder.

Bürger, P. (1984). *Theory of the avant garde* (M. Shaw, Trans.). Minneapolis, MN: University of Minnesota Press.

Calinescu, M. (1987). *Five faces of modernity: Modernism, avant-garde, decadence, kitsch, postmodernism*. Durham, NC: Duke University Press.

Greenberg, C. (1939). Avant-garde and kitsch. *Partisan Review*, 6(5), 34–49. Retrieved from http://www.sharecom.ca/greenberg/kitsch.html

Hautamaki, I. (2003). *Origin of Avant-garde, modern aesthetics from Baudelaire to Warhol*. Helsinki: Gaudeamus (in Finnish). Introduction (in English) at http://mustekala.kaapeli.fi/artikkelit/1070380027/index_html.

Hayek, F. (1960). *The constitution of liberty*. Chicago, IL: The University of Chicago Press.

Jung, J. (1998, August). *The future of philosophy*. Paper presented at the Twentieth World Congress of Philosophy, Boston, MA. Retrieved from http://www.bu.edu/wcp/MainCont.htm.

Jung, R. E., Gasparovic, C., Chavez, R. S., Flores, R. A., Smith, S. M., Caprihan, A., & Yeo, R. A. (2009). Biochemical support for the "threshold" theory of creativity: A magnetic resonance spectroscopy study. *Journal of Neuroscience*, 29, 5319–5325.

Kiralyfalvi, B. (1990). The aesthetic effect: A search for common grounds between Brecht and Lukacs. *Journal of Dramatic Theory and Criticism*, 4, 19–30.

Marginson, S., Murphy, P., & Peters, M. A. (2009). *Global creation: Space, connection and universities in the age of the knowledge economy*. New York, NY: Peter Lang.

McCrae, R. R., & Costa, P. T. (1987). Validation of the five-factor model of personality across instruments and observers. *Journal of Personality and Social Psychology*, 52, 81–90.

Murphy, P., Peters, M. A., & Marginson, S. (2010). *Imagination: Three models of imagination in the age of the knowledge economy.* New York, NY: Peter Lang.

Negri, A. (2008). The labor of the multitude and the fabric of biopolitics (S. Mayo, P. Graefe, & M. Coté, Trans.). *Mediations, 23*(2), 8–25. Retrieved from www.mediations journal.org/the-labor-of-the-multitude-andthe-fabric-of-biopolitics.

Nietzsche, F. (1966). *Beyond good and evil* (W. Kaufmann, Trans.). New York, NY: Viking Press.

Nietzsche, F. (1968). *The will to power: In science, nature, society and art.* New York, NY: Random House.

Nietzsche, F. (1989). *Human, all-too-human* (R. J. Hollingdale, Trans.). Cambridge, United Kingdom: Cambridge University Press.[7]

Peters, M. (2009). Futures of philosophy of education. *Analysis and Metaphysics, 7,* 14–26.

Peters, M. (2010). Open works, open cultures, and open learning systems. In T. Lukes (Ed.), *Putting knowledge to work and letting information play* (at http://www.cddc.vt.edu/10th-book/putting_knowledge_to_work.pdf). Blacksburg, VA: Center for Digital Discourse and Culture, Virginia Tech.

Peters, M., & Besley, T. (2006). *Building knowledge cultures: Education and development in the age of knowledge capitalism.* Lanham, MD: Rowman & Littlefield.

Peters, M., & Besley, T. (2010). The narrative turn and the poetics of resistance: Towards a new language for critical educational studies. In I. Gur-Ze'ev (Ed.), *The possibility of a new critical language in education* (pp.261–274). Rotterdam, the Netherlands: Sense Publishers.

Peters, M., Murphy, P., & Marginson, S. (2009). *Creativity and the global knowledge economy.* New York, NY: Peter Lang.

Peters, M., & Roberts, P. (2010). *The virtues of openness.* Boulder, CO: Paradigm Publishers.

Pike, D. (1985). *Lukács and Brecht.* Chapel Hill, NC: UNC Press Books

Pink, D. (2004). *A whole new mind: Why right-brainers will rule the future.* New York, NY: Riverhead Trade.

Poggioli, R. (1981). *The theory of the avant-garde* (G. Fitzgerald, Trans.). Cambridge, MA: Belknap Press of Harvard University Press.

Puchner, M. (2005). *Poetry of the revolution: Marx, manifestos and the avant-gardes.* Princeton, NJ: Princeton University Press.

Saulsman, L. M., & Page, A. C. (2004). The five-factor model and personality disorder empirical literature: A meta-analytic review. *Clinical Psychology Review, 23*(8), 1055–1085.

Stalder, F. (2004). *Open cultures and the nature of networks.* New Media Center_kuda.org, at http://felix.openflows.com/html/kuda_book.html.

United Nations Creative Economy Report (2008) at unctad.org/fr/Docs/ditc20082cer_en.pdf

Index

Academy of Science (Paris), 172–173
access, open. *See* open access
The Accidental Billionaires (Mezich), 125
accumulation, 26, 27, 28, 202
action, ethical, 107
Adams, J., 5, 240
administrative reason, 199
advertising, Web-based, 132
aesthetics, Marxist, 280
affective capitalism, 23
Africa, 239
agriculture, 101
Alberts, Bruce M., 180, 181
algorithmic trading, 119–121
Ampere, A. M., 16
Anderson, Warwick, 177
anthropocentrism, 80–81, 82
An Anthropological Introduction to YouTube (Wesch), 126
argumentation, philosophical, 60
Arrow, Kenneth, 139
art, avant-garde, 278–280
arts, role of in economic development, 142
Ashby, W. Ross, 16
Ashmole, Elias, 223
Asia, 5, 239, 241, 247
authority, 265–266
avant-garde, 278–280

Baber, Z., 93
Bacon, Francis, 171–172, 223
Banks, Joseph, 174–175
Barlow, John Perry, 146, 265, 266
Bauwens, Michel, 270–271
Becker, Gary, 62, 135, 198
Beer, Stafford, 16
belief, control of, 266
Bell, Daniel, 41, 43, 63, 135
Beller, Jonathan, 127
Benkler, Yochai, 53, 69–70, 72, 144, 145–146, 148, 207, 225–226, 235, 244

Berlin, Isaiah, 47–48
Berners-Lee, Tim, 130, 225
Besley, Tina, 8, 45
Beverungen, Armin, 198–199
Beyond Good and Evil (Nietzsche), 281
bibliometrics, 3, 177, 238, 239
Bifo, Franco Berardi, 123–124
Big Bang, 80
biocapital, 107
   as force in society, 97–98
   Freiburg school of, 105–106
   and patent laws, 104
   and resistance, 109
   rise of, 102
   and subjectivity, 108
biocapitalism, 24, 34, 195
   concept of, 116
   emergence of, 93–94
   features of, 101–102
   genealogy of, 103
   and neoliberalism, 104–106
   scholarship in, 102–104
   strategies of power, 104
Biocapital (Rajan), 102
bioeconomy, emergence of, 98
biology, 75–76, 94–97
biopolitics, 100
'Biopolitics/Bioeconomics' (Lazzarato), 105
biopower, 102
biotechnology, 98–101
   domestication of, 97
   merge with infotechnology, 101
   and patent laws, 104
   philosophy of ethical care in, 107
   as third industrial revolution, 115–118
Blankenburg, Stephanie, 196
Blue Heron, 116
Boltanski, L., 45, 46
Bolter, Jay, 258
Bounty, 175

Bourdieu, Pierre, 63, 136
Boutang, Yann Moulier, 32
Boyle, James, 71, 146, 147–148, 226
Brazil, 5
Brecht, Bertolt, 279
Breton, A., 277
Bria, Francesca, 202
Brown, Gordon, 143
Budapest OA statement, 130
budget, U.K., 198
budget, U.S., 197–198
Building Knowledge Cultures (Peters and Besley), 8, 219
Burckhardt, Jacob, 200
Bürger, Peter, 278, 279
Bush, George W., 208

Calinescu, Matei, 279
Cameron, David, 198
Cape Town Education Declaration, 220–221
capital, human, 198
capital, intellectual, 242
capital, natural, 83
capitalism
  financialization of, 21, 61
  greening of, 83
  mutations in spirit of, 46
  networked model of, 194
  new culture of, 23
  new spirit of, 23
  transformation of, 191, 192–193
capitalism, aesthetic, 44–45
capitalism, affective, 23
capitalism, algorithmic, 121
capitalism, cloud, 121
capitalism, cognitive, 9, 23, 121–123, 195
  class in, 204–205
  compared to industrial capitalism, 32
  and education, 124
  and immaterial labor, 29–33, 203–205
  knowledge labor in, 204–205
  resistance to, 124
capitalism, cultural, 23, 195

capitalism, cybernetic, 33–34, 121–123
capitalism, designer, 44–45
capitalism, digital, 22
capitalism, educational, 42
capitalism, fast, 23
capitalism, finance, 24, 34, 195, 197
capitalism, financialization of, 21, 61, 99, 195, 196–199
capitalism, genomic. *See* biocapitalism
capitalism, global, 20–21
capitalism, high-tech, 23
capitalism, industrial, 32, 191
capitalism, informational, 22–23, 24–29, 126, 194
Capitalism, Integrated World, 269
capitalism, knowing, 23, 45–46
capitalism, knowledge, 8–9, 22
  debate concerning, 208
  role of creativity in, 202
  substitution of capital for labor in, 203
  and universities, 199
  use of term, 191–192
capitalism, mercantile, 191
capitalism, postmodern, 193–194
capitalism, virtual, 23
Caplan, Arthur L., 114–115
care of self, 107–109
Caribbean, 239
Castells, Manuel, 24, 25, 26, 27–28, 77, 126, 194
catastrophe theory, 18
Center for the Study of the Public Domain, 71, 147–148
change, 260
chaos theory, 17, 18
Chartier, Roger, 258, 259, 260
Chiapello, E., 45, 46
China, 5, 240, 247
civil society, 223–225
class, in cognitive capitalism, 204–205
classification, 175
climate change, 82
Clinton, Bill, 72, 148
'Cognitarian Subjectivation,' 123–124

INDEX

cognitive capitalism. *See* capitalism, cognitive
Cohen, Hal, 181
Coleman, James, 63, 76, 136
collaboration, 180–183
   competitive, 182, 183
   growth in, 239
   international, 167, 248
   networks of, 247
   non-competitive, 182–183
   via Web, 7, 155, 250
collaboration, European, 178–179
communication
   and democratization of media, 144
communications environment, open, 207
communications technologies
   and collaboration, 180–183
   in globalization, 25
Communist Manifesto (Marx), 278
complexity, 18–20, 72, 149, 245
The Constitution of Liberty (Hayek), 282
consumption, postindustrial mode of, 128
control, 70, 147
Cooper, Melinda, 99, 100
copyleft, 51, 70, 147, 268
copyright, 70, 71, 147, 152, 232, 242, 266, 267–268
"The Copyright Grab" (Samuelson), 72, 148
corporations, multi-national, 194
courseware, open, 220–220, 250
   See also OpenCourseWare (OCW)
Craig Venter Institute, 95, 113, 114, 116–118
Creative Commons, 268
creative economy, 41–43, 46–47, 67–69
Creative Economy Report (United Nations), 141–142, 286
creativity
   commodification of, 50–51
   as communal project, 268
   concept of, 48–49
   and copyright law, 267
   dangers to, 71

   as development paradigm, 286
   in economic definitions, 50
   emphasis on, 139, 140
   encouraging in schools, 142–143
   and intellectual property rights, 50–51
   interest in, 46
   in knowledge capitalism, 202
   and knowledge economy, 68–69, 141
   in legal definitions, 50
   models of, 42
   openness associated with, 285–286
   as Romantic, 48
   teaching of, 47, 51, 68, 140–141
   as value, 46
   See also innovation
Crick, Francis, 94, 95
crisis, concept of, 199–201
crisis, economic, 61, 200, 201–202, 209
crisis studies, 200
cultural capitalism, 23, 195
cultural economy, 23
culture, knowledge-based, 28, 281, 282
culture, networked, 77
culture, open, 153
cyber-capitalism, 22
cybernetic capitalism, 21–24
cybernetics, 15–18
Cybernetics (Weiner), 15

Darwinian paradigm, 96–97, 101
data, linked, 225
David, Paul A., 251
Declaration of the Independence of Cyberspace, 266
Defillippi, R., 48
Deleuze, G., 123, 124
democracy, 143–145, 245
design, in knowledge economy, 68–69
Designing the Green Economy (Milani), 79
design principle, 42–43
Dewey, J., 223
digital capitalism, 22
digital information goods, 242–243
digital rights management, 284

digitization, 284
DNA, 95, 98, 100
    See also genomics
Drucker, Peter, 43, 63, 135
Dunne, Stephen, 198-199
Dyer-Witheford, Nick, 30, 32
Dyson, Freeman, 96-97

ecologies, knowledge, 218
ecologies, open knowledge, 130
economic rationalism, 199
economics, neoclassical, 80
The Economics of Knowledge (Foray), 8-9
economy, creative, 41-43, 46-47, 67-69
    as new development paradigm, 141-142
economy, cultural, 23
economy, gift, 28, 29
economy, green
    conceptions of, 79-80
    education in, 82-83
economy, information, 207
economy, informational, 24
economy, knowledge, 8-9
    changing concepts of, 155
    concept of, 41-42, 62-64, 137
    creative economy, 67-69, 140-143
    and creativity, 141
    and design, 141
    greening of, 78
    history of, 43-46, 135-137
    and innovation, 141
    learning economy, 64-67, 137-139
    monopolies in, 121
    and open science, 251 (*See also*
        economy, open science)
    theoretical studies of, 135-137, 193
    as transformation of Western
        capitalism, 191
    types of, 191
    See also economy, green
economy, learning, 64-67, 137-139, 205
economy, open knowledge, 143-149
economy, open science, 69-73, 154-155,
    203, 209, 243-250, 251-252

economy, proprietary, 28, 29
economy, spectator, 127
economy, U.S.
    crisis in, 61
    decline of, 247
    Obama era, 61-62
    Obama on, 60-61
ecopolitics, 82
ecosophy, defined, 59
education
    banking metaphor of, 265
    and cognitive capitalism, 124
    and creative economy, 142
    environmental education research, 60
    and financialization, 197
    future of, 280
    in gift economy, 29
    and Google, 131, 203
    in green economy, 82-83
    intellectual labor within, 204-205
    and international collaboration, 182-
        183
    link to capitalism, 68, 140
    manifesto for, 287
    neoliberal restructuring of, 33
    and new media, 262
    Nietzsche on, 281
    and openness, 146, 151, 231
    privatization of, 201
    in proprietary economy, 29
    restoring publicness of, 205-206, 210
    and technologies of openness, 129
    in transnational networks of
        capitalism, 28-29
    See also universities
education, distance, 73, 74, 150
education, environmental, 60
education, open, 73-74, 149-151
    defined, 220
    downsides of, 222
    emergence of, 221, 233-238
    growth of, 245
    and innovation, 235
    potential of, 221-222

reports in, 235–238
education, public
  crisis in, 205
  restoration of, 205–206, 210
  See also universities
educational capitalism, 42
election, presidential, 197
Electronic Frontier Foundation, 266
El-Hani, Charbel Niño, 75–76
Emmeche, Claus, 75–76
Empire (Hardt and Negri), 31
Endeavour, 175
energy crisis, 82
energy use, 82
England
  Royal Society, 5, 167, 171, 172, 173–174, 175, 223
  See also United Kingdom
Enlightenment, 258
environment
  as dynamic concept, 83
  threats to, 82
environment, information, 207
environmental education research, 60
environmental ethics, 81–82
Ephemera, 198–199
epistemology, 242
ethics
  Foucault on, 104
  in genomic science, 115
ethics, environmental, 81–82
Eucken, W., 106
European Research Council (ERC), 152, 247
European Science Foundation, 178
Euroscience, 179–180
experience, openness to, 285–286

Facebook, 124, 125–126, 266–267, 272
Falkner, R., 101
fast capitalism, 23
file sharing, 266
  See also peer-to-peer networks
finance capitalism, 24, 34, 195, 197

financialization
  as crisis of accumulation, 202
  and universities, 198–199
financialization of capitalism, 21, 61, 99, 195, 196–199
Fjällbrant, N., 174
Florida, Richard, 41, 140
food, 101
Foray, Dominique, 8–9
Fortunati, Leopoldina, 30
fossil fuel, 82
Foucault, Michel, 94, 97, 102, 104, 105, 106–107, 206
Framework 6, 180
France, 172
François, Charles, 16–17
freedom, 70–71, 72, 106, 128, 147, 149, 207, 219, 244, 267, 282–283, 284
Freedom of Information, 144
freedoms, academic, 282
Freiburg School, 104, 105–106
Freire, Paulo, 265
Freud, Sigmund, 277
Friedman, Thomas, 82
"From Biopower to Biopolitics" (Foucault), 105
Fuchs, C., 24, 25, 26, 194, 203
future, 280–282
Future Antérieur, 30
The Future of Ideas (Lessig), 71, 147

Gates, Bill, 143
Gaylor, Brett, 267–268
genetics, 93–95
  See also biology
genomic capitalism. *See* biocapitalism
genomics, 98, 116
genomics industry, 98, 107
genomics research, 93–95
  See also biocapitalism
geography of science, 171
Germany, 4, 240
Gibbs, Richard, 93
Gibson, Daniel G., 113

gift economy, 28, 29
giftedness, 68, 141
Giving Knowledge for Free, 235–236
globalization
  Castells's analysis of, 24
  as connectivity, 286
  as expression of finance, 197
  and global capitalism, 20–21
  theories of, 170–171
GNU project, 70, 146–147
Goldenfield, Nigel, 96
Google, 121, 131–133, 203, 267
The Googlization of Education
  (Vaidhyanathan), 131
The Googlization of Everything
  (Vaidhyanathan), 131–133
The Googlization of Universities
  (Vaidhyanathan), 131
Goonatilake, S., 176
Granovetter, Mark, 63, 76, 135
Greaves, M., 51–52
Greenberg, Clement, 278
green economy. *See* economy, green
Greenspan, Alan, 196
Guattari, F., 269–270
Guterman, Lila, 246

Habermas, Jürgen, 206, 223, 224
Hall, Jerry, 94
Harding, S., 176
Hardt, Michael, 26, 29, 30, 31, 206
Harvard University, 152, 217, 218, 232, 246, 247
Harvey, D., 27, 136
Harvie, David, 33
Hautamaki, Irmelia, 279
Hawking, Stephen, 80
Hayek, Friedrich von, 8, 41, 43, 62, 135, 282
hedge funds, 61
hegemony, scientific, 179
Heidegger, Martin, 168, 169
Heim, Michael, 259
Helms, S. J., 18

Helmreich, Stefan, 102–104
high-tech capitalism, 23
Hobbes, Thomas, 170
Hoedemaekers, C., 198–199
homo economicus, 76, 79, 198, 199
Horak, E., 24, 25
How Europe's Economies Learn (Lorenz and Lundvall), 138
Howkins, John, 41, 140
Hoyle, Fred, 80
Hubble, Edwin, 80
Huffington, Arianna, 269
Huffington Post, 269
human capital, 198
Human Capital (Becker), 198
Human Genome Project, 93, 94
Hume, David, 191
hydrogen, 82

Iati, Rob, 120
identity and networked culture, 77
imagination, 49, 127
  See also innovation
"Imagining the New Media Encounter" (Liu), 261
immaterial labor. *See* labor, immaterial
India, 5, 240, 247
information, 128
  and biology, 75–76
  and democracy, 143–145
  freedom of, 144
  and knowledge, 143
  versus knowledge, 65, 138
  as vital, 72, 149
informational capitalism, 22–23, 24–29, 126, 194
informationalism, 26
information democracy, 143
information environment, networked, 207
information goods, 242–243
information state, 143–144
infotechnology, 101
innovation
  emphasis on, 139

and knowledge economy, 68–69, 141
and need for learning, 65, 139
as networked endeavor, 75
and open education, 235
openness as source of, 151, 153, 231
role of, 204
See also creativity; imagination
The Institute for Genomic Research, 95
Integrated World Capitalism, 269
intellectual property, 50–51, 68, 70, 72, 104, 125, 140, 147–148, 154, 208, 209, 242, 251, 260, 284
and open science, 128
political economy of, 71
threat of to public domain, 71
International Council for Science, 181
Internet. *See* Web
interpretation, 67
intertextuality, 50
invention, 67

Jameson, Fredric, 194
journals, scientific, 173–174
See also publishing
justice, 145

Kelty, Christopher, 127
Kemple, Thomas M., 45
Kew Gardens, 175
King, David A., 3–4, 239–240
Kiralyfalvi, Bela, 279
knowing capitalism, 23, 45–46
Knowing Capitalism (Thrift), 45–46
knowledge
as barely excludable, 69, 141, 242
classical account of, 242
as commodity, 26
conflict with authority, 266
defined, 263
democratization of, 265
design of, 280
as economic good, 241
ideational stage of, 242
and information, 143

versus information, 65, 138
as non-rivalrous, 69, 141, 242
as not transparent, 242
open knowledge production systems, 20 (*See also* open access)
personal, 66
populist perspectives on, 264–265
privatization of, 201
tacit, 65, 66–67
Knowledge, Networks, and Nations (Royal Society), 5
knowledge capitalism. *See* capitalism, knowledge
knowledge cultures, 28, 281, 282
knowledge economy. *See* economy, knowledge
knowledge goods, collective, 225
knowledge management, 135
knowledge production, 193
Koselleck, Reinhart, 200, 201
Kuhn, Thomas, 67, 170

labor
internationalization of, 28–29
in production of immaterial goods, 26
transformation of, 29
labor, immaterial, 23
attempts to quantify value produced by, 33
and cognitive capitalism, 29–33, 203–205
critiques of, 31–32
defined, 30
emergence of, 45
and networks, 205
types of, 31
La Naissance de la Biopolitique (Foucault), 104
Landow, George, 258
Landry, Charles, 140
language, significance of, 194
Latin America, 239
Lazaratto, Maurizio, 30
Leadbeater, Charles, 121

learned societies
 Academy of Science, 172-173
 establishment of, 223
 Royal Society, 5, 167, 171, 172, 173-174, 175, 223
learning, consumer, 139
learning, in service of innovation, 139
learning, institutional, 139
learning, life-long, 65, 138
learning, organisational, 139
learning, producer, 139
learning, types of, 67
learning by doing, 139
learning by interacting, 139
learning by using, 139
Lessig, Larry, 53, 70-71, 146, 147, 244, 268-269
Lewontin, Richard, 93
liberty, 282
life, synthetic, 113, 116
Lin, Kwei-Jay, 52
linked data, 225
linked-up policy analysis, 59
Linneaus, Carl, 175
Little Science, Big Science (Price), 2-3, 177
Liu, Alan, 261
Lukács, György, 279
Lundvall, Bengt-Åke, 64-65, 137, 139
Lyotard, Jean-François, 44, 63, 136, 193-194

Machlup, Fritz, 8, 41, 43, 62, 135
Macy conferences, 17-18
making, vs. speculating, 61-62
malleability, 27
Mandelbrot, Benoit, 21
Manifeste du Surréalisme (Breton), 277
manifestos, 146, 278, 287
Manovich, Lev, 259
Marazzi, Christian, 201-202
market, free, 106
market forces, 132
market order, 105
markets, finance, 195

Marx, Karl, 200, 201, 277, 278
Marxism
 aesthetics of, 280
 and cybernetic capitalism, 21-22
McCulloch, Warren, 18
McKenzie, D. F., 260
media
 as de-centralized, 144-145
 democratization of, 144
 as de-territorialized, 127
media, new, 259, 272
 anti-democratizing trends in, 267-269
 connectedness, 266-267
 features of, 262-263
 and governments, 143-144
 narratives of, 262
 potential for, 271
 in schools, 262
 value of, 272
media, social, 125-129, 272
Mezich, Ben, 125
middle class, U.K., 62
Middle East, 239
Milani, Brian, 79
MIT, 74, 130, 150-151, 152, 209, 218, 232, 247
Modern Capitalism (Sombart), 30
monopolies, 121
Murdoch, Rupert, 143
Murray, Stuart, 107-108
music piracy, 266

La Naissance de la Biopolitique (Foucault), 104
National Institutes of Health (NIH), 130, 152, 234, 246-247
Negri, Antonio, 26, 29, 30, 31, 206, 287
Neidich, Warren, 123, 124
neoliberal era, 61
neoliberalism, 132
 and biocapitalism, 104-106
 concept of, 197
 as expression of finance, 197
 and finance capitalism, 195

Freiburg school of, 105–106
    postmodern critique of, 78–79
network, 25, 258
    concept of, 77
    and immaterial labor, 205
network, social, 125
network logic, 74–78
network perspective, 75
networks, collaborative, 247
networks, peer to peer, 71, 245–246, 270–271
network theory, 78
'The Neurobiopolitics of Global Consciousness' (Neidich), 124
neutrality, 176
The New Spirit of Capitalism (Boltanski and Chiapello), 45
Nietzsche, Friedrich, 199, 280, 281
Nissenbaum, H., 145–146, 225

OA. *See* open access
Obama, Barack, 60, 61–62, 197
observation, 67
OCW. *See* OpenCourseWare (OCW)
OCW Consortium, 150, 152, 232
OECD, 196, 221, 235–236
Oldenburg, Henry, 173
On the Future of Our Educational Institutions (Nietzsche), 280–281
open access, 207, 243–244
    defined, 217
    developments in, 217–219
    growth of, 245
    and intellectual property, 232, 260
    mandates for, 152, 222, 232–233, 246–247
    potential for, 217, 226
    and public sphere, 223
    statements and manifestos, 130
    threats to, 251–252
    University Publishing in a Digital Age, 218–219
    See also OpenCourseWare (OCW); openness

OpenCourseWare Consortium, 150, 152, 232
OpenCourseWare (OCW), 74, 130, 150–151, 152, 218, 232, 247
open culture, 153
open education. *See* education, open
Open Educational Practices and Resources, 236–237
Open e-Learning Content Observatory Services (OLCOS), 235, 236–237
open era, 219
openness, 128, 243–247
    as alternative mode of social production, 151, 153, 283
    as architecture of alternative educational globalization, 231
    associated with creativity, 285–286
    in communication networks, 75
    concept of, 151, 231
    and democracy, 144
    economics of, 128
    to experience, 285–286
    and freedom, 284
    of Internet, 130
    as mode of production, 129, 231, 243–244
    possibilities of, 20
    as source of innovation, 151, 153, 231
    See also open access
open source, 7, 20, 129, 206, 231, 243–244, 270
    as alternative mode of text production, 283
    and changed political economy for education, 146
    and copyright, 267–268
    growth of, 245
    and new models of production, 154
    See also open access
Open Standards, Open Source, and Open Innovation, 233–234
Open University, 74, 150
OpenWetWare, 209
Operaismo, 202

order, concept of, 106
ordoliberalism, 104, 105, 106
O'Reilly, Tim, 52
'Our Biotech Future' (Dyson), 96

Palma, José Gabriel, 196
Paris, 172
Park, Paula, 181
Pasinetti, L., 139
patent, 242
Patrinos, Aristides A. N., 117
peer-to-peer networks (P2P), 71, 147, 245–246, 270–271
 and virtue, 145–146
personal anarcho-aesthetics, 42
personality theory, 285
Personal Knowledge (Polyani), 65–67
Peters, M., 8
Philosophical Transactions of the Royal Society, 173, 174
philosophy, systems, 16–17
Peirce, Charles Sanders, 223
Pike, D., 279
piracy, music, 266
poetry, 278
Poetry of the Revolution (Puchner), 278
Poggioli, Renato, 278
policies, economic, 197
political economy, network approach in, 76
The Political Economy of Peer Production (Bauwens), 270
The Politics of Life Itself (Rose), 102
Polyani, Michael, 65–67
Porat, Marc, 63, 135
The Post-Industrial Society (Touraine), 63, 135
The Postmodern Condition (Lyotard), 63, 136
Postmodernism (Jameson), 194
Powell, W. W., 154, 249–250
power, 104, 105, 106
P2P, 71, 147, 245–246, 270–271
Price, Derek J. de Solla, 2–3, 177
problem solving, 132

production
 Castells's view of, 27–28
 metaphysics of, 244
 openness as mode of, 129
 transformation of, 284
production, cinematic mode of, 127
production, commons-based peer, 128, 145–146
production, industrial mode of, 128
production, mode of, 219
production, nonmarket, 245
production, nonproprietary, 245
production, open, 243–247
production, open knowledge, 203
production, peer, 245–246, 270–271
production, social, 151, 153, 225, 231, 235, 283
productivity
 evaluation of, 3, 177
 measuring, 238
 and open source initiatives, 7
property, concept of, 260
property, private, 206
proprietary economy, 28, 29
public domain, 71, 226
 threats to, 148
Public Domain Manifesto, 226
public sphere, 206, 223–225
publishing, 173–174, 238–239
 changes in, 153
 concerns for, 2, 166
 open access mandates for, 152, 232–233
 open source initiatives, 7 (*See also* open access)
 See also productivity
publishing, commercial, 218
publishing, electronic, 260
PubMed Central, 130
Puchner, Martin, 278
Putnam, R., 76, 136

Quah, Danny, 44
Queiroz, João, 75–76

Rajan, Kaushik Sunder, 99, 101, 102
rationalism, economic, 199
reason, administrative, 199
reason, technical, 199
Regents of the University of California v. Bakke, 282
Research and Development (U.S. National Science Board), 4–6, 240–241
resistance, 278
resources, non-renewable, 82
A Review of the Open Educational Resources (OER) Movement, 235, 237–238
revolution, virtual, 263–264
Rhoten, D., 154, 249–250
Rifkin, Jeremy, 82, 101
Rimbaud, Arthur, 277
RiP! (Gaylor), 267–268
The Rise of the Creative Class (Florida), 41
The Rise of the Network Society (Castells), 24
romanticism
    Berlin on, 47–48
    critiques of, 49–50
    and shift to subjective, 49
Romer, Paul, 41, 63, 136
The Roots of Romanticism (Berlin), 47
Rose, Nikolas, 98, 102, 104
Royal Botanical Gardens at Kew, 175
Royal Society, 5, 167, 171, 172, 173–174, 175, 223

Samuelson, Pamela, 71, 72, 146, 147
scarcity, 69, 141, 243
science
    distribution of, 3–4, 238, 240, 247
    economics of, 165
    funding of, 180, 183, 208–209, 240
    geography, 171
    geography of, 171
    history of, 167–170
    metanarrative of, 1–2, 165–166
    productivity of, 165, 177, 248 (*See also* publishing)
    relation with State, 175
    relation with technology, 168–169
    restoring publicness of, 210
    spending on, 240
Science 2.0, 7, 154, 209, 250
science, big, 6, 177–179, 208, 248
science, classical, 171–175
science, colonial, 171, 175–177
science, free, 1–2
science, global
    age of, 165
    classical science, 171–175
    and collaboration, 167, 178–179, 180–183 (*See also* collaboration)
    and colonial science, 171, 174, 175–177
    emergence of, 2, 169
    emergence of big science, 177–179
    emerging political economy of, 1
    as international science, 167
    major forces in, 6
    political economy of, 238–241
    rise of, 170–179
    shift in architecture of, 5
    use of term, 2, 166–167
science, open, 128, 153–155, 203, 208, 220, 251
    characteristics of, 209–210
    economics of, 241–243
    forces in, 247
    and knowledge economy, 251
    new models of, 249
    notion of, 224
    possibilities of, 209
    role of, 209
    transnational, 208
    vs. intellectual property, 209, 251
    and Web, 224–225
science, post-normal, 2
science, small, 6–7
science, transnational, 248–249
Science Citation Index, 238, 239
Science Commons, 224
science policy, 165, 175

Scientific American, 154
scientometrics, 177
self
    capitalization of, 199
    care of, 107–109
self-regulation, 194
semio-capitalism, 24
Sen, Amartya, 179
Sennett, Richard, 29
smallness, advantages of, 248
Smith, Adam, 106, 191
Smith, Hamilton O., 117
social media, 125–129, 272
The Social Network, 125, 272
social network, idea of, 125
social sciences
    complexity in, 19–20
    in service of empire, 170
societies of control, 123
society, civil, 223–225
society, knowledge-based, 28
society, networked, 194
software, free, 70, 127, 129, 147
    See also open source
software, open source, 270
    See also open source
Sombart, Werner, 30
Soros, George, 61
South Africa, 4
South Korea, 247
spatiality, 34
spectatorship, 127
speech, free, 284
Stallman, Richard, 70, 146–147
states of domination, 106, 107
Stiglitz, Joseph, 63, 136
Stillman, Robert, 94
The Structural Transformation of the Public Sphere (Habermas), 206
The Structure of Scientific Revolutions (Kuhn), 67, 170
struggle, call for, 106–107
Suber, Peter, 222
subjective, 49, 50

subjectivity, 108, 109, 263
Surrealism, 277
surveillance, 267
sustainability, 65, 83, 138
Synthetic Genomics, 116
systems, large-scale, 59–60
systems analysis, globalization of, 20
systems theory, 19

Taleb, Nassim, 21
Tarde, Gabriel, 30
Tea Party movement, 197
technical reason, 199
technological determinism, 143
technology
    appropriation of, 27
    in globalization, 24–25
    and immaterial labor, 30
    malleability of, 27
    relation with science, 168–169
    shift from print to digital, 258–263
Teeple, G., 20–21
text production, 283
textuality, electronic, 259–263
Theory Culture and Society, 19
Theory of the Avant-garde (Bürger), 278
The Theory of the Avant-Garde (Poggioli), 278
thinking, critical, 265
Thrift, Nigel, 45–46
Thurstone, L. L., 285
time, beginning of, 80
Toffler, Alvin, 43, 63, 135
Touraine, Alain, 41, 43, 63, 135
trading, algorithmic, 119–121
Twitter, 272

UIS Bulletin on Science and Technology Statistics (UNESCO), 3, 238–239
United Kingdom
    budget, 198
    in distribution of science, 4, 240
    middle class, 62
    Open University, 74, 150

See also England
United Nations, 141–142
United Nations Conference on Trade and Development (UNCTAD), 142
United States
  budget, 197–198
  decline of science in, 4–5, 241
  in distribution of science, 3–4, 240
  economy of, 247
  science budget in, 240–241
universe, beginning of, 80
universities
  budgets, 198
  commercialization of, 251
  economic interest vested in, 199
  and financialization, 198–199
  intellectual labor within, 204–205
  and international collaboration, 182–183
  as networked environment, 207
  philosophical critique of, 199
  and public good, 206
  and public sphere, 223
  See also education
university, neoliberal, 199
'The University of Finance,' 198–199
University Publishing in a Digital Age, 130, 218–219, 246
Urry, John, 19
U.S. National Science Board, 4–6

Vaidhyanathan, Siva, 131–133, 203
Valery, Paul, 280–282
value, 33, 34, 46
Venter, Craig, 94–95, 114, 116
  Craig Venter Institute, 95, 113, 114, 116–118
The Violence of Financial Capitalism (Marazzi), 201–202
virtual capitalism, 23
virtual reality, 259
The Virtual Revolution, 263
Voltaire, 172

Wade, Nicolas, 116

Waldrop, M. Mitchell, 154, 250
Wales, Jimmy, 264–265
Watson, James, 93, 94, 95
Watts, Susan, 115
The Wealth of Networks (Benkler), 69–70, 72, 146, 148
Web
  advertising on, 132
  as challenge to authority, 265–266
  collaboration over, 7, 155, 250
  democratization of knowledge, 265
  openness of, 130
  and open science, 224–225
  potential for democratization, 269
  See also media, new
Web 2.0, 51–53, 126, 129, 149, 154, 203, 209
"Web 2.0...The Machine Is Using Us" (Wesch), 126
Weiner, Norbert, 15
Wesch, Michael, 126
WikiLeaks, 272
Wikipedia, 264–265
Willinsky, John, 251
Will to Power (Nietzsche), 281
Wilsdon, J., 5, 240
Woese, Carl R., 95
word, written, 260
work, transformation of, 29
Workerism, 202
World Economic Forum (2007), 143
World Wide Web. *See* Web

YouTube, 126, 132, 267

Zuckerberg, Mark, 125, 272

GLOBAL STUDIES IN EDUCATION

A.C. (Tina) Besley, Michael A. Peters,
Cameron McCarthy, Fazal Rizvi
General Editors

Global Studies in Education is a book series that addresses the implications of the powerful dynamics associated with globalization for re-conceptualizing educational theory, policy and practice. The general orientation of the series is interdisciplinary. It welcomes conceptual, empirical and critical studies that explore the dynamics of the rapidly changing global processes, connectivities and imagination, and how these are reshaping issues of knowledge creation and management and economic and political institutions, leading to new social identities and cultural formations associated with education.

We are particularly interested in manuscripts that offer: a) new theoretical, and methodological, approaches to the study of globalization and its impact on education; b) ethnographic case studies or textual/discourse based analyses that examine the cultural identity experiences of youth and educators inside and outside of educational institutions; c) studies of education policy processes that address the impact and operation of global agencies and networks; d) analyses of the nature and scope of transnational flows of capital, people and ideas and how these are affecting educational processes; e) studies of shifts in knowledge and media formations, and how these point to new conceptions of educational processes; f) exploration of global economic, social and educational inequalities and social movements promoting ethical renewal.

For additional information about this series or for the submission of manuscripts, please contact one of the series editors:

A.C. (Tina) Besley: tbesley@illinois.edu
Cameron McCarthy: cmccart1@illinois.edu
Michael A. Peters: mpet001@illinois.edu
Fazal Rizvi: frizvi@unimelb.edu.au

Department of Educational Policy Studies
University of Illinois at Urbana-Champaign
1310 South Sixth Street
Champaign, IL 61820   USA

To order other books in this series, please contact our Customer Service Department:

(800) 770-LANG (within the U.S.)
(212) 647-7706 (outside the U.S.)
(212) 647-7707 FAX

Or browse online by series:
www.peterlang.com